Organization Theory and Governance for the 21st Century

CQ Press, an imprint of SAGE, is the leading publisher of books, periodicals, and electronic products on American government and international affairs. CQ Press consistently ranks among the top commercial publishers in terms of quality, as evidenced by the numerous awards its products have won over the years. CQ Press owes its existence to Nelson Poynter, former publisher of the *St. Petersburg Times,* and his wife Henrietta, with whom he founded Congressional Quarterly in 1945. Poynter established CQ with the mission of promoting democracy through education and in 1975 founded the Modern Media Institute, renamed The Poynter Institute for Media Studies after his death. The Poynter Institute (*www.poynter.org*) is a nonprofit organization dedicated to training journalists and media leaders.

In 2008, CQ Press was acquired by SAGE, a leading international publisher of journals, books, and electronic media for academic, educational, and professional markets. Since 1965, SAGE has helped inform and educate a global community of scholars, practitioners, researchers, and students spanning a wide range of subject areas, including business, humanities, social sciences, and science, technology, and medicine. A privately owned corporation, SAGE has offices in Los Angeles, London, New Delhi, and Singapore, in addition to the Washington DC office of CQ Press.

Organization Theory and Governance for the 21st Century

Sandra Parkes Pershing
University of Utah

Eric K. Austin
Montana State University

Los Angeles | London | New Delhi
Singapore | Washington DC

Los Angeles | London | New Delhi
Singapore | Washington DC

FOR INFORMATION:

CQ Press

An Imprint of SAGE Publications, Inc.

2455 Teller Road

Thousand Oaks, California 91320

E-mail: order@sagepub.com

SAGE Publications Ltd.

1 Oliver's Yard

55 City Road

London EC1Y 1SP

United Kingdom

SAGE Publications India Pvt. Ltd.

B 1/I 1 Mohan Cooperative Industrial Area

Mathura Road, New Delhi 110 044

India

SAGE Publications Asia-Pacific Pte. Ltd.

3 Church Street

#10-04 Samsung Hub

Singapore 049483

Acquisitions Editor: Sarah Calabi

Developmental Editor: Nancy Loh

Editorial Assistant: Davia Grant

Production Editor: Libby Larson

Copy Editor: Megan Markanich

Typesetter: C&M Digitals (P) Ltd.

Proofreader: Sally Jaskold

Indexer: Kathy Paparchontis

Cover Designer: Anupama Krishnan

Marketing Manager: Amy Whitaker

Printed in the United States of America

Library of Congress Cataloging-in-Publication Data

Pershing, Sandra Parkes

Organization theory and governance for the 21st century / Sandra Parkes Pershing, Eric K. Austin, Montana State University, University of Utah.

pages cm
Includes index.

ISBN 978-1-60426-984-0 (pbk. : alk. paper)

1. Organizational sociology. 2. Organizational behavior. 3. Management. I. Austin, Eric K. II. Title.

HM786.P4357 2015
302.3'5—dc23

This book is printed on acid-free paper.

14 15 16 17 18 10 9 8 7 6 5 4 3 2 1

Contents

Foreword

Organization theory is one of the most interesting, useful, and dynamic fields in the broader fields of public administration and its cousins in business, education, healthcare, and social work administration. No student of any form of administration should complete their degree without at least one course in organization theory. Yet many undergraduate and graduate students think about organization theory as a field that died or at least went dormant in the second half of the 20th century with giants such as Herbert Simon (1946), J. D. Thompson (1967), and Douglas McGregor (1957)—if not all the way back in the eras of Max Weber (1922), Frederick Winslow Taylor (1911), and Luther Gulick (1937). Certainly no theories as old as these can be of more than historic interest in today's world of fluid, rapidly changing, and electronically connected organizations. Obviously, the authors of *Organization Theory and Governance in the 21st Century,* Sandra Pershing and Eric Austin, and I disagree.

Interestingly, the older organization theories remain vital and useful in today's world because of the solid understanding of organizations as stable institutions provided to us by the likes of Weber, Taylor, Gulick, Simon, Thompson, McGregor, and their contemporaries. They continue to serve as foundational models in theory and practice in different ways. Sometimes these early theories are useful as models of what might be or what might have been, while at other times they can provide a basis of comparison for more fluid alternative models of organizations that fit better with the current environment in the 21st century. In both instances, these legendary theories remain rock-solid points of departure for today's exciting, newly emerging organizational forms and functions—in practice as well as in theory.

Therefore, the early theories should not be ignored. Neither should they be used as constraints against trying creative new forms. Organizations are means, not ends. Organizations should be designed to serve people and societies. They are vehicles for accomplishing coordinated activities that lead to desired ends whether the ultimate end is profit, effective and efficient delivery of services, or enabling individuals to collectively challenge the status quo. Older notions of organizations need to be adapted to the times. As the title of John Meyer and Brian Rowan's (1977) article aptly states: "Institutionalized Organizations: Formal Structure as Myth and Ceremony." In many respects, the older theories are not much more than myths and artifacts. Certainly Max Weber never considered government agencies that deliver essentially all of their services through contracted nonprofit organizations. Whereas Chester Barnard (1938) focused on chief executives holding their organizations together by creating an environment or culture of cooperation and collaboration among employees, consider how different this challenge is when employees are only temporary—engaged only for the duration of a project—and are spread around the globe (DeSanctis & Fulk, 1999). They never meet in person, for relatively short periods of time, and only through electronic communication systems. What provides the basis for member collaboration or loyalty? I propose that it is often inaccurate to even use the word "employee" with many of today's organizations. It is completely misleading. Barnard provided the foundation, but it is also time for alternative theories.

Thus, new theories of organization that deal with today's world are needed and are emerging rapidly. New post-positivist theories are addressing types of issues the founding giants of organization theory could not possibly foresee. They are keeping organization theory interesting, useful, dynamic—and relevant—in the 21st century. Whereas J.D. Thompson (1967) is widely credited with introducing the notion of organizations as "open systems," theorists today are wrestling with boundary-less organizations where organizations are integral elements of their community. Therefore, corporate social responsibility is an essential element of an organization's mission, purpose, and business model—not a public relations ploy (Carroll & Buchholtz, 1989). Likewise, many nonprofit organizations today borrow their organizational models from the for-profit world of business but employ them for completely different purposes. They are not seeking profits as a business does but instead are seeking supplements for the inadequate charitable contributions needed to finance their public benefit works. This explains why over the past several decades organizational models have evolved that blend profitability from entrepreneurial ventures with social consciousness (Light, 2008).

As Pershing and Austin state in the *Preface,* countless other texts are available to introduce readers to the field organization theory. So why should students and instructors choose *Organization Theory and Governance in the 21st Century?* There are several sound reasons. First, Pershing and Austin do a better job of blending theory, historical foundations, and current contextual influences than any text I have seen in recent years. They weave together the influences of the early giants with the fluidity of the current context. Second, the volume remains true to the authors' stated purpose of making organization theory practical. Pershing and Austin bring strong academic credentials and decades of administrative experience in the public sector to this volume. The chapters bring theories to life through the authors' well-internalized understanding of organizations and organizational life, case studies, and contemporary expressions. Theories are applied and operationalized. Third, Pershing and Austin are unapologetic proponents of *public* organizations. In the current environment of unrelenting bureaucracy-bashing, Pershing and Austin focus on the often unnoticed strides that have been made and are being made to realign old-style government bureaucracies with today's political, social, and economic complexities and fluidities. Public bureaucracies serve vitally important purposes grounded in the Constitution of the United States, the constitutions of individual states, and the practice of democratic governance, but they are relatively ineffective institutions for accomplishing many of the tasks and responsibilities assigned to them today. Pershing and Austin do a superb job of balancing between traditional and post-positivist assumptions and epistemologies, and they do so with an elegant writing style.

In short, *Organization Theory and Governance in the 21st Century* is worthy of your intellectual investment. It will make you a better manager for the public benefit, whether you are employed or contracted by a government agency, a nonprofit organization, or a responsible for-profit business. I hope you enjoy it.

J. Steven Ott

University of Utah

References

Barnard, C. I. (1938). *The functions of the executive.* Cambridge, Mass: Harvard University Press.

Carroll, A. B., & A. K.Buchholtz (1989). *Business and society: Ethics and stakeholder management.* Boston, Mass.: South-Western.

DeSanctis, G. & J. Fulk, eds. (1999). *Shaping organization form: Communication, connection, and community.* Thousand Oaks, Calif.: Sage.

Gulick L. (1937). Notes on the theory of organization. In L. Gulick & L. Urwick, eds., *Papers on the science of administration* (pp. 3–34). New York: Institute of Public Administration.

Light, P. C. (2008). *The search for social entrepreneurship.* Washington, D.C.: The Brookings Institution Press.

McGregor, D. M. (1957). The human side of enterprise. *Management Review, 46,* 88–92.

Meyer, J. W., & B. Rowan. (1977). Institutionalized organizations: Formal structure as myth and ceremony. *American Journal of Sociology, 83,* 340–363.

Simon, H. A. (1946), The proverbs of administration. *Public Administration Review, 6,* 53–67.

Thompson, J. D. (1967). *Organizations in action.* New York: McGraw-Hill.

Weber, M. (1922). Bureaucracy. In H. Gerth & C. W. Mills, eds., *Max Weber: Essays in sociology.* Oxford, UK: Oxford University Press.

Taylor, F. W. (1911). *The principles of scientific management.* New York: Norton.

Preface

Organization theory is a large, diverse, and expansive field of study that has connections to a range of academic disciplines including public administration, political science, business, sociology, psychology, economics, and others. Organization theory is a central area of study in these fields in no small part because organizations are the setting in which the bulk of political, social, economic, interpersonal, and other activities occur. In order to understand and effectively navigate the world today, a reasonably sophisticated sense of organizations and their operations is crucial. For students and practitioners interested in public administration and governance, organizations are likely to be both the venue and mechanism by which they can positively affect the world around them. More broadly though, nearly everyone who lives in nations with fairly developed economies spends their working lives, and much of the rest of their lives, in and directly interacting with formal organizations. We believe that it's not entirely hyperbole to suggest that, because so much of our lives are spent formally in and informally interacting with organizations, developing some level of understanding of their structure and function enables us to be more successful.

At this point, there are probably at least as many text books introducing organization theory as there are theories to explore. Why then, do we need another book on this topic? Based on several decades of combined managerial, teaching, and research experience in the field, we have sought to craft a survey of organization theory in a way that balances theory, history, and contextual influences such that students can position themselves to be effective in applying concepts in the jobs they have now and in the immediate future, but also over the longer arch of their careers as they move through different roles and levels of the organizations they occupy.

In pursuit of that balance, this book has a number of features that, in combination, make it unique. Making sense of organizations' actions in the abstract has value, but we have strived to select and describe theories so that they are applicable *and* actionable. To start, we conduct our examination of organization theory in a way that presents the heterodox and sophisticated range of influential ideas **contextualized** such that students can explore and develop ways to operationalize organization theory. This book embraces a conscious and thoughtful awareness of the history, political events, social and cultural dynamics, and technological changes that coincide and contribute to the evolving nature of organizations.

Much of the work that surveys organization theory leaves its own internal—and more broadly, the discipline's—**epistemology and ontology** implicit and assumed. These underlying assumptions have implications in practice—which courses of action are selected, which are avoided, and moreover, which are never even given consideration in the first place. In illuminating the epistemological and ontological assumptions, we both explore their consequences in practice and open a space in which we consider the consequences of these embedded assumptions for both organizational practice as well as democratic governance.

Over the span of the book we combine emerging perspectives and theories with their historic roots and, recognizing the critical intersection between theory and practice, with an emphasis on **prescriptive theory and practical application** for the effective transfer of learning. To support students' ability to find the applicability of theory, the text is developed to provide students' experiential perspective from which to analyze organizational settings and take effective action in the unique setting of contemporary governance. We have included a wide range of **case studies** and **contemporary expressions** and applications of the theories we cover, in order for students and instructors to explore the sorts of concrete steps needed to move from theory to practice.

Throughout the text, we pose a series of **reflection questions** that support class and group discussion of the ideas and their application, and also encourage students to pause and ponder the operationalization of ideas on their own.

There are a number of areas that we believe have come to have a significant influence on public administration and governance, but could receive more extensive treatment in their relationship to organization theory. One set of works that we feel deserves significantly more attention are **economic theories** of organization, especially agency theory and transaction cost economics. These areas are particularly important because beyond being underexplored in most survey texts, there's been little treatment of how these theories are implicit in important management initiatives like new public management and its expression in policies and programs like the National Performance Review and the Government Performance and Results Act.

Although they remain both controversial and challenging, since the late 1960s a range of new theory has emerged from Continental philosophy, social theories that have slowly made their way into organization theory. Currently, many of the treatments of **post-positivist** thinking are quite brief and superficially lump together a substantial volume of heterodox material. Our approach to this collection of work is intended to reveal several important attributes of the theory. First, we show that many of the ideas of precedents in "mainstream" organization theory aren't radically different in concept or practice. Second, one of the justifiable critiques of post-positivist theory is that it is difficult and too little operationalized to be of use to practitioners. In part by examining the conceptual links to mainstream theory, but also by focusing on practices that already have the potential to embody the assumptions of post-positivist theory, we show that these concepts not only can be used, but that they can be used to support organizational effectiveness in unique conditions of governance and democratic public administration.

In total, then, what we aspire to is a book that draws students into the study of organization theory in ways that reveal the breadth, sophistication, and, indeed, elegance of our thinking about organizations. We hope to have done this in a way that grounds students' thinking about organizations in both contextual and conceptual ways that will remain with them beyond the end of a class. Finally, we envisage that our approach enables them to use and apply that theory to craft courses of action that help them be more effective, support the efficacy of their organizations, and ultimately contribute to the good life of citizens in their communities.

As with all projects of this size, this book could not have been completed without the help of a number of people. First and foremost, our editors Nancy Loh and Libby Larson at CQ Press have been invaluable in helping facilitate the process of writing the book, and has shown extraordinary patience and encouragement throughout. We received valuable feedback and recommendations from several anonymous reviewers, which significantly improved the content and clarity of the book. We also benefited enormously from the help of three graduate students in Montana State University's MPA program: Lisa Hammer, Jennifer Avery, and Kelly Mildenberger. Last, and definitely not least, we want to thank our families for their support and encouragement through what has been a longer and windier road than we expected at the outset of this journey.

Chapter 1

An Introduction and Orientation to Organization Theory

This book explores the complex topic of public organizations. Organizations are made up of a group or groups of people who are brought together to accomplish ends beyond that which a single individual can achieve alone. **Public organizations** are distinct in that they must respond to citizens, law, politics, and change in ways different than most private organizations. We build organizations because of what they can do for us. We are born and raised in and then spend most of our lives directly or indirectly affiliated with them. Understanding the way organizations work in an increasingly complex, global, diverse, technological, and changing world is critical to our ability to thrive in the world both personally and professionally. This book explores how we have come to know and understand public organizations over time and will help readers to explore their own thinking and experiences in and around them.

Organization theory (OT) is a multidisciplinary set of ideas and concepts that seek to explain or predict relationships among things in and around organizations. OT carefully focuses on topics that concern the organization as a whole, such as environment, culture, goals, effectiveness, strategy, decision making, change, innovation, structure, and life cycle. OT is not to be confused with organizational behavior, a subset of OT that focuses on understanding the actual behavior of individuals and groups in organizations and is a framework for understanding how such things make an organization tick.

To study organizations is to study the social world, which in many ways can be a more challenging subject matter than studying natural entities, be it microbes or galaxies. In our explorations throughout this book, we observe social and organizational life in order to discern and understand patterns. Such patterns are often fluid and difficult to measure, and we believe that identifying—let alone making sense of them—is made easier through the use a variety of theoretical lenses. Before introducing the lenses we'll be using, we need to first say a bit more about the institutional context of the organizations we're interested in.

The Complex World of Public Organizations: A Primer

Public organizations reflect the society they serve. We must appreciate the contextual factors that influence the practice in order to better understand it. In an age of intense public scrutiny, rapid technological advancements, and changing organizational demographics, administrators face many complex challenges, requiring them to wear many hats. The changing nature of work and the workforce, in addition to the expectations of the public, requires that public administrators think about many things beyond the walls of the organization. Before exploring the current political and administrative climate, we want to briefly examine the conceptual background or public administration and public organizations.

Many of us who are interested in studying organizations do so because we are students and scholars of public administration. Exactly what *is* **public administration?** The root word of *public* is *populous,* which essentially means "the people." The root word of *administration* is *minos,* which means "detail and service." So, in essence, public administration means "the details or service of the people." How is this different than private administration? Public administration, more so than private administration, is culturally bound, legally based, and institutionally founded. Public administration in the United States exists within a federal system, and governance is based on shared powers, separation of powers, and authority across many branches. Public administration is part of our governmental system, and public organizations, which carry out policies and implement programs, reflect the underlying values, laws, ideologies, structures, and technologies of the United States.

The creation of the United States was shaped, to a great extent, by values of classical liberalism. These values include individualism, freedom, equality, capitalism, democratic ideals, and limited representative government. Although we have a strong intuitive sense of what each of these values entails, they can be difficult to precisely define and they can often exist in tension with one another. For example, it's often noted that efforts to ensure equality can have the effect of diminishing individual freedom. Resolution of these tensions is a political process, and politics, for our purposes, has to do with achieving the good life.

Despite the possibility of tension among our founding values, the United States has maintained a substantial level of ideological agreement over our history, and our disagreements occur largely at the margins.[1] It is important to remember that public organizations exist within this context and that the people in the organization are a product of this culture as well. Public organizations operate in fairly transparent goldfish bowls, unlike much of the rest of the world that can draw the curtains so that their activities are more difficult to observe. It is often public administrators, rather than politicians, judges, or the public, who are responsible for finding ways to balance these ideas and values.

Americans often talk about ideology and culture as something that other countries have and the United States does not. In a sense, the United States is nonideological—but only to the extent that the majority of us ascribe to similar ideologies. Public administrators reflect the culture in which they grow up, in which they live, in which they are educated, and in which our government structures were developed. Our political culture-ideology determines basic orientations toward ourselves and others, ideas about economics, the role of individuals and government, and what we value and what we see and fail to see.

We have a federal constitution that is now over 200 years old. Essentially a written framework for our government and outline of our political values, the Constitution established a strong national government made up of legislative, executive, and judicial branches and provided for the control and operation of that government. It articulates many of our political norms and ideologies and institutionalizes the assumptions and values of our political and social culture. The Constitution provided fundamental law, was the legal basis for public administration (but it is not specified there), established supremacy of national government, set up a federal system of shared power (federalism), and separated government into three branches (bicameral legislative, executive, and judicial branches). Within this constitutional context and its inherent values, we find the development of the field of public administration.

Paul Appleby described the distinction between public and private organizations when he explained that public servants must possess a "governmental attitude" in which the public's needs are put first, there is a sense of action, and there is a feeling of the need for decisions.[2] He also explained that the government function and attitude should have at least three complementary aspects that differentiate government from all other institutions and activities. They are breadth of scope, impact, and consideration; public accountability (meaning no action of government is immune to public debate, scrutiny, or investigation); and political character (government is politics). Appleby argued that government is different because government is politics. He insisted that to have governmental processes that were not political contradicts the experience of being American. He stated, "Governments exist so that there is someone in society charged with promoting and protecting the public interest."[3] It is within this context that we find public organizations.

With this conceptual foundation in mind, we can highlight several sociopolitical and economic factors that also influence the actions of governance organizations in important ways. First, the roles and functions of public administrators are political in that they determine the allocation of government resources.[4, 5] They must abide by rules and regulations set forth by the political system and policy process and, ultimately, influence policy. Public administrators are expected to uphold the democratic values upon which our political system is based, while simultaneously being held accountable to individual concerns within their organizations.

Second, the roles and functions of public administrators are constitutional, because they must recognize the rights and privileges espoused within the Constitution as they examine the way they deal with people both inside and outside of public organizations. Administrators must consider equity, justice, public interest, rights, and the underlying values of the American government system and also be accountable and responsive to the public and to employees within those boundaries.[6, 7]

Third, the roles and responsibilities are legal, in that their actions are limited by precedents and court decisions.[8, 9] Organizations may depend upon decisions made at other levels of government, and often rely upon those other levels for a variety of resources.[10, 11] Their roles are also legal in that public organizations may be granted quasi-legislative or quasi-judicial authority to make rules and adjudicate violations of those rules.[12]

Fourth, their roles and functions are social because their decisions and actions often result from the demands of citizens and the characteristics of their communities. Public interest frequently initiates reform efforts, and public administrators must pay attention to these forces within their organizations and communities.

Finally, they are organizational in that public administrators need to work within political, constitutional, legal, and social constraints in the name of effective and efficient organizations. They must allocate resources in such a way as to maximize effectiveness and productivity and not tip the scales of balance away from adherence to public expectations. And here we find ourselves back at the organizational. This book will look closely at the theories in and around public organizations. In the public sector, administrators have to think about many things beyond the walls of the organization.

The environment that lies beyond the boundaries of the organization has become more complex in recent times. The simple distinction between public and private, while useful, is insufficient for capturing the variety of organizations, which have a role in what we might more broadly consider public affairs. The breadth of organizations given consideration in this text includes not only traditional public organizations but also nonprofit organizations, quasi-public organizations, and some private organizations because these nonpublic organizations have a direct role in carrying out public policy.

The attention to what might loosely be termed *traditional public agencies* is reasonably straightforward. This group includes those organizations, whether at the federal, state, or local level, that are funded directly through public revenues of some form. Personnel who staff these organizations may take oaths of office in which they commit to upholding the Constitution and are typically provided with some level of legal protection in the exercise of their duties.

Increasingly, the distinction between public organizations and other sorts of organizations has become blurred. For example, nonprofit organizations have long had a role in public affairs. Churches and charity organizations have carried out activities that parallel or sometimes even replace those of public social service agencies. Over time, the relationship between public and nonprofit organizations has in some cases become more formalized through the creation of contracts for products or services. As politics and policy have prompted public organizations to reduce staff size and move some activities into the private sector, the range of specific programs executed by nonpublic organizations has grown and the relationships between public and private organizations has become more formal and extensive.

It is worth noting that the nonprofit designation is a legal one that is established under the federal tax code and is overseen by the Internal Revenue Service (IRS). While service organizations of all sorts, including schools, health care providers, social service organizations, and others are granted nonprofit status—often under 501(c)(3) designation—tax-exempt status also includes a wide range of separate designations for other organizations and activities including labor or agricultural organizations under the 501(c)(5) designation, business leagues under 501(c)(6), child care organizations under 501(k), the now-notorious 501(c)(4) political organizations, and many others. Tax-exempt, nonprofit, or nongovernmental organizations (NGOs) are generally defined as private institutions, independent of the government, that provide services to populations for whom public programs are unavailable or insufficient. We argue that in the current climate, which includes political and social trends such as devolution and globalization, NGOs must be included in any study of public organizations because they are a major part of the answer to questions of who provides services as well as where and how those services are provided to the public.

To complicate the picture even further, political authorities, from city councils to the US Congress have created other nonpublic organizations as mechanisms for carrying out public policy. At the local level, city councils may create nonprofit development authorities to facilitate the process of economic development. At the federal level, Congress has created a number of different organizations, such as Fannie Mae and Sallie Mae. Some of these organizations are both shareholder owned, like many for-profit corporations, and backed by the full faith and credit of the US Treasury, like traditional federal agencies. Such organizations advance ends that are clearly to the benefit of the public, like expanding home ownership and higher education, but their operations simultaneously raise important questions about oversight and accountability that are critical features of how public organizations function.[13]

Finally, there are those organizations that fall squarely on the private side of the old public-private dichotomy. Private contractors, such as those providing construction services, and others, like defense contractors, fit into this category. The range of products and services provided by these organizations is ever growing and expanding, from high-profile logistical and security services provided to the military for overseas operations by organizations like Halliburton and Academi (formerly known as Blackwater) to the civil government and training contracts provided by organizations such as Lockheed Martin.

Although it is implied in the elements described in the preceding paragraphs, organizational diversity also includes the myriad objectives and activities of organizations. While the work of public organizations includes obvious and traditional activities such as the promotion and protection of health, education, safety, and defense, they also include a much wider range of less traditional work. A brief selection includes discovery (National Science Foundation [NSF], National Aeronautics and Space Administration [NASA]), socialization (community centers), preservation (museums and monuments), recreation (parks), and transportation (state and federal departments of transportation, Federal Aviation Administration [FAA]).

One purpose of this book is to introduce students to the complexity and variety of organizations as a way of pointing out that there are commonalities among organizations of any size, shape, or purpose. The following section presents a preliminary set of characteristics of organizations and ways of knowing about organizations.

Size and Structure

Public organizations have dramatically changed in size and shape over the past several centuries, and many started quite humbly. When the US Department of State was created following the ratification of the Constitution in 1789, the department was composed of seven employees including the secretary. More than 100 years later, when the Division of Grazing, a predecessor to the current Bureau of Land Management, was created, the first agency head had to borrow all of its seventeen staff members from the US Forest Service to manage the 142 million acres of public lands it was to administer.[14]

These early public organizations stand in stark contrast to the size and complexity of contemporary agencies. For example, the Department of State, with its modest beginnings, had grown to more than 39,000 employees by 2010 and more than fifty separate offices and bureaus across the globe.[15, 16] In 2004 there were some 1.43 million active duty uniformed military personnel. Local governments reflect these trends as well. Fairfax County, Virginia, an urban-suburban county in the greater Washington, DC, area employs some 10,000 full-time equivalent (FTE) employees across more than forty major departments and agencies.[17]

At the opposite end of the spectrum, myriad small public organizations provide the entire range of public services, especially in tiny, rural communities. Small, incorporated cities may have populations as small as 1,000 residents and often have payrolls of just a dozen or fewer employees. While the organizations that comprise the governments of these small public entities represent only a fraction of the public workforce, there are thousands of these units across the nation providing services to millions of people. The impact and breadth of activities undertaken by these organizations merit consideration and study and also reveal the need for considerable conceptual flexibility among scholars and practitioners who are interested in working across the diversity of contemporary organizations.

A Brief History of Organizational Studies

Formal study of organizations began around the turn of the last century, though obviously the history and existence of formal organizations dates back much further. While all organizations have in common the fact that they exist to accomplish goals, the complexity and variety of such goals has clearly expanded dramatically in the past century. Growth in industry, technology, population, and services to the public have dramatically impacted organizations structurally, functionally, socially, demographically, and even politically. According to Mary Jo Hatch, there are four historic perspectives on OT.[18] These are classical, modern, symbolic interpretive, and postmodern. We examine these ideas in more depth later in the text, but the following outline provides some historical context and content useful in framing our study of organizations.

Classical OT focuses on both sociological and classical management theories. Early on, organizational thinkers sought to discover universal principles that could be applied to organizations scientifically in the name of efficiency and productivity. In the early 1900s, engineer Frederick Taylor developed **scientific management theory,** which espoused that there was "one best way" to accomplish a task that could be scientifically studied, understood, taught, and applied.[19] Taylor viewed organizations as machines of which people were the moving parts, and he was preoccupied with the question of how to get more work out of those machines. He lived at a time of corruption, inefficiency, political immorality, and growing industrialization, which gave way to a gospel of efficiency—for efficiency was synonymous with good. He was one of the leading spokesmen who preached to businesspeople, workers, doctors, housewives, teachers, and clergy about efficiently running their organizations. Taylor's underlying values were efficiency, rationality, productivity, and profit. While the impact of Taylor's classical thinking has clearly left a lasting impression on modern-day organizations, his thinking is often criticized for being rigid, rationally focused, and impersonal.

Best known for his work on bureaucracy, a German lawyer, historian, sociologist, and economist named Max Weber defined bureaucratic organizations as hierarchical, legally based, controlled, neutral, rule bound, based on career service, and impersonal.[20] Weber's bureaucracy was characterized by careful division of labor, specialization by function, chain of command, formal framework of rules and procedures, maintenance of records, and professionalization. The central purposes of these characteristics, as Weber described, were control, uniformity, discipline, and efficiency. His explanation was consistent with developments in government in the late 1800s and early 1900s. The field of public administration grew with these principles clearly in sight, and his influence can still be seen in today's organizations. Other classical theorists, including Henri Fayol, Chester Barnard, Elton Mayo, and others extended and further developed classical concepts of authority, control, and communications first articulated by Taylor and Weber.

This early approach to the study of organizations largely ignored the human dimension, focusing instead on efficiency, rationality, money, and authority. In 1927, a Harvard psychologist in the School of Business, Elton Mayo, and his student assistant, Fritz Roethlisberger, started a five-year study of factors effecting productivity in Western Electric's Hawthorne Works plant near Chicago.[21, 22] For example, they sought to determine if better working conditions, brighter lighting, formal or informal structural changes, more breaks, or different work spaces increased employee output. As they studied the different conditions, they found that productivity did go up. At this point, their results became confusing. After increasing illumination, the researchers began to turn the lighting down further and further until employees were almost in the dark, and productivity still went up. They isolated workers and productivity improved. They then put workers into work groups and worker output increased.

The phenomenon they ultimately recognized has been come to be known as the **Hawthorne effect,** which means that people change their behavior when they know they are being observed or paid attention to. They also found that informal social groups had a strong effect on productivity and that cohesive work groups can effect productivity. They started off looking at the situation from one perspective and ended up refining that to include an understanding of the human dimension in organizations. The Hawthorne studies opened the way to investigate factors beyond the formal organization and established the importance of social structure, organizational culture, and worker interaction as vital elements of productive organizations.

According to Hatch's model, from the classical school of thinking came the modern perspective, whose foundations could be traced back to systems theory.[23, 24, 25] Systems theory looks at factors both internal and external to the organization to see how and why people perform their jobs the way they do. Daniel Katz and Kahn argued that social organizations were living systems that continually interacted with their environment and, thus, were highly dependent on their external environment to maintain their internal one.[26] As a result, organizations constantly adjust and adapt in response to their environment in order to avoid entropy. This reasoning led them to accurately predict that organizations would attempt to enhance their capacities for assessing environmental factors.

Systems are sets of variable, dynamic, complicated, and interrelated components that interact with the world. A system takes energy and resources from the environment in the form of inputs and transforms it into outputs (services, information, etc.). Systems theory recognizes the dependence of organizations on their environments, recognizes that a number of approaches may be successful, and emphasizes the importance of information. Systems theory looks at differentiation rather than specialization and values the synergy that comes from dealing with thousands of interdependent relationships—linkages to people, groups, or organizations with diverse goals, opinions, and beliefs.

The third perspective in Hatch's model is the symbolic interpretive perspective, in which it is espoused that reality is socially constructed. Additionally, this approach recognizes that actions are often a result of the meanings that individuals attach to a particular social construct.

The final perspective presented by Hatch is postmodernism. Postmodern organizational theories tend to value multiple ways of knowing and resist the belief that there is one best way or one universal truth to be found in an organization. Additionally, postmodernism typically implies a deep skepticism of hierarchy and focuses, instead, on complexity, varying forms of diversity and difference, and the growing experience of ambiguity in organizations.

What Hatch's framework reveals beyond the loose historical eras that characterize organization studies is that we have multiple perspectives from which to view them. It is important to understand that there are different forms of organizations that perform more or less effectively in different environments and under different conditions. Organizations cannot ignore formality or context. They must have specialized employees but must be flexible enough to deal with adversity, change, and competition. They must be closed in the sense that boundaries are identifiable and activities predictable yet be open to change within the organization and the environment. With that, let's explore the uniqueness of public organizations, to further establish the context for this text.

A Brief Political History

If, as we are arguing, the study of public organizations stands apart from the study of other sorts of organization in critical ways, then it is important to identify some source of the difference. Obviously, organizations are not insulated from the social conditions and trends of the societies in which they operate. And while political and social dynamics are likely to be related, the political environment shapes the behaviors and structures of public organizations in ways that deserve separate focus.

According to Frederick Mosher in *Democracy and the Public Service,* the governance of our country has undergone significant shifts over time.[27] These shifts are helpful in understanding the context of our government, public administration, and modern public organizations. These are fundamental shifts in "the purposes, phases, and methods of federal operations."[28] Mosher identifies the following shifts in experiences in and around governance and organizations in the United States.

1789–1829: Government by the Gentlemen

It was during this time that the Constitution was ratified. Only those of the highest socio-economic status took part in governance. This stratification based on socioeconomic status is consistent with James Madison's description of a "natural aristocracy" that he believed would emerge in American society, based on merit. Rather than the hereditary aristocracy, or ruling class, that existed in England, those who would rise to prominence in American government would do so because of their economic and intellectual prowess. It was, however, white, wealthy, male property owners who became largely responsible for defining governance during this era.

1829–1883: Government by Common Man

During this period in our history, President Jackson was elected on a platform of reform. Jackson was in favor of replacing the caucus system in elections and encouraging the common man to be involved in government. Unions were expanding, and the frontier spirit was consistent with increased democratization. States were removing property requirements from voting, and Wyoming, in 1869, even let women vote. A lot of these changes were accomplished through political parties.

As a result, one did not necessarily have to be a man or a wealthy property owner in order to participate in governance. One only had to be a loyal party member. While this made the face of government and workforces more representative, it also brought about spoils and patronage systems in which family, friends, and loyal party members used their connections to find work in governance. This, of course, led to corruption and, subsequently, to loss of respect for government and public servants. Allegations were that increasing numbers of unqualified people were appointed to government positions.

As a result of the corruption associated with the spoils system, the country underwent the civil service reform movement—the Progressive reform movement—which was antiparty, spoils, and patronage and attempted to deal with these problems. The "good guys" during this reform movement were those who were antipolitical party, while the "bad guys" were in favor of political parties. This movement culminated with passage of the Pendleton Act in 1883, which was designed to take power away from the parties by saying that it was illegal to hire-fire on the basis of party affiliation and created a new criterion for government service, nonpartisanship. So the good guys won. Mosher called this shift "government by the good."

1883–1906: Government by the Good

The notion of the "good" during this period can be understood and seen in two different ways. First, this was an era of the morally upright in government. This is in part a response to the corruption that was seen as an outcome of the spoils system. The second form of good comes to be defined as competent and nonpartisan. Public administration was defined as neutral and independent from politics and nonpartisan.

The question that emerged about this definition was the following: How do administrators stay neutral yet responsive to elected officials and democratic controls? Woodrow Wilson offered a solution in 1887. Wilson described a separation of political decision making from administrative implementation, what we now call the **politics-administration dichotomy**. He explained that the core elements and objectives of policy were to be determined by elected representatives and that administration would be neutrally or scientifically carried out by administrators. There would, according to Wilson, be little threat of abuse from administrative discretion. Wilson argued that politics may set tasks and goals for administration but should not manipulate the process. He had modest aims for his work, which is now considered to be the beginning of public administration as a field of study and practice.

Wilson's dichotomy was a conceptual separation—the administrative function was separate and distinct. This brought back some prestige and respect to public service. It suggested that we should look at the two separately and consider carefully the expertise needed to truly manage government and the protection of administration from politics—putting democratic principles and policymaking on top and subordinated public administration to public opinion.

Goodnow, founder and first president of the American Political Science Association, extended and articulated the notion of bureaucratic neutrality.[29] He is known for saying that "there is no 'republican' way to build a road." Goodnow believed that executing authority was subordinate to creating authority and was an advocate of Wilson's politics-administration dichotomy. He believed that politics and administration could be distinguished as "expression of the will of the state and the execution of that will," though did feel that politics should have some control over administration, however, which was a slight shift away from the dichotomy.

1906–1937: Government by the Efficient

Civil service reform and neutral competence (expertise independent from politics) fit nicely with what was happening in the private sector. By early 1906, the Industrial Revolution was in full swing and resulted in the emergence of a new type of organization, one that separated ownership and management. The search for more scientific management procedures, as discussed in Chapter 2, created a new focus on efficiency and production. Much of the moral tone from the previously discussed era stayed intact—but it went from morality as nonpartisanship to morality as efficiency. Government tried to become more businesslike and rational through the use of planning, specialization of workers, and standardization. This still has a profound effect on current ideas about how government should be fixed, which are based on the assumption that management is separate from politics, so there *must* be some set of management truths that work equally well in government as they do in private businesses.

Based on Mosher's model our country had gone from an aristocracy, to one in which the common man was included in governance, to morally upright and nonpartisan, to efficient.[30] One era did not really replace the other; they simply built upon each other. As the century progressed, the government was growing and changing. Not only was it providing required public services, but after World War I and the Great Depression, the government became involved in managing social and economic change. The focus on efficiency, therefore, gave way to the next era.

1937–1955: Government by the Administrators

During this period, public administrators were not mere technicians but rather they were generalist managers in charge of large, complex, social programs, which had grown during the New Deal period. Schools of public administration were well established, and managers were more sensitive to politics. There existed a growing acceptance of the fact that politics and administration were not entirely separate and an increasing concern about presidential control of bureaucracy. Two presidents, Roosevelt and Eisenhower, commissioned committees to look at the organization of government to help the president get control of and manage the bureaucracy.

World War II ended during this time frame. After the war, the United States and the Soviet Union emerged as world superpowers. Competition around knowledge building, space travel, defense systems, and technology was high between the countries. Modern organizations were impacted heavily by this because they were now exposed to different ideas, cultures, trade arrangements, and technologies that broadened our views of who we were and what we could be. Again, Mosher's model did not replace one era with another—it layered them. Public servants were to be statesmen, common men, and morally upright, efficient administrators.

1955–1968: Government by the Professionals

During this period of time, schools of public administration were well established. Public administration and public organizations grew and expanded optimistically. This was the era of the educated. Sputnick was launched by the USSR in 1957, and the United States believed that they were technologically and educationally behind. There was a revolution in the utilization of the professionals, the experts, and the white-collar worker with specialized knowledge with training in medicine, engineering, law, and psychology that generated some tension between public values and administrative values.

1968–Present: Government by the?

In part as a result of the turbulence of the 1960s, new answers to dealing with the tension between public and administrative values began to emerge. One movement was New Public Administration (NPA) and was the first of several calls to make public administration more public oriented and more political. During this time, agencies were reviewed, in an attempt to reverse some of the growth of previous decades. This was a more conservative agenda than had existed in the past. Advocates argued that public administration was not value free and that it ought to openly advance values such as social equity, democracy, and environmental quality. To this day, there is still not a lot of agreement about what sort of values or models are dominant or should be held as the responsibilities of public agencies. During this era, there was a blurring distinction between public and private, reform, and technology. This is a lengthy era, in which the country experienced post–Cold War shifts, the tearing down of the Berlin Wall, various pursuits of free markets, serious political changes, and war, each serving to redefine and reform our thinking and practice in various ways (see Figure 1.1).

While these eras are loose conceptualizations of the major administrative trends at any period of time, and there is necessarily some overlap between them, they are useful in identifying both significant and changing currents in the field.

Sociology of Knowledge: Ways of Knowing about Organizations

As we noted earlier, organizations reflect the societal context in which they operate. Knowledge—what we know and what we don't—as well as how we acquire that knowledge shape how organizations respond to the world they are in. Gareth Morgan makes the case that it is possible to use several different metaphors to understand how organizations work.[31] Metaphors are the comparison of two dissimilar entities in order to highlight a particular and important attribute of the thing being studied. Among others, Morgan compares organizations with machines, natural organisms, brains, and political systems. Each metaphor highlights different attributes of how organizations behave and what shapes that behavior. While some metaphors are more widely used than others, no one metaphor is exhaustive in its ability to capture the rich and sophisticated activities of organizations. Just as no one metaphor is sufficient to capture all of the variations of organizational behavior, neither is there one theory or one body of knowledge that can do so either. Beyond metaphors, this section of the chapter identifies two other categories of knowledge—paradigms and disciplines; each has been used to frame our thinking about organizations.

Thomas Kuhn, in his book *The Structure of Scientific Revolutions*, outlines the theory of paradigms as they relate to the nature and development of scientific knowledge.[32] According to Kuhn, paradigms are mutually exclusive and incommensurable; one cannot believe in two paradigms simultaneously. For example, a clear case of contending scientific paradigms and the shift from one to another is found in a move from a geocentric—earth-centered—view of the solar system to a heliocentric—sun-centered—view. There are a number of important aspects to this example. First, it shows how paradigms are mutually exclusive and incommensurable. The earth and sun cannot simultaneously be the center of the solar system. Moreover, one cannot simultaneously believe that both are true. Extending the example further, it reveals how paradigmatic commitments shape not only how one sees the world but what questions are asked in order to understand the world and what actions are possible to live within that world. Understanding how this is the case requires moving from this

Figure 1.1 A Brief Timeline of Organization Theory and Frederick Mosher's Eras of Governance

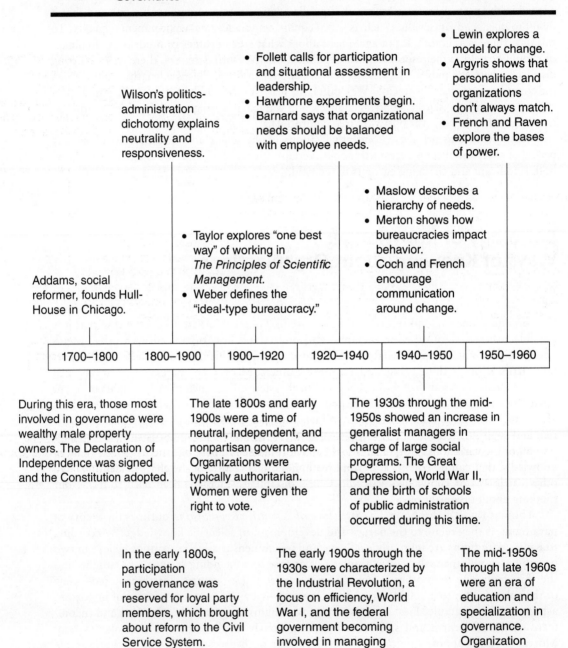

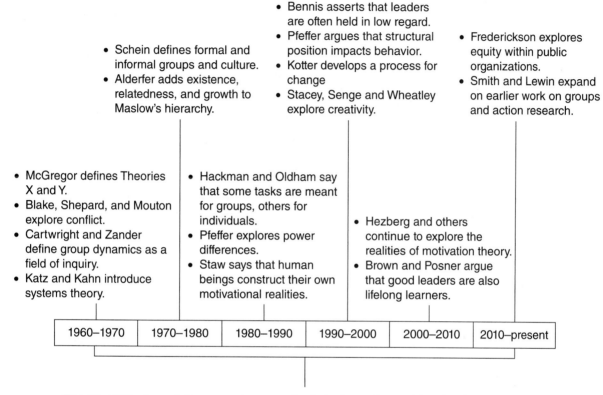

- Schein defines formal and informal groups and culture.
- Alderfer adds existence, relatedness, and growth to Maslow's hierarchy.

- Bennis asserts that leaders are often held in low regard.
- Pfeffer argues that structural position impacts behavior.
- Kotter develops a process for change
- Stacey, Senge and Wheatley explore creativity.

- Frederickson explores equity within public organizations.
- Smith and Lewin expand on earlier work on groups and action research.

- McGregor defines Theories X and Y.
- Blake, Shepard, and Mouton explore conflict.
- Cartwright and Zander define group dynamics as a field of inquiry.
- Katz and Kahn introduce systems theory.

- Hackman and Oldham say that some tasks are meant for groups, others for individuals.
- Pfeffer explores power differences.
- Staw says that human beings construct their own motivational realities.

- Hezberg and others continue to explore the realities of motivation theory.
- Brown and Posner argue that good leaders are also lifelong learners.

| 1960–1970 | 1970–1980 | 1980–1990 | 1990–2000 | 2000–2010 | 2010–present |

The late 1960s through the present represent a time of massive social and technological change. Public administration was encouraged to be more responsive and to openly advance the values of classic liberalism. Management trends such as total quality management came on the scene, while virtual and self-directed teams were also explored. Diversity of all types became much more broadly embraced throughout society and within organizations.

celestial example to a more terrestrial case. Consider the behavior of light. Light has the unique ability to behave both like a wave and like a particle. Which light one chooses to work from (wave or particle) will determine what sorts of questions can be asked about the behavior of light and how the answers can be determined. Asking particle questions will not yield wave answers or vice versa. Similarly, in the social sciences, if one believes that human behavior can be understood as wholly rational, this choice implies different questions *and* yields different answers than does the understanding of human behavior as nonrational (emotional, intuitive, etc.).

At first glance, the inclusion of a philosopher of science in an OT text may seem a bit odd, but we believe that the notion of paradigms reveals important insights into the range of thinking about organizations and their functions. Burrell and Morgan suggest that there are several sociological paradigms that can be used to understand organizations.[33] According to Burrell and Morgan, theories of organization all fall into one of four distinct paradigms that are useful in not only understanding organization's behavior but also in understanding how people study and understand those organizations in the first place.[34]

There are difficulties associated with the conceptual use of paradigms in the social sciences. One difficulty is that unlike the physical sciences—wherein scientific revolutions or paradigm shifts occur when the empirical evidence of the new paradigm comes to outweigh, better describe, and predict the behavior of a physical system than does the old paradigm—in the social sciences the empirical evidence supporting one paradigm in relation to another continues to be contradictory and shows little likelihood of being resolved. A second problem is that the line between one paradigm and another in the social sciences—the extent to which paradigms are truly mutually exclusive and incommensurable—is less clear. The rational-nonrational example of human behavior is a case in point. It can be, and often is argued, that rational-nonrational is a false dichotomy and that human behavior is more complex. Perhaps it is the case that humans behave rationally in some cases and nonrationally in other instances or that rationality exists along a sort of continuum from wholly rational, to bounded-rationality, to nonrational, to irrational.

Given this fundamental and apparently insurmountable problem, why continue to use the concept of paradigms? The claim we make is that paradigms do something that other concepts, such as models and metaphors, don't do nearly as well. Paradigms clearly and intentionally reveal what philosophers call epistemology and ontology. In simple terms, epistemology is a theory of knowledge. It is a study of what can be known about the world and how we can know it. Ontology, sometimes used interchangeably (and somewhat imprecisely) with the term *metaphysics*, is a theory about the nature of the world and how it works. So the exploration of multiple paradigms reveals the fundamentally different understandings held by the range of social and organizational theorists about the nature of the world and what we can know about it.

More specifically, different paradigms have different, incommensurable, and mutually exclusive views about the nature of the world and what can be known about it. By extension then, paradigmatic commitments also imply something about what sorts of actions are possible and appropriate.

The conceptual use of paradigms does at least two things for students of organization. First, it helps reveal the ontological and epistemological commitments of adherents of any given paradigm. This is useful for analyzing and describing what organizations do and why.

The second benefit can be described more indirectly. A common, popular culture definition of *insanity* is doing the same thing over and over and expecting different outcomes. If paradigms presume or predetermine what questions we ask and what answers are possible, it seems likely that paradigms also prescribe and limit the range of actions and strategies that are conceivable. If our organizations do the same thing over and over again and continue to see suboptimal outcomes, perhaps shifting the paradigms we use to study and understand organizations can reveal new options for action.

A Note about Categories

At least as early as the work of Aristotle, Western empiricism has been engaged in an evolving effort to develop an ever more sophisticated and accurate taxonomy or framework of categories into which the world around us can be divided. The general trend in this process has been to develop taxonomies in which categories are mutually exclusive and exhaustive. Every entity, whether a bacterium or battleship, can fit into one specific category and no more than one category. For example, the system of classification for biological entities first developed by Linnaeus functions in this way.[35] Every living entity can fit into one and only one kingdom, phylum, order, family, genus, and species. This same tendency exists in the social sciences where we have worked to create exhaustive and mutually exclusive sets of disciplines (e.g., sociology, psychology, economics, political science) or organization types (e.g., public, private, nonprofit). Although such categories are useful as a sort of shorthand in our efforts to rapidly and systematically make sense of the world, and there are real differences between the things under consideration, the distinctions between categories frequently blur, blend, and even break.

However, if the study of organizations is to be something more than a big, jumbled mess, it is necessary to establish and use various taxonomies. Readers should be aware that we, as organization theorists and teachers attempting to help students learn about the messy and fascinating world of organizations, have chosen any number of categorization schemes and do our best to conform to the definitions associated with those schemes. However, we also recognize that many of the categories and definitions we use collapse under close examination. Our intent is to be as consistent as we can with the categories and definitions we use. At the same time, we believe that it is necessary, and we strive to help our students to practice the conceptual flexibility to become comfortable with the sorts of tensions and even paradoxes that emerge between and within the categorical schemes that we and others use.

Influential Theories and Paradigms in the Social Sciences

The notion of paradigms is applicable as we begin to examine the intellectual disciplines that shape the thinking about organizations. While there are arguably other influential bodies of knowledge, three broad areas—the social sciences, the physical sciences, and the humanities—can be used to frame the primary influences on OT.

Social Sciences: Sociology, Psychology, Economics, and Political Science

Within the social sciences, this book will focus primarily on the contributions from four different disciplines—sociology, psychology, economics, and political science. Some of the earliest thinking about organizations is found in the work of Max Weber.[36] As noted earlier in the chapter, Weber was interested in the way groups of people come together and behave in groups. Weber's understandings of bureaucracy and authority (see Chapter 2) have been enormously influential and continue to have an impact on OT and practice. Many other sociologists have taken up where Weber left off, examining questions of power, culture, and socialization—all of which are connected to the behavior of people in groups.

If organizations are no more than collections of people, then another means of shedding light on their actions is through the examination of individual and collective psychology. Theorists from this discipline are interested in questions such as the following: What drives individuals' perceptions of the world around them? How do individuals and groups make sense of those situations? How do individuals and groups behave as they pursue particular goals and objectives?

The third scholarly discipline that has had a clear influence on organizational thinking is economics. A fundamental question for economists is the following: What motivates people to act? Based on the answers to this question, economists interested in organizations begin to explore topics that include the following: How can groups of people be motivated to accomplish organizational ends? What are the most efficient ways of structuring and operating organizations?

The final academic discipline considered in this collection of social sciences is included not for its contribution but instead for its notable lack of interest and input in the study of organizations. Given that political scientists are generally interested in questions of power and authority and associated structures and processes and also that public organizations are very much at the heart of efforts to accomplish political ends, the lack of original contributions to the field is indeed interesting. Although political scientists have had comparatively little to say about organizations specifically, they have a great deal they can add to the discussion of organizations and democracy. They have contributions to make in two related areas that are important to OT generally and to theories of public organizations specifically. Broadly, the two issues where political science has a clear contribution to make are in questions of how public organizations do or can contribute to a functional democracy and how, if at all, the ideals of democracy can be embodied in the internal processes of organizations.

Physical-Natural Sciences: Chaos Theory, Ecological Sciences, and Cybernetics-Artificial Intelligence

Interestingly, OT also has a robust history of drawing from the physical and natural sciences. There are a range of instances where parallels and perhaps even more direct connections can be drawn between social and natural phenomena. One of the most recent instances of this is the use of concepts developed in chaos and complexity theories (realizing that these are not synonymous areas of study). Ideas such as sensitivity to initial conditions and self-organizing systems seem to describe social systems nearly as well as metrological or fluid systems. Another example of OT use of the natural sciences includes concepts such as resource competition and population dynamics from the biological and ecological sciences. Here, the general notion is that individual and groups of organizations can be understood based on our knowledge of how biological entities survive in natural environments. Finally, an example of applied sciences can be found in the application of cognitive sciences, cybernetics, and artificial intelligence to the way organizations manage information and make decisions. The extent to which the influence of the physical sciences has been conceptual and metaphorical rather than a direct application of mathematical or empirical modeling is an open, and sometimes contentious, question. Nevertheless, the influence of the physical sciences to date is undeniable and is likely to continue.

The Humanities: Philosophy and Literature

More recently, thinking emerging from the humanities, and especially literary theory and philosophy, has come to be influential on social and organization theory. For example, literary theorists such as Fredric Jameson and Jacques Derrida and philosophers such as Michel Foucault have introduced concepts generally associated with postmodernism into the social sciences and public administration specifically. Work in the humanities has been influential in prompting public administration scholars—and to a lesser extent, practitioners—to more intentionally examine their paradigmatic commitments and the consequences of those commitments. Recent work drawing on these influences strives to find new ways to operationalize the theories into administrative and organizational practices. Though many of the ideas remain controversial, recent thinking drawn from the humanities has certainly broadened the discourse within the field.

Levels of Analysis

Looking across the fields of study that influence organizational thinking, one issue that should be apparent is that many of these approaches use different units of analysis, ranging from a single decision to entire populations of organizations. Within each of the disciplines that were previously described, researchers examine different aspects of the organization and select a unit of analysis that allows them to answer their questions of interests. Rather than identifying discrete units of analysis, we utilize a framework of five levels of analysis into which the theories we consider will loosely fall.

- *Individual and small group:* Questions at this level include developing an understanding of individual behavior, motivation, and responses to authority.
- *Structural:* At this level, the focus is on internal organizational structures, such as formal and informal authority, communications, and decision making.
- *Environmental:* Attention at this level centers on the relationship between the organization and its immediate environment including clients, constituents, suppliers, regulators, and oversight organizations.
- *Industrial:* Attention at the industrial level is given to how groups of similar organizations, such as school districts, operate and what influences that operation.
- *Societal:* At this level, questions center on how organizations influence entire societies and vice versa.[37]

Using these categories as a way of framing how we examine organizations is useful because it makes explicit an intuitive understanding of organizations that we already use. When we think about our experience in organizations, we often think about our interaction with particular employees (individual and small group), our encounters with formal procedures or authority, whether too much or too little (structural), or the ability or inability of entire agencies to meet community needs (environmental). Making these experiential and intuitive categories explicit gives us the ability to better organize and distinguish both theories and their resulting strategies.

The Book's Approach

This book seeks to provide the reader with a sense of coherence and connectedness among various theories of organizations and will specifically place those theories into the context of public organizations. We explore the development of the field in terms of both theory and practice. Toward that end, the historical, institutional, and political context of the OT is examined throughout our treatment, as are current trends and issues in the field. We also emphasize both explicit and implicit values underlying the evolution of public administration and the implications of those values for the future of the field. This emphasis allows readers to familiarize themselves with the writings of prominent scholars and practitioners and the practical or operational implications of their ideas. The book intends to be practical and to suggest multiple ways to view organizations through different lenses such that students can craft strategies to take effective action in the organizations with which they find themselves working. Our attention to explicit and implicit values works at a more political level as well, and we want to push readers to consider the role and place of public administration in our social and political, or governance, system.

Voice of the Book

There are several premises that should be articulated here at the beginning of the book and that will be important for interpreting what appears in the subsequent chapters. First, we point out that there are multiple paradigms present in the OT research and literature. These paradigms are actively held and utilized both for understanding and for managing public organizations. Kuhn, who developed the notion of scientific paradigms in seeking to understand and describe the development of empirical sciences, argued that paradigms are mutually exclusive and incommensurable; one could not adhere to two paradigms simultaneously. In an overly simple example from astronomy, one cannot simultaneously seek to understand the solar system as geocentric and heliocentric. More recently, social scientists like Burrell and Morgan have sought to demonstrate how social theory conforms with Kuhn's notion of paradigms. Our thinking on this point follows David Farmer's extensive exploration of epistemic pluralism.[38] We argue that while it may in fact be true that paradigms are logically incommensurable, as students and inhabitants of organizations, we make sense of and come to know about organizations in many different ways. We explicitly and implicitly use plural bodies of knowledge—epistemological paradigms—as a way of understanding and operating in organizations.

Second, we believe that these paradigms are best understood as being socially constructed. While there are clear and important real-world consequences of organizational actions, we understand the structures, processes, and interpretations of organizations to be built and maintained primarily in the minds and behaviors of those who are involved with organizations in some way. A metaphor from the game of chess may be of some use here in making this concept clear. While the eight-square-by-eight-square chessboard provides some real constraints on how the game of chess is played and there are a clear and formal set of rules governing play, the majority and most interesting structure (patterns of behavior) to the game is provided by the complex but widely known strategies that are held in the heads of the players. What makes chess fascinating is not simply the game as constrained by the board and formal rules but the stable patterns that have been developed and shared among players worldwide over the long history of the game. Similarly, while there are real constraints and influences on organizations, the interesting patterns, strategies, and informal rules that govern behavior in an organization exist primarily in the gray matter between people's ears, not the white matter between the covers of policy manuals or elsewhere in the real world. We believe that the best way to identify and examine these gray matter rules is by following an analytical theme that reveals paradigmatic commitments, consequences, contributions, and critiques of organization theories that will be treated throughout the book.

We are also committed to the retention of the possibility of human agency—intentional, directed human action. We hold to the belief that individuals and groups can choose to act together in such a way that organizations and the broader community can benefit. Besides, what fun would it be to live in a world where we can examine our situation but do nothing about it?

The following chapters focus primarily on the descriptive and prescriptive aspects of the theories under consideration. We have intentionally chosen to avoid attention to predictive theories—largely because we feel that as a practical matter prediction is largely too resource intense and imprecise to merit extensive attention. Given that even with the best science and computer modeling meteorologists have at their disposal, detailed weather forecasting is notoriously unreliable beyond just a few days. Throwing in the element of human behavior, and the prediction of organizational behavior seems a sketchy proposition.

More theoretically, a reluctance to engage in prediction is consistent with our paradigmatic commitments. Positioning ourselves as we have as constructivists, claims about the ability to make accurate predictions of individual or organizational behavior would push us toward a sort of positivist paradigm that we have largely rejected. Paradigmatically, the extreme position of logical positivists is that given enough information about any physical or social system—and a sufficient understanding of the causal laws—scientists can predict the position of all actors in the system at any point in the future. The world is nothing more than a highly complex, multidimensional billiards game. The difficulty is that such a commitment to prediction simultaneously undermines a commitment to human agency. If we can predict what every element of the system will do in the future, what room does that leave for human will?

It should be acknowledged that this is a simplified caricature of positivism; there are few, if any, social scientists who hold such a position. However, this thought experiment does place in stark contrast the logical consequences of one particular paradigmatic commitment.

Organization and Content of the Book

With this background in mind, the remaining task of this first chapter is to give a brief description of what will be covered and how we'll proceed through the remainder of the book.

Structurally, the book is organized into three distinct parts. These parts focus on providing a brief introduction to the field, presenting a rough historical sketch of OT, revealing how the major theories deal with several practical managerial and organizational functions, and finally, suggesting ways in which emerging post-traditional theories might offer new and promising opportunities.

This chapter provides an introduction and orientation to OT as well as an overview of the approach and content of the book.

Part I: Theories of Organization

Part I (Chapters 2–4) presents a historical overview of the development of OT. Each chapter presents a collection of theorists and theories that represent the dominant lines of thought during the time period, the contributions that these theories add to the understanding of organizations, and description of current examples of their influence. Each chapter also includes a shorter description of "other voices" that emerged at roughly the same time. These other voices represent alternative discourses, paradigms, or orientations to the mainstream thinking. The chapters in Part I each include cases that reveal how the concepts and ideas from each chapter have been expressed in real-world governance institutions.

Chapter 2—Classical Foundations: The Historical Context of a New Field of Study: Explores early organization and management theories including ideal types of bureaucracy and authority, principles of scientific management, and early approaches to the systematic study and practice of management. The other or alternative voice in this period is drawn from the work of Mary Parker Follett and notions of the law of the situation and power with rather than power over.

Chapter 3—Behavioral Revolution: Examines the alternatives developing out of and in response to classical approaches to organizations. The historical developments followed in this chapter start with the Hawthorne experiments and Chester Barnard's ideas and trace their innovations into a wide range of work done following the Second World War, including human relations theories (HRTs), Herbert Simon's work on bounded rationality and satisficing, and concluding with the development of systems theory. Other voices in this period are represented by the emergence of institutionalism and other structural functionalist thinking as well as Dwight Waldo's normative challenges in public administration.

Chapter 4—Life after Berger and Luckmann—A Theoretically Diverse World: Introduces the idea of social construction in OT and then summarizes several of the ontologically diverse theories of organization that have emerged from contemporary thinking about organizations. Particular attention is given to two economic theories of organization—transaction cost economics and agency theory and their influence on thinking about public organizations. Other theories examined include chaos and complexity theories, resource dependence and contingency theories, and network theory. The chapter also gives attention to more constructivist or interpretivist theories such as sensemaking.

Part II: Issues, Strategies, and Tactics

The focus of Part II (Chapters 5–8) shifts from a historical overview of the emergence of major organizational theories to the application of those theories to broad areas of organizational activity. Attention is given to how each theory included helps the reader to understand the activity; the assumptions that underpin the theories being examined; benefits and limitations of the theory's application; and Current Expressions, or case examples of the theory as applied in contemporary governance organizations.

Chapter 5—Managing Individual Behavior: This chapter reviews many of the dominant approaches to managing individual behavior. It explores and compares assumptions about motivations and incentives and connects them to historical and contemporary management approaches.

Chapter 6—Understanding and Shaping Group Dynamics: Chapter 6 shifts its level of analysis from the individual to the group and examines different approaches to understanding formal and informal mechanisms of group development including the development of social norms, organization culture, and institutional dynamics.

Chapter 7—Affecting Organization Change: With concepts of individual and group dynamics in mind, this chapter examines a range of approaches for initiating and managing intentional effective organization change. The chapter gives attention to the role of organization development (OD) approaches, participation, and leadership-centered changes.

Chapter 8—Managing Organization-Environment Relations: The final chapter in Part II again shifts levels of analysis and examines approaches organizations might use to manage their relationship with a wider environment including clients, citizens, regulators, legislators, political executives, and others.

Part III: Toward Post-Positivist Organizations

The final part of the book intentionally shifts its attention to post-positivist thinking and applications. This final section introduces many of the critical and affirmative aspects of post-positivist thinking and explores ways to apply these aspects in real settings of contemporary organizations.

Chapter 9—Escaping the Void: History of Post-Positivism: This chapter presents a brief introduction to the history and heterodox thinking that has emerged in the past twenty years with an emphasis on their appearance in public administration. Chapter 9 also connects back to Part I in demonstrating how elements of the "other voices" identified in the first part of the book can be traced to post-traditional theory.

Chapter 10—Learning to Fly: Applying Post-Positivist Theory: The second chapter in Part III turns its attention to an exploration of how post-positivist theories can be, and in some cases already are being, applied in organizations involved in governance. The intention of this chapter is severalfold. First, it demonstrates that post-positivist theory is applicable in useful rather than narrowly esoteric ways. It reveals how the theory and application may not constitute a radical departure from existing practice but still differs in subtle but important ways. Finally, it suggests new and emerging opportunities to further apply post-traditional theory in ways that support governance organizations and broader democratic society.

Chapter 11—Conclusion: This Is the Beginning: The final chapter of the book returns to several of the themes introduced in this chapter and commends readers not to adopt any particular approach to organizations but rather to embrace a reflexive and flexible attitude. The chapter also further explores implications of traditional and post-traditional OT for democratic processes in an increasingly complex and diverse society.

Diving In

There are two last comments we want to make before you leap headfirst into the book and its ideas. One is that because many of these ideas are likely to be new to you, give yourself plenty of time to read and reflect. Give some thought, for example, to how the ideas you read about appear in organizations you're familiar with and what factors or attributes support or hinder that application. Toward that end, we posed a range of reflection and discussion questions throughout all of the chapters. that can be used to prompt the sort of consideration and reflection we have in mind or that can be used to generate discussion in the classroom. Try to use these—and other questions that come to your mind as you read—to inform and extend your consideration of the ideas we introduce.

We also want to note that while we think the order and structure of the book is well suited to building a formidable and useful understanding of OT, it is certainly possible to arrange or rearrange the readings into other orders or in other arrangements that support grasping the ideas just as effectively as our framework. For example, one might use the chapters in Part II to structure reading of the book and supplement the reading of Chapters 5 through 8 with selected readings from chapters in Part I and even Part III. Regardless of the approach you use, at this point, we invite you to dive in and see where your exploration leads you. We encourage you, as a student of OT, to follow your curiosity and see where it leads you through the Contents and Index. Don't hesitate to read ahead or look back to material you've already covered. OT and organization practice are endlessly fascinating areas to study. We hope that you find that study as useful and interesting as we do. ■

Notes

1. Our notion of ideology is a bit broader than the widely held connotation centered on liberal or conservative, Democratic or Republican political ideology. Following McSwite, we view ideology as being a wide ranging set of beliefs and assumptions, largely held unconsciously, that make the world sensible to us.
2. Paul Appleby, *Citizens as Sovereigns* (Syracuse, NY: Syracuse University Press, 1962).
3. Ibid.
4. W. C. Rich, *The Politics of Urban Personnel Policy: Reformers, Politicians, and Bureaucrats* (Port Washington, NY: Kennikat Press, 1982).
5. F. J. Thompson, "The Politics of Public Personnel Administration," in *Public Personnel Administration: Problems and Prospects*, 3rd ed., ed. Steven W. Hays and Richard C. Kearney (Englewood Cliffs, NJ: Prentice Hall, 1995), 4–16.

6. Y. S. Lee, *Public Personnel Administration and Constitutional Values* (Westport, CT: Quorum Books, 1992).

7. D. H. Rosenbloom, "What Every Personnel Manager Should Know about the Constitution," in *Public Personnel Administration: Problems and Prospects,* 3rd ed., ed. Steven W. Hays and Richard C. Kearney (Englewood Cliffs, NJ: Prentice Hall, 1995), 20–36.

8. N. J. Cayer, *Public Personnel Administration in the U.S.,* 2nd ed. (New York: St. Martin's Press, 1996).

9. Rosenbloom, "What Every Personnel Manager Should Know about the Constitution."

10. G. S. Hartman, G. W. Homer, and J. E. Menditto, "Human Resource Management Legal Issues: An Overview," in *Handbook of Human Resource Management in Government,* ed. S. E. Condrey (San Francisco: Jossey-Bass, 1998), 145–164.

11. A. Salzstein, "Personnel Management in the Local Government Setting," in *Public Personnel Administration: Problems and Prospects,* 3rd ed., ed. Steven W. Hays and Richard C. Kearney (Englewood Cliffs, NJ: Prentice Hall, 1995), 37–53.

12. John Rohr, *To Run a Constitution: The Legitimacy of the Administrative State* (Lawrence: University of Kansas Press, 1986).

13. Harold Seidman, "The Quasi World of the Federal Government," *The Brookings Review* (Summer 1988): 23–27.

14. Philip O. Foss, *Politics and Grass* (Seattle: University of Washington Press, 1960).

15. "Office of Personnel Management," March 26, 2014, http://www.census.gov/compendia/statab/cats/federal_govt_finances_employment/federal_civilian_employment.html.

16. "U.S. Department of State," December 5, 2010, http://www.state.gov.

17. "Fairfax County, Virginia," December 5, 2010, http://www.fairfaxcounty.gov.

18. Mary Jo Hatch, *Organization Theory: Modern, Symbolic and Postmodern Perspectives* (New York: Oxford University Press, 1997).

19. Frederick W. Taylor, *The Principles of Scientific Management* (New York: Harper Brothers, 1911).

20. Max Weber, *From Max Weber: Essays In Sociology,* trans. H. H. Gerth and C. Wright (Oxford, UK: Oxford University Press, 1946).

21. Elton Mayo, *The Human Problems of Industrialized Civilization* (New York: Macmillan, 1933).

22. Fritz Roethlisberger and W. J. Dickson, *Management and the Worker: An Account of the Research Program Conducted by the Western Electric Company, Hawthorne Works, Chicago* (Cambridge, MA: Harvard University Press, 1939).

23. Hatch, *Organization Theory.*

24. Ludwig von Bertalanffy, *General System Theory: Foundations, Development, Applications* (New York: George Braziller, 1968).

25. Daniel Katz and Robert L. Kahn, *The Social Psychology of Organization* (New York: Wiley, 1966).

26. Ibid.

27. Frederick C. Mosher, *Democracy and the Public Service,* 2nd ed. (New York: Oxford University Press, 1982).

28. Ibid.

29. Frank K. Goodnow, *Politics and Administration: A Study in Government* (New York: Russell and Russell, 1900).

30. Mosher, *Democracy and the Public Service.*

31. Gareth Morgan, *Images of Organization* (Thousand Oaks, CA: Sage, 1997).

32. Thomas Kuhn, *The Structure of Scientific Revolutions* (Chicago: University of Chicago Press, 1970).

33. Gibson Burrell and Gareth Morgan, *Sociological Paradigms and Organizational Analysis* (Burlington, VT: Ashgate Publishing Limited, 1998).

34. Ibid.
35. Carl Linnaeus, *Systema Naturae (1753)*; repr. in facsimile, William Rudolf Sabbott, 1978).
36. Weber, *From Max Weber.*
37. Richard W. Scott, *Organizations: Rational, Natural and Open Systems* (Upper Saddle River, NJ: Prentice Hall, 2003).
38. David John Farmer, *Public Administration in Perspective: Theory and Practice through Multiple Lenses* (Armonk, NY: M.E. Sharpe, 2010).

Part I

Theories of Organization

I n an era when highly developed industrial production and global distribution efficiencies make high-quality, low-cost goods ubiquitous, it's difficult to imagine a time or a way of living in which we would have had to produce much of our own food, build our own tools, sew our own clothes, and even produce our own forms of entertainment. The benefits of industrialization for the quality of life in developed nations are so much a part of our experience that life without them is little more than an abstract thought experiment. With just a little reflection, however, it's not difficult to see that the confluence of factors that enabled the Industrial Revolution to occur is quite extraordinary in human experience.

The availability of cheap, portable, large-scale power production first through the steam engine and later internal combustion engines is one piece of the puzzle. Steam allows production to move away from water sources—the use of moving water for power—and to grow in scale, enabling production at unprecedented levels. In other words, steam allows for here to fore unseen economies of scale. At the same time, transportation technology had to improve to support the movement of raw materials and finished products to and from production sites and markets. Agricultural technology had to change at roughly the same moment. New agricultural processes create a labor force that would have been unavailable otherwise, and at the same time ensures that the food supply is large enough, stable enough, and cheap enough to sustain a workforce engaged in new forms of work. And to support all of these developments, sufficient levels of capital had to be available, in this case through a growing and vibrant middle class who had newly available monies to invest outside their own households.

Why, you might be wondering, are we starting a study of organization theory with a description of socioeconomic and technological changes that lead from the Model-T to the MP3? In part, we're doing so because in addition to having an astonishing impact on the quality and shape of our lives, the industrial revolution also resulted in the emergence of large and complex organizations on a new scale, demanding that for the first time, we give systematic attention to how these emerging entities function. In short, without the industrial revolution, there would be few large or complex organizations, and little reason to study organization theory. We're also starting with this description because we believe that the study of organizations cannot be divorced from the historical or societal context in which these organizations operate.

As such, we've crafted Part I of the book to include three core threads. One is a roughly historical depiction of how organization theory—both practical and academic approaches to it—emerges and evolves over the last one hundred plus years in the context of various socioeconomic, political, and technological influences. Organizations, and the theories used to understand and improve their performance, reflect the circumstances of the time, rather than emerging in a vacuum or laboratory setting with no outside influences. In addition to these broader, societal influences on organization theory, there is also a degree of self-reflectiveness in this work as well. In other words, organization theorists are, to some degree, engaged in an ongoing dialog in which they examine and assess the work of their colleagues and respond to the strengths and weaknesses in that work. Tracing the genealogy of this dialog is also part of this first thread.

A second thread in Part I, and really the most obvious, is the description of many of the central, influential, and actionable theories of organization, and their expression in governance settings. The three chapters in Part I take up what we view to be the core ideas that meet our criteria for inclusion, namely that they are not only useful in describing organizations' behavior, but that they also enable managers to craft strategies to enhance their own effectiveness, as well as that of their workers and their organizations as a whole.

The third thread that you'll see in Part I, and then continuing through the remainder of the book, is a governance thread. We've very intentionally selected theories for inclusion because of their presence and applicability in governance settings, be that traditional public organizations at the local, state or federal levels, their fit and presence non-public organizations including tax exempt service organizations, philanthropic groups, cultural associations or any number of other entities involved in governance, or what can be understood as the pursuit of the good life for ourselves and our communities.

The arc of these first three chapters is roughly historical. Chapter 2 examines some of the earliest ideas about how organizations are or should be structured as they emerged in the United States and other industrializing countries. Chapter 2 also traces the development of these ideas well into the twentieth century, and well into the structure and operation of public organizations. Chapter 3 extends both the historical progression of organization theory, as well as the intellectual dialog of organization theory as scholars and practitioners seek to integrate new learnings from research, as well as changing contexts and influences through the mid and late 1900s. The theory we treat in Chapter 4 is more heterodox, reflecting again the intellectual discourses taking place and the societal context. Nevertheless, a loosely historical trajectory can be found in the organization studies and practices of the late twentieth and early twenty-first centuries. By the end of Part I, our objective is for students to have a solid grounding in a wide range of organizational thinking, a grounding that will serve as a foundation from which to drill down and investigate the application of theory to a range of practical, organizational activities in Part II.

Chapter 2

Classical Foundations

The Historical Context
of a New Field of Study

Although various forms of organization existed for thousands of years prior to the emergence of classical management and organization theories, it was not until the end of the nineteenth century that the study of organizations became a more formalized discipline. In large part this emerging awareness and study can be understood as being tied to the second Industrial Revolution—that is, the shift away from dependence on water power that characterized early industrialization, to steam power, and the advent of mass produced and cheap steel. Simultaneously, there was a shift in economic power and productivity from Great Britain to the United States and Germany. In the United States, the period following the conclusion of the Civil War and Reconstruction supported substantial growth in science, technology, and engineering. Laissez-faire, or let-it-be, approaches to economic development and regulation come to predominate economic thinking—at least until the depression of the 1890s when the Progressive movement began to emerge in the United States.

Among the significant changes that emerge as a part of this second Industrial Revolution were technological developments in energy production as well as improvements in infrastructure and transportation. Central to these changes is the advent and wide availability of steam power. The shift to steam power meant that industrial production and distribution was no longer dependent on the availability of water power, which allowed industry to move away from the northeastern United States, especially in the post–Civil War Reconstruction period. The dramatic expansion of transportation infrastructure and the availability of cost-effective (though not necessarily cheap) transportation allows for new economies of scale. Organizations that produced all sorts of goods could now reach new and much larger markets as a result of rail access. This scaling up of production allowed producers to realize economies of scale—the idea that producers can reduce the per-unit costs of goods or services by producing a greater volume of those goods or services—and enabled consumers to access a wider range of cheaper goods. For example, Henry Bessemer developed a new way to produce large volumes of inexpensive but high-quality steel, which in turn allowed for the production of a whole new range of technologies. In Germany Gottlieb Daimler developed a cost-effective internal combustion engine that ran on refined petroleum—gasoline. Henry Ford combined these innovations in steel and power generation with assembly line production, and the transportation of goods and people expanded that much further.

In response to these industrial, economic, and social changes, early social scientists began giving attention to the description and prescription of organizational practices. In some ways, this attention can be seen as reflecting both optimism and pessimism regarding the implications of rapidly growing and expanding organizations. One reading of these trends—the growth and extension of science and engineering and application and effectiveness of their principles—suggests that the enthusiasm about their effectiveness contributed to optimism about the application of those same principles to other areas, including social concerns. This reading suggests, and many social and organizational theorists of the time believed, that rigorous study and the systemization of practice would yield similar benefits in all settings, be they organizational or societal.

It's clear that new tools opened up new opportunities, and organizations grew and diversified in corresponding ways. It also became apparent to some scholars that organizations, in addition to having great potential to accomplish ends well beyond any individual, had the capacity to collect and use resources that could and sometimes were used outside the explicit objectives of the organization. Organizations' resources could be used for individual rather than organizational purposes, or what Charles Perrow called "feathering the nest."[1] Those in positions of power have often used that power, either internally or externally, to advance their own self-interest rather than the interests of the organization or of a wider population. Tax collectors, for example, have been historically notorious for using their organizational authority to expand their own wealth. As we'll explore in the following pages, scholars of organizations began to think about how organizations might be structured and function so that such abuses might be minimized or even eliminated.

Concurrent with these social and economic trends were a set of political changes and reforms. It is during this period that the notion of *government by the good* becomes an identifiable trend.[2] Woodrow Wilson's centennial essay called for both a split between the political and administrative institutions and for the intentional and systematic study of what would be come known as the science of administration. This era saw the enactment of legislation such as the Sherman Antitrust Act and the creation of regulatory agencies such as the Interstate Commerce Commission in response to the perceived excesses of an unconstrained market. Similarly, the Pendleton Civil Service Reform Act was passed in order both to eliminate the ill effects of the spoils system and to enhance the competence of the civil service.

It is in this climate that the major players of the classical era are working. The following set of organizational and management theorists have perhaps had the most influence on both the thinking about and practice

Reflection Questions

What events or features of the sociopolitical context of the late nineteenth and early twentieth century do you think were most important in shaping the form and approach of newly industrialized organizations?

How do these features shape contemporary public and private organizations?

How have technological developments impacted organizations in the public sector in positive ways? What challenges arise due to advances in technology?

of management in modern organizations. Beyond their particular influence, these thinkers are also indicative of the general sense of promise associated with the application of rationalized, technical, and scientific practices.

Max Weber—Authority and Bureaucracy

Born in 1864 in Erfurt, Germany, Max Weber is perhaps best known for his conceptualization of ideal types of authority and bureaucracy.[3] His work, however, spans the fields of sociology, economics, law, religion, and a range of other related disciplines. One of the central themes of this work—and which ties closely to his work on authority and bureaucracy—is the processes and influences that contribute to the rationalization of society. Throughout his work, Weber[4] explores issues associated with how society becomes increasingly systematized or routinized by comparison to earlier periods in history.

As a part of this line of thought, Weber develops descriptions of three ideal types of authority and corresponding administrative forms.[5, 6] As ideal types, none of these forms exist in a pure form in organizational practice but represent a conceptual model for consideration in both administrative practice and study.

Charismatic Authority

Charismatic authority is grounded in particular individuals who exhibit exceptional personality or personal qualities. Charismatic leaders often derive their authority from past deeds, personal heritage, articulation of a dramatic view of the future, or some other combination of personal appeal. This form of authority, and the administrative practices that correspond to it, is likely to be somewhat unstable and unpredictable over time in that it is rooted in a single individual who may or may not remain in position over time. Any legitimacy of such a system is narrowly drawn from the leader and is unsystematically delegated or allocated to other members of the organization—likely those who are the most devoted or committed to the organization's leader. Under this form of organization, there are no systematically established, rational structures, sets of duties, or performance standards. The system relies on the charismatic leader to establish both the goals, or objectives, and the processes to accomplish those ends—all of which may be determined arbitrarily based on the concerns of the leader. Commonly noted examples of charismatic authority would include Martin Luther King Jr. and Mahatma Gandhi on the positive side and Adolf Hitler and David Koresh on the negative side.

Traditional Authority

Traditional authority is associated with long-standing practices and perceived legitimacy and is frequently established and retained through adherence to historically ground and sustained practices and norms. Traditional authority is frequently based on heredity or historical affiliation. Traditional systems remain stable so long as leaders are reasonably consistent with established practices of the past. Weber suggests that there are several related sets of administrative systems affiliated with traditional authority, including patriarchal and patrimonial forms.

Patriarchal forms—such as those that might be seen within a household or small, family-owned business—are characterized by authority that is grounded in a single individual who rules over a relatively small number of family members and staff. Patrimonial forms of authority may be larger in scale, extending up to monarchy. While there is likely to be some division of labor under both of these administrative forms associated with traditional authority, in neither case is that division established rationally or systematically. Division of labor is instead based on family ties, personal or historical connections. Here again, decisions may be arbitrary and no standard set of rules or regulations exist to determine the delegation or distribution of resources.

Legal-Rational Authority

As the name of this form suggests, legal-rational authority is grounded on laws and rules that apply broadly or universally regardless of individual traits or history. Authority and other resources are delegated on the basis of these rules and regulations, and loyalty is owed to the system rather than to individual office holders. The legitimacy of the system and of office holders therein is based on the extent to which actors operate within the authorities that are granted to them and that they exercise in a way that is consistent with the established rules and policies. Loyalty is directed to the office rather than an individual officeholder, regardless of traits or history. Bureaucratic forms of administration under the legal-rational form of authority not only create a rational and systematic distribution of control and discretion but also do so in a way that provides far greater stability and predictability than do either charismatic or traditional forms.

Bureaucracy as an Organizational Form

In describing legal-rational authority, Weber presents a rational argument for a particular way of distributing power, authority, decision making, and other attributes of management in leadership. Weber also develops an important description of bureaucracy as a specific set of organizational forms that correspond with the expression of legal-rational approaches to organization.[7]

Although organizations that include some attributes of bureaucracy predate modern, industrial experience, Weber believes that the increasing complexity and need for coordination under industrialization resulted in increasingly rationalized forms of bureaucracy. According to Weber, the characteristics of this ideal type bureaucracy include the following:

1. *A formal, hierarchical structure*—Each successive level of the organization controls the level below and is controlled by the level above. This hierarchy is the basis of centralized control and coordination for all productive activities of the organization.

2. *Management by rules*—An extensive and rationally developed set of rules are applied universally through the organization. This system of rules allows decisions made at high levels to be executed consistently by all lower levels.

3. *Internal organization by functional specialty*—The core work of the organization is to be done by specialists, and specializations are organized into units based on the type of work they do or skills they have.

4. *Clear goal specificity and orientation*—The objectives of the organization are clearly understood by all members and units in the organization, and the resources of the organization are universally oriented to the accomplishment of that goal.

[handwritten: Vision/ Mission stmt]

5. *Purposely impersonal*—All members of the organization, regardless of rank, are treated equally. Any arbitrary decisions or treatment due to personal relationships or personal traits is systematically eliminated from the organization.

6. *Selection and promotion are based on technical qualifications*—Personnel decisions, because of the importance of specialization, are based on technical merit rather than other personal qualities. Although one of the major influences on the development of the merit civil service system in the United States was the corruption of the spoils system and party machine system at the local level, the need for technical merit emerged simultaneously and is consistent with it.

Although Weber's contribution to our thinking about contemporary organizations is undeniable, his work is sometimes criticized for its apparently dehumanizing effects. Two caveats to these critiques should be remembered, however. First, and as a practical matter, in many ways bureaucratic structures and processes are more humane and egalitarian than those existing under charismatic or traditional organizational forms. For example, in a bureaucratic organization, the rules and policies apply to all members of the organization, even those in positions of authority, as opposed to being applied randomly or arbitrarily. Further, personnel actions are taken for reasons relevant to the organization—that is, based on empirical assessments of merit and performance rather than familial affiliation. It is not a coincidence that many elements of the merit system first introduced in the United States with the Pendleton Civil Service Reform Act institutionalize attributes of bureaucracy.

> ## Reflection Question
>
> What are some of the challenges or tensions between bureaucratic organizational structures within democratic systems of government?

Second, while Weber does describe the rationalization of organizations and organizational life via the development of bureaucracy, he is well aware of the impacts that such rationalization would have in a modern society. It was, after all, Weber who coined the term *iron cage* to describe the experience of work life in a rationalized bureaucracy.

Henri Fayol

Henri Fayol was born in Istanbul in 1888, was subsequently educated as a mining engineer, and spent much of the rest of his working life as a manager a large French mining conglomerate. Upon retiring at age seventy-seven, he published his comprehensive theory of administration in which he described and classified administrative management activities, functions, and principles. Fayol also founded the Center of Administrative Studies with the intent of encouraging the study and development of management practice.

His theorizing about administration grew out of direct observation and experience of what worked well in terms of organization. His intent for an "administrative science" was the creation of a consistent set of principles that all organizations must apply in order to run properly and effectively.

Principles of Management

Fayol developed the following doctrines of organization, which are *principles of management*:[8]

- *Specialization of labor*—The organization of the major operating tasks of the organization should be divided into an exhaustive set of discrete or specific tasks that require a particular skill set not shared by all members of the production process. Specialization enhances efficiency and effectiveness by utilizing expertise in each discrete area in an effort to maximize effectiveness. One effect of specialization is that it encourages continuous improvement in skills and the development of improvements in methods.
- *Division of work*—Complementing the idea of specialization, the division of work principle leads to arrangements wherein the work of complex organizations should be divided into discrete or distinct tasks. Workers should be trained for and assigned to tasks in a way that allows the organization to benefit from specialization.
- *Authority and responsibility*—The authority to direct the activities of other members of the organization is coupled with the responsibility to ensure compliance.
- *Discipline*—It is the responsibility of leaders and managers to ensure consistent, if not unyielding compliance with the rules, responsibilities, and obligations of the organization.
- *Unity of command*—Each member of the organization should have one and only one boss. Having multiple supervisors undermines coordination and authority and reduces efficiency.
- *Unity of direction*—Final planning and decision making are carried out by single individuals in order to ensure consistency and continuity.
- *Subordination of individual interests*—The resources of the organization are committed to the objectives of the organization and not to extraneous goals or individual members' goals. Ideally, workers would not utilize their organization's resources toward their own interests or concerns.
- *Remuneration*—Employees should receive fair and standard payment for services. Payment should also be sufficient to act as an incentive for high performance.
- *Centralization*—Management functions, such as direction and supervision, should be consolidated in a central source. Decisions should be made at the appropriate level of the organizational hierarchy.
- *Scalar chain (lines of authority)*—Organizational hierarchy follows a formal chain of command running from top to bottom of the organization. All communication runs from one level to the next, whether ascending or descending, rather than skipping levels.
- *Order*—All resources of the organization are allocated and maintained in a standard, prescribed system.
- *Equity*—All members of the organization should be treated in a fair and consistent way.

- *Personnel tenure*—Tenure in the organization should be based on merit rather than other arbitrary factors. Moreover, normal turnover should be managed to ensure as much stability and consistency as is possible.
- *Initiative*—While authority, unity of command, and discipline are central features of complex organizations, encouraging employees to exercise initiative—the capacity to develop and implement new ideas or approaches to their work—contributes to motivation and commitment.
- *Esprit de corps*—Steps should be taken, to the extent possible, to promote harmony, cohesion, and ideally synergy among personnel.

Activities and Functions

Beyond these general principles, Fayol also distinguishes between the governance of organizations and the management of them (see Table 2.1). Managerial activities represent only one of six sets necessary for the effective function of the organization (see Table 2.2).[9]

Table 2.1 Fayol's Management Activities

Activity Type	Description
Managerial	Planning, organizing, commanding, coordinating, controlling
Technical	Producing, manufacturing, adapting
Commercial	Procuring, distributing, and exchanging
Financial	Acquiring, utilizing, and controlling capital
Security	Protecting property, personnel, and other resources
Accounting	Maintaining inventory control, fiscal oversight of revenues, and expenditures

Focusing more narrowly on management activities, Fayol developed a set of five management functions.

In total, the principles, activities, and functions developed by Fayol constitute an amazingly comprehensive, though largely command and control, picture of the structures and processes of many, even contemporary, organizations.

Frederick Winslow Taylor

Frederick Winslow Taylor was born in Philadelphia, Pennsylvania, in 1856.[10] Taylor initially planned a career in law but because of degenerating eyesight became an

Reflection Questions

How do Fayol's principles of management play out in today's public sector organizations?

Are some of these principles more applicable in modern organizations than others? How so?

Table 2.2 Fayol's Management Functions

Function	Description
Planning	Looking to the future, assessing likely conditions, and planning for them
Organizing	Dividing the resources—human, material and otherwise—of the organization. This includes establishing a division of labor and acquiring materials to ensure the best or most efficient use of resources.
Commanding	Issuing orders and instructions with the intent of keeping the organization actively striving toward the best possible performance
Coordinating	Working to ensure the greatest possible integration, cooperation, and harmony across divisions and departments within the organization
Controlling	Making efforts to ensure that the standards and objectives of the organization are being maintained over time

industrial apprentice patternmaker at a pump manufacturing company in Philadelphia. He later became a machine shop laborer at a steel plant, where he subsequently worked his way from gang boss, to foreman, to research director, and eventually the chief engineer. At the same time, Taylor was studying engineering and in 1883 obtained a degree in mechanical engineering. After ten years of working as an engineer, Taylor became an independent consultant providing manufacturing and management support. In 1898, Taylor joined Bethlehem Steel as an independent consultant, where he did much of the work that would eventually become a part of *The Principles of Scientific Management.*[11]

Interestingly, it was Louis Brandeis, who, before being selected to the Supreme Court, coined the term *scientific management* while arguing a case before the Interstate Commerce Commission in 1910. Brandeis argued that railroads managed under Taylor's principles did not need to raise rates to increase wages. The following year, Taylor adopted Brandeis' term in the title of his monograph, the now-famous *The Principles of Scientific Management.*

Although the details of Taylor's concepts of scientific management are extensively developed in his writings, there are four core principles that run throughout. First is the need to eliminate rule of thumb work methods. Organizations should conduct a scientific study of the tasks performed by workers, typically through the use of detailed time and motion studies to determine the "one best way" for all workers to complete their assigned tasks.

Once that best way has been determined, it is then necessary to employ a process for the scientific selection and training of personnel. Workers should be scientifically assessed for employment, and only those prospective employees who have the right skills, validly measured, are selected for employment. Once hired, the organization should train and develop each employee actively and in an ongoing way rather than passively leaving them to train themselves.

Toward this end, the organization should develop and provide detailed instruction for and supervision of workers both as they learn a given task as well as in the performance of that task over time. Supervision, under Taylor, is no longer seen as a right for those afforded positions of relative privilege in society. Rather, supervision is a critical role in the organization, and like every other role, those in supervisory roles should be selected based on valid measures of merit for the position.

Finally, the work of the organization should be nearly equally divided between managers and workers. The logic of this prescription held that the managers apply scientific management principles to the planning of work and the workers actually perform the tasks. In total, Taylor provides much greater emphasis on the role that management has in supporting and developing the capacity of and supporting the workforce in the accomplishment of its work.

Luther Gulick

Luther Gulick was born in Osaka, Japan, in 1892. He received his PhD from Columbia University in 1920, after which he spent much of his career working at the New York Bureau of Municipal Research and teaching at Columbia.[12]

Among the core organizational issues that Gulick is interested in is the division of work.[13] Because scope of work is larger than what one individual can undertake, a central challenge facing organizations is how to organize and coordinate that work. Gulick, like Weber and Taylor before, recognizes that workers have different capabilities and physical limitations: we can't be in two places at once, nor do two things at once, and have a limited range of knowledge and skills. One of the consequences of this is the development of specialization with respect to the tools that are used, materials and conceptual knowledge, or the expertise in principles and processes used to produce the output of the organization. In other words, the limits in human capacity should be understood as structural limits in what can be achieved, and specialization is the means for overcoming individual limits. Further, as we continue to develop greater knowledge through science, we are able to improve and further specialize in ways that overcome limits.

There are, of course, limits to division of labor. One is that there is nothing to be gained from dividing labor beyond individual capacities. In other words, if one person can do it, don't subdivide the work further. A second limitation is driven by technology and custom. Technology, here, should be understood more broadly than the machines and tools of a job; technology is the means of turning inputs into outputs. So the means or technology and customs, such as trade or craft divisions of work, will limit how things can be divided. There are also practical limits or limitations of core character. Reality limits how far things can be subdivided. Among Gulick's more colorful examples is the observation that one can't have a cow graze and be milked simultaneously. More importantly though, he raises the question of whether something critical may be lost in potential division of labor. For example, if one were engaged in a technical writing and editing project, one has to look for multiple elements—grammar and mechanics, technical accuracy, and appropriateness to the audience. All of these have to be balanced, and it may not make sense to break this into three processes or among three workers. Another concern in the subdivision of labor is ensuring that the whole remains part of and recognizable in the parts. To ensure that the whole, the critical character of the overall project, remains part of the individual parts, there is the need for specialists focused on the coordination of the diverse elements: someone has to be sure that everything connects back together correctly. This has to happen by design and intent, not by accident.

Gulick also introduces the notion of *Caveamus Expertum,* or "beware of the expert." While specialization is necessary and is a means of overcoming human limitations, Gulick understood that there are dangers associated with the use of specialized experts. Among the concerns are the possibility that a sense that "we know best" or overextension of expertise. In response, he suggests that experts should be on tap not on top. Organizations must balance the need for valid reliable information for efficient decision-making with the corresponding need for accountability and supervision.

A further concern of Gulick is the coordination of work, and here his thinking echoes much of that developed by earlier thinkers, especially Fayol and Weber. Among the strategies to be used to coordinate work is the use of authority, which Gulick further subdivided into two familiar concepts: *span of control* and *unity of command.* Span of control refers to the number of subordinates any one supervisor oversees. There are limits, according to Gulick, to the breadth of this span. One is the bounds of knowledge a manager has, which constrains the range of activities he can reasonably supervise. Managers should have sufficient knowledge of all the tasks and activities of their subordinates in order to provide adequate oversight. Another limit is found in the amount of time and energy the manager has available. Span of control must be only so wide as to allow the manager to commit sufficient attention to all subordinates.

Gulick also proposes a number of general principles to determine the appropriate span. First, the more routine, repetitive, measurable, and homogenous the tasks within a manager's span of control, the wider a span might be. Conversely, a more diverse, qualitative, and geographically scattered range of activities the narrower the span should be. Appropriate span also depends on the nature of the executive—his or her capacity.

Following Fayol, Gulick also identifies a second element associated with control and coordination, namely the importance of maintaining a clear unity of command. If one is to have work coordinated effectively, there can be no ambiguity about lines of authority. Not only do inefficiencies result from confusion about unity of command but coordination is likely to suffer, potentially leading to more severe organizational failures.

Gulick also describes a collection of organizational patterns or strategies for organization. He noted at earlier points the need for someone to take responsibility for coordination, and the executive, according to Gulick, is the person to undertake that responsibility. So, rather than technical expertise, he advocates organizational expertise. The central elements in that expertise could be captured in the now famous acronym POSDCoRB:

Planning

Organizing

Staffing

Directing

Coordinating

Reporting

Budgeting

These are elements designed to ensure coordination as opposed to technical expertise associated with carrying out specific, instrumental tasks. Consistent with Gulick's notion of span of control—in larger, more heterogeneous organizations—these functions could be further divided.

Reflection Questions

What similarities exist between Gulick's and Weber's notions?

Where do they differ?

Woodrow Wilson

Although best known for his presidency leading up to and through the First World War, Woodrow Wilson's writing as an academic has had a much more profound impact on public administration and public organizations. Born in Staunton, Virginia, in 1856, Wilson's family spent much of his childhood in Augusta, Georgia, where he witnessed the devastation of the Civil War and the challenges of Reconstruction. Wilson studied at Princeton before earning his law degree at the University of Virginia and, subsequently, his doctorate at Johns Hopkins in political science in 1885. Wilson wrote his doctoral dissertation, entitled "Congressional Government," on the difficulties that result from the constitutional separation of executive and legislative powers. This was an issue that would continue to animate his research through his early academic career and formed the intellectual backdrop for his 1887 essay on public administration. Wilson taught at Bryn Mawr and Wesleyan College for several years before returning to Princeton, where he advanced rapidly, ultimately become the president of the university in 1902. He served in that role until entering politics, first winning a gubernatorial race in New Jersey and later winning the presidency when William Howard Taft and Theodore Roosevelt split the Republican vote.

Wilson's essay, "The Study of Administration," is best known for its articulation of the politics-administration dichotomy, which continues to be influential both in scholarly treatment of public administration as well as popular sentiments and expectations of government.[14] And while this is a central element of the essay, we want to point out that Wilson's description of and argument for the dichotomy reveals a particular conception of legitimacy that informs both practical and instrumental approaches to organizations. It also frames those approaches in a particular orientation of governance. Our exploration of Wilson's essay highlights both of these concerns and their interrelationship.

Written in 1887, the piece appeared just four years after the Pendleton Civil Service Reform Act was passed, just at the front end of the era Mosher refers to as Government by the Good. Wilson is clearly immersed in the discourse of the era, and begins his essay by arguing that reform must pick up and address the "science" of administration as well as the mere processes of personnel management. In an effort to build an administrative apparatus that meets these criteria, he begins by posing two rhetorical and orienting questions. First, he asks, what can government successfully and properly do? Second, how can it do these things most efficiently?

To address the first question, Wilson describes the sources and background of our constitutional and administrative heritage. In a move reminiscent of Publius in the *Federalist Papers*, he points out that administration is the most obvious part of government.[15] It is what we experience on a day-to-day basis and while we tend to think about Washington, DC, when we think explicitly about government, what we *experience* is administration. To that point, Wilson suggests that most literature and discussion—especially political science (and even public administration)—is focused on the Constitution—forms and structures of government, even saying that the discipline had, at the time, become "dogmatized" about the constitution of government.

Attention to administration in the United States is neglected because it was comparatively simple, which was a reflection of the fact that society was itself relatively simple as well. However, in the aftermath of Reconstruction and in the beginnings of massive industrialization in the United States, things were rapidly becoming complex. There were, to Wilson's mind, more issues to deal with that were more technically complex, and there were, because of immigration and liberalization, more opinions and positions regarding any issue.

To respond to this increasing complexity, Wilson argues that we need to build the sort of administrative knowledge and experience that is not available here in the United States because we're too young and have had comparatively simple government. Instead, we have to look to nations like Germany and France, which have had more experience with building and managing more developed administrative devices. However, we have to temper the learnings from small, centralized states like these, to large, diverse, and more free states like the United States.

Because of these circumstances and conditions, he calls for scholars of political science to establish stable principles and foundations for administration and then prescribe the best methods for organizing and acting for administrative (executive) organizations. In an effort to begin the development of such principles and foundations, he crafts an assessment of the conditions at that time and resulting courses of action. Wilson begins to develop a model that sees politics as being in those things great and universal, and administration is the activity of the state in individual and small things—those things that are mundane to running a Constitution. Making the distinction clearer, the establishment of general laws is the realm of politics, and the detailed execution of those plans is administration. In other words, administration can be narrowly instrumental.

Nevertheless, Wilson reminds us that this focus on administration shouldn't minimize the importance of constitutional questions or political questions—ones that support the establishment and maintenance of liberty. Administration, for Wilson, no matter how effective and benevolent, "cannot live apart from constitutional principle."[16] There is still a constitutional element here that responds more directly to a variation of the original question: What is the proper or appropriate distribution of authority? Consistent with his call for a "science of administration," Wilson sees this as an empirical, practical question. What is the most efficient and effective distribution of executive authority—one that can be a critical contribution? Moreover, how do we ensure responsibility in actions of the executive? If responsibility is clearly established, it will develop into "trustworthiness" or a collective sense of legitimacy. A further question though is to what extent does public opinion have a legitimate role in the activities of administration? To be clear, this link to a collective or public sense of legitimacy takes place within a strongly representative system and does not imply more direct expressions of democratic engagement. The public serves as a sort of authoritative critic, the suggestion being that the means of expressing legitimacy wouldn't be through direct participation but rather by voting processes.

This results in what is a central challenge for the study of administration—the development of effective, efficient practices that continue to be sensitive to citizens' opinion. Wilson's response is to move pubic administration toward technocracy. Such technical expertise, when experienced directly by the people, will be a central mechanism of creating trust, which in turn will reinforce and expand the role for technical capacity. Wilson also addresses an organizational and managerial principle that Weber also notes—and one that continues to be at the heart of public personnel training. In public bureaucracies, we must provide service while maintaining good behavior, that being allegiance to policy of government. Responsiveness to public opinion isn't about how policy is carried out, nor is it about which policy is carried out. Wilson's argument for separating the politics of decision making from efficacious implementation supports his assertion that responsiveness to what the public wants comes via a close connection to those who are elected. Further, such a connection in conjunction with expert implementation has the added advantage of avoiding charges of arbitrariness.

Although his efforts to flesh out the politics-administration dichotomy were significant, and have had a substantial impact to this day, Wilson understood that we still have much to learn; despite our long experience with democracy, we're not good at the sort of administration that's needed in complex times. However, we need not fear that good administration threatens democracy or liberty. We can avoid tyranny, but to do so we must identify "one rule of good government." Within the realm of politics, we can still debate the myriad options for policy—politics and administration are still separate.

What Wilson leaves us with is a founding essay that makes two critical points. It illuminates the links of classical principles and practices of organization—the science of administration. It also establishes the role of administrative organizations in governance, namely that politics happens outside of technical administration. In doing so, he reinforces the philosophies of classical management theory in the public sector, and he frames the legitimacy debate for the subsequent eight decades.

Other Voices

The trajectory of thinking in the authors presented so far demonstrates the centrality of rational, linear, scientific, and systematic approaches to organizations. These management trends are consistent with the social, economic, and scientific trends of the period. Although these lines of thought and practice have been profoundly influential, they are not monolithic, and other voices were present at the same time. Exploring these other voices reveals alternative possibilities for thinking and practice.

We have selected three thinkers, each of whom presents an alternative or a critique to the dominant approaches we've covered thus far. These three are quite different in the central concerns, approaches, and intellectual orientation from which they come. The first, Mary Parker Follett, is perhaps the most dramatic departure from the theories and theorists covered so far. While her critique is subtler, the alternative she presents is the most extensive departure of these "other voices." Jane Addams' work is the most applied of the three and embodies a philosophical pragmatism that makes her community level work distinct from that of her classical contemporaries. Karl Marx is likely the best known of the other voices and most controversial of them. Our interest in Marx is focused fairly narrowly here on his critiques of the consequences of capitalism and the extent to which he recognized what might be necessary, or unavoidable consequences of the economic and organizational structures resulting from capitalism.

Mary Parker Follett

Mary Parker Follett was born in Quincy, Massachusetts, in 1868, to a wealthy Quaker family. In 1892 she began attending the Society for the Collegiate Instruction of Women in Cambridge, which later became Radcliffe College. There she studied economics, government, law, and philosophy. In 1900 she began doing social work in the Roxbury neighborhood of Boston, where she eventually became active in efforts to develop community centers and public schools. Her work took advantage of the diversity of the community as she used face-to-face social processes that integrated churches, trade associations, local civic groups, and other community organizations.[17]

In her book *The New State,* Follett extends what she learned working in the community to develop an argument that social interaction and local networks of individuals could be the basis of effective democratic process.[18] In this work, she claims that experience can be the basis of governance processes and that conceptual dichotomies, such as individual and group, citizen and state, and freedom and determinism, are false in conditions of rich social interaction. She emphasizes the importance of relationship and notes that the individual is not isolated and radically autonomous but is created by social interaction and social process. Here, drawing from the thinking of American pragmatists such as William James, she describes the individual as "a complex of radiating and converging, crossing and re-crossing energies."[19] Through such inherently relational processes, Follett sees democracy as a socially emergent phenomenon rather than a form of rationalized selection of representation.

In her subsequent work, *Creative Experience,* Follett extends a number of themes introduced in *The New State.*[20] Follett has said the following about experience:

> [Experience] becomes what it was plus you: you are responding to the situation plus yourself, that is, to the relation between it and yourself . . . Life is not a move for us; you can never watch life because you are always *in* life.[21]

In thinking about our experiences and considering their meaning and implications with respect to our own role and interpretation of them, it is possible to learn and go beyond previous understandings and conceivable actions. It is possible to exercise new forms of creativity. Just as her earlier work emphasized relationship, *Creative Experience* stressed engagement and encounter as a central feature of process.

While much of her writing focuses its attention on social process, community level democracy, and citizen engagement, much attention to her work has come from organizational and managerial arenas. One implication of her work is that organizations, like communities, could be understood as social systems of individuals and small collections of individuals. In such a setting, the social processes she developed and advocated could contribute to the organization's ability to self-govern and to the growth of individuals and the groups to which they belong. In this way, organizations can be not only more productive but also more just.

Many management and organizational scholars have interpreted Follett's work as a precursor to participatory work emerging from behavioralism.[22] Others view her work as dramatically departing from the thinking of the time.[23] In making this claim, they point to a number of elements in her thinking, including the pragmatist influences on her thinking. For example, her work tends to be antifoundational in that she does not argue for one best way. In other words, and in opposition to positivist notions, antifoundationalist orientations suggest that no one single, right understanding, or Truth of approach, can be rationally, abstractly, or universally determined for *all* scenarios. Instead, the optimal course of action in any situation emerges from the interaction of the individuals involved, the context or as Follett termed it, *the law of the situation,* and the social process by which knowledge and understanding develops. Further, her thinking tends to collapse the subject-object distinction, meaning that there is no neutral position from which to observe or study a situation purely objectively. Rather, social actors are always and inherently in context or in the midst, and as such, there is the possibility of new creativity and synergy beyond a sort of mechanical summation of forces.

It should also be recognized that the conceptual work done by Mary Parker Follett, as well as the street-level application of that thinking by Jane Addams and others in the settlement house movement, not only emphasized engagement, community, and participation but it also demonstrated the early influences of women on the theory and practice of public administration. While during this time in history, the contributions of women were not as widely recognized by mainstream society, these two women are credited with influencing social and organizational reform in ways that were enlightened and forward thinking.[24]

Jane Addams and the Settlement House Movement

Social settlements began in the 1880s in London in an effort to respond to ills resulting from urbanization, industrialization, and immigration. The idea moved to other industrialized countries and notably the US settlement houses, which typically attracted educated, native born, middle-class, and upper-middle class women and men, known as "residents," to live or settle in poor, urban neighborhoods. Some social settlements were linked to religious institutions, but many others, like Hull-House, were secular. By the turn of the twentieth century, the United States had over hundred settlement houses, and within another ten years, the city of Chicago alone had thirty five.

In the 1890s, Jane Addams' Hull-House was founded in the heart of a densely populated, multiethnic and largely immigrant urban neighborhood. During the 1920s, African Americans and Latin Americans began to settle more extensively in the neighborhood and subsequently joined more of the clubs and other activities at Hull-House. Addams and other Hull-House residents provided educational opportunities, day care facilities for the children of working mothers, and an employment and worker assistance program. In time, Hull-House's services included libraries; English and citizenship classes; and even theater, music, and art classes. At its peak, the complex grew to include more than a dozen buildings and added even more clubs and activities, such as a Labor Museum, the Jane Club for single working girls, meeting places for trade union groups, and a wide array of cultural events.[25]

By contrast to the bureaucratic reforms seen in the thinking of classical theorists, the central metaphor in the settlement house movement is one of *home*.[26] Consistent with the processes and dynamics described by Mary Parker Follett, this alternate metaphor created an emphasis on an attitude of initiating substantive new programs focused on the living conditions of those in the community rather than abstracted principles developed for universal application. The settlement house movement reformers were strong believers in empirical research, but it was a practical, contextualized, and experiential form of research, the results of which were directly

Reflection Questions

How did Mary Parker Follett's work impact the way we think about organizations today?

Do you think her ideas were well accepted at the time? Why or why not?

What was the role of women in public administration in the early 1900s?

oriented toward active responses to those same lived conditions. Notions of democracy and citizenship were grounded in involvement, and the "official" actor was a community member who directly engaged in the processes of governance that connected agencies and people.

Karl Marx

Karl Marx died in 1883, the same year that the Pendleton Civil Service Reform Act was passed. While most of his work appeared prior to or at the very beginning of the classical era as we've marked it, the socioeconomic dynamics he was concerned about—and the corresponding labor and organizational attributes he identified—appeared earlier and by many measures have accelerated since his death. The ideas he explored over the three volumes of *Capital* are far beyond what we can reasonably explore here.[27] We briefly introduce just three of them—alienation, commodities, and exploitation—in order to indicate how Marx's analysis revealed what he believed to be unavoidable, structural failures of capitalism and capitalist organizations.

With the movement out of earlier forms of political-economy, Marx argued that the relationship between labor and human expression changed. Rather than working to fulfil basic needs, or to express ideas, labor became *alienated* from the products or outputs of its efforts. Instead of owning, using, or selling them for their own purposes, products under capitalism belong to the organization, or for Marx, the capitalist. For this same reason, labor is also alienated from one another in that they no longer cooperate to produce something they share in. As specialization increases and the rationalization and separation of line, supervision, and ownership extend—consistent with the forms and ideals described in Weberian bureaucracy— these dynamics become magnified further.

This alienation is manifest in the emergence of *commodities* as well. Commodities, for Marx, are not just goods produced by labor for their own use. Commodities are items produced for exchange and exchange largely beyond those who contribute to production. This shift from use to exchange disconnects the price of a product from its value; because there is a gap between producer and user, commodities lose their natural value, take on an independent or external reality, and correspondingly, price and value lose their correspondence. As organizational efficiency increases, especially through economies of scale and reduction of internal inefficiencies— through optimizing span of control and chain of command—it is possible for the organization to improve productivity in ways not equitably passed on to the labor force.

One way that organizations are able to improve their overall efficiency—the ratio of inputs and outputs—is by *exploiting* labor. If the organization can pay labor less than the value of their output, the difference is retained by the organization as profit. While this is the basic equation of production and profitability in capitalism, Marx argues that the modus operandi of capitalist firms was to unfairly maximize or exploit that difference by artificially holding wages down or by increasing performance expectations while holding compensation stable. The stereotypical contemporary example is the organizational expectation that a salaried worker routinely work more than forty hours a week while compensating the individual for only forty hours. The additional work done by the employee is surplus labor—labor and outputs that benefit the organization but not the worker.

As a normative theorist of political-economy, Marx argues that there are structural or systemic attributes of capitalism that have necessary, unavoidable consequences. As an organizational critic, Marx's articulation of these and other aspects of capitalism reveal organizational consequences unexplored from within classical theories.

Case 2.1

The President's Committee on Administrative Management (the Brownlow Committee and Report)

The following case demonstrates the practical expression of many of the major concepts developed by the classical era theorists we've described in the preceding pages. The president's Committee on Administrative Management embodies many of the notions of structural efficiency and rationality first expressed at the turn of the twentieth century; they are core to ideas of classical management theory. As you read the following case, and those in subsequent chapters, consider the extent to which the ideas and corresponding practices are present.

In 1937, in the midst of the Great Depression and the ongoing political struggles to enact New Deal programs, President Franklin Roosevelt convened the Committee on Administrative Management, or the Brownlow Committee. The Brownlow Committee was brought together in the context of the political economy of the Great Depression and the New Deal in an effort to consolidate administrative authority with the president and to maximize the effectiveness of New Deal programs. Politically, the Brownlow Report is an expression of the ongoing tensions between the president and the Congress to establish and extend control over the federal bureaucracy. Struggles for control over bureaucracy have long been a part of American political discourse—at least as early as Alexander Hamilton's, James Madison's, and John Jay's arguments in the *Federalist Papers* for the importance of good management as a critical element of good and effective government, which in turn they saw as part of the justification for the ratification of the Constitution.[28] This struggle for control has continued all the way in to the most recent debates about executive primacy advanced by George W. Bush's administration. The link between good administration and functional democracy initially advanced by Publius (Hamilton, Madison, and Jay) is clearly apparent in the Brownlow Committee's work. According to the final report of the committee, "The forward march of American democracy at this point of our history depends more upon effective management than upon any other single factor."[29] Setting the questions about political institutions aside, the language of the Brownlow Report also makes explicit the importance of effectiveness and efficiency as core values. Toward the end of substantively improving the performance of the federal government, the report advanced five key points:

- Reorganize the White House administrative and management processes by giving the president additional support staff to *aid him in dealing with* the executive departments and agencies (span of control).

- Enhance the budgetary and efficiency research, as well as the planning and the personnel services of the government, so that these may be effective managerial arms for the president. Doing so enables the president to *better coordinate, direct, and manage* all of the work of the executive branch for which he is responsible under the Constitution (currently expressed in the existence of federal offices focused on management effectiveness including the Executive Office of the President, Office of Management and Budget, and Office of Personnel Management).

- Place the entire federal government service on a *career basis and under the merit system* by extending the civil service system upward, outward, and downward to include all non-policy-determining positions and jobs (objective needs and effectiveness measures as well as personnel decisions rationally driven by knowledge, skills, and abilities [KSAs]).

- Restructure the executive branch so as to *consolidate* the range of disconnected and dispersed offices and commissions into the twelve regular departments, which would include the existing ten departments and two new departments, a Department of Social Welfare and a Department of Public Works (span of control and specialization).

- Improve executive branch accountability to Congress by creating a postaudit of fiscal activities by an independent auditor general who would report fraud, waste, and abuse to Congress *without himself becoming involved in the management of departmental policy* and transfer the duties of the present comptroller in part to the auditor, to the Treasury, and to the attorney general (effectiveness, span of control, and specialization).[30]

What should be readily apparent in these recommendations is the importance of making rational, empirical decisions that lead directly to the improved effectiveness and efficiency of not only specific executive branch agencies but the executive branch as a whole. Central to means by which these recommendations are supposed to achieve greater efficiency and effectiveness are structural attributes that link directly with ideas advocated by the classical organization theorists described in this chapter. Among the ideas emphasized are the centralization of critical management processes in the executive, consolidation of control through clearer establishment of clear chains of command, use of specialization, and optimized spans of control.

As was previously noted, the expression of these principles also appears in the existence of various managerial units including the following: the executive office of the president, which enables the president to exercise much more direct control over administrative agencies including planning, administration personnel, and budgeting; the former Bureau of the Budget, now the Office of Management and Budget; and the shift to an executive budget as the starting place and central fiscal process for the federal government, and the Office of Personnel Management (formerly the US Civil Service Commission).

Case Reflection Questions

What are some specific, current examples of federal level practices or structures that are reflective of the Brownlow Report recommendations?

Are there agencies or settings where the recommendations from the Brownlow Report continue to be valuable in enhancing operations? If so, what are they and how do the recommendations help?

Are there current settings where the recommendations of the Brownlow Report are more problematic? If so, where? What are the difficulties, and why do you think they are present?

Summary and Conclusions

IT IS INTERESTING TO NOTE THAT ALTHOUGH WEBER, Fayol, and Taylor were all working at, roughly the same time, because they were working in Germany, France, and the United States, respectively, there is no indication that they were aware of each other's ideas. In fact, Weber's and Fayol's works were not translated into English until the 1940s. This suggests that the context they worked in, namely highly structured, industrial, increasingly complex, and simultaneously routinized settings, which evolved as a part of industrialization, had a parallel influence on their understanding of what management principles should apply. While other voices, like that of Mary Parker Follett, did emerge at the same time, divergent thinking and gender issues may have kept society from giving careful consideration to these ideas in a timely way.

It is important to recognize that sociologists, economists, and other social scientists were not the only figures working to respond to the growth and sometimes excesses of newly emerging organizations. The Progressive Era can be understood as a wider social movement that was broadly concerned with these same dynamics.[31] For public administration, this is the *governance response,* an effort to govern or coordinate, to keep stable and functional the activities not just of organizations but of society more broadly. It can be seen in the creation of early regulatory agencies such as the Interstate Commerce Commission and the Federal Trade Commission.[32] Similarly, the passage of the Pendleton Civil Service Reform Act in 1883 moved public administration away from the political influence, and in some cases outright corruption of the spoils system, and took important steps toward creating and institutionalizing a merit based, systematically assessed, and developed civil service. It was at this same moment in history, marked by the appearance of Woodrow Wilson's 1887 essay, that the field of public administration emerges as a self-identified discipline.[33] Not only does Wilson's essay establish the concept of the politics-administration dichotomy (see Chapter 3 for a more extensive discussion of this dichotomy) but it also introduces the notion of scientific or systematic study and application of administrative principles. ■

Discussion Questions

1. What are some of the shared features that emerged across the work of management theorists in Europe and the United States at the turn of the last century?

2. What are some of the residual elements of these classical foundations that are still found in contemporary organizations?

3. What are some of the positive and negative consequences of these residual elements for contemporary organizations?

4. Which of the theoretical ideas presented in the chapter do you see evidenced in the cases? How so?

Notes

1. Charles Perrow, *Organizations: A Critical Essay,* 3rd ed. (New York: McGraw-Hill, 1983).

2. Frederick Mosher, *Democracy and Public Service,* 1st ed. (New York: Oxford University Press, 1968).

3. Marianne Weber, *Max Weber: A Biography* (New Brunswick, NJ: Transaction Publishers, 2009).

4. Max Weber, *Max Weber: Essays in Sociology,* trans. and ed. H. H. Gerth and C. Wright Mills (New York: Oxford University Press, 1946); Max Weber, *The Theory of Social and Economic Organization,* trans. A. M. Henderson and Talcott Parsons (New York: The Free Press, 1930); Max Weber, *The Protestant Ethic and the Spirit of Capitalism,* trans. Talcott Parsons, foreword by R. H. Tawney (London: Allen & Unwin, 1947).

5. Max Weber, "Objectivity in Social Science and Social Policy," in *The Methodology of the Social Sciences,* trans. and ed. E. A. Shils and H. A. Finch (New York: Free Press, 1949).

6. Max Weber, "The Three Types of Legitimate Rule," trans. Hans Gerth, *Berkeley Publications in Society and Institutions* 4, no. 1 (1958): 1–11.

7. Weber, *Max Weber.*

8. Fayol's work is developed and reiterated across many of his works, including the following: Henri Fayol, *Industrial and General Administration,* trans. J. A. Coubrough (London: Sir Isaac Pitman & Sons, 1930); Henri Fayol, "The Administrative Theory in the State," in *Papers on the Science of Administration,* trans. Sarah Greer, ed. Luther Gulick and L. Urwick (New York: Institute of Public Administration, 1937), 99–114; Henri Fayol, *General and Industrial Management,* trans. C. Storrs (London: Sir Isaac Pitman & Sons, 1949).

9. Derek Pugh, David J. Hickson, and C. R. Hinings, *The Great Writers on Organizations* (Burlington, VT: Ashgate, 2007); David Evans, *Supervisory Management: Principles and Practice* (London: Thomson, 2004).

10. Frank Barkley Copley, *Frederick W. Taylor, Father of Scientific Management* (New York: Harper & Brothers, 1923).

11. Frederick W. Taylor, *The Principles of Scientific Management* (Easton, PA: Hive Publishing Company, 1985).

12. Jacques Steinberg, "Dr. Luther H. Gulick, 100, Dies; Adviser to Roosevelt and Mayors," *New York Times,* January 11, 1993.

13. Luther Gulick, "Notes on the Theory of Organization," in *Papers on the Science of Administration,* ed. Luther Gulick and Lyndall Urwick (New York: Institute of Public Administration, Columbia University, 1937).

14. Woodrow Wilson, "The Study of Administration," *Political Science Quarterly* 2, no. 2 (1887): 197–222, www.jstor.org/stable/2151276.

15. In building a constitutional argument for the legitimacy of public administration, John Rohr pointed out that Publius makes more references to the need for and character of good administration than he does to the three branches of US constitutional government combined. See John Rohr, *To Run a Constitution: The Legitimacy of the Administrative State* (Lawrence: University of Kansas Press, 1986).

16. Wilson, "The Study of Administration," 212.

17. Pauline Graham, *Mary Parker Follett: Prophet of Management* (Washington, DC: Beard Books, 2003).

18. Mary P. Follett, *The New State—Group Organization, the Solution for Popular Government* (New York: Longmans, Green and Company, 1918).

19. Ibid., 75.

20. Mary P. Follett, *Creative Experience* (New York: Longmans, Green and Company, 1924).

21. Ibid., 133–134.
22. Graham, *Mary Parker Follett*.
23. See, for example, the following as interpretations of Follett's work as being fundamentally—onto-logically—different than other social and organizational theorists of the time: O. C. McSwite, *Legitimacy in Public Administration: A Discourse Analysis* (Thousand Oaks, CA: Sage, 1997); Camilla Stivers, *Bureau Men, Settlement Women: Constructing Public Administration in the Progressive Era* (Lawrence: University Press of Kansas, 2000).
24. See, for example, Camilla Stivers, *Gender Images in Public Administration: Legitimacy and the Administrative State* (Thousand Oaks, CA: Sage, 1993).
25. Victoria Bissell Brown, "Jane Addams," in *Women Building Chicago 1790–1990: A Biographical Dictionary*, ed. Rima Lunin Schultz and Adele Hast (Bloomington: Indiana University Press, 2001), 14–22.
26. Stivers, *Gender Images*.
27. Karl Marx, *Capital: A Critique of Political Economy*, trans. Ben Fowkes and D. Fernbach, vol. 1–3 (New York: Vintage Books, 1977).
28. See, for example, *Federalist* No. 70 and No. 72.
29. President's Committee on Administrative Management, *Administrative Management in the Government of the United States* (Washington, DC: Government Printing Office, 1937), 47.
30. John Woolley and Gerhard Peters, "Franklin D. Roosevelt, Summary of the Report of the Committee on Administrative Management, January 12, 1937," American Presidency Project, University of California, Santa Barbara, www.presidency.ucsb.edu /?pid=15342.
31. Robert Wiebe, *The Search for Order: 1877—1920* (New York: Hill and Wang, 1986).
32. For a thorough discussion of the development of the modern administrative or regulatory state in the United States, see John Rohr, *To Run a Constitution: The Legitimacy of the Administrative State* (Lawrence: University Press of Kansas, 1986).
33. Wilson, "The Study of Administration."

Chapter 3

Behavioral Revolution

Historical Context:
Prewar Hints and Postwar Proliferation

Many of the earliest organization theorists in public administration gave little, if any, explicit attention to public organizations. This is evident in the fact that only two of the major theorists covered thus far, Luther Gulick and Mary Parker Follett to a lesser degree, gave specific attention to the function of public organizations. Much early thinking about organizations in the field of public administration works from an assumption consistent with Wilson's politics-administration dichotomy.[1] The notion that politics should occur solely within and between the legislature and political executive as well as the administration and implementation of political and policy decisions should then be entirely apolitical. In this way, the processes of administration and the structure and function of administrative organizations can therefore be conceived entirely in technical and scientific terms. Partly as a result of the widespread acceptance of the politics-administration dichotomy, many scholars of organization worked under the assumption that there were no significant differences between the operation or study of organizations in the public and private sectors. Among the questions to be explored in this chapter is whether and why that assumption is valid or not.

Setting the blurred distinction between public and private organizations aside for a moment, perhaps the most important shift that emerges out of behavioralism is the development of models of behavior that extend beyond narrow models of rationality. A first hint that something besides narrowly rational behavior and efficient construction of bureaucratic structures might affect the performance of organizations emerged from what has become known as the Hawthorne experiments. The Hawthorne experiments will be described in more detail later in this chapter, but for the moment, it's sufficient to recognize that what started as a study in scientific management—for instance, the optimal lighting levels for maximizing performance—eventually revealed the complexity of social behavior in a work environment. This early glimpse into the complexity of behavior contributed greatly to the proliferation of behavioral studies for several decades to come.

Returning to Frederick Mosher's historical eras, much of the early work in behavioralism coincides closely with Mosher's *government by the administrators*.[2] During this era, public administrators were more than technicians who scientifically assessed and maximized the outputs of their organizations. Rather, they were proficient generalist managers in charge of large, complex social programs, which had grown during both the New Deal period and the Second World War. Mosher points out that this new model did not replace the classical model oriented toward efficiency but instead layered the two together. Public servants were to be statesmen, common men who were morally upright as well as being efficient, technically competent administrators.

One of the first public administration scholars who recognized a distinction between the public and private sector was Paul Appleby. Appleby believed that administration of government was inherently different because of the character of the work done in the pubic sector, and the orientation of those who do it.[3] According to Graham Allison, we live in an era that is often referred to as post-industrial.[4] Just as industrialization changed administration, our current era also shapes the context of public administration and the political environment in which it exists. If administration of government *is* different, as Appleby and Allison suggest, a remaining question is, what are the characteristics of the public sector that make it different from the private sector? Moreover, what are the characteristics of public administration that make it distinctly American? Allison compared the context and environments of public and private management, showed how they were different, and examined the implications of running government as a business.[5] Allison set the stage for understanding what public management is by examining public managers and their environments.

Perhaps the best way to understand all of this is that public administration has collected over the years a series of expectations and standards. Consistent with the political and social culture, this step implies that public servants must be of the highest stature and integrity, representative of the larger public and the common man, highly educated administrators, efficient, concerned about public opinion and politics, and scrupulously neutral and nonpartisan.

This is indeed an extensive list and one that goes back to the tension mentioned earlier—How do you make a bureaucracy that has a primary value of efficiency work in a democracy that places the primary value on participation and responsiveness? This is an enduring question with no clear answers; it simply creates part of the backdrop for the job of public administrators who must manage programs to solve very complex problems, serve clients, respond to legislators, react to market failures, facilitate community involvement, protect the public's money, and be politically neutral while they do it.

Public organizations clearly call for employees who can wear many hats and who are able to work within a complex system of competing values, expectations, politics, and contexts. In any organization, public or private, the people are the most vital resource. This has not always been a common understanding in theory and is still not always accepted in practice. Much has evolved. We do need to recognize that talents and potential are often underestimated and skills underutilized and that respect, trust, collaboration, and problem solving are critical to each work environment. Managers need to build organizations where people can utilize their talents to accomplish organizational goals. So, given that perspective, it is important to also recognize the importance of understanding behavior in organizations and how it relates to the quality of service provided and how effective or, ultimately, excellent the organization becomes. Organizations are social creations that must respond to customers, law, politics, and change.

We build organizations because of what they can do for us. Individual performance is the foundation of organizational performance, so understanding it is crucial for effective management. Human resources are powerful. The way people work, think, and act determines the direction of an organization. In an increasingly global, diverse, technological changing world, this is important to understand and address. Organizations need employees that are excellent, creative, and hardworking. Public organizations clearly place additional expectations on the employees.

This chapter examines the alternatives developing out of and in response to classical approaches to organizations discussed in Chapter 2 and historic developments discussed earlier in this chapter. Here, we will introduce the concepts, theories, and historical developments associated with the behavioral revolution.

Organization theory (OT) is a set of propositions that seek to explain or predict relationships among things in and around organizations. OT focuses on concerns important to the entire organization or even sets of organizations, such as environments, goals, effectiveness, strategic direction and decision making, change and improvement, structure and design, and birth and death.

Modern study of organizations and management began around 1900, though its history as a process dates back much longer. The goal has always been to find a way to accomplish a goal. The Industrial Revolution and the political shifts that were previously described dramatically expanded industry and the need to plan, organize, and control. While there has been a century-long theoretical history in organizations and management and a long tradition of interest in behavior in organizations, it has only been since about 1957 that the behavioral perspective came into being. This means we began to look at organizations through the lenses of the people, groups, and relationships.

In the early 1900s, management thinkers sought to discover universal principles of administration that could be applied. The metaphor during this period of time was that organizations were machines and people were the parts. This time in our history was a time of corruption, inefficiency, political immorality, and growing industrialization that gave way to a gospel of efficiency. Individuals like Frederick Taylor and Max Weber, covered in the previous chapter, were important contributors to our thinking around the efficiency of organizations at this time.

The strong focus on efficiency in the early 1900s resulted in organizations that paid more attention to production, profit, scientific management, and authority than they did to the individuals working within them. The early approach to thinking in and around organizations was based on the notion that, through carefully collecting data, one could uncover the best way to accomplish a task. The behavioral revolution or human relations movement called for a change from this earlier, formal model.

Chester Barnard

One of the key representatives of the shift recognizing and emphasizing the human elements of organizations was Chester Barnard. Although not a behaviorist himself, his thinking does mark an important shift away from the classical models described in the last chapter. He is also one of the few scholars and writers who was also a highly successful practitioner, including serving as the president of Bell Telephone, heading the United Service Organizations (USO) during World War II, and working as the president of the Rockefeller Foundation. From this experience and his reflections on the structures and processes of organization, Barnard advocates organizations as cooperative systems. He breaks away from scientific management and emphasized the importance *nonscientific* of the individual, small groups, systems, communications, and decision making. Barnard thinks that formal theory was overly descriptive and superficial. He argues that administrators should understand several critical attributes of organizations related to executive's responsibilities.

- Despite the presence of top-down structures, organizations are actually cooperative. As such, authority is not imposed from above but is granted to supervisors by employees.
- Managerial decision making should involve searching for and focusing on strategic factors. Barnard claims that managers should not decide on questions that are impertinent to overall organizational success, should not decide prematurely, and should not make mundane decisions that others at more appropriate levels should make.
- Communication is a central function of an executive.
- The individual is a key strategic factor in organizations, but regardless of his or her uniqueness, individuals must be induced to cooperate.
- In addition to material goods, opportunities for individuals to show pride in workmanship and have satisfactory social relationships are important to individual and organizational success.[6]

Barnard also pioneered work in the importance of informal groups. He emphasizes the role of leadership by saying that leadership cannot be solely exercised by those at the top—and not only at their discretion. Leadership is dependent upon the willingness of workers to follow, accept, and respond to the direction. He suggests that followers have a great deal to do with the nature of leadership. Barnard pictures motivation as a matter of interactive exchange of capacity rather than the narrow pursuit of self-interest. In such interactive relations, leaders and followers have something to offer the other and seek to negotiate these roles. In shifting attention away from narrowly rational organizational structures and behaviors, and to the importance of cooperation and interactive relationships, Barnard represents an important bridge to what would become the behavioralist movement.

Elton Mayo, Fritz Roethlisberger, and the Hawthorne Experiments

During the early part of the century, organizations in the United States were very taken by Taylor's *The Principles of Scientific Management*, discussed in the previous chapter. Organizations regularly examined the impact of the environment on their employees. Systematic organizational experiments were completed in an effort to clearly understand the interplay between environmental factors and employee efficiency. In an enormously ambitious and extensive undertaking, researchers from Harvard University and Western Electric, including Elton Mayo and Fritz Roethlisberger, began a nine-year series of efficiency studies at Hawthorne Works outside of Chicago, Illinois, which would profoundly influence future thinking about organizational dynamics, though not in the way they anticipated.

Some of the earliest research at the Hawthorne Works began as a fairly direct effort to study and optimize the relationship between lighting levels on the work floor and worker productivity. Working from an assumption out of scientific management that workers were motivated by external factors such as pay and the quality of the physical environment, the researchers hypothesized that worker productivity would increase as illumination increased. To their surprise, researchers found that regardless of the changes made to illumination levels, productivity increased. Confused by these results, the researchers then conducted a further series of experiments using control groups in order to more accurately assess the effect of changes.

> [These more controlled experiments] resulted in very appreciable production increases in both groups and of almost identical magnitude. The difference in efficiency of the two groups was so small as to be less than the probable error of the values. Consequently, we were again unable to determine what definite part of the improvement in performance should be ascribed to improved illumination.[7]

Confounded by these results, it was at this point that the researchers asked Mayo to participate in the studies. Trained in mental and moral philosophy, and having conducted research on behavior and psychology, the Australian-born Mayo brought a human dynamics rather than an industrial engineering perspective to the research team. With the addition of Mayo, and his protégé Roethlisberger, the research team began to reach the conclusion that social factors might be an additional if not more important factor than physical variables in effecting performance. The illumination studies revealed, then, what has become known as the Hawthorne effect, or that behavior is affected by outside observation itself. This is an issue both for researchers and managers in that if we want to understand and improve employee performance, it is necessary to be much more sophisticated in observing employee behavior and determining the factors that affect that behavior.

Given the length and breadth of studies done at Hawthorne Works, an exhaustive description of the nearly decadelong effort is beyond the scope of this section. However, three other experiments within the Hawthorne studies are worth noting here.

The Relay Assembly Room

Based on their experiences with lighting investigation, researchers decided to move a group of workers into a separate room, the idea being that experimental conditions could be manipulated with less chance of outside or other organization routines or conditions affecting workers' behavior. The relays being assembled were composed of about thirty-five small parts, and the study sought to determine the effects of fatigue on productivity and the extent to which rest periods and the duration of the workday affected productivity. After studying thirteen different combinations of rest periods and workday lengths, the researchers concluded that productivity, measured as output per hour, was affected to some degree by fatigue. More importantly, however, the researchers also found that workers' attitudes toward each other, toward the group as a whole, and toward supervisors also influenced their productivity.

The Bank Wiring Room

A further phase of the study, the bank wiring room, was designed to examine the social effects and the mechanics of small-group processes. Researchers were attempting "to obtain more exact information about social groups within the company."[8] Using a methodology similar to the relay assembly room, a small group of workers were taken out of their regular work setting and placed in a separate room. In order to further control the conditions of the experiment, efforts were made to ensure that no other changes were made in the working conditions other than the location. Researchers first found that when workers reached what they felt was an acceptable or appropriate day's work, their individual productivity would decline. In other words, informal performance standards developed beyond the formal or explicit performance incentive systems developed by the organization. Further, the results of the bank wiring room also revealed that not only were interpersonal dynamics a factor in performance but that the emergence of informal social organization could be a major limiting factor on performance. Initially researchers hypothesized that social pressure from the group would be brought to bear on low performers, giving them incentive to improve. What was found, however, was the opposite. A common body of sentiments developed among the workers wherein pressure was brought to bear on high performance workers not to be "rate busters." These social norms had effects both internal and external to the group. Internally, the developing norms had the effect of creating stable controls or regulations. Over time, clear, constant expectations of behavior emerged and were maintained. Externally, these norms served to protect the group from change or potential change imposed from the outside.

The Interview Program

The relay assembly room experiment revealed, in part, that relationships between the workers and their supervisor had an effect on morale and productivity. Based on these findings, the researchers began a series of interviews with workers intended to better understand the nature of worker concerns and how the supervisor's behavior affects worker morale and productivity. In this portion of the studies some 21,000 interviews with employees were conducted. Roethlisberger states the following:

> It became clear that many employee comments which had formerly been interpreted in terms of the interviewees' personal situation could be better understood if they were interpreted in light of the employee's existing social relations within the plant: the social organization of the group with which he worked and his position in that group.[9]

Yet again, social rather than physical or remunerative factors were revealed to be significant in worker productivity.

In sum, the Hawthorne studies were the major impetus for the move away from the narrowly focused rationalism described in Chapter 2. What would emerge from this shift are at least two related but distinct ways of thinking about social and organizational behavior: **systems theory** and **human relations theory (HRT)**.

Reflection Question

Describe the importance of informal groups as they relate to an organization with which you have some familiarity. How do they impact behavior in organizations?

Systems Theory

Systems theory views organizations as dynamic and interactive systems in which each part is dependent upon another for its inputs and outputs. Systems theory is often traced back to Ludwig von Bertalanffy in the late 1920s and was then expanded upon by Daniel Katz and Robert Kahn.[10, 11] In the 1920s, Taylor's *The Principles of Scientific Management* had grown with the understanding that each component of an organization could be understood and controlled independently and linearly. Von Bertalanffy disagrees with this understanding and instead claims that an organization is a system in which various individuals and components—internally and externally—interact together to accomplish outcomes and depended upon such interaction within an environment for growth and success.

This very biological way of thinking about organizations was a far cry from the more traditional and closed systems view propagated in earlier years. Such early theories viewed organizations as closed, isolatable, and independent. In the 1960s, such ideas were less favorable, and instead, more systemic, holistic, environmental, open, and humanistic approaches were embraced.

Importantly for public sector organizations, systems theory tells us that while organizations may be made up of many parts or stakeholders, rarely do those parts operate independently from one another. Each piece of a system influences, informs, or reacts to another. With this as a framework, we are encouraged to look at the whole picture to truly understand interdependencies, inputs, and outcomes. If we look at a university as an example of a system, for instance, many relationships define the ultimate effectiveness and efficiency of that system. To illustrate, Figure 3.1 demonstrates but a few examples of the multiple stakeholders associated with a university. It is clear that each piece of the system informs and is informed by the other.

> ## Reflection Question
>
> Using a systems theory framework, who are the stakeholders associated with your local or municipal government?

Human Relations Theory

As noted at the beginning of this chapter, one of the most far-reaching effects of the Hawthorne experiments and the findings that were initially so confounding was the emergence of Human Relations Theory (HRT) which drew on developing knowledge about the social and psychological influences on organizational performance. More specifically, it became clear that beyond the formal structures and processes of the organization, informal aspects also affected worker behavior—as did the norms and sentiments of workers and work groups. If the findings from Hawthorne reveal that multiple factors affect the performance of individuals in the organization, then how might we understand what those factors are, how they operate, and most importantly, how to adapt organization processes to improve that performance?

The theorists in this section, all of whom fall under the broad umbrella of human relations, each explore specific aspects of how social and psychological factors as well as formal and informal relations are expressed and impact organizational and individual performance. Among the concepts developed by human relations scholars are many of the contemporary concerns of management, including cohesion, morale, motivation, direction, and leadership.

Given that human behavior inside the organization is more complicated than was initially believed, researchers began to turn their attention to what we can learn about the complexities of that behavior and how can we structure the organization in such a way as to improve or maximize organizational performance.[12] Many of these same researchers also explored a second set of concerns, the normative issues of how we treat those in the organization.

Figure 3.1 System of University Stakeholders

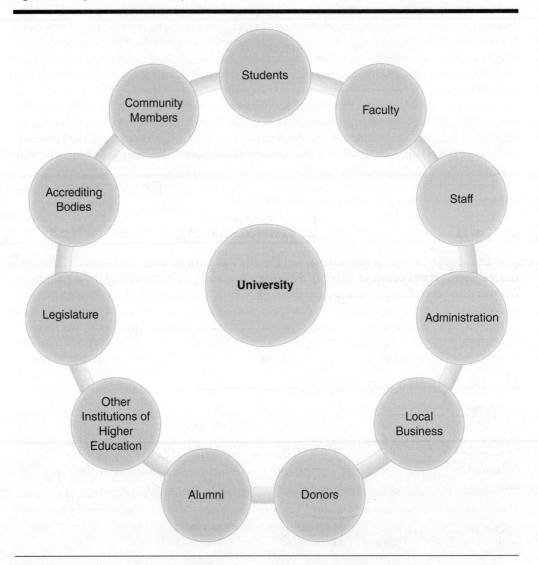

Theoretical and empirical work within HRT is both diverse and voluminous. Given the breadth and depth of this body of research, any broad-brush description of it will necessarily be imprecise. However, a substantial portion of the scholarship in HRT is oriented to the relationships between and among leadership, motivation, attitudes, and social cohesion. Broadly, the notion is that if organizations can improve some combination of these factors, not only will organizational performance correspondingly improve but that improvement will happen in a way that makes the conditions and experience of workers better too.

In what follows, we briefly introduce several of the seminal theorists associated with HRT and behavioralism more broadly. Our intent with these descriptions is to familiarize readers with many of the major figures and their ideas. A more detailed exploration of the consequences of their ideas on organizational concepts like leadership, management of individual and small-group behavior, and managing organization change will come in Part II of this book.

HRT constitutes what is probably the single largest body of research in the study of organizations, and perhaps social sciences more widely.[13] Broadly, this research can be divided into two lines of inquiry. One, which is primarily empirical and includes work done by theorists including **Kurt Lewin** and **Rensis Likert**, is typified by the studies conducted at the University of Michigan's Research Center for Group Dynamics, the Ohio State University, and the Tavistock Institute in Great Britain. The second line of study was conceptual in nature and includes that done by **Douglas McGregor, Abraham Maslow,** and **Chris Argyris.**

Empirical Work—Kurt Lewin and Rensis Likert

Kurt Lewin (the German pronunciation is Le-veen) was born in what was western Germany, an area now part of Poland, in 1890. After earning his doctorate in psychology he served in the German army and was wounded during the First World War. Following the war Lewin served as a lecturer at the University of Berlin, but because he was Jewish, he was unable to become a full faculty member. He immigrated to the United States in 1933 as the National Socialists were consolidating power in Germany and taught first at Cornell University and then later at the University of Iowa. A driven researcher, Lewin founded institutes at MIT and through the American Jewish Congress in New York, while at the same time working with Eric Trist at the Tavistock Institute in England. Succumbing to the pace and volume of this workload, Lewin died of a heart attack in 1947 at the age of fifty-six.[14]

Lewin's contribution to social psychology is substantial, and he is perhaps best known in OT for his ideas about change management. His conceptualization of change management will be discussed in detail in Chapter 7. The following description of Lewin's work focuses on his understanding of the structure of organizations and the interrelationship of individuals with each other and with the organization.

Field Theory and Force Field Analysis

Rather than viewing individuals as atomistic actors operating in either a rational or boundedly rational way, Lewin presents a model of behavior based on the idea of fields.[15] Fields, for Lewin, are comprised of all of the forces or factors, including individual needs and desires, that shape an individual's behavior. Force field analysis is a means by which the factors or forces that influence a situation can be examined and understood. It makes sense to think of these forces as being mutually interdependent and the force field is the exhaustive environment, or "life space" of the individual. Behavior, according to Lewin, is a result of the interplay of these various forces. Force field analysis looks at forces that are either driving movement toward an objective or hindering movement toward a goal.

Leadership Climates and Organizational Efficiency

With this model of behavior in place, Lewin, collaborating with Ronald Lippitt and others, studied the efficiency of various management styles.[16] They identified three styles or climates, which they described as authoritarian, democratic, and laissez-faire. As might be expected, authoritarian approaches are characterized by classical hierarchical structures and processes wherein leaders make decisions that are then implemented through traditional structures of hierarchy and spans of control. Leaders in such organizations are not inherently unreceptive but are disengaged from mundane work processes. Democratic settings, by contrast, are characterized by decision making that takes place through collective processes. Organizational actions are informed by information and perspectives drawn from group discussion and technical advice from a leader. Members of the organization are given voice and choice in decisions regarding organizational processes. Finally, laissez-faire environments allow substantial freedom within work groups without any formal or requisite participation from the leader. Leaders are uninvolved in work decisions unless asked and do not participate in work processes.[17]

The results of the research found that groups that operated from democratic processes had better results than did those that worked from either authoritarian or laissez-faire orientations.[18] Among other outcomes, democratic groups, according to Lewin's and Lippitt's findings, demonstrated more originality, group-mindedness, and friendliness than did groups operating from the two other orientations.

Change Management and Action Research

Lewin, perhaps more than many of his contemporaries, was not only interested in the structures and processes that lead to organizational effectiveness but was also keenly aware of the need to help organizations change and in order to effectively adopt new practices and processes. Lewin's ideas about managing change will be a major topic of exploration in Chapter 7, but for now it will be sufficient to make a few brief comments. Lewin's model of change views organizational change in terms of a three-stage process.[19] The first stage he called "unfreezing." In this stage, organizations focus on recognizing and overcoming the inertia that develops around practices and at the same time seek to dismantle the existing mind-set of those in the organization. In the second stage the change occurs. The change period is often characterized by a certain amount of uncertainty, confusion, and transition. The third stage, when new, functional patterns of behavior are stabilized, is described as "freezing" (not *refreezing* as it is sometimes termed).

In support of this change process, Lewin develops a research process that allowed the organization to collect specific, practical data related to the practices and mind-set in place in the organization in order to most effectively effect change. A more detailed description of action research first appears in his 1946 paper "Action Research and Minority Problems," where he indicates that action research is "comparative research on the conditions and effects of various forms of social action and research leading to social action" that uses "a spiral of steps, each of which is composed of a circle of planning, action, and fact-finding about the result of the action."[20] It's worth noting that, consistent with Lewin's notions of democratic leadership, the change management process and the research approach used to support it are both interactive and participative in ways that parallel the work processes Lewin found to be most effective.

Rensis Likert was born in 1903, in Cheyenne, Wyoming. He first attended the University of Michigan, where he received his bachelor's degree, before going on to Columbia University for his doctoral studies. Like many scholars of his generation, in addition to conducting research and teaching, Likert also brought his expertise to bear in support of efforts to fight World War II. In Likert's case, he worked with Kurt Lewin in the Department of Navy during the war.

Reflection Question

Think of an example of a change that you have experienced. Does Levin's three-stage process adequately represent the way the change occurred? Why or why not?

Near the end of the war, Likert, along with Lewin and McGregor, met to begin planning and developing what would become one of the first social sciences research institutes—at MIT. Following Lewin's death in 1947, Likert helped move and merge the MIT center with another existing center at the University of Michigan. The combined center would become the Institute of Social Research.

Likert is perhaps most widely known for his work developing specialized instruments for the measurement of social attitudes, including the use of the now-famous Likert scale response format. However, Likert and his colleagues spent nearly three decades studying management styles across hundreds of organizations. These studies led to the development of a four-part model of management systems. The four systems of management, or the four leadership styles, identified by Likert are as follows:

- *System 1—Exploitative authoritative:* In this system, responsibility lies solely at the top of the organization's hierarchy. Managers have little if any trust in the capacity of subordinates. Decisions are made by supervisors and imposed on lower levels of the organization. Direction and communication tend to flow down to the worker, and workers do not engage substantively back up the chain of command with their supervisor. Coordination is primarily structural or mechanical, very little if any substantive teamwork exists, and motivation is primarily based on threats.
- *System 2—Benevolent authoritative:* As with the previous system, responsibility resides with managers and supervisors and not line workers. Supervisors have minimal and condescending confidence and trust in workers. Communication remains primarily top down, and teamwork or communication is very minimal; though, here, motivation is based on a system of rewards rather than threats.
- *System 3—Consultative:* In contrast to the prior two systems, here, responsibility is distributed throughout the organizational hierarchy. Superiors have substantial but not total trust and confidence in workers. Communications patterns reveal some job related interaction taking place between the managers and workers as well horizontally between workers. It is in this system that substantive teamwork appears for the first time. The approach to motivation is driven by systems of rewards and by creating a sense of involvement in the job among workers.
- *System 4—Participative group:* In this final system, responsibility for accomplishing goals is widely distributed across the entire organization. Supervisors have a high level of trust and confidence in workers, and there is extensive communication, teamwork, and substantive engagement across the breadth and height of the organization.[21]

In studying the organizations that led to the development of this four-stage model, Likert and his colleagues also developed a set of seven process variables that were operationalized in order to determine where organizations fell in the broader model. The seven process variables are as follows:

1. leadership processes

2. motivational forces

3. communication process

4. interaction-influence process

5. decision-making process

6. goal setting or ordering

7. control processes

Likert and his researchers examined how organizations led, motivated, communicated, and so forth in order to determine which of the four systems best characterized their overall management approach.

Likert's studies revealed that organizations, divisions, or work units employing management approaches from Systems 1 and 2 were the least productive, and those units using management practices consistent with Systems 3 and 4 were the most productive. System 4, or participative group organizations, achieved and sustained the highest levels of productivity.

Later, in *New Patterns of Management,* Likert described the practices and structures of System 4 organizations in further detail.[22] In such organizations, leaders would create an environment where groups would participate in the establishment and achievement of their own goals rather than simply imposing standards from the top (see Figure 3.2). Communication, support, and respect are among the core values, and mutual influence would contribute to greater innovation and flexibility.

Work groups form the core of System 4 organizations, and they are characterized by several dynamics that clearly reflect the process variables noted previously. Members would have a well-developed capacity for both leadership and membership roles, which contribute to functional relationships and interaction. The group has been in place long enough for relaxed and well-developed working relationships to have been formed. Group members are loyal to both the group and to each other and have built a high level of trust. The norms, values, and goals of the group reflect the values and needs of its members.[23]

The idea of being competent at both leadership and membership roles leads to one other concept from Likert's research. The *linking pin model* is an idea developed by understanding the organization as a number of overlapping operating divisions or departments in which a member of that unit is the leader of another unit (see Figure 3.3).[24] In this conceptualization, a supervisor is simultaneously responsible for maintaining group coherence among the work group being supervised and at the same time representing that unit in meetings with superiors and management staff from the same level. Individuals in these positions are *linking pins* of the organization.

Figure 3.2   Typical Organization Chart

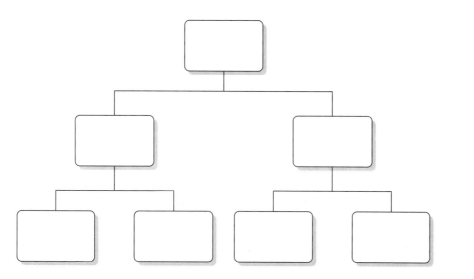

A typical organization chart with separate and mutually exclusive units

Figure 3.3   Linking Pin Organization Chart

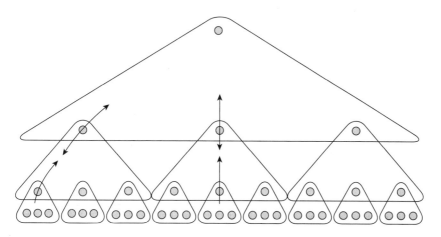

An organization chart revealing the overlapping and interconnected *linking pin* roles

Source: Rensis Likert, *New Patterns of Management* (New York: McGraw-Hill, 1961), 113.

To reiterate several points, Likert's research and concepts fit with the broader human relations model along several lines. First, one of the critical characteristics of System 4 organizations is its stress on creating supportive relationships as a means of enhancing effectiveness. System 4 organizations also establish high performance goals but importantly do not do so simply in a top-down approach but rather in a way that engages workers across the organization in framing those goals. And finally, System 4 organizations emphasize the use of groups and teamwork for supervisory processes and for goal accomplishment.

Likert found that performance tended to improve under System 4, or participative organizational structures. Likert believed that this had to do with group participation in the establishment of goals and decision making. Further, his work indicated that a sense of affinity or loyalty to the group had the effect of motivating them to work harder in support of the group's efforts. For Likert, two elements of such group dynamics were particularly important. First, group members received recognition from their peers, which satisfied their social needs, and second, they developed a sense of ownership for the means and ends decisions they contributed to.

Working from a hypothesis that leadership can improve morale, attitudes, and motivation, which in turn improves performance, studies by Ralph White and Lippitt as well as Ralph Stogdill and Alvin Coons also found that workers were more effective in participatory or System 4 organizations.[25, 26] Their results also indicated that those who had higher performance had higher morale.

Raymond Miles' research also found a relationship among these factors, but his study indicated that productivity affects morale, not vice versa.[27] Morale is connected to being a contributing member of the group—being liked, respected, making a contribution, etc.—and higher morale will be the result. But morale is not a causal factor in increasing performance. Moreover, participation is a way to increase morale and is the least cost method of obtaining buy in for decisions. Even though the causal relationship was not confirmed in Miles' studies, in its emphasis on democratic or participatory processes and a focus on employees rather than production, the importance of relationships and connections over bureaucratic rules remained consistent with other human relations theorists' work. Similarly, Arthur Brayfield and Walter Crockett's meta-analysis (study of studies) found little if any evidence that attitudes bore any causal relation to performance.[28]

Conceptual Work—Abraham Maslow

It is the attention to employees and their normative value in the organization that helps establish a link with the work of Abraham Maslow, perhaps the most well-known psychologist beyond Sigmund Freud to make a contribution to management and OT. As a student at the University of Wisconsin, Maslow conducted his early research on rhesus monkeys, where he first recognized the behavior that suggested that a prioritized or hierarchical set of needs were involved in shaping what the monkeys, as well as humans, do. With this recognition, together with the addition of the concept of self-actualization first suggested by Kurt Goldstein, he developed the now famous *hierarchy of needs*.[29] Beyond the profound impact Maslow's theory has had on American psychology, the same concepts have influenced thinking about leadership and management in organizations as well. In 1962, Maslow spent a summer observing and studying a small manufacturing firm, the results of which were published in his book *Eupsychian Management* (later retitled, and much easier to pronounce, *Maslow on Management*).[30]

The basic idea of Maslow's hierarchy is that humans pursue the needs described in the hierarchy and do so in a particular prioritized way. If one's basic, or physiological, needs haven't been met, the individual will not consider or pursue his safety needs, which are at a higher level of Maslow's hierarchy. Extending the theory to an organizational setting, the claim is that if the organization can structure itself in such a way that most of the individual's needs can be fulfilled inside the organization, then that individual will be able to focus his energy on his job duties. If more of the employee's energy can be directed to job duties and tasks, then the organization will benefit: organizational performance will be higher (see Table 3.1).

Table 3.1 Maslow's Hierarchy of Needs

Maslow's Hierarchical Levels	Example Workplace Expressions
Physiological needs	Provide lunch breaks, rest breaks, and wages that are sufficient to purchase the essentials of life.
Safety needs	Provide a safe working environment, retirement benefits, and job security.
Social needs	Create a sense of community via team-based projects and social events, Friday afternoon clubs, softball teams or recreational opportunities, company picnics, and holiday parties.
Esteem needs	Recognize achievements to make employees feel appreciated and valued; offer job titles that convey the importance of the position.
Self-actualization needs	Provide employees a challenge and the opportunity to reach their full career potential.

In addition to the hierarchy of needs, Maslow also developed a set of principles that he argued should shape or inform the practice of enlightened management (see Box 3.1).

Box 3.1 Maslow's Principles

1. Assume everyone is to be trusted.

2. Assume everyone is to be informed as completely as possible of as many facts and truths as possible—that is, everything relevant to the situation.

3. Assume in all your people the impulse to achieve.

(Continued)

(Continued)

4. Assume that there is no dominance-subordination hierarchy in the jungle sense or authoritarian sense (or "baboon" sense).

5. Assume that everyone will have the same ultimate managerial objectives and will identify with them no matter where they are in the organization or in the hierarchy.

6. Eupsychian (having a good mind or soul) economics must assume good will among all the members of the organization rather than rivalry or jealousy. Synergy is also assumed.

7. Assume that the individuals involved are healthy enough.

8. Assume that the organization is healthy enough, whatever this means.

9. Assume the "ability to admire."

10. We must assume that the people in eupsychian plants are not fixated at the safety-need level.

11. Assume an active trend to self-actualization—freedom to effectuate one's own ideas, to select one's own friends and one's own kind of people, to "grow," to try things out, to make experiments and mistakes, etc.

12. Assume that everyone can enjoy good teamwork, friendship, good group spirit, good group harmony, good belongingness, and group love.

13. Assume hostility to be primarily reactive rather than character-based.

14. Assume that people can take it, that they are tough, stronger than most people give them credit for.

15. Eupsychian management assumes that people are improvable.

16. Assume that everyone prefers to feel important, needed, useful, successful, proud, respected rather than unimportant, interchangeable, anonymous, wasted, unused, expendable, disrespected.

17. Assume that everyone prefers or perhaps even needs to love his boss (rather than to hate him) and that everyone prefers to respect his boss (rather than to disrespect him).

18. Assume that everyone dislikes fearing anyone (more than he likes fearing anyone) but that he prefers fearing the boss to despising the boss.

19. Eupsychian management assumes everyone prefers to be a prime mover rather than a passive helper, a tool, a cork tossed about on the waves.

20. Assume a tendency to improve things, to straighten the crooked picture on the wall, to clean up the dirty mess, to put things right, make things better, to do things better.

21. Assume that growth occurs through delight and through boredom.

22. Assume preference for being a whole person and not a part, not a thing or an implement, or tool, or "hand."

23. Assume the preference for working rather than being idle.

24. All human beings, not only eupsychian ones, prefer meaningful work to meaningless work.

25. Assume the preference for personhood, uniqueness as a person, identity (in contrast to being anonymous or interchangeable).

26. We must make the assumption that the person is courageous enough for eupsychian processes.

27. We must make the specific assumptions of nonpsychopathy (a person must have a conscience, must be able to feel shame, embarrassment, sadness, etc.).

28. We must assume the wisdom and the efficacy of self-choice.

29. We must assume that everyone likes to be justly and fairly appreciated, preferably in public.

30. We must assume the defense and growth dialectic for all these positive trends that we have already listed previously.

31. Assume that everyone but especially the more developed persons prefer responsibility to dependency and passivity most of the time.

32. The general assumption is that people will get more pleasure out of loving than they will out of hating (although the pleasures of hating are real and should not be overlooked).

33. Assume that fairly well-developed people would rather create than destroy.

34. Assume that fairly well-developed people would rather be interested than be bored.

35. We must ultimately assume at the highest theoretical levels of eupsychian theory, a preference or a tendency to identify with more and more of the world, moving toward the ultimate of mysticism, a fusion with the world, or peak experience, cosmic consciousness, etc.

36. Finally we shall have to work out the assumption of the metamotives and the metapathologies, of the yearning for the "B-values," i.e., truth, beauy, justice, perfection, and so on.

Source: Abraham Maslow, *Maslow on Management* (New York: Wiley, 1998).

Douglas McGregor

Another researcher who contributed to our understanding of the noneconomic factors that influence behavior and satisfaction was Douglas McGregor. McGregor was born just after the turn of the twentieth century and grew up on the outskirts of Detroit, Michigan, just as the area was becoming the central hub of the American automotive industry. While growing up, McGregor was heavily involved in his family's business, which provided support for transient workers in the Detroit area. After bouncing among several jobs and schools, McGregor eventually enrolled at Harvard where he earned an MA and PhD in psychology. McGregor spent his academic career at MIT and Antioch College, where he developed his ideas on management, serving as a researcher, consultant, and administrator.

In 1960 McGregor wrote *The Human Side of Enterprise* in which he presented two models that describe how managers fulfill their role of bringing together the factors of production for the benefit of the organization.[31, 32] The first, Theory X, is based on the mechanistic, formal assumptions about people. Theory Y, by contrast, is based on the behavioralist model, including Maslow's work, that human behavior is more than narrow mechanical, or self-interest-based utility maximization. Both models are driven by a set of ontological claims, or assumptions about the fundamental nature of individuals and how they behave in the world.

McGregor begins with a series of assumptions about the nature of employees and then extrapolates the implications of those assumptions for processes and structures used by the organization to coordinate the factors of production. Among the assumptions of Theory X are that employees dislike work and attempt to avoid it, have no ambition, want no responsibility, and would rather follow than lead. It is further assumed that the worker is self-centered and therefore does not care about organizational goals, will resist change, and is generally gullible and not particularly intelligent. The consequence is that organizations can generally and effectively adopt a carrot-and-stick approach that relies on positive and negative inducements or incentives to prompt employees to act in ways that are consistent with or that advance the ends of the organization.

Theory Y, by contrast, starts from the assumption that work can be as natural as play and rest. Workers will be self-directed to meet goals in the workplace if they are committed to them and, further, will be committed to those objectives if rewards are in place that address higher level needs such as self-fulfillment. Under these conditions, people will not only seek responsibility but can handle responsibility because both creativity and ingenuity are common in the population.

McGregor explains that individual needs are satisfied at work, and a manager's perception of a person can greatly impact their effectiveness. A manager who views employees from a Theory X perspective will view employees as those who do not like to work and must be coerced to be effective. This differs from a Theory Y manager, who believes that work is natural and people are committed, responsible, and creative but that need to have their talents utilized more fully. Theory Y organizations, therefore, bring together an emphasis on humanist forms of leadership that build both morale and collective connection or cohesion to each other and to the organization in ways that make the organization more effective and make employees' lives more fulfilled. McGregor's theories recognized the relevance of the perspective of the manager toward the employees and its impact on behavior and productivity.

Chris Argyris

Chris Argyris was born in New Jersey in 1923. He served in the US Army during the Second World War before earning an undergraduate degree in psychology from Clark University. He then went on to earn a master's degree in psychology and economics at Kansas University before pursuing a PhD in organizational behavior from Cornell University. While at Cornell, he studied with William Whyte, one of the central figures in the development of the human relations school of OT, as well as being a pioneer, along with Kurt Lewin, of action research. Subsequent to his graduation for Cornell, he took a position at Yale University, where he taught for twenty years before moving to Harvard in 1971.

Argyris' work shares with other human relations theorists the assumption that all workers have needs that they work to satisfy.[33] As humans develop over the course of their lives, they strive to become better at satisfying those needs. Argyris' thinking about these needs parallels the thinking of Maslow and other behavioralists in that his notion of human needs includes higher-order concepts including building self-esteem and becoming self-actualized. If Argyris' assumptions about human character and behavior are correct, it becomes clear that classically structured organizations can substantially limit these tendencies. Organizations wanting to perform to their highest potential benefit from helping satisfy workers' needs while at the same time meeting organizational goals.

In more detail then, Argyris claims that humans, as they develop throughout their lives, strive to become better at satisfying these needs. There are a number of tendencies that typify this aspect of human development from childhood to adulthood. This development includes the tendency to do the following:

- Become more active and less passive.
- Move from dependence to independence.
- Develop more and more complex ways of behaving.
- Shift from superficial and rapidly changing interests to deeper, more substantive interests.
- Develop time horizons that are longer rather than shorter term.
- Move from subordinate positions in relationships to coequal or superordinate positions.
- Establish greater awareness of and ability to exercise self-control.[34]

The implication of these tendencies, as Argyris describes in *Personality and Organization*, is that traditional or classically structured organizations have the effect of limiting the development of its members.[35] Structures that typify classical organizations function in such a way that limits the ability of individuals to develop along these lines. For example, the classical admonition to adopt ridged, predetermined structures of specialization have the effect of truncating the capacities of those in the organization. While it may be practically true that particular tasks require specialized knowledge, skills, and abilities (KSAs), framing positions narrowly around discrete KSAs will have the effect of limiting the position holder's ability to bring other preexisting capacities to bear on a position as well as limiting the position holders ability to develop or enhance these capacities in a way that support their efforts to meet their developmental needs. More importantly however, when the organization limits such opportunities for personal development, it simultaneously diminishes its own development and capacity for greater effectiveness. This same tendency will hold true for other classical structures, including unity of command and span of control.

Argyris' work focused not only on formal structures of the organization and their effect on development but also on leadership and management controls as well.[36] Classical management and leadership, which tended to rely narrowly on directive practices of issuing commands, according to Argyris, tend to foreclose opportunities for individual growth and development. By contrast, healthy and effective organizations require that workers also develop interpersonal competencies. The capacity to build and sustain authentic relationships, like structures that support individual growth and development, not only support individual development but they also have the effect of enhancing the ability of the organization to effectively respond to interpersonal problems that inevitably arise in social and organizational settings.

Reflection Questions

As you think about a governance organization you are familiar with, how does that organization's management practices reflect the use of Argyris' ideas?

What practices in that organization ignore or miss out on Argyris' ideas?

What impact do you think the inclusion or exclusion of these ideas has on organization performance or on the experience of staff members?

While Argyris clearly wants to see organization structures function such that they support individual development in a way that benefits individual growth as well as organizational effectiveness, he does not deny the need for stable organizational structures in order to ensure order and effective coordination. However, he wants those structures to function in a way that leads to greater satisfaction of needs among members *as well as* enhance organizational outcomes.

Robert Merton

Robert Merton, a sociologist who trained first with George Simpson at Temple College and then with Pitirim Sorokin at Harvard, began writing, among other sociological dynamics, about bureaucratic structure, personality, and their consequences on behavior.[37] Heavily influenced by both Weber and Emile Durkheim, Merton introduced a number of concepts that directly and indirectly move the study of organizations away from a narrowly empiricist approach.

Merton was among the first to acknowledge that behavior can be functional and dysfunctional and that dysfunctional behavior is not merely a result of ignorance or error that could be understood as fixable problems within the organization.[38] Merton also recognized three additional causes of unintended consequences that might be mitigated but not permanently resolved such as the tension between immediate term versus long-term interests, conflicts with basic values, and self-defeating or self-fulfilling prophecies. While these organizational features seem obvious to anyone who has spent time in even moderately complex organizations, they were not given systematic attention as important aspects of the behavior or organizations prior to Merton's work. In conceptualizing more complex structural dynamics, Merton brings to bear the idea of manifest functions, or those that are intentional and expected as well as latent functions or those that are unintentional and unexpected. Merton recognized that Weberian bureaucracy would produce dysfunctional behavior such as trained incapacities and inflexibility in the face of change. For example, he recognized that strict adherence to rules has the effect, as Weber described, of increasing the reliability and predictability of the bureaucrats' behavior but that it also causes rules to become an end rather than a means to an end, which can displace organizational goals and decrease accountability. Such latent, or unintended, consequences are, according to Merton, an unavoidable occurrence. Ultimately, Merton was among the first organization scholars to understand that in order to identify and explain alternatives to dysfunctional behaviors, we must recognize and give systematic attention to the presence and meaning of those behaviors.

Merton's work also introduces a conceptual shift in the study of organizations, their behaviors, and their outcomes. Whereas classical management theorists, and to some degree early behavioralists, sought to develop grand or universal theories of organization and behavior, Merton was critical of both strict and narrow empiricism as well as abstract theorizing. As an alternative, he introduced the notion of **middle range theory**, which bridged the gap between theory and empirical evidence. In *Social Theory and Social Structure* Merton writes the following:

Our major task today is to develop special theories applicable to limited conceptual ranges—theories, for example, of . . . the unanticipated consequences of purpose action, social perception, reference groups, social control, the interdependence of social institutions—rather than to see the total conceptual structure that is adequate to derive these and other theories of the middle range.[39]

In making this claim, Merton first gives us a means of more broadly and rigorously thinking about what was increasingly recognized as a complex yet still understandable social setting. Just as importantly, Merton also sets out a preliminary framework of behavioral and structural indicators to give order to that study.

Herbert Simon

Another thinker who dramatically broadened our thinking about organizations by exploring an extraordinary range of disciplines including economics, decision theory, artificial intelligence, and psychology was Herbert Simon. Born in Milwaukee, Wisconsin, in 1916, Simon earned a PhD in political science from the University of Chicago in 1943. Simon held teaching and research positions at a number of institutions but spent the vast majority of his career on the faculty at Carnegie Mellon University. Simon's impact across fields is unparalleled among recent scholars. He was awarded the Turing Award for his contributions to founding work in artificial intelligence, received the Dwight Waldo Award from the American Society of Public Administration (somewhat ironically because of an active intellectual debate he had with Waldo earlier in his career) for his contributions to public administration, and even won the Nobel Prize for Economics in 1978.

Simon critiqued the claims of Taylor, Gulick, and classical management thinkers with regards to scientific management but did believe that efficiency was critical. Simon's work, while significantly differing from the bulk of HRT, fits squarely with behavioralism because of his intense focus on individual and organizational behavior. Early, formal theory makes us think about our goals, encourages us to break tasks and responsibilities into components, offers a mechanism to provide stability and specialization, and highlights the importance of machine-like efficiency. The formal approach to the study of public administration and organizations ignored the human dimension and did so for many years because of the focus on efficiency and authority. The informal, behavioral tradition differs from the formal both in assumptions and in direction of research. Formal, classical theory assumed that workers were rational and motivated only by their pocketbooks. Informal theory viewed workers as also having noneconomic needs and therefore motivated by satisfaction of noneconomic needs. So research sought to define what noneconomic factors have an impact and what kind of impact. Breaking from classical theory, Simon proposed a theory of bounded rationality, which claimed that individuals cannot be completely, independently, and linearly rational.[40] Simon explained that while we have needs, goals, and aspirations and that we are intendedly rational, decisions and understandings are limited by the complexities and interrelationships that exist within our systems and environments. Simon claims that we simply do not have the ability to understand every detail within our systems, and our thoughts are limited to what we have the ability to know and understand.

Simon's interest, however, is not merely the behavior of individuals. Rather, he is concerned with the individual within the organization and the means by which the organization can maximize efficiency. Simon, first in *Administrative Behavior,* and later in *Organizations* with James March, describes how individuals "adapt their decisions to the organization's objectives" and how they are provided, in the organization, with the information required to make correct *organizational* decisions.[41, 42, 43] For Simon, this arrangement benefits the organization, which notably differs from Barnard's notion of collective exercise of rationality, by which the individual benefits.

For Simon, individual behavior within the limits of bounded rationality is characterized as satisficing; the individual creates simplified models of reality based on past experiences and particularized or selective views of the situation. One then conducts a limited search for and assessment of options and satisfice—that is, select the first satisfactory option available to them. According to Perrow, the standards for satisficing solutions emerge out of the descriptions and models of the situation.[44] These definitions and models can be established and controlled by the organization as a way of standardizing actions across the organization. This has the added benefit of reducing the potential search costs of a more comprehensive or more fully rational decision process.

The organizational result looks familiar. Organizational goals are established by leaders and are broken down and operationalized at successively lower levels of the organizations. Individuals work toward the operationalized goals not because of concurrence or coincidence with their own goals (like Barnard's model) but because the organization has mechanisms to ensure compliance, largely unobtrusively. The existence of structures such as standard operating procedures and routinized programs and processes serve to ensure consistency and compliance without requiring supervisors to directly or coercively direct individual behavior.[45]

Unobtrusive controls fall at one end of a continuum of control mechanisms that operate in different ways and have different costs. On the opposite end of the continuum are direct, fully obtrusive forms of controls, under which supervisors have direct and continuous oversight of workers' activities. It is the world that Taylor describes where workers do what they're told from morning until night with no back talk.[46] While direct, obtrusive control systems may be effective in ensuring organizationally beneficial behaviors, the costs are high in that they require continual time and effort from the organization. Further, they tend to be reactive rather than proactive, which is problematic in fluid, variable environments. Somewhere in the middle of this control continuum one finds bureaucratic controls, which tend to be less obtrusive and more effective in their ability to limit narrowly self-interested behavior of employees at a lower cost than direct, obtrusive controls.

At the other end of this continuum are full unobtrusive controls, in which factors such as organizational premises and vocabularies, tasks, subprograms and procedures, standardization of resources and channels, or patterns of communication are so thoroughly internalized that even fewer organizational resources are required. If the organization can maintain the same level of outputs, with fewer resources, it is by definition more efficient.

Reflection Questions

What is your reaction to or intuition about Simon's theory of bounded rationality?

How does this notion impact our expectation of behavior within public organizations?

Other Voices: Dwight Waldo

Dwight Waldo was born in the small Nebraska farming town of DeWitt in 1913. One of five children, Waldo's childhood in DeWitt was characterized by many of the features of nineteenth-century agricultural life and community including communal harvesting, barn raising, and Sunday church socials.[47] Upon graduating high school in the midst of the Great Depression, he attended the Nebraska State Teachers College with the intent of becoming a high school teacher. Unable to find a job after finishing college, and by a twist of fate, he went on to study political theory first as a master's student at the University of Nebraska and then earned a scholarship to pursue his PhD at Yale (which he claimed to have accepted because it was the furthest east, away from his experiences at that point in his life). Waldo's studies at Yale were heavily influenced by the political theorist Francis Cooker and Harvey Mansfield, who, among other things, served as a staff researcher for the Brownlow Committee. Cooker encouraged Waldo to explore the problems posed by the emerging importance of expertise in government, and Mansfield's first-hand knowledge of the actual workings of the federal administration added crucial real-world context to Waldo's thinking.[48] Waldo's dissertation at Yale would eventually be published as *The Administrative State,* a groundbreaking work that would set the tone and direction for the remainder of his career.[49]

The Administrative State, as well as Waldo's larger body of work, can be read as an exploration of the ideology underpinning the government's role as an active agent in the constitution of America as a state.[50] *The Administrative State* opens by examining many of the same issues and conceptual influences that the bulk of administrative and organizational scholars at the time address, including the advent and practices of scientific management, the role of empiricism in administration, the personnel and administrative reform initiatives of the Progressive Era, and others. What Waldo recognizes is that the emergence of the administrative state in the United States is the unique and critical influence that scientific management has as compared to a positive law foundation. Most states are based on a positive law tradition, whereas in the United States, "Scientific management served as a uniquely adaptable, empirically realistic, and above all 'a scientifically respectable basis' for an administrative system grafted into a federal constitutional order in a bottom up manner."[51] In the final section in *The Administrative State,* and especially for our purposes, in Chapter 9—Principles, Theory of Organization, and Scientific Method—Waldo presents a critique of rationalism and universalized managerial principles as embodied in Gulick and Urwick's work, the Brownlow report, and concepts like POSDCoRB. He points out that "purpose," "task," and "aim" in organizations, especially public organizations, are not neutral or objective concepts but are inherently normative or value based. As such, this normative character reveals the extent to which the structures and behaviors of public organizations are political rather than narrowly rational or scientific.

These same themes are revealed in Waldo's famous interchange with Simon.[52] In the debate, Waldo points out that the form of decision theory developed by Simon relies on a separation of facts and values that, to Waldo, is akin to the politics-administration dichotomy. This distinction has the effect of allowing Simon and those who follow his line of thinking to ignore the value issues inherent in *public* administration. Where Waldo's work differentiates itself further from other administrative theorists is in highlighting the value tensions from this foundation, tensions that are as present today as they were in 1942. Waldo, unlike Simon, Taylor, and others who serve as the dominant voices of this and earlier stages of administrative

Reflection Question

What evidence of Waldo's ideas do you see in public administration practice and debates about public organizations or public programs?

and organizational thinking, does not focus narrowly on efficiency, nor does he finesse away the tension with other values. Rather, he points out that there is "no presumption that the administrative state should serve one or few deductively derived ends, other than those inductively discovered pluralist values"[53] that are present in ongoing, normal political/administrative debates.

There is no overarching state—or organizational—purpose based on first principles. Whereas the behavioralists can be read as striving to become more empirically scientific in their study of human behavior, as a means of making organizations more effective, Waldo recognizes the need to acknowledge and engage in the normative conversations that are critical to an administrative state that remains democratic.

Case 3.1

The New York Department of Sanitation—Bureau of Motor Equipment

On September 23, 1992, the *New York Times* ran a story reporting that the New York City Department of Sanitation had won a national award recognizing the improved performance of its fleet of 6,200 vehicles. As far back as the late 1960s, the Department's Bureau of Motor Equipment (BME) had suffered a laundry list of organizational and managerial problems. In one infamous instance, then mayor John Lindsay nearly lost a bid for reelection when city streets went unplowed for days following a particularly severe 1969 snowstorm. Over the next ten years, if anything, performance of the agency only got worse, and by 1978 a state audit found that the BME was spending $3.5 million a year on overtime, and despite these huge expenditures, half of the BME fleet was out for repairs on any given day. At that point, Commissioner of Sanitation Normal Steisel hired Ronald Contino to head the BME, and Contino selected Roger Lewer as his deputy.

When Contino was hired, morale was low, and communication channels were largely cut off as a result of contentiousness between line workers and administrators. Contino spearheaded a change initiative that included a number of critical factors. First, it garnered support and commitment from top management. It also created shifts in line-staff relationships. Minimally, greater consideration was given to suggestions made by line workers for changes. More substantively, this was done in part by giving staff the opportunity to work on projects to solve operation and working condition problems. The idea here was that supervisors were able to benefit from the collective working knowledge and expertise that resides among line workers. One result of this shift was a substantial, technical contribution by line workers to decision making about the fleet and its technical capacity. Among the specific outcomes were the creation of new garbage truck designs to support early city recycling efforts and the early adoption of compressed natural gas trucks for the fleet.

Another expression of this effort was the creation of diverse labor management teams and committees that had access to systems and workers to collect data. This data was used as the basis of practical work process problem solving. Another critical element of these teams and committees is that BME management went directly to the union to identify members to represent frontline workers on a labor-management committee rather than selecting members unilaterally. In other words, management didn't ignore or go around the union, which in turn fostered communication, understanding, and maybe even trust.

Contino and Lewer's efforts also shifted the dynamics of the line-staff relationship by establishing regular meetings as well as access to and communication with managers. The initiative also reduced emphasis on hierarchy. Here is one account:

> In the past, sanitation men received their orders on a hierarchical basis and were expected to carry them out. Now the men are given an opportunity to influence their supervisors. Simultaneously, supervisors get an opportunity to regularly benefit from the collective working knowledge and experience of the men.[54]

More broadly, the newly established committees were linked to each other as a means of ensuring more rigorous communication and more effective coordination between and across efforts. This also resulted in greater emphasis being placed on operating problems instead of cost reductions. The innovation and change that came about out of these efforts was pragmatic; the first changes were among the most basic—management fixed leaky roofs and resolved other basic working condition problems. But even beyond these first, practical issues, the group problem-solving efforts were focused on a shared understanding of what the mission means and how to collectively achieve it.

One final change in management's orientation, as the labor management committee moved beyond initial working condition issues and dealt with more challenging and potentially contentious issues like productivity, raised the issue of work standards—a set of measures detested by labor. Labor and management agreed to ignore individual worker performance against the standards and stopped collecting the data. Rather, BME moved to broader systems assessments and focused on the total productivity of each shop. This allows, for example, the comparison of the average cost for the radiator shop with the equivalent private sector cost. The focus moved from the evaluation of individual performance to a systems level assessment of the performance of the entire shop. The result was that it was the team of mechanics that mattered. Toward this end, the new data they collected was at the system level rather than the individual level—shop by shop comparisons, supplier performance, work flow processes, and so forth.

Case Reflection Questions

What specific elements of HRT do you see in the changes made in the BME case?

In what ways does the BME case embody aspects of classical managerialism, behavioralism, and Waldo's normative understanding of public organizations?

In the first several years of the program, changes saved the city an estimated $49 million. At the time of the publication of the *New York Times* article, fairly dramatic change had occurred. By 1992, about 84 percent of the BME fleet was on the road any given day, up from barely 50 percent. Of those vehicles on the road, only 1 percent don't return under their own power. Millions of dollars in overtime expenditures have been cut from the budget, and the BME actually provides maintenance services under contract to other municipal agencies.[55]

Summary and Conclusions

As we noted at the outset, this book intends to be practical and to suggest ways to think about organizations from the perspective of those who not only inhabit them but are tasked with making them as effective as possible. It encourages readers to look at the structure, context, and environment of an organization. We encourage readers to view situations through different lenses or frames so that they can best understand the structures, environments, politics, history, and relationships associated with a variety of topics and situations.

Positive contributions of the human relations movement were that it marked a turning point in the approach toward management; it served as a bridge to early organizational humanism; and it created a new focus on individual contributions, needs, and characteristics within an organizational setting. In theory and in practice, public managers continue to question the rigidity of the traditional, rule-bound bureaucratic model. While it offers predictability and efficiency in many cases, it does not provide the flexibility necessary to move public organizations into the next century.

Criticisms of the human relations movement, which arose when it replaced discipline with manipulation, discounted the effect of the formal organization, structure, and economic incentives (that it was only important to *feel* important). It ignored the conflict between management and employees, which may exist over goals, methods, and assignments; it is more conceptual than experiential.

It is important to understand that different forms of organization are more or less effective in different types of environments.[56] We cannot ignore formality, specialization, or hierarchy from the early theorists, but we also must be flexible enough to deal with adversity, change, emerging competition, or other variation in our environment. Our organizations should be closed in the sense that boundaries are identifiable and activities predictable yet be open to change within the organization and the environment.

As society changes, organizations must change. Demographic, technological, and structural changes each bring with them unique and complex challenges for the public manager. Demographic changes bring with them the need for managers to adapt to and recognize the unique skills and abilities of individuals within their organizations. As the American population grows, diversifies, and ages, public managers must recognize and utilize the uniqueness of their employees and their contexts in order to raise the quality of public service.

Challenges often occur because managers cannot foresee the issues, even when they are routine ones. Organizations are often complex, surprising, ambiguous, learning environments. Our ability to make sense of them depends largely upon the perspectives and attitudes that we bring to the task. Our judgments depend on our expectations and beliefs. Rather than making the world conform to our beliefs, we need to go deeper and ask what is really going on here. This takes time and effort and risk.

Rather than blaming people, the bureaucracy, or a thirst for power, we look through more diverse and sophisticated lenses and look from more than one angle. Use of all the lenses takes advantage of strengths of each when suitable.

In a nutshell, perhaps the most important thing we will learn is how complex public organizations are and that often there is no single theory that is best in any given situation.[57] But we will be able to look at situations through several lenses to examine and diagnose. So we will "meet" some of the big thinkers and learn about their theories, but we try always to put them in a practical context that allows you to reflect on the concept. ■

Discussion Questions

1. What social and political changes impacted the shift toward a more behaviorist orientation toward OT?

2. How are the specific changes you identified manifest in today's organizations?

3. Based on the ideas covered thus far, what are some ideas and approaches that have been used make a bureaucracy, with the primary value of efficiency, work in a democracy, which has the primary values on participation and responsiveness?

4. If you were a manager in a large public organization, which ideas from this broad set of behaviorist approaches would be most appealing? Why? How would you incorporate these ideas into your work?

Notes

1. Woodrow Wilson, "The Study of Administration," *Political Science Quarterly* 2, no. 2 (1887): 197–222, www.jstor.org/stable/2151276.
2. Frederick Mosher, *Democracy and Public Service*, 1st ed. (New York: Oxford University Press, 1968).
3. Frederick Mosher, *Democracy and the Public Service*, 2nd ed. (New York: Oxford University Press, 1982).
4. Graham T. Allison, "Public and Private Management: Are They Fundamentally Alike in All Unimportant Respects?" in Richard J. Stillman III, *Public Administration: Concepts and Cases*, 5th ed. (Boston: Houghton Mifflin, 1992), 282–288; James Q. Wilson, *Bureaucracy: What Government Agencies Do and Why They Do It* (New York: Basic Books, 1989).
5. Ibid.
6. Chester I. Barnard, *Functions of the Executive*, 30th anniversary ed. (Cambridge, MA: Harvard University Press, 1968).
7. Fritz L. Roethlisberger and William Dickson, *Management and the Worker* (Cambridge, MA: Harvard University Press, 1939), 16.
8. Ibid., 385.
9. Ibid., 374.
10. Ludwig von Bertalanffy, *General System Theory: Foundations, Development, Applications* (New York: George Braziller, 1968).
11. Daniel Katz and Robert Kahn, *Social Psychology of Organizing* (New York: Wiley, 1966).
12. The notion of structure should be understood as *stable repeating patterns of behavior*. Structures can be formal, like official hierarchies, or informal, like culture.
13. Charles Perrow, *Complex Organizations: A Critical Essay*, 3rd ed. (New York: McGraw-Hill, 1986).
14. David Bargal, "Personal and Intellectual Influences Leading to Lewin's Paradigm of Action Research: Towards the 60th Anniversary of Lewin's 'Action Research and Minority Problems' (1946)" *Action Research* 4, no. 4 (2006): 367–388.
15. Kurt Lewin, *Field Theory in Social Science: Selected Theoretical Papers*, ed. Dorwin Cartwright (Oxford, UK: Harpers, 1951).
16. Kurt Lewin, Ronald Lippitt, and Ralph K. White, "Patterns of Aggressive Behavior in Experimentally Created Social Climates," *Journal of Social Psychology* 10, no. 2 (1939): 271–301.

17. John B. Miner, *Organizational Behavior: Behavior 1: Essential Theories of Motivation and Leadership* (Armonk, NY: M.E. Sharpe, 2005).
18. Kenneth E. Reid, *From Character Building to Social Treatment. The History of the Use of Groups in Social Work* (Westpoint, CT: Greenwood Press, 1981).
19. Kurt Lewin, "Frontiers in Group Dynamics: Concept, Method and Reality in Social Science; Social Equilibria and Social Change," *Human Relations* 1, no. 1 (1947): 5–41.
20. Kurt Lewin, "Action Research and Minority Problems," *Journal of Social Issues* 2, no. 4 (1946): 34–46.
21. Rensis Likert, "System 4: A Resource for Improving Public Administration," *Public Administration Review* 41, no. 6 (1981): 674–678; Rensis Likert, *New Patterns of Management* (New York: McGraw-Hill, 1961); and Rensis Likert, *The Human Organization: Its Management and Value* (New York: McGraw-Hill, 1967).
22. Likert, *New Patterns of Management*.
23. Mark K. Smith, "Kurt Lewin: Groups, Experiential Learning and Action Research," *The Encyclopedia of Informal Education*, September 22, 2011, www.infed.org/thinkers/et-lewin.htm.
24. Likert, *The Human Organization*.
25. Ronald Lippitt and Ralph K. White, "An Experimental Study of Leadership and Group Life," in *Reading in Psychology,* 3rd ed., ed. Elenor E. Maccoby, Theodore. M. Newcomb, and Eucene L. Hartley (New York: Holt, Reinhart and Winston, 1958), 496–511.
26. Ralph Melvin Stogdill and Alvin E. Coons, *Leader Behavior: Its Description and Measurement, Bureau of Business Research* (Columbus: Ohio State University, 1957).
27. Raymond E. Miles, "Conflicting Elements in Managerial Ideologies," *Industrial Relations* 1, no. 1 (October 1964): 77–91.
28. Arthur H. Brayfield and Walter H. Crockett, "Employee Attitudes and Employee Performance," *Psychological Bulletin* 52, no. 5 (1955): 396–424.
29. Kurt Goldstein, *The Organism: A Holistic Approach to Biology Derived from Pathological Data in Man* (New York: Zone Books, 1934).
30. Abraham Maslow, *Eupsychian Management: A Journal* (Homewood, IL: Irwin, 1965); Abraham Maslow, *Maslow on Management* (New York: Wiley, 1998).
31. Douglas McGregor, *The Human Side of Enterprise* (New York: McGraw-Hill, 1960).
32. The factors of production, most broadly, are understood to be land, labor, and capital.
33. Chris Argyris, *Personality and Organization* (New York: Harper, 1957). See also Chris Argyris, *Reasoning, Learning and Action: Individual and Organizational* (San Francisco: Jossey-Bass, 1982); Chris Argyris, *Interpersonal Competence and Organizational Effectiveness* (Homewood, IL: Dorsey Press, 1962).
34. Argyris, *Personality and Organization*.
35. Ibid.
36. Chris Argyris, *Increasing Leadership Effectiveness* (New York: Wiley, 1976).
37. Sorokin's development of the empirical *logico-meaningful method,* as distinct from the *logical-positive method,* is important here in that it represents a shift in sociological thinking about how to study and understand behaviors. Giving consideration to what's meaningful is a crucial step in moving from the findings of the Hawthorne experiments, to more structuralist approaches such as Merton's and even to poststructural approaches that will be addressed in Chapters 9 and 10.
38. Robert Merton, *Social Theory and Social Structure,* rev. ed. (New York: Free Press, 1957).
39. Ibid., 51.
40. Herbert Simon, *Administrative Behavior* (1945; repr., New York: Free Press, 1997).
41. Ibid.
42. James March and Herbert Simon, *Organizations* (New York: Wiley, 1958).
43. Simon, *Administrative Behavior,* 79.

44. Charles Perrow, *Organizations: A Critical Essay*, 3rd ed. (New York: McGraw-Hill, 1983).

45. Simon understands structures fairly broadly, or as "those aspects of the pattern of behavior in the organization that are relatively stable and that change only slowly." James March and Johan P. Olsen, *Rediscovering Institutions: The Organizational Basis of Politics* (New York: Free Press, 1989), 185.

46. Frederick W. Taylor, *The Principles of Scientific Management* (New York: Harper & Brothers, 1911).

47. Richard J. Stillman, "Dwight Waldo's The Administrative State: A Neglected American Administrative State Theory for Our Times," *Public Administration* 86, no. 2 (2008): 581–590.

48. Ibid.

49. Dwight Waldo, *The Administrative State: The Study of the Political Theory of American Public Administration* (Transaction Publishers: New Brunswick, 2007).

50. See also Dwight Waldo, *Public Administration in a Time of Turbulence* (Novato, CA: Chandler and Sharp, 1971); Dwight Waldo, *The Enterprise of Public Administration* (Novato, CA: Chandler and Sharp, 1980).

51. Stillman, "Dwight Waldo's The Administrative State," 587.

52. Herbert A. Simon, Peter F. Drucker, and Dwight Waldo. "Development of Theory of Democratic Administration: Replies and Comments," *American Political Science Review* 46, no. 2 (1952): 494–503.

53. Stillman, "Dwight Waldo's The Administrative State,".

54. Marc Hozer, "Productivity In, Garbage Out: Sanitation Gains in New York," *Public Productivity Review* 11, no. 3 (1988): 37–50.

55. Details of this case have been pulled together from Robert D. Behn, "Innovative Organization: Ten Hints for Involving Frontline Workers," *State and Local Government Review* 27, no. 3 (1995); Kathleen Teltsch, "Sanitation Department Is Honored for Innovation," *New York Times*, September 23, 1992; Robert D. Behn, "The Myth of Managerial Luck: Success From an Unlikely Place," *Governing Magazine*, November, 1993; Hozer, "Productivity In, Garbage Out," 37–50.

56. See the discussion of contingency theory and the concept of equifinality in Chapter 4.

57. Here again, David Farmer's notion of *epistemic pluralism* is particularly useful in conceptualizing the different ways of knowing about organizations and the varying consequences of those forms of knowledge. David John Farmer, *Public Administration in Perspective: Theory and Practice Through Multiple Lenses* (Armonk, NY: M.E. Sharpe, 2010).

Chapter 4

Life after Berger and Luckmann

A Theoretically Diverse World

I n this chapter we explore the growing diversity of thinking about organizations, and their place in society, that begins to emerge in the late twentieth century. We begin the chapter by giving a brief summary of the changing political, economic, and social conditions beginning in the 1960s as a way of showing how a broadening set of social dynamics parallels the emergence of a diverse set of organizational theories that respond to and aspire to comport with a widening set of organizational concerns. The chapter presents this diverse set of theories via the interpretive lens of **social construction.** Social construction is the idea that society—and the organizations that comprise an important part of it—is formed over time as members of society engage in patterned roles and behaviors that become habituated or institutionalized. As roles and patterns of behavior are institutionalized and replicated over time, knowledge and people's shared understanding of reality become integrated into the fabric of society. As such, the elements of society do not exist outside the individuals that comprise that society, but instead, those elements exist in our heads and are expressed and made real as we interact with one another. As such, social reality is said to be socially constructed.

The chapter explores various theories that emerge during this period and then summarizes several of the ontologically diverse theories of organization that have emerged from contemporary thinking about organizations. Admittedly, the material we explore in this chapter is quite varied and emerges over a longer period of time than those covered in either of the prior two chapters. Although there are schemas that we could use to break this body of work into smaller and more conceptually consistent segments, our intent in selecting a broader framework and including more diverse ideas in this chapter is to emphasize what we believe to be increasingly complex conditions and the corresponding variation in theoretical and practical approaches that coincide with those changes.

We start by giving particular attention to two economic theories of organization—transaction cost economics and agency theory and their influence on thinking about public organizations. Other theories examined include chaos and complexity theories, resource dependence theory (RDT) and contingency theory, and network theory. The chapter also gives attention to more intentionally constructivist or interpretivist theories such as *sensemaking*. Unlike the previous two chapters, we are not presenting an "other voice" in this chapter, the reason being that with the explosion of conceptual or ontological diversity during this period, the idea that there is something "other," something conceptually outside this collection of ideas, makes no sense. As Anthony Giddens sees it, "The orthodox consensus terminated in the late 1960s and 1970s as the middle ground shared by otherwise competing perspectives gave way and was replaced by a baffling variety of competing perspectives."[1] In such a setting, everything is an "other voice."

Social and Historical Climate—Things Get More Complicated

Beginning in the late 1950s and early 1960s a variety of political, social, and economic events occurred both domestically and internationally that reflect and contribute to the theoretical variation seen in the organizational theories presented in this chapter. Among the changes that began immediately following the end of World War II was the trend among European, imperial powers to grant independence to their colonies. In Africa, Asia, and Latin America, the British, French, and other colonial powers gave—or were forced to give—independence to many of their former colonies, resulting in the emergence of a new set of nation-states and the corresponding appearance of a wider range of cultural, ethnic, geographic, and other influences that then, in turn, began to filter into social and political discourse. One effect of these changes was the growth and increase in diversity of international organizations such as the United Nations. Further, many of these newly independent states became the focus of the United States and Soviet Union during the Cold War. The US involvement first in Korea and then later in Vietnam (a former French colony), as well as in Chile, El Salvador, and elsewhere, was in response to the perceived threat of expanding communist, and especially Soviet, influence and control. While the influence of these developing and newly independent nations did little to affect the overall dynamics and interaction between the United States and the USSR as global superpowers, the growth in the number and diversity of nation states did and continues to have an impact on international governance and economics.

Economically, the predominance of the United States as the preeminent economic power was first challenged by Japan and then later by other emerging Asian economies, especially China. This trend put new pressures on American companies, which in turn prompted many to reexamine their management and organizational strategies. This reexamination eventually found its way into the public sectors as well. With respect to the US domestic economy, demographic changes including the baby boom and white flight from older urban centers to newer, more geographically dispersed suburbs corresponded with the rise of new concerns about urban poverty. The civil rights movement, combined with growing unease about poverty, led to social unrest and even violence in some urban centers. These same dynamics led also to the creation of new, large social programs—and corresponding growth in administrative programs—such as the Great Society and War on Poverty programs.

Mosher suggests that much of this period can be described as *government by professionals*, as the importance of specialized training in administration but also physical sciences and engineering (e.g., in the National Aeronautics and Space Administration [NASA] and the military), natural and biological sciences (e.g., in the Environmental Protection Agency [EPA]), and sociology and social programming (e.g., in the then Department of Health Education and Welfare) reaches its zenith at this time.[2] However, the first cracks in the public's historically high regard for the civil service and public organizations also appear during this period, in no small part because of opposition to the Vietnam War and later the reaction to the Watergate break-in.

These social and political forces had a direct effect on the study and practice of public administration. In 1968, Dwight Waldo, concerned that neither the study nor the practice of public administration was responding adequately to the escalating turmoil and the complications that emerged from those conditions, organized the first Minnowbrook Conference. New Public Administration (NPA), a relatively coherent body of thinking about public administration and democracy, emerged from the work done at the conference. Advocates of NPA argued that the purported value neutrality of public administration was neither possible nor desirable. Instead, NPA advocated the adoption of normative values in public administration including social equity, citizen or client focus (rather than efficiency and effectiveness narrowly), and change in terms of the relative distribution of power and influence.[3]

Intellectually, the behavioralist work described in the previous chapter continues to develop in breadth and sophistication, but sociopolitical trends including the civil rights and antiwar movements begin to have an effect on the scholarly work at the time. While hints of the intellectual diversity described here developed over several decades and can be found in many disciplines including literature, sociology, political science, psychology, philosophy, and elsewhere, they are perhaps most clearly and profoundly given voice with the publication of Peter Berger and Thomas Luckmann's *The Social Construction of Reality*.[4] In it, Berger and Luckmann describe how people and groups interacting in a social system over time establish concepts or mental representations of each other's behaviors, as a way of understanding, and fitting themselves into those behaviors. These mental concepts and representations eventually become habituated into mutually reinforcing roles played by the individuals in relation to each other. When these roles are made available to other members of society, the reciprocal interactions are said to be *institutionalized*. In the process of this institutionalization, meaning—which allows for the understanding of and relating to others' behaviors—becomes dispersed throughout society. This means knowledge and people's understanding of what reality is becomes embedded in the institutional fabric of society. As such, reality, at least social reality, can be understood as being socially constructed.

This understanding of social organization and behavior has profound implications for the study of organizations. From this perspective, organizations are nothing more or less than the sum total of institutionalized interactions of those in and around the organization and the meanings given to those interactions. If this is true, then the study of organizations can no longer be approached as simply an engineering and efficiency puzzle, or as just a behavioral puzzle. It implies that no longer can we assume that one best way will emerge from the study of structures or behaviors. The factors that can and do impact the effectiveness of any organizational arrangement are likely to be far more diverse than was previously realized. Not only are those factors more diverse but what would have been considered mutually exclusive models of organization and behavior in the past now might be better understood as simultaneously present. In other words, organizations now present us with irresolvable paradoxes. As a result, it can be argued that this is a period that began as a continuation of government by the professionals but that then changed and fragmented to the point where it's difficult to ascribe any single, overarching, or predominant theory of organization.

Theoretical Diversity in a Constructed World

The following sections describe a series of diverse, important, and influential organization theories, all of which emerged during this period. Each of these theories strives to answer particular sorts of organizational questions and in total do so in a wide range of ways. What links these theories together is not a shared intellectual or theoretical perspective but instead that they are so different and yet emerged at roughly the same time and under the same socioeconomic conditions. To be clear, the claim being made here is not that all of the theories and theorists presented here are constructivist in their approach to the study of organizations. In fact, some, such as chaos and complexity theories, are decidedly empiricist and anti-constructivist. Rather, the diversity of these theories presented in this chapter—and their respective ontological and epistemological commitments—reveals the breadth of conceptualizations of organizations.

Because of the conceptual diversity present in the following theories, and because of the questions addressed across the breadth of that diversity, a new orienting framework may be useful here. The behavioral and structural questions that were common across the approaches appearing in the preceding chapters remain, and new questions appear. W. Richard Scott suggests one approach to organizing the breadth of thinking that emerges at this time.[5] Rather than using questions of structure or behavior as a means of organizing concepts, Scott suggests the possibility of using levels of analysis as the basis of an organizational schema. There are five levels of analysis that might be considered here:

1. The examination of individual or small-group behavior inside the organization. Questions at this level of analysis include factors of motivation affecting individual or work unit performance.

2. The examination of internal, structural arrangements. What are the optimal forms of hierarchy, communications, authority, and so forth?

3. The examination of the relationship between the organization and its immediate environment. How can the organization best relate to its clients, oversight institutions, stakeholders, etc.?

4. The examination of the organization in relation to other, similar organizations. How, for example, does a specific, local mental health organization compare to other, similar organizations?

5. The examination of the effect of organizations on society as a whole. What is the impact of large-scale, ubiquitous organizations on the social, psychological, economic, and political dynamics of the wider society?[6]

The application of these levels of analysis framework is particularly helpful in differentiating how and where different theories apply. For example, the theories described in Chapters 2 and 3 function primarily at the first two levels of analysis—individual or small-group interaction and internal structural arrangements of the organization. Clearly, questions of effectiveness at these two levels are important for organizational success; operating at that level alone is not sufficient to ensure the success of the organization. The theories presented in the remainder of this chapter operate at several

Reflection Question

What do you believe are the critical social, economic, and political factors that contribute to the emergence of each of the theories in this chapter?

different levels of this framework. One question to hold in mind as you read about and consider these theories is as follows: How do they contribute to the ability of a manager to help or maintain the organizations effectiveness?

Economic Theories of Organization: Transaction Cost Economics and Agency Theory

It should be clear by this point that much of the early—and ongoing—thinking about organizations and individual behavior within organizations is heavily influenced by a roughly economic model of man. Humans are either rational or intendedly rational, and organizational systems and structures can or should be established to reflect that model of behavior. Despite the centrality of economic rationale, classical economics has historically given very little attention to the role, function, or impact of organizations until fairly recently. Not only are these economic theories—transaction cost economics and agency theory—specifically interested in organizations but their central logic bears directly on public organizations and their role in democratic governance.

Transaction Cost Economics

Transaction cost economics is, in simple terms, the study of the emergence of and increasing tendency toward large organizations that internalize most or large portions of the production process and do so because it's the most efficient means of production. Organizations tend to grow in size as they develop new organizational arrangements in order to reduce transaction costs. Transaction costs are defined as the costs all organizations have associated with writing and monitoring long-term contracts that are complex because of the contingencies that must be anticipated. Transaction costs also include administrative and logistical costs of planning, adapting, and monitoring task completion. Administrative and logistical costs would include human resources functions like managing payroll, health and retirement benefits, accounting functions, contract management activities, and any other work that doesn't directly and explicitly contribute to the production of the goods or services of the organization. It is these transaction costs that organization scholars in public administration concern themselves with, since it is these costs that necessarily reduce the efficiency with which the organization uses public resources to provide services to citizens.

Before exploring the application of transaction costs economics to the public sector, it's worth looking at the theory in more detail.[7] Oliver Williamson's attention to organizations, efficiency, and transaction costs stems from his analysis of particular, structural attributes of developed economies.[8] For Williamson, organizations would ideally use spot contracts, or short term or one-time contracts, that typify exchange relationships in a functional market economy—that is, one that is perfectly competitive or near perfectly competitive. However, when goods become specialized, competition is reduced as only a small number of suppliers can provide needed products. This results in small numbers bargaining, which occurs in less than ideal, or highly competitive, circumstances and is not optimal for efficiency or costs. Add to these conditions concerns with uncertainty regarding the stability and futures of the market and the characteristic behavior under conditions of bounded rationality to take advantage of the other in a contract relationship—getting more for less than market value, and the result is market failure. In this case, market failure is the situation in which spot contracts fail to retain acceptable levels of efficiency when opportunism-bounded rationality combine with small numbers bargaining such that buyers are "cheated."

The result is the emergence of **organizational man** who Williamson claims is different from economic man because of his attention to organizational structures and arrangements but who is at his core still self-interested and utility maximizing. For the organization then, theoretically, the two means of reducing costs and maintaining or increasing productivity (i.e., becoming more efficient) are by establishing economies of scale, and economies of scope in either case via some form of integration. The notion of an economy of scale can be seen in the idea that the infrastructure required to build one unit of a product is the same as that required to build hundreds of units of the same product. So by producing more units, the organization can do so at a cheaper cost per unit. By contrast, an economy of scope can be seen in the production of a wider range of similar products. For example, a company producing baseballs could potentially recognize an economy of scope by producing softballs. The same basic materials, infrastructure, and administrative requirements apply to both, so the marginal cost of adding softballs is relatively small. Beyond the reductions in costs and efficiency gains there are strategic benefits to the organization from integration or internalization. One benefit is that it gives the organization more control and influence over the factors of production. Another benefit is that the assets become more dedicated to integrated organization instead of going to or being influenced by other organizations.

Integration or internalization can take any of several different forms. The first is forward integration or expansion of organizational activities into activities such as distribution, wholesaling, and retailing. Backward integration, then, is the acquisition of raw materials. Finally, lateral or horizontal integration is the decision to make for oneself, or to buy out producers of the same or similar products. While such integration clearly provides an organization competitive advantage by eliminating competition, the more important outcome to recognize here is the efficiencies the new, larger organization can realize. The logic here suggests that if two organizations producing the same goods integrate, no longer does the new, combined organization need two personnel departments, two accounting departments, two contracting departments, etc. The new, unified organization can produce as much as the two old organizations but do so with lower transaction costs.

In the public sector, there are two ways that the logic of transaction cost economics is expressed. In the first, public sector organizations undergo some sort of reorganization that consolidates similar sets of activities that historically have existed across multiple agencies or departments. Such efforts at reorganization or restructuring are made, at least in part, in order to improve economies of scope—placing similar sets of activities "under one roof"—and at the same time reducing the administrative or transaction costs of conducting these similar activities. It's useful to recognize that the costs that such efforts attempt to reduce are not only monetary but may include costs such as the loss of information or the delay of information delivery associated with inefficient communications systems between organizations. This rationale can be seen as one of the justifications for the establishment of the US Department of Homeland Security (DHS) following the 9/11 attacks. The logic of transaction costs indicates that one of the reasons intelligence agencies were unable to effectively convey information to one another was that the formal interactions between and among agencies had become too high and inefficient. In order to make the process more efficient, the multiple agencies that had existed in various cabinet level departments were placed under the authority of a new, single department. Concerns about administrative efficiencies—or lack thereof—have been a major part of presidential politics since the late 1970s, and nearly every new president elected since then has brought with him some restructuring initiative designed to improve the efficiency of the federal government.

Beyond reorganization or restructuring efforts, the logic of transaction cost economics has also been operative in other administrative reform efforts at all levels of government. The recurrent criticism that government is inefficient seems, on closer examination, to be making the argument that the vast array of transaction costs associated with many public sector activities that are too high. For example, efforts to "streamline" regulatory or oversight activities of the EPA, Mining Heath and Safety Administration (MHSA), Federal Aviation Administration (FAA), or other regulatory agencies are efforts to reduce the transaction costs of the implementation of environmental and other forms of health and safety regulation. Similarly, efforts to reform procurement or purchasing policies so that organizations can establish contracts more quickly and effectively are also endeavors to reduce transaction costs. While such process reform or redesign efforts generally receive less attention than major structural reorganizations, a strong argument can be made that these more mundane process reforms are part of a much more profound and pervasive effort that has had an enormous impact in both the scholarship and practice of public administration since the early 1990s. The central concerns of new public management broadly and the Government Performance and Results Act and National Performance Review initiatives specifically are strongly informed by an underlying logic of transaction cost economics.

Agency Theory

A second economic theory of organizations that emerged during this period and has had an influence on thinking about and work in public organizations is **agency theory** or **principal-agent theory**. Unlike transaction cost economics, agency theory places its analytic focus on the relationships between and among workers inside the organization.

An underlying assumption of agency theory is that social life is characterized by a series of contractual relationships. Again, in a simple marketplace, relationships take the form of spot, exchange contracts between principals who buy goods or services from producers or agents. In this simple exchange relationship, it is assumed that both the principal-buyer and agent-seller have good information about the value of the product or service, by which a mutually agreeable, or appropriate, price can be set. The question from an organizational perspective (remember that organizations are created in order to achieve ends beyond the capacity of single individuals—i.e., as collections of individuals who work together, they are inherently cooperative) is one of imperfect information. When a collection of agents cooperates to produce increasingly large or complex goods, each agent should be compensated based on his or her relative contribution. The informational challenge is how do we know what the relative contribution of every other agent is? Anyone who has ever worked on a team project understands the difficulty of compensating or evaluating the relative contribution of each individual to a final product. This is particularly a concern when there is the perception that members of the group are *shirking,* or not sufficiently contributing.

Not surprisingly, agency theory suggests that the solution to this sort of informational problem can be found by further utilizing self-interested behavior and developing additional contract relations. A fairly simple thought experiment presents one way to conceive of how agency theory explains the formation and function of organizations under these conditions. So again, in order to produce increasingly complex goods and services, workers cooperate, but because they cannot do the work and monitor the contribution of others at the same time, they use the surplus profits from their productive activities to contract with or hire a monitor. The monitor's contractual obligation is to oversee the activities of the workers and also assess and determine the compensation. It's important to recognize that these relationships depend on the functionality of the contract and structured distribution of profits. The monitor is paid from the residual profits of the organization rather than receiving a salary, which ensures that the monitor has incentive to do the job well—that is, not shirk because based on self-interest; the greater the organization's profits are, the greater the residual profit is.[9]

Reflection Question

What examples of organizational practices can you identify that function based on the logic of agency theory?

Issues Arising Out of the Theory

One of the central elements of agency theory is that individuals are self-interested, and the best way to utilize that self-interest in such a way that it works to the advantage of all parties is to establish mutually beneficial contracts as the basis of any exchange relationship. In other words, the basis of one's employment is a contract and probably one that is fairly explicit. And in fact, when looking at our employment experiences, those of us who are not self-employed often have some form of contract that details the nature of the employment relationship. For example, the two coauthors of this book have a contract with the publisher that details the basic content of the work, terms and timelines for delivery, and so forth. In exchange, there are explicit terms about the compensation we receive for that work. Moreover, we also negotiate the terms of our working relationship such that the compensation we receive is commensurate with the work we each contribute to the final product. Perhaps more commonly, we are all familiar with the basic content of position descriptions, which detail the responsibilities or terms of the job we've been hired or contracted to do. In some organizations, these descriptions of the work to be done and corresponding compensation do in fact take the form of a contract, signed and explicitly agreed to by both parties—principals and agents.

However, in practice, there are limits in the extent to which our employment relationships adhere to the elements of agency theory. In part this is an expression of the fact that most organizations mix some of the principles of agency theory with principles of Weberian bureaucracy.

In bureaucratic organizations, position descriptions and compensation are standardized or systematized. Workers are hired to do a specific job, based on the fit between the needs of the job and their individual merit—their knowledge, skills, and abilities (KSAs) to do a particular job. Moreover, employees in such organizations are paid a standardized rate to do that particular job, and either they perform sufficiently well and get paid or they get fired. They are not paid based on their relative contribution.[10] This bureaucratic arrangement of positions is created based on a rationale of structural efficiency. Given that there are fairly standardized classes or categories of jobs in most hierarchical organizations, this rationale suggests that it's more efficient to create uniform standards for activities and performance evaluations than to maintain unique expectations and corresponding contracts.[11]

In many other organizations, the contract describing the obligations and compensation is much more implicit. In those situations where the employment relationship does not include or, more importantly, operate under an explicit contract, an important question is as follows: Do organizations operate by authority or contract? A contract implies a symmetrical relationship—balance (or at least an agreed upon balance) of rights between parties. However, much of our organizational experience suggests that it the supervisor-subordinate relationship is one based on asymmetrical power and authority rather than a symmetric, mutually agreeable contract.

Beyond the mixing of economic and bureaucratic organizational principles, there are other challenges that are linked more narrowly to concerns of economic or rational decision making by organizations' managers. The first challenge is the problem known as adverse selection. Adverse selection describes the situation wherein the employer (principal) necessarily has incomplete information regarding the qualifications of potential employees (agents). Potential employees have essentially complete info about their own KSAs to do a potential job, but they don't have an incentive to share that information with prospective employers. Moreover, prospective employees have better information about the employer, especially with regard to levels of pay. The result is that employers lose potential employees who have the right job skills to do the work but who feel those skills are above the salary or that they can get paid more elsewhere. Potential employees who may not have the necessary skills have an incentive to "pad" their resumes to make it appear that they are more skilled than they are, or at the very least, leave those resumes ambiguous in hopes that the employer will misinterpret or not verify actual skills. The result is that it is extremely difficult for the employer to discriminate, based on limited—incomplete or biased—information, between good prospects and poor prospects for employment.

A second information problem, described as moral hazard, is the situation in which an employer really cannot be sure if an employee is doing his or her job or not. A classic example of moral hazard can be seen in the movie *Office Space*, when the main character, Peter, describes the ploys he uses to appear as if he's doing real work but in fact is not and concludes by saying, "I'd say in a given week I probably only do about fifteen minutes of real, actual work."[12] The phenomenon of moral hazard is particularly problematic in that one of the central problems that agency theory purports to respond to is that of shirking. If agency theory provides a model for understanding how organizations operate in such a way that individual contributions to the organization can be maximized—and a central problem of shirking is to be identified and avoided—it does not seem to prescribe an effective way of identifying, let alone responding to that sort of behavior.

Further, agency theory doesn't seem to sufficiently recognize the reverse problem—exploitation of agents: misrepresentation of work, safety, and the required skills needed by managers or supervisors. It assumes that principals are at the mercy of agents but fails to give consideration to how principals can control information to the detriment of agents.

Charles Perrow suggests that a structural analysis or an assessment of technology and processes is better suited to understand the relative importance of adverse selection and moral hazard in the scheme of organizational dynamics. A structural or technological examination helps answer questions like the following: What's the type of work done in the organization? What's the nature of the resource pool, including employees and their ability to do their jobs? What are the expectations of the labor pool? For Perrow, agency theory doesn't add anything new here. Moreover, the problems of adverse selection and moral hazard are based on assumptions about human nature being inherently self-interested, which new research in cognitive science and neuroscience are increasingly calling into question. Perrow also argues that concerns about recognizing and utilizing self-interested human nature may not be the real issue in the organization. For Perrow, a structural analysis can better get at the real issues, and as we'll explore in Part III of this book, there are other, post-traditional approaches that may better describe and prescribe organizational strategies.[13]

Given that there are these difficulties associated with the logic and application of agency theory, one is left wondering why we should give the theory attention either in a descriptive or prescriptive form. Perrow predicted that the theory would continue to be influential over the twenty years that followed the publication of his work and that bridge the twentieth and twenty-first century. A brief assessment of the literature suggests that he was correct in his prediction.[14] A recent search of the organization theory (OT) literature found more than fifty articles in business and academic journals use agency theory in a substantive way. At least one-fourth of those articles appeared in management publications, suggesting a continuing influence on practitioners and scholars.

While the continuing scholarly popularity of the theory is interesting, the more important question for practitioners is what substantive elements of the theory merit consideration for how they might affect the way managers conduct their day-in and day-out work. One aspect of the sustained interest in agency theory for practitioners is that it forces managers to give attention to the existence of self-interested behavior. It may be the case that even if it's not the dominant issue in organizations, self-interested behavior may still be present in such a way that it should be acknowledged if managers want to maximize the effectiveness of their workers and therefore their organizations. Agency theory gets the questions of when, why, or under what conditions does self-interested behavior occur and how might it be managed effectively. Along similar lines, agency theory enables an organizational analyst, whether a manager or consultant, to see where self-interested behavior takes place.

One additional issue serves both to raise a critique of agency theory and to reveal a potential use of the theory as well. The critique is one that is leveled at most economic theory and that is that self-interest is insufficiently precise to be useful as an analytical tool. The concern here is that in retrospect, *any* behavior can be described as self-interested. Even the most self-sacrificing behavior can be attributed to some form of rationalized self-interest by an outside observer. As such, in order to make the theory useful, attention should be given to short-run analysis of self-interest. Such attention could be given to questions that more carefully explore what situations generate self-interested behavior and that generate other regarding behaviors. Further, attention can be given to what factors contribute to inhibit self-interested behavior, such as the following:

- the extent of ongoing, direct interactions with others (which go beyond rationally established spot or one-time contracts)
- the use of individual versus group rewards as a means of performance management and compensation
- the application of individual or group performance evaluation processes
- the presence of independent work processes by comparison to team or collaborative processes
- the presence of stable, generalized hierarchy or other authority structures

The presence or absence of these structures and processes can affect the appearance of self or other regarding behavior, but Perrow suggests that efforts to maintain other regarding structures and processes are difficult for several reasons. One difficulty is that "if you've got a hammer, everything looks like a nail."[15] In other words, everything can look like self-interested behavior both in the short and long term, and the extent to which we "find" self-interested behavior may be more of a feature of our perception than of empirical reality. In fact, we may all be stronger ideological adherents of agency theory than we realize.[16] While we have yet to examine organization in any detail yet (see Chapter 6), even without an in-depth knowledge of how organization culture functions, it's not difficult to understand how an organization's culture is embedded and shaped by the wider social culture of which it is a part. Organizations reflect wider society's perceptions about race, gender, economics, etc. As a result, our generally held view of the world is dominated by assumptions that give preference to individual autonomy and rationality rather than assumptions of interconnectedness and collectivism. That perspective shapes individual behaviors, but more importantly, it affects group-organizational behavior. In short, if based on our social, economic, and political culture we assume that we act in ways consistent with agency theory, our individual and group behavior will reflect that set of assumptions. We'll begin an examination of research and theory that questions our culturally held beliefs about human behavior and motivation later in this chapter. A much more extensive exploration of alternative conceptualizations of behavior will come in Part II.

Network Theory

As we move away from economic theories of organization and to an examination of networks, there are two analytical shifts taking place as well. First, the economic theories we've examined so far in this chapter have been concerned with the internal functions of the organization. Transaction cost economics focus on questions of how an organization can increase its efficiency in the absence of new technologies, and although a central means of accomplishing this end based on transaction cost economics is by integrating or absorbing the operations of other organizations, the analytical position from which this assessment is made, is clearly from *within* specific organizations that are trying to improve their own efficiencies. Similarly, agency theory is concerned with information problems within the organization or as new members enter the organization. By contrast, network theories focus in the relationship between the organization and its wider environmental field, or its relationship to other organizations. Another difference in network theory, unlike the classical theories covered in Chapter 2, is that it assumes the organization to be open to the environment. A central tenet of the theory is that the processes and functions that are central to the theory reflect that the organization itself is always engaged in exchange relationships with the wider environment.

Scott suggests that networking between organizations is a bridging strategy that enables organizations to build greater security and stability through interdependence.[17] More specifically, such interdependence takes place through bargaining, contracting, co-opting joint ventures, and making alliances and mergers. In contrast, Harold Gortner and others use networking as a conceptual tool for examining the patterns and direction of communication within and between organizations.[18]

While these characterizations of networks are undoubtedly present in various contemporary governance processes, Lawrence O'Toole's recognition of the use of networks as a means of responding to highly complex interconnection policy problems is particularly important for students of public administration.[19] O'Toole points out that public organizations increasingly find themselves being asked to respond to what can be described as *wicked problems*.[20] Horst Rittel and Melvin Webber describe wicked problems as those that include a wide range of political, economic, and social problems. They argue that wicked problems are likely to be linked to other problems and to changes in not only physical but also social dynamics. Further, wicked problems are characterized by conflicts in which stakeholders bring significantly different perspectives to the table. The perspectives represent a range of ideological, cultural, political, and economic constraints. As a result, responses to wicked problems are not right or wrong but rather better or worse within a specific context. Over time, wicked problems are not permanently resolved but are affected by iterative initiatives that shape and create new dynamics to be addressed.[21] It is not difficult to see how many social, economic, environmental, and other problems fit this description.

If, as O'Toole suggests, public organizations increasingly have to engage in the responses to such problems, traditional, static, and hierarchical organizational models are inappropriate to meet the complex demands of such settings. Beyond the complexity of wicked problems, there are other reasons for the growth of networked arrangements as well. Keith Provan and H. Brinton Milward also recognize the link between wicked problem settings and fiscal or other resource constraints in arguing that cooperation or collaboration is going to be more effective, especially if profit motive is absent and information about intentions and perceptions is available.[22] The fiscal and political limitations often placed on the direct influence or reach of public organizations act as another incentive for networked approaches. Networks, or collaborative arrangements, are viable options especially where resources are scare, problems are complex, and service providers are narrowly focused functionally and financially.

Although there are compelling reasons to recognize the importance of networked arrangements of organizations—and there is reason to believe that the instance of such arrangements is unlikely to shrink anytime soon—networks do pose substantial challenges to public managers. O'Toole highlights several specific challenges:

1. Traditional, hierarchical forms of authority are unlikely to be operative in networked settings, and attempts to rely on authority for direction and coordination may weaken individual manager's influence rather than increasing it.

2. Because networks will likely be fluid and sometimes informal, administrators will need to routinely assess the breadth and scope of the network and understand that the network may extend beyond their immediate set of relationships.

3. Coordination challenges will be perpetual, and administrators will benefit from identifying points of coordination and overlap—common practices, procedures, perspectives, etc., that serve all or most interests in the network.

4. Given the lack of direct authority and influence, administrators should consider other means of influence, including the following:

    a. acting within the network cluster to advance the interests of program success
    b. considering and adapting the network structure as possible to move toward more favorable arrangements[23]

The rationale for the use of networks in complex environments that are also afflicted by limited resources should seem reasonably clear. The notion of a network being a more or less interconnected set of organizations with parallel, though not identical, goals also seems a reasonable strategy. However, a more detailed framework, especially that recognizes O'Toole's concerns about the breadth, fluidity, and lack of authority in networks, would be useful.[24] Provan and Milward, in an effort to establish a means of evaluating network effectiveness, establish such a framework.[25]

Provan and Milward's framework expands the conceptualization of networks beyond just the network itself to three distinct levels of analysis. Working from the most macro to the most micro level, they begin by considering the wider community, or the area that is served by the network. Assessing networks from a community level of analysis prompts consideration of both clients groups as well as wider stakeholder groups. Interestingly (and consistent with the notion of social construction that we began the chapter with), Provan and Milward also introduce the idea of social capital to their framework as a way of giving consideration to the possibility that because wicked problems are so interconnected and borderless that networks contribute to the collective capacity of a community to deal with wider or future problems.[26]

The second level of analysis is at the level of the network itself. Uniquely, Provan and Milward depart from a simple consideration of immediate outcomes and include questions about the form, structure, and function of the network. An important aspect of their model is the conceptualization of a network administrative organization (NAO).[27] In its simplest terms, the NAO is the lead organization that provides coordination and supports the necessary infrastructure for the network's efforts. The presence of an NAO provides a focal point for considering the network's coordination, diversification of services, and interconnectivity. Part of such an assessment has to do with the growth network and retention of member organizations as well as the network's ability to accomplish the provision of services that are the ones actually needed by clients. A final concern at this level of analysis is the strength of relationship and extent of coordination and interaction not only between individual organizations in the network but also across the entire network. If one were to map out the organizations and relationships in the network, how much **multiplexity** is present? Multiplexity is a way of examining the extent to which multiple ties between organizations have been established and maintained, and this, in turn, is a potential indication of greater strength and robustness across the entire network.

The last level of analysis is at the level of the individual organizational participant or individual organizations. The concern recognized by Provan and Milward here is that while networked approaches have the potential to extend impact in responding to wicked problems in a way that neither single organizations, nor uncoordinated efforts could accomplish, ultimately the members of the network are individual organizations with distinct missions. Any efforts of the network must be balanced with or in parallel to the mission of the individual organizations. Members of individual organizations have to be attuned to the impact that membership in the network has on organizational processes such as resource acquisition, perceived legitimacy, opportunity costs, and specific client outcomes.

There are, of course, integration issues that span across all levels of analysis. A primary concern here is that a network's success is contingent on success and integration across all three levels. Consideration of a single level or single outcome measure misunderstands the nature of wicked problems and the potential synergistic benefits (like social capital development) that networks can have. Another issue to note here is that network outcomes may be counter to individual organizational outcomes. Network success also demands at least some continuity of perspectives on means and ends (or at least the conditions that will allow for consensus to develop)—it's also conceivable that the departure of an organization or dissolution of an organization with inconsistent or divisive perspectives might be to the advantage of the network.[28]

Reflection Question

What are some examples of wicked problems in governance settings?

The consideration of networks of organizational actors clearly has utility for public administrators in a number of ways. Recognizing the complexity and interconnectedness of policy or program initiatives is important for administrators and will only become more so in the foreseeable future. Attention to the forms and structures of those networks like that provided by Provan and Milward is likely to be helpful in considering how the relations between and among organizations is created and maintained. Developing a more sophisticated understanding of complex policy environments is something that the next contemporary theory may help even further.

Contingency Theory

Contingency theory, or structural contingency theory, emerged in the late 1950s and 1960s and reflects thinking both from behavioral theories and from systems theories. The term was coined by Paul Lawrence and Jay Lorsch in 1967, who argued that the amount of uncertainty and pace of change in an environment impacts the development of internal features in organizations.[29] While some work in contingency theory has focused on leadership and management, the primary concern in our treatment of the theory is its application to organizational structures.[30]

The central claim of contingency theory is that there's no best way to structure an organization. Contingency theorists argue that earlier structural theories, especially rational or classical theories such as Max Weber's bureaucracy and Frederick Taylor's scientific management, fail in practice because they attempted to apply abstract, universal structural principles and neglected that organizational structures are and should be influenced by various aspects of the environment—that is, contingency factors. In other words, there could not be one best way for leadership or organization.[31]

Broadly, contingency theory has focused on the development of broad generalizations about the formal structures that are typically associated with or best fit the use of different technologies (again, the means of turning inputs into outputs—not specific tools). This line of thinking first appeared with the work of Joan Woodward, who argued that technologies directly determine differences in organizational arrangements or structures including span of control; centralization of authority; and the formalization of policies, processes, rules, and procedures.[32]

Contingency theorists, like Herbert Simon, argue that organizational structures cannot be universalized.[33] As a neoclassical or rational theorist, Simon argues that we need to describe and diagnose administrative situations. It is then possible to reframe organizational principles such that they're understood as criteria and then determine the relative weights assigned to those criteria so that it's possible to make sense of them in practice—or so that we can strive toward the "guiding criterion," overall efficiency.[34] Rather, the optimal course of action is contingent (dependent) upon the internal and external situation. Woodward also presents an alternative conceptualization to the notion that there is one best way in suggesting that not all structures and approaches are appropriate to all organizations—for example, production mass versus small batch—and the use of a bureaucratic structure.[35] She further noted that given any technology, any range of organization form may be employed. Choices to match technology with a given structure are strategic choices rather than an *a priori* given.[36]

Scott describes contingency theory in the following manner: "The best way to organize depends on the nature of the environment to which the organization must relate."[37] There are several core ideas associated with contingency theory as including several specific characteristics. First, consistent with Daniel Katz and Robert Kahn and open systems theory, contingency theory sees organizations as being open to the environment and as such, needing strategic and intentional management to satisfy and balance internal needs and to adapt to environmental circumstances.

Core to contingency is the idea that there is no one best way of structuring or organizing. The appropriate forms or structures depend on a variety of factors, including the nature of the organization's tasks or operations and the nature of the environment in which the organization operates. Extending further, there are several dimensions of the organization that reflect the influence of the environment. The first dimension is about the tasks within the organization, which are understood to lie along a continuum from highly standardized and stable to characterized by rapid change. Beyond a focus on tasks, there is also close attention to the organization of work, communication systems, and the nature of authority. This includes the clarity of roles in the organizations, positions, clear structure, and hierarchy versus interactive, ambiguous, and varied organization or structure.

Given these characteristics, the task of managers is to be aware of and work to achieve alignments and good fits between the organization's structures and the environment. "Contingency theory is guided by the general orienting hypothesis that organizations whose internal features best match the demands of their environments will achieve the best adaptation."[38]

Lawrence and Lorsch's 1967 study in the plastics industry presents evidence that in complex environments, organizations developed separate departments to deal with varying environmental conditions.[39] But these separate departments created coordination problems. Therefore, the extent that the companies could differentiate to the level required by the environment *and* at the same time integrate these different departments into collective action determined the organization's success rate.

Different subunits within an organization may confront different external demands.

To cope with these various environments, organizations create specialized subunits with differing structural features, (for example, differing levels of formalization, centralized vs. decentralized, planning time horizon) the more varied the types of environments confronted by an organization, the more differentiated its structure needs to be.[40]

Furthermore, the more differentiated the organization is, the more difficult it will be to coordinate the activities of the subunits and more resources need to be applied for coordination.

In addition to the difficulties of coordination, interunit variation can also result in conflict within the organization. The interdepartmental tensions resulting from differentiation are often caused by mutual task dependence, task-related asymmetries, conflicting performance measures, reliance on common resources, communication barriers, and uncertain or unclear goals. Rational theories of organization see conflict as disruptive and best resolved. By contrast, contingency theory, like other natural or open theories, tends to view conflict as part of the ongoing negotiation process between elements of the organization and their conflicting interests and can have beneficial outcomes. Along these lines, Tom Burns and George Stalker advance the idea of the ongoing process of organizing rather than static organization. This moves the conception of the organization from an object to a process (from a noun to a verb).[41]

Jay Galbraith's view is similar to systems design in that it stresses information flow but adds that as uncertainty increases, the amount of information required for decision making also increases. "Various structural arrangements, such as rules, hierarchy, and decentralization are mechanisms determining the information-processing capacity of the system."[42]

Other research, including that done by Lawrence and Lorsch and James Thompson, is consistent with this notion and are also more interested in the impact of contingency factors on organizational structure.[43] Their structural contingency theory was the dominant paradigm of organizational structural theories for most of the 1970s. Johannes M. Pennings, who examined the interaction between environmental uncertainty, organization structure, and various aspects of performance, furnished a major empirical test.[44]

Chaos and Complexity Theories

Beginning in the 1970s and 1980s, researchers in a variety of physical and natural sciences began to extend some of the ideas that had emerged decades earlier from general and open systems theory. Scientists working to understand dynamic natural and physical systems such as weather patterns, fluid dynamics, ecological systems, and others started to recognize the possibility that while such systems were highly dynamic and complicated, they were not, in fact, random.[45] Their study of these systems led to the development of a number of new concepts that were then applied to still other complex and dynamic systems.

In outlining and framing the contribution that chaos and complexity theories have made to organizational and administrative thinking, Francis Neumann links the physical and natural science concepts to existing organizational approaches.[46] He identifies a connection with systems theory in the extent to which Ludwig von Bertalanffy sought to replace a linear, reductionist view of the world with one that is more comprehensive or holistic. Neumann goes further and describes how Fred Emery and Eric Trist's conception of turbulent fields also seeks to capture the nonlinear attributes of social behavior that is central to much of chaos and complexity theories. These linkages reveal the extent to which existing problems in OT (i.e., how to understand and explain particularly complicated social behavior) are present already in the field. Because the conceptual work in chaos and complexity theory is quite extensive and fairly diverse, it offers apparently fertile ground from which to draw ideas. Despite that diversity, there are several concepts that have received ongoing attention for application to organizational and management questions.[47]

Beyond Open Systems

As we noted previously, these ideas developed out of the study of many different types of systems. For the sake of simplicity and space, what follows describes the development of these ideas primarily as applied to public administration and related organization and management questions rather than from the fields where they developed. In the 1960s Edward Lorenz and other meteorologists began using newly developing computing technology as a means of modeling weather patterns in hopes of improving forecasting accuracy. One of the central premises of their work was that more and better information would improve the accuracy of their predictions. Lorenz programmed a set of atmospheric data into a modeling program developed for early mainframe computers and ran the model. Subsequently he reran the model but truncated one of the variables from .506127 to .506.[48] The result of this tiny change was that the first and second runs of the model were quite similar for the first several periods of the run, at which point the two runs began to diverge to the point where the two resulting forecasts were radically different. This result gave rise to the notion of the *butterfly effect,* or *sensitivity to initial conditions,* wherein complex systems behave not in random ways but rather in ways that can be dramatically affected in nonlinear ways by small variations in any of the systems critical variables (see Figure 4.1).

Two other concepts that are often applied in related ways are *self-organization* or *emergence,* and *strange attractors.* The notion of emergence or self-organization can be seen in the schooling and flocking behaviors of fish and birds. The idea of self-organization recognizes that macroscale patterns emerge in large, interdependent, complex systems as a result of interactions that take place solely at the micro or lower levels of the system. The behaviors of individual birds and fish result in sophisticated, complex, and patterned behaviors within the larger groups. The "rules" that determine the interactions that take place within the system are executed using only micro level information without direct or explicit intent to create a macro or global pattern. In other words, self-organization—the emergence of patterns—happens spontaneously (bottom-up) without any intentionality or centralized control (top-down). *Attractors,* or *strange attractors,* including Lorenz's butterfly, are similar in that systems that behave in nonlinear, nonrepeating ways reveal stable patterns when viewed over longer periods or from broader perspectives (see Figure 4.2).

Figure 4.1 The Lorenz Attractor

Source: By Creative Commons Attribution-Share Alike 3.0 Unported license (CC BY-SA 3.0), http://creativecommons.org/licenses/by-sa/3.0/deed.en.)

Figure 4.2 Flock of Birds—Avian Emergence
Behavior

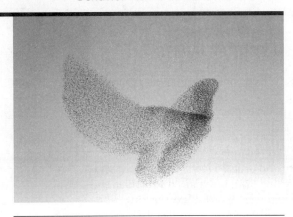

Source: Associated Press.

One final concept drawn from chaos theory that has found its way into organization and management applications is the idea of *bifurcation points* within systems. This idea gives some clarity to the behavior of systems that are characterized as being in qualitatively different conditions or phase states. For example, a container of water can be solid, liquid, or gaseous, and the transition from one state to another takes place at a bifurcation point. Further, the dramatically different qualitative states are achieved by incremental quantitative changes—that is, incremental quantitative changes from 1 degree Celsius to -1 degree Celsius or from 99 degrees Celsius to 101 degrees Celsius each result in dramatic qualitative phase state changes.

Drawing on these ideas, and emerging research in the physical and biological sciences, management and organization scholars in the 1980s and 1990s began to explore the possibility that concepts might also operate in social systems. Early efforts in this area include Margaret Wheatley's *Leadership and the New Science* and Ralph Stacey's *Complexity and Creativity in Organizations*.[49] Efforts to apply concepts for chaos and complexity theories in public organizations and governance settings have followed.

For example, L. Douglas Kiel and others have made the case that public administration has traditionally focused on incremental-linear and stable-equilibrium models of organization and management.[50] Although such models may have been applicable in the past, he suggests that these models fail to account for circumstances in which significant, dramatic change can take place. This line of thinking proceeds by suggesting that nonlinear and nonequilibrium understandings of social process and dynamics are more descriptive of organizational and political systems that are open to inputs of energy—be that inputs of resources, political attention, economic variation—and can experience rapid and dramatic upheaval as a result.

Specific examples include Kiel's efforts to apply concepts of nonlinear dynamics to both describe the activities and outputs of public agencies and to prescribe ways public managers can orient themselves to the challenging but natural nonlinear behavior of organizations.[51] From Kiel's perspective, chaotic processes are useful elements that allow organizations to become increasingly adaptive to fluid environments and to make changes in a functional, managed way rather than a traumatic, dysfunctional one. Similarly, Alexander Dawoody looks at the relationship between organizational decisions and the broader policy environment and finds that a nonlinear analysis better depicts the complex relationships among influential factors.[52] Göktuğ Morçöl takes up a similar conceptual approach to explore questions about organization and environment interactions.[53]

A critical question to consider as practitioners is the applicability of chaos and complexity theories. Lorenz's work in meteorology reveals one example of how the modeling techniques can be applied to practical forecasting efforts. Do the same conditions exist in organizational and managerial settings? Can elements of the theory move from a sophisticated and revealing description to useful prescriptions for administrators? For example, can administrators accurately determine the bifurcation points where social systems move from one phase state to another, or is the theory a useful retrospective, descriptive metaphor to make sense of what has already occurred?

Structural Functionalism and Structuration Theory

One of the primary findings of the Hawthorne studies was that human behavior in organizations is more complicated than was previously recognized among managers and organizational scholars. Structural functionalism—and later, structuration theory—can be recognized as efforts to understand the complexity of not just individual behavior but social behavior. Given that Hawthorne reveals that there is much more to the behavior of individuals and groups than the overt operation of incentives, structural functionalism explores questions including the following: What is the source of this stability and order? How is it sustained and/or changed over time? A primary concern of structural functionalism is the social structures and institutions in society broadly and organizations more narrowly. Scott points out that while as members of organizations we may focus much of our attention on the unpredictability and deviations of behavior, structural functionalism highlights and examines the rather extraordinary stability order present in most organizations, most of the time.

A simple definition of *social structures* is that they are stable, repeating patterns of behavior. They include but are by no means limited to economic, educational, legal, and gender structures. Emile Durkheim proposed that modern, industrialized societies are characterized by high levels of segmentation or specialization and that because no one individual can fulfill all their own needs they are also highly interdependent. Such societies are, according to Durkheim, held together by shared values or common symbols.[54] The shared values and symbols—and corresponding understandings and behaviors they support—are the embodiment of social structures.

Social structures exist at many levels of analysis. For example, the economic, educational, and other structures described in the previous paragraph reveal themselves in families, organizations, communities, and entire societies. For the purposes of OT, the expressions of these structures within the organization and in the relationship between the organization and its wider environment are particularly important.

It's also important to recognize that structures can be formal and informal. Formal structures are ones in which the social positions, roles, and relationships among them have been explicitly specified and are defined outside the characteristics or relations of those occupying the positions. Such formal structures would include organizational hierarchies as embodied in organization charts or decision processes established through formal policy and procedure statements. Informal social structures, by contrast, are likely to emerge unintentionally and be closely linked to the individuals and relationships in a group at any point in time. This should not suggest that informal structures are purely subjective but rather that informal structures typically develop out of specific relations and while stable and repeating are more likely to change in response to changing participation than are formal structures. Structures (social phenomenon in the form of stable repeating patterns of behavior) are seen as functional in the sense of working together. Over time patterns of behavior remain largely intact despite changes to group membership, leaving structures to effectively take on lives of their own. The patterns are expressed in but persist somewhat independently of individuals' behaviors.

Reflection Questions

What are some examples of chaotic or complex systems that involve governance organizations?

How does chaos and complexity theory help you better understand *and* respond to these situations?

The notion of functionalism highlights the idea that society—and the subgroups that comprise it—has needs. There are a variety of activities or functions that must be carried out in order for any social group to remain viable. Goods and services must be produced and distributed in order for members of the group to survive. There must be some means of administering justice, as high levels of violence against individuals or property threaten individual and collective existence. There must be some means of establishing and maintaining political and family systems so as to sustain the population and coordinate, however loosely, their activities. In short, for groups to survive, certain functions have to occur in order for needs to be met. In this way, structural functionalism draws on natural and open systems thinking. Organizations, like organisms, behave in complex and evolving ways, in relationship to their environment, in order to sustain themselves.

Structural functionalism holds that standardized social and cultural beliefs (structures), and the behaviors derived from such beliefs, serve some need or function. That function may be in support of individual, organizational, or even societal needs, but so long as the function is achieved, the structure will remain more or less stable.

Two important questions about social structures are the following: How do they develop? How are they maintained over time and as membership in the group changes? Certainly the creation of formal structures resembles the explicit and intentional characterizations present in previous chapters. As organizations are created and evolve, key actors assess the circumstances and objectives of the organization, make choices about the nature and arrangement of relationships, and codify those relationships into organization documentation. The maintenance of those formal structures, as well as the creation and maintenance of informal structures, occurs in a different way. Sanctioning is the mechanism by which these processes occur.

The maintenance of structures is associated with *sanctions*, or social consequences for conforming to or violating norms. When organizational members encounter and respond to a social norm, we may be rewarded by a positive sanction. Positive sanctions range from an approving smile to a public ceremony in our honor. By contrast, when we violate a social norm, we may be punished by a negative sanction, which may range from a disapproving look to the death penalty or life in prison. Sanctions are also the mechanism by which new behaviors become structures. When members of a social group encounter a novel situation—one that is outside their individual and collective experience—some behavior will result. The sanction that occurs in response to that behavior will either serve to help pattern that behavior (ensure that it's replicated in future situations) or ensure that the behavior will not be part of the acceptable repertoire of responses in future situations.

Most sanctions are spontaneous expressions of approval or disapproval by groups and individuals; these are referred to as informal sanctions. Sanctions that are carried out according to some recognized or formal procedure are referred to as formal sanctions. Types of sanctions, then, include positive informal sanctions, positive formal sanctions, negative informal sanctions, and negative formal sanctions (see Table 4.1).

Structural functionalism reveals insights about both the internal and external behaviors of organizations. Internally, it's easy to see how the sanctioning process and the emergence of constraining and enabling social structures are helpful in describing the sorts of behaviors Fritz Roethlisberger and his fellow researchers describe sanctioning in the bank wiring and relay assembly rooms.[55] Structural functionalism is also helpful in understanding complex relationships as our analysis moves up and outside of the organization as well. Not only are internal interactions insufficiently described by narrowly rationalist or behavioralist models, the behavior of social groups, and, in this case, organizations but they also exceed prior theoretical descriptions.

Table 4.1   Types and Examples of Sanctions

	Positive	Negative
Informal	Being praised by one's colleagues for arriving at or starting a meeting on time	Receiving negative body language or being ostracized for arriving after a meeting has begun
Formal	Being selected for an employee award for performance in support of the organization	Being formally "written up" for violating organizational policy

Institutionalism

Perrow makes the case that institutionalism, as described in his own research, as well as that of Philip Selznick, Burton Clark, Mayer Zald, and others, is the area of organization-specific studies where structural functionalism is most clearly expressed.[56] Institutionalism reflects the open and natural systems elements of structural functionalism in that it examines the organization as a sort of organic whole and often extends the study of that organization to include its relationship with the broader environment. Institutionalism does study specific, discrete processes in the organization but does so in a way that recognizes the nested nature of those processes into a larger whole that gives them meaning. Moreover, because structures and the functions they serve develop over time, a sort of "natural history" of the organization is warranted.[57] A historical assessment along these lines reveals patterns of influences or forces that result in formal and informal structures.

This shift in how organizations are studied and what organization theorists look for has several consequences. One result of this approach is an enhanced recognition of the structural uniqueness of each organization. The way forces and influences come together and the structural arrangements that result can be highly variable. What this also means is that rather than looking at the structures as the basis of organizational analysis, as Luther Gulick and other classical theorists did, structural functionalism and institutional theorists look for patterns in the forces and influences.

This, in turn, helps us realize a number of new attributes of how organizations function over time. One is that because the influential forces and resulting structures are both intentionally and unintentionally applied, organizations are very susceptible to unintended and unexpected outcomes. Organizations, or institutions, can take on a life of their own; they can exceed the explicit or intentional purposes for which they were created. This also reinforces the importance of, and the attention given to, the wider environment. Organizations, from this analytical perspective, are understood as being open to, and potentially highly influenced by, other actors in their immediate environment.

Structuration Theory

Structural functionalism has come under critique for at least two related difficulties with the theory. First, it has been criticized for being overly static and not sensitive enough to the possibility and nature of change. Second, that same rigidity, it is argued, leaves no room for human agency. In other words, structural functionalism is critiqued for being too static and too

Image 4.1 Drawing Hands

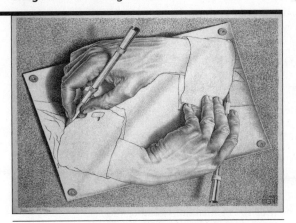

Source: © Christie's Images/Corbis.

deterministic. Giddens, a British sociologist, takes on these concerns directly in his conceptualization of structuration theory.[58] Giddens acknowledges the existence and importance of social structures but departs from early structural functionalism in his development of a theory that describes the *duality of structure.* Namely, social structures do in fact constrain the choices that humans can make about their activities, but at the same time, structures are created and sustained by the very activities they constrain. Structures and the behavior of agents are within them—therefore, mutually influential.[59] Mary Jo Hatch nicely links this process of mutual creation to the famous M. C. Escher image of two hands drawing one another.[60]

One of the outgrowths of Giddens' theory in organizational settings is that his more dynamic, agency-centered model is framed so as to give much greater attention to how influence and effect run both directions and that what is underlying in apparently stable structures is a dynamic set of relations through which the organization is sustained in particular structural form. Richard Whittington, for example, uses structuration theory to develop an account of managerial agency, which exists within and is constrained by existing structures yet still exercises influence on organizational action.[61] More recently, others have taken up Giddens' structuration theory as a way for actors to more effectively understand the patterns of organizational action and develop actionable knowledge about these patterns over time.[62]

In sum, what the related theories of structural functionalism, institutionalism, and structuration theory do is give a language and logic to the informal patterns of behavior first formally described by Roethlisberger and his colleagues in the Hawthorne experiments. The question they uncovered—and the behavioralists were unable to sufficiently answer—was how do we understand and explain the existence of patterned collective behaviors? The behavioralist theories of motivation presented in the previous chapter present an effort to explain behavior at the individual level but don't adequately scale that up to group, collective, or organizational levels. Structural functionalism and subsequent variations of it move us further in that direction.

Reflection Questions

Can you think of a governance organization in your community that has become an institution? How has this change benefited or challenged the organization?

Can you think of practices in your organization that have become institutionalized? How has this enhanced or limited the organization's operations?

Cognitive and Psychological Models—Sensemaking

Karl Weick first emerged as an organizational scholar with the publication of *The Social Psychology of Organizing.*[63] This book, the title of which is a play on Katz and Kahn's *The Social Psychology of Organization,* shifts the thinking about organization from a static entity, to that of a dynamic, ongoing process. In other words, organization is not a noun, but rather a verb. It's important to note that in making this move, Weick is extending a constructivist view of organizations. He uses the term *enactment* to denote the idea that organizations are created by being talked about and acted out. "Managers construct, rearrange, single out, and demolish many 'objective' features of their surroundings. When people act they unrandomize variables, insert vestiges of orderliness, and literally create their own constraints."[64]

Weick's later work further emphasizes this shift in his conceptualization of *sensemaking*, which is a particular, structured psychological information processing and behavior model. For Weick, sensemaking is the processes and means by which individuals make sense of their situation. It describes specific ways of structuring the unknown by placing stimuli into a framework. More, it is the mechanism by which members of an organization account for surprises, uncertainty, and ambiguity—conditions that are increasingly common in contemporary organizations.

The processes of sensemaking involve seven overlapping characteristics:

1. *Grounded in identity construction*—The way by which one makes sense of a situation is grounded in part in whom that person is and how he views himself.

2. *Retrospective*—Making sense of that which has already occurred. One makes sense of past experiences and situations.

3. *Enactive of sensible environments*—People enact or produce the social environments that they face. Those environments, including organizational ones—are sensible in that they are tangible or describable in some way. We create environments that we have a sense of.

4. *Social*—Sensemaking is done in the context of an array of relationships, and those relationships shape, and are shaped by, how we view and fit ourselves into the world. However we make sense of a situation, that sense is likely shared in some way with those around us.

5. *Ongoing*—The process of sensemaking never starts or stops. Sensemaking and enactment is never inactive nor are individuals ever separate from their environment. Even electing not to act is an action. One cannot step outside of the situation to observe or avoid action.

6. *Focused on and by extracted cues*—We use individual, simple, and familiar cues as the basis of sensemaking. And we do so regardless of other data available. Cues are a point of reference used to orient oneself, and they establish context from which to act. The perception of these cues is not purely objective, meaning that the cues we recognize and respond to are those that are part of our perceptual experience and existing understandings.

7. *Driven by plausibility rather than accuracy*—Sensemaking will plausibly fit data—it doesn't have to be an accurate match to the data (danger of using cues).[65]

In one of his most well-known case studies, Weick studies the importance of sensemaking—or more precisely, the consequences of the collapse of sensemaking for organizations. Weick examines the Mann Gulch fire as a way of revealing the importance of stable sensemaking for organizational performance.[66]

In 1949, a team of fifteen smoke jumpers were deployed into the Mann Gulch drainage of the Helena National Forest, just outside Helena, Montana, to fight a lightning-caused forest fire. Once on the ground, the smoke jumpers joined up with another US Forest Service fire guard who had reported the fire and was making initial attempts to control it. What the group initially believed to be a 10:00 fire, or one that could be controlled by 10:00 the following morning, quickly changed behavior and overran the crew. One of the crew was able to set an escape fire—or was able to burn a large enough area of grass so that the larger fire would burn around him but leave him safe. The use of escape fires was a technique that had been used in the prairies to escape grass fires but had never been used by the US Forest Service and was not part of the smoke jumpers' training. Two other members of the crew were able to scramble through a crevice into a neighboring gulch and rock field, where they survived. All of the other members of the team perished in, or as a result of, the fire. Ultimately, the fire burned 4,500 acres and took 450 men five days to control it.

Weick begins his analysis by describing six structural characteristics of a smoke jumper unit that he believes make it typical of other, more common types of organization.[67] Smoke jumpers, like most organizations, operate through the use of sets of existing roles and interlocking routines. Their work is characterized by habituated action patterns—same people (or same roles), same places (same types of places), same work. The group functions within a simple but formal organizational structure. There was a commander, second in command, and set of line workers. Within this simple structure, the group is characterized by generic subjectivity typical of bureaucratic organizations. The individuals on the crew could be interchanged with other individuals who had the same skill sets and training. These attributes, according to Weick, are common in most contemporary organizations.

If the cognitive processes of sensemaking enable organizational members to create a sense of stability and order in a highly complex environment, then the Mann Gulch fire reveals what can happen to organizations when the shared processes of sensemaking cease to provide that perception of stability and comprehensible order. In other words, organizations perform reasonably well when sensemaking processes are intact and functionally operational, but organizations are susceptible to sudden losses of meaning that constitute a significant threat to their functionality. These losses of meaning, or cosmology events, are essentially an experience of *vu jade*, or "I've never been here before," and consequentially, they have no basis of figuring out what to do. Organizations and individuals within them depend on a comprehensibleness of their day-to-day experiences and then can find themselves in situations that are totally out of the ordinary. The experience of the breakdown in continuity of everyday events constitutes a grave threat to the functionality of the organization.

While, thankfully, such cosmology events aren't typical of our everyday experience, they are, perhaps, not as uncommon as one might think. Consider, for just a moment, the number of organizational events, or outright collapses, that have occurred in recent memory. For example, the collapse first of Enron and Arthur Andersen or of Goldman Sachs and Lehman Brothers seemed unimaginable up until almost the very moment they occurred. Interviews with former members of these organizations reveal the outright confusion—collapse of sensemaking—that occurred around those events. Other less catastrophic but no less traumatic events might include the heart transplant debacle at the Duke Medical Center or NASA following the *Columbia* disaster. Again, consider the profound uncertainty that occurs when discovering that the identity, experiences, and all of the associated practices of organizations like these cease to provide a sense of stability and order.

Weick does propose a model that he believes can engender much more robustness and resilience in organizational sensemaking. We will examine that model in more detail in Chapters 6 and 7, but for the moment, it's enough to recognize sensemaking as a cognitive model of organizational analysis.

Case 4.1

The Tennessee Valley Authority: An Examination of Parallel Theories

Selznick's examination of the Tennessee Valley Authority (TVA) is perhaps one of the best-known, oft cited case studies of institutionalism in public administration and OT. As presented here, the TVA represents an opportunity to think not only about the processes and characteristics of institutionalism but the expression of other theories as well. As you read the following case, consider how other theories that function at the organization structure and environmental field levels are revealed in the history and behavior of the agency.

The TVA was created by Congress in May 1933 to provide power generation, flood control, agricultural support, and economic development in the Tennessee Valley, a region particularly affected by the Great Depression. The organization was conceived not only as an energy provider but also as a regional economic development agency that would use federal experts and electricity to rapidly modernize the region's economy and society. To some degree, the TVA is typical of most large, bureaucratic organizations. It has a clear hierarchy, relies on technical expertise and specialization, and adheres to well-established practices and policies and so forth. The traditional hierarchy of the TVA is revealed in its organization chart (see Figure 4.3).

In another way, however, the TVA represented a significant shift from the structures, strategies, and approaches of other agencies at the time. First, it was a "relatively autonomous public corporation" generally free from "the normal financial and administrative controls exercised over federal organs."[68] In advocating for the creation of the TVA, President Roosevelt argued that an organization "clothed with the power of government but possessed of the flexibility and initiative of private enterprise" was necessary to develop the Tennessee River.[69] Most importantly, the act that established the TVA provided the organization extensive discretion to accomplish its mission, based on the justification that it "would invite those in charge to recognize the social consequences of specific activities."[70] The TVA also had "freedom to devise methods of dealing with local people and institutions."[71]

From even before its formal establishment, the creation of the TVA was understood as having importance beyond its instrumental purposes. For example, progressives and liberals viewed the TVA as an important symbol. Selznick notes that "it is primarily as a symbol that TVA excites allegiances and denunciation."[72] As a result progressive and liberal activists defended the institution during "controversies over finance and accountability," and they promoted the idea of the TVA as "a model for regional development in other areas."[73] Even within the TVA, this extra-instrumental character was important, for example, as its administrative leaders recognized the need to develop an "official doctrine." This doctrine, eventually operationalized in the TVA response to its environment, was "grassroots administration."

Figure 4.3 Partial Tennessee Valley Authority Organization Chart

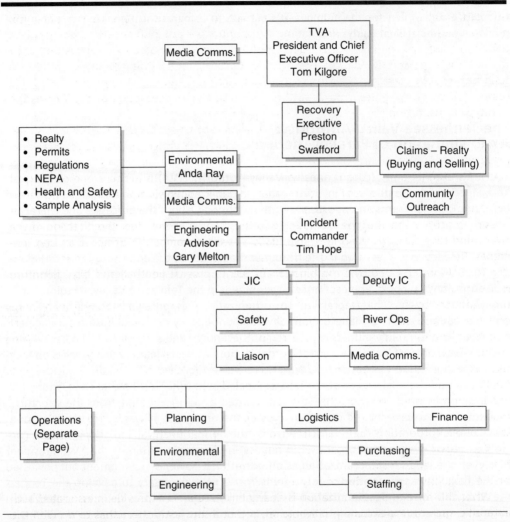

Source: Tennessee Valley Authority.

Through the first five years of the agency's existence, several members of the board of directors advanced contending visions for the TVA institutional identify. Finally in March 1938, President Roosevelt removed A. E. Morgan from the board and replaced him with David Lilienthal. Subsequently, Lilienthal moved forward using a grassroots approach, and the TVA priorities and strategies shifted. Importantly, these new approaches included the use of co-optation as a means of overcoming resistance from local communities.[74] This was critical in part because of the corresponding emphasis on power generation, industrialization, and an agricultural program that relied on the region's preexisting institutions. Further, TVA officials used the idea of decentralized administration and regional democracy to *legitimate* their institution. In support of their efforts, administrators asked for and received substantial independence from the federal government and its operating procedures. For example, the TVA was not subject to Civil Service Commission regulations, allowing it significant flexibility in developing personnel practices that ultimately support the establishment of a unique, TVA specific institutional character. The legacy of the TVA original board of directors and their strategic choice continued to be a powerful ideological force within the organization—so much so, Hargrove contends, that their successors became "prisoners of [the] myth" they had created.[75] These, among many other factors, led to Selznick's description of the TVA as the prototypical institution.

An alternative interpretation of this early period is revealed in Weick's notions of sensemaking and enactment. Weick points out that organizational participants, especially those with power, are in positions to impose their enactments, or sensemaking frameworks, on others. The influence of sensemaking frameworks can be seen from the very founding of the agency in the perspectives of A. E. Morgan, chairman, and his antagonists, board members David Lilienthal and H. A. Morgan (no relation). Erwin Hargrove describes the early history of the agency and the internal struggle for power and control over the direction of the TVA would take through the 1930s and 1940s as well as competing perspectives and ideologies. Respectively, these ideological frameworks can be described as utopian social planning (A. E. Morgan) versus the combination of giant power (Lilienthal) and big agriculture (H. A. Morgan). A. E. Morgan arrived at the TVA from Antioch College, where he had previously served as the school's president. Prior to being appointed to the TVA board, Lilienthal had served on the Wisconsin Public Service Commission. Agriculturist H. A. Morgan's selection to the TVA board signified Roosevelt's desire to have local-regional interests represented. A former president of the University of Tennessee, H. A. Morgan championed policies that favored the Valley's large-scale farmers and was important to efforts to develop relationships with the states' land-grant colleges and universities, extension services, and county agents.[76]

Case Reflection Questions

As you think about the tasks or operations of the TVA, how does switching theories change the sorts of issues managers focus on and change the courses of action managers might select?

What opportunities and challenges might managers face if they attempt to use multiple theoretical orientations?

While this form of decentralization is clearly linked to a normative claim associated with pragmatic, grassroots democracy, it would seem that a secondary theme has to do with the effectiveness of a decentralized approach. While the notion of a network had not been applied to organization studies in the 1940s, a preliminary assessment of the environment reveals a certain level of complexity with respect to agency activities as well as social and political contexts throughout the Tennessee Valley. Such complexity and the corresponding decentralization and interconnectedness of the structures of the TVA fit with O'Toole's claims about networks.

There is also evidence to suggest that the efficiency logic of transaction costs may also be a valid means of assessing the behaviors of the TVA. For example, Michael Taylor points out that outside both the coordinative benefits of networks and the political legitimacy benefits of institutions, there are efficiencies to be realized.[77] The establishment of stable, ongoing working arrangements as described by Provan and Milward or the grassroots co-optation identified by Selznick also serve as a means of reducing the transaction costs of relationship maintenance. In later episodes, the agency has taken other management level steps to reduce its transaction costs. For example, more recently, the TVA has changed some of its purchasing processes to reduce the transaction costs of procurement.[78]

Summary and Conclusions

ONE OF THE KEY TAKEAWAYS from this chapter is recognition of the substantial theoretical diversity that emerged in the later half of the twentieth century. This diversity results in part from the breadth of ideas—from biological and physical sciences, to other social and behavioral sciences like psychology and economics—that have come to influence the study of organizations. This diversity is also a result of new and evolving concerns within the field. Growth in the complexity and scope of organizational efforts during and after the war, evolving political and economic dynamics around the Cold War and collapse of European empires, emerging technological influences in communications and information management, and many other factors appear during this period and result in fresh theoretical and analytical responses.

Despite, or perhaps because of, this diversity, the theories we've described in this chapter have remained influential and continue to have effects in the contemporary study of and practices of organizations. The practical uses of these theories are explored further in Part II of the book, so we won't review the contemporary influences and effects of each of these theories here. Instead, we want to highlight a different sort of impact that two of the theories we've covered in this chapter—economic theory and structural functionalism—have.

Economic theory—and particularly principal agent and transaction cost theories—is especially powerful in both the practices and the orientation of contemporary governance organizations. New public management's efforts to use incentive mechanisms to shape behavior both in and outside of the organization and contemporary rhetoric focused on reducing red tape and regulatory inefficacies reveal the widespread influence of economic thinking in governance organizations.

Structural functionalism, by contrast, is notable not so much for its influence on current political and managerial rhetoric and practice but instead because it lays important experiential and analytical foundations that are taken up and extended by researchers at the end of the twentieth century. Elements of structural functionalism described by Selznick and others are important because they give researchers and practitioners a means of understanding some of the nonrational, nonlinear, and symbolic behaviors of organizations that emerge beyond the intent or control of leaders and members of the organization. Structural functionalism not only confirms our experience and intuition of how organizations take on lives of their own but reveals how that occurs in ways that can be used to enhance organization performance. Structural functionalism also lays the groundwork for ideas that we'll examine in Part III of the book, namely the move into poststructuralism, or the possibility not only that organizations and practices take on a life of their own but that this phenomenon is far more fluid and variable than Selznick, Zald, or other institutionalists ever anticipated. What that fluidity and variability look like, however, is a question you'll need to hold on to until Chapters 9 and 10. ■

Discussion Questions

1. As you consider each of the respective theories presented in this chapter, what do think is the central organizational problem or question to which each theory seeks to respond?

2. How might diversity of thought, culture, theory, and discourse enhance democratic governance?

3. What level of analysis (individual or small-group, structural, environmental, organization type, or sociocultural) do each of the theories covered in this chapter correspond with?

4. Which of the theories do you see supporting or reinforcing each other? Which are in tension or conflict with one another? What effect do the supports or tensions you identified have on the theory's use?

Notes

1. Philip Cassell, *The Giddens Reader* (Stanford, CA: Stanford University Press, 1993).
2. Frederick Mosher, *Democracy and Public Service*, 1st ed. (New York: Oxford University Press, 1968).
3. H. George Frederickson, *Social Equity and Public Administration: Origins, Developments and Applications* (Armonk, NY: M.E. Sharpe, 2010); Mary Timney Bailey and Richard T. Mayer, *Public Management in an Interconnected World: Essays in the Minnowbrook Tradition* (New York: Greenwood Press, 1992).
4. Peter L. Berger and Thomas Luckmann, *The Social Construction of Reality: A Treatise in the Sociology of Knowledge* (Garden City, NY: Anchor Books, 1966).
5. W. Richard Scott, *Organizations: Rational, Natural and Open Systems*, 5th ed. (Upper Saddle River, NJ: Prentice Hall, 2003).
6. Ibid.
7. Oliver Williamson, *Markets and Hierarchies* (New York: Free Press, 1975); Oliver Williamson, "Transaction Cost Economics: The Governance of Contractual Relations," *Journal of Law and Economics* 1 (March 1980): 5–38.
8. Oliver Williamson, along with political scientist Elinor Ostrom, was awarded the 2010 Nobel Prize for Economics.
9. See Armen A. Alchain and Harold Demsetz, "Production, Information Costs and Economic Organization," *American Economic Review* 62, no. 5 (1972): 777–795.
10. See Chapter 5 for details on pay-for-performance compensation systems.
11. Given the critiques of bureaucracies as inefficient, it is somewhat ironic that this type of standardization is intended to make the organization more efficient by reducing the transaction costs of position management and performance evaluation.
12. *Office Space*, directed by Mike Judge (Los Angeles: 20th Century Fox, 1999).
13. Charles Perrow, *Complex Organizations: A Critical Essay*, 3rd ed. (New York: McGraw-Hill, 1986).
14. Ibid.
15. Abraham H. Maslow, *The Psychology of Science: A Reconnaissance* (Madison, WI: Harper & Row, 1966), 15.
16. Here again, ideology should be understood as a largely unconscious system of beliefs and understandings that make the world sensible. Ideology is not being used in a narrowly political sense.

17. Scott, *Organizations,* 5th ed.
18. Harold F. Gortner, Julianne Mahler, and Jeanne Bell Nicholson, *Organizational Theory: A Public Perspective* (Chicago: Dorsey, 1987).
19. Lawrence O'Toole, "Treating Networks Seriously: Practical and Research-Based Agendas in Public Administration," *Public Administration Review* 57, no. 1 (1997): 45–51.
20. Horst Rittel and Melvin Webber, "Dilemmas in a General Theory of Planning," *Policy Sciences* 4 (1973): 155–169.
21. Jeff Conklin, *Dialogue Mapping: Building Shared Understanding of Wicked Problems* (West Sussex, UK: Wiley, 2006).
22. Keith G. Provan and H. Brinton Milward, "Do Networks Really Work? A Framework for Evaluating Public-Sector Organizational Networks," *Public Administration Review* 61, no. 4 (2001): 414–423.
23. O'Toole, "Treating Networks Seriously."
24. Ibid.
25. Provan and Milward, "Do Networks Really Work?"
26. Ibid.
27. Ibid.
28. Ibid.
29. Paul R. Lawrence and Jay W. Lorsch, *Organization and Environment: Managing Differentiation and Integration* (Cambridge, MA: Harvard University Press, 1967).
30. See for example, F. E. Fiedler, "A Contingency Model of Leadership Effectiveness," *Advances in Experimental Social Psychology* 1 (1964): 149–190.
31. See F. Kast and J. Rosenzweig, *Contingency Views of Organization and Management* (Chicago: Science Research Associates, 1973); D. T. Otley, "The Contingency Theory of Management Accounting: Achievement and Prognosis. Accounting," *Organizations and Society* 5, no. 4 (1980): 413–428.
32. Joan Woodward, *Management and Technology* (London: Her Majesty's Stationary Office, 1958).
33. Herbert A. Simon, "The Proverbs of Administration," *Public Administration Review* 6 (1946): 53–67.
34. Ibid.
35. Woodward, *Management and Technology.*
36. Ibid.
37. W. Richard Scott, *Organizations: Rational, Natural, and Open Systems,* 1st ed. (Englewood Cliffs, NJ: Prentice Hall, 1981).
38. Scott, *Organizations,* 1st ed., 89.
39. Lawrence and Lorsch, *Organization and Environment.*
40. Scott, *Organizations,* 1st ed., 89.
41. Tom R. Burns and George M. Stalker, *The Management of Innovation* (London: Tavistock, 1961).
42. As quoted in Scott, *Organizations,* 1st ed., 90.
43. Lawrence and Lorsch, *Organization and Environment;* James D. Thompson, *Organizations in Action* (New York: McGraw-Hill, 1967).
44. Johannes M. Pennings, "Measures of Organization Structure: A Methodological Note," *American Journal of Sociology* 79 (1973): 686–704.
45. Edward Lorenz, *The Essence of Chaos* (Seattle: University of Washington Press, 1993); Ilya Prigogine and Isabelle Stengers, *Order Out of Chaos* (New York: Bantam Books, 1984); R. M. May. "Biological Populations with Non-Overlapping Generations: Stable Points, Stable Cycles and Chaos," *Science* 186 (1974): 645–647.
46. Francis X. Neumann Jr., "Organizational Structures to Match the New Information-Rich Environments: Lessons from the Study of Chaos," *Public Productivity and Management Review* 21, no. 1 (1997): 86–100.

47. Ibid.

48. Nancy Mathis, *Storm Warning: The Story of a Killer Tornado* (New York: Touchstone, 2007), x.

49. Margaret Wheatley, *Leadership and the New Science: Discovering Order in a Chaotic World* (San Francisco, CA: Berrett-Koehler Publishers, 1999); Ralph Stacey *Complexity and Creativity in Organizations* (San Francisco, CA: Berrett-Koehler Publishers, 1996).

50. L. Douglas Keil, "Nonequilibrium Theory and Its Implications for Public Administration," *Public Administration Review* 49 (1989): 544–551; Alexander Dawoody, "Examining the Preemptive War on Iraq," *Public Integrity* 9, no. 1 (Winter 2006–2007): 63–77; Göktuğ Morçöl, "What Is Complexity Science? Postmodernist or Postpositivist?" *Emergence* 3, no. 1 (2001): 104–119.

51. L. Douglas Kiel, *Managing Chaos and Complexity in Government: A New Paradigm for Managing Change, Innovation and Organizational Renewal* (San Francisco: Jossey-Bass, 1994).

52. Dawoody, "Examining the Preemptive War on Iraq"; Alexander Dawoody, "Teaching Public Policy as a Nonlinear System," *Journal of US-China Public Administration* 8, no. 4 (2011): 372–386.

53. Göktuğ Morçöl, "Issues in Reconceptualizing Public Policy from the Perspective of Complexity Theory," *Emergence: Complexity and Organization* 12, no. 1 (2010): 52; Göktuğ Morçöl, "Complexity of Public Policy and Administration: Introduction to the Special Issue," *Public Administration Quarterly* 32, no. 3 (2008): 305; Göktuğ Morçöl, "In the Wake of Chaos: Unpredictable Order in Dynamical Systems," *Journal of Public Administration Research and Theory* 6, no. 2 (1996): 315.

54. Jonathan S. Fish, *Defending the Durkheimian Tradition: Religion, Emotion and Morality* (Aldershot, UK: Ashgate Publishing, 2005).

55. Fritz Roethlisberger and W. J. Dickson, *Management and the Worker: An Account of the Research Program Conducted by the Western Electric Company, Hawthorne Works, Chicago* (Cambridge, MA: Harvard University Press, 1939).

56. Perrow, *Complex Organizations,* 3rd ed.; Philip Selznick, *TVA and the Grass Roots* (Berkeley: University of California Press, 1949); Charles Perrow, "Goals and Power Structures," *The Hospital in Modern Society,* ed. Eliot Freidson (New York: Free Press, 1963); Burton Clark, *Adult Education in Transition* (Berkeley: University of California Press, 1956); Mayer N. Zald, "The Correctional Institution for Juvenile Offenders: An Analysis of Organizational Character," *Social Problems* 8, no. 1 (1960): 57–67.

57. Perrow, *Complex Organizations,* 3rd ed.

58. Anthony Giddens, *Central Problems in Social Theory: Action, Structure and Contradiction in Social Analysis* (Berkeley: University of California Press, 1979).

59. Ibid.

60. Mary Jo Hatch, *Organization Theory: Modern, Symbolic and Postmodern Perspectives* (New York: Oxford University Press, 1997).

61. Richard Whittington, "Putting Giddens into Action: Social Systems and Managerial Agency," *Journal of Management Studies* 29, no. 6 (1992): 693–712.

62. Robert D. McPhee, "Text, Agency and Organization in Light of Structration Theory," *Organization* 11 (2004): 355–371; Christian Fuchs, "Structuration Theory and Self-Organization," *Systematic Practice and Action Research* 16, no. 2 (2003): 133–167.

63. Karl E. Weick, *The Social Psychology of Organizing* (Reading, MA: Addison-Wesley, 1969).

64. Ibid., 243.

65. Karl E. Weick, *Sensemaking in Organizations* (Thousand Oaks, CA: Sage, 1995).

66. Karl E. Weick, "The Collapse of Sensemaking in Organizations," *Administrative Science Quarterly* 38, no. 4 (1993): 628–652.

67. Ibid.

68. Selznick, *TVA and the Grass Roots,* 5.

69. Ibid., XX.

70. Selznick, *TVA and the Grass Roots,* 6.

71. Ibid., 6.

72. Ibid., 19.

73. Ibid.

74. Selznick defines co-optation as "the process of absorbing new elements into the leadership or policy-determining structure of an organization as a means of averting the threats to its stability or existence." Selznick, *TVA and the Grass Roots,* 13.

75. Erwin Hargrove, *Prisoners of the Myth: The Leadership of the Tennessee Valley Authority* (Knoxville: University of Tennessee Press, 2001), 64. See also John W. Meyer and Brian Rowan, "Institutional Organizations: Formal Structure as Myth and Ceremony," *American Journal of Sociology* 83 (1977): 340–363.

76. Hargrove, *Prisoners of the Myth.*

77. Michael Taylor, "Structure, Culture and Action in the Explanation of Social Change," *Politics and Society* 17 (June 1989): 115–162. See also Joel M. Podolny and Karen L. Page, "Network Forms of Organization," *Annual Review of Sociology* 24 (1998): 57–76.

78. M. Verdin (1999), "TVA Revamps Procurement Process," *TMA Journal* 19, no. 1, 39–40; Mihir A Parikh and Kailash Hoshi, "Purchasing Process Transformation: Restructuring for Small Purchases," *International Journal of Operations and Production Management* 25, no. 1 (2005): 1042–1061.

Part II

Issues, Strategies, and Tactics

I n Part I we presented a historical and conceptual overview of organization theory (OT), tracing the evolution of thinking about how to maximize the effectiveness of organizations, especially in the public sector. Part II shifts gears and is both practical and problem oriented in its content and structure. It presents a basic *taxonomy*, or framework, of issues or activities that administrators must routinely contend with. Each of the chapters in Part II do so by working across levels of analysis from the individual, to systems, to organizations writ large and finally to organization-environment relations in an effort to explore the implications of the theories from Part I for organizations as they operate in twenty-first-century governance settings.

The purpose of organizing Part II in this way is twofold. First, it is intended to give students a clearer sense of how OT is operationalized in prescriptive ways, or in terms that can be taken up and used by practicing administrators. Second, and more conceptually, the theoretically driven practical strategies presented across the chapters in Part II are framed such that their practical limits are more apparent. We argue that no single OT is comprehensive in its capacity to respond to all problems at all levels of analysis. Therefore, the presentation of the theories in this part is designed to make the limits of these theories more apparent, giving practitioners the ability to reflect more intentionally on how to integrate theories and practices such that it is possible to respond more effectively across levels of analysis.

With those objectives in mind, each chapter presents a working description of the topic derived out of the literature in the field. It's important to know that this is a working description rather than the definitive definition. Before proceeding, it's worth reiterating that *working descriptions and definitions* are useful starting places to understand concepts but as our understanding becomes deeper as well as more nuanced and subtle, then the definitions fall away, and we're left with a more intuitive understanding of that nuance and subtlety.

Each chapter then explores a set of the central, theoretically grounded approaches associated with this activity. The exploration of these approaches spans many of the historical and conceptual categories-models described in Part I. The idea here is to both present a practical overview of "how to" and to relate that "how to" to the historical-conceptual literature so that you, as a current or future administrator, can consider strategies and tactics for responding to real problems you are likely to face in your organizations but also reflect on the normative, conceptual, or theoretical assumptions embedded in those strategies, or tactics.

To be clear, the taxonomy developed here is one of many that are possible. This is not the only framework that might be valid. However, we believe it is a thorough one, both practically (prescriptively—for figuring out what to do) and conceptually (descriptively—for figuring out what and why things happen in organizations and management). As we noted in Chapter 1, such frameworks serve as a simplification of highly complex environments such that actors within them have the ability to rapidly make sense of and craft responses to them. As such, framing organizational activities in terms of individual, group, change, and organization-environment dynamics is not exhaustive, nor are these categories mutually exclusive. However, in combination, many of the concerns of working administrators fall within these categories, and the theories associated with these categories havebeen, and we believe, will continue to be, useful in establishing effective responses to organizational challenges.

We also want reemphasize the idea of **governance** here. As public administration scholars, our notion of governance tends to be fairly broad in its conception of organizations, and is certainly wider than just traditional, public sector—municipal, state, and federal—organizations. Increasingly, because of trends in the last decades of the twentieth century, including privatization, contracting, devolution, new federalism, and so forth, a wider range of organizations have become involved in providing what might have once been core, narrowly public activities. It is not our intent to suggest that we can provide a valid primer on OT that is applicable across nonprofit organizations. Instead, we want to recognize that the sort of organizations involved in governance activities is increasingly diverse and that what links these organizations may be less about their public-private or tax-exempt status and more about their orientations toward the settings they operate in.

Each chapter in Part II proceeds by exploring the activity at hand via a recurrent structure, starting with the smallest or narrowest level of analysis—individual behavior—and then moving on to broader and wider levels including systems and groups, organizations, and organization change, and finally, organization-environment relations.

Each chapter is organized around what we believe to be the core theories that are, or can be, prescriptively applied to the development of strategies and tactics to respond to management and organizational challenges. The chapters present a focused, working, or operational description of the relevant theories, a description of their expression in organizations, and a set of contemporary, real-world examples of how they have appeared in actual practice and include reflections on the theories' challenges, critiques, and limits.

Chapter 5

Managing Individual Behavior

The Management Attribute

Management is defined and described in a variety of ways—most of which typically include some combination of activities focused on directing processes, people, or things. While organizations are necessarily comprised of formal processes, policies, and technologies, the perspective we take here is that what fundamentally makes an organization an organization is people. Without people, organization is an abstraction. So one of the critical aspects of organizations and organization theory (OT) is understanding and adopting strategies to coordinate people—managing individual behavior toward organizational objectives.

There are at least two variations on managing individual behavior. The first has to do with ensuring compliance with requirements—laws, policies, and procedures. A second variation has to do with shaping employees' behavior such that it maximizes their contribution to the organization. It should be obvious that these two variations are not mutually exclusive; there are policies and procedures that are designed to optimize organizational performance. James Wilson, in his work on public organizations, makes a similar distinction in his discussion of discipline in schools and prisons in terms of maintaining order.[1]

The maintenance of order is consistent with our description here, distinct from management of behavior for performance purposes. However, we believe it's worth distinguishing between these two variations because there are also many policies and procedures that have to do with things other than task performance.[2] In this chapter, we are narrowly focused on management for the purposes of improved performance.

The central question is as follows: How do managers get staff members to behave in a way that contributes in a stable, predictable, and coordinated way to the ends of the organization?

As noted in the introduction to this section of the book, we are not arguing that the taxonomy or framework used here is *the* schema for either understanding or managing organizations. Rather, it is one among many models. As such, like Max Weber's ideal models of authority, the models we present here do not exist in pure form in organizations. We present them in starker distinction than actually exists in organizations. Nevertheless, the basic distinctions we make are useful in thinking about and acting in organizations.

Classical and Rationalist Approaches

The management practices described here are those that are either directly affiliated with, or evolved from, the classical management approaches described in Part I. We've dropped the "classical foundations" moniker because "classical" isn't an apt way to discuss contemporary approaches like those of new public management. However, what links these theories together is a set of shared assumptions about the nature of organizations and the people who populated them, all of which is associated with rationalism.

Assumptions

As noted in the introduction to the chapter and this section, we are presenting these ideas in fairly stark terms and understand that they don't appear in real organizations in similarly stark practice. The experiential reality is that most organizations adopt multiple (and perhaps conceptually incommensurable) approaches. That said, one way of disentangling or deconstructing these approaches in practice is to examine the assumptions that underpin the approaches and trace the consequences of these assumptions into operational practices.

The rationalist approach presumes the existence of a stable and fixed human nature and the presence of an autonomous, rational actor. Shaping the behavior of that actor required utilizing self-interest toward organizational ends. Given the ability of individuals to calculate the consequences of different courses of action, the obvious implication for management is that supervisors can structure the task environments such that it is in the rational interest of workers to not only contribute to but maximize their contribution to the organization.

Frederick Taylor was the first to articulate a comprehensive, rationalist approach to management. In Taylor's assessment, workers would make rational decisions that were in their self-interest, and it was the responsibility of managers and supervisors to create a setting with incentives to induce workers to maximize their efficiency. Moreover, doing so was itself a rational, scientific endeavor. Creating the setting and incentive system was a question of empirical evidence above all else. Taylor argues the following:

> In the past the prevailing idea has been well expressed in the saying that "Captains of industry are born, not made"; and the theory has been that if one could get the right ma, methods could be safely left to him. In the future it will be appreciated that our leaders must be trained right as well as born right, and that no great man can (with the old system of personal management) hope to compete with a number of ordinary men that have been properly organized so as efficiently to cooperate.[3]

To be clear, these were attributes of managers and leaders, not line workers. Taylor goes on to describe a situation when he is providing instructions to a pig iron loader named Fritz. Taylor says the following to Fritz:

> Well, if you are a high-priced man, you will do exactly as this man tells you to-morrow, from morning till night. When he tells you to pick up a pig and walk, you pick it up and you walk, and when he tells you to sit down and rest, you sit down. You do that right straight through the day. And what's more, no back talk. Now a high-priced man does just what he's told to do, and no back talk. Do you understand that? When this man tells you to walk, you walk; when he tells you to sit down, you sit down, and you don't talk back at him. Now you come on to work here to-morrow morning and I'll know before night whether you are really a high-priced man or not.[4]

Although his focus is on organizational and social structures, Weber shares similar assumptions. Rationality is conceived as "human evolution on a course of universal progress culminating in a sort of feast of reason, in the sense of a flowering of true justice, genuine virtue, equality, peace, etc."[5] By contrast, rationalization as Weber saw it (and was critical of it) is described as the following:

> The product of the scientific specialization and technical differentiation peculiar to Western culture, and Weber sometimes associated it with the notion of intellectualization. It might be defined as the organization of life through a divisional and coordination of activities on the basis of an exact study of men's relations with each other, with their tools and their environment for the purpose of achieving greater efficiency and productivity. Hence it is a purely practical development brought about by man's technological genius.[6]

This logic can also be seen in Taylor's strict adherence to rational, empiricist methods for analyzing and maximizing task efficiency. As we will describe in more detail at the end of the chapter, this logic is not only inherent in Taylor's studies in scientific management but will evolve and appear in modified form later in new public management initiatives that emerge in the late twentieth and early twenty-first century.

We'll further explore Herbert Simon's prescription for organizations later in this chapter. However, at this point, it's worth noting that while Simon's conception of effective organizations functions largely through structural attributes, he illuminates several key assumptions shared with other managerial rationalists. Although Simon argues that human behavior is intendedly rational, or bounded, Simon does believe that the world itself functions in a *positivist* way. The difficulty is that humans don't have the cognitive capacity to behave in a purely rational way given the complexity of the world. There are simply too many factors—too many variables—for humans to collect and analyze. Simon's model of how the world functions—his ontology—is grounded in the same assumptions as the rationalists described in this chapter, although the assessments of our possible or optimal behaviors within that system are significantly different.

Concepts

Rationalist approaches to managing individual behavior largely fall into two categorical approaches—incentives and formalized structures. Incentives are predetermined outcomes or consequences linked directly to individual actions. The logic of incentives, also sometimes called inducements, is to use the threat of a negative outcome or promise of a positive outcome to increase the likelihood of a desired particular behavior. The metaphor of sticks and carrots is derived from an agrarian past wherein literal carrots and sticks were used to get pack and draft animals to do what their owners wanted. Carrots were a positive reward for the correct behavior, while the stick was used as a negative, physical inducement to get a recalcitrant animal on track. The use of structures, by contrast, entails using practices, policies, procedures, and other stable attributes of organizational experience as a more unobtrusive means of shaping worker behaviors.

Negative Incentives: Sanctions and Sticks

Despite Taylor's apparently authoritarian claim that workers should work from morning 'til night with no back talk, there is surprisingly little attention to the use of sticks, sanctions, or formal and coercive power as a means of ensuring that workers do, in fact, do what they're told. The few references to formal sanctions in organizations first appear with Weber's articulation of rational-legal organization.[7] In this instance, however, sanctions are not primarily focused in ensuring or maximizing individual compliance with organizational mandates associated with maximizing productive work. Instead, legal sanctions, for Weber, have to do with responding to violations of the organization's rational-legal mandate.

Others do recognize a role for discipline in management. Frank Gilbreth, for example, describes the disciplinarian as "a trained specialist, who holds his job during good and efficient behavior. He should be free from the politics of election by a self-governing body.[8] He should also be 'of the management' in selecting employees, fixing base rates of wages, and determining promotion of deserving workers and foremen." In other words, even the disciplinarian is focused on administration—wages and promotion—rather than directly shaping the productive behavior of workers.

More recently, Amitai Etzioni frames the notion of sanctions in terms of the uses of power to ensure compliance with organizational mandates. Etzioni uses the term *coercive-alienative* relations to suggest that the negative uses of power through the use of direct and even physical force or other coercive means. These are, according to Etzioni, relatively rare and occur in only a few, very unique organizations. Another expression of power used for compliance, *remunerative-calculative,* operates based on management's ability to systematically assess what can be offered or withheld to workers as a way to directly influence behavior. This form of power may appear more frequently than coercive-alienative relations and is likely to include both negative (sanctions) and positive (incentives) attributes.[9]

Jeffrey Pfeffer also gives attention to the use of sanctions in organization settings, as part of a wider discussion on mechanisms of social control (i.e., getting people to do what they're told).[10] Pfeffer's treatment of sanctions, however, is couched in terms of approaches organizations use to generate commitment of employees to the organization and in doing so presumably increase the productivity and effectiveness of those employees.[11] Sanctions, whether explicit and formal disciplinary actions or implied through monitoring and surveillance, not surprisingly, have the opposite effect, diminishing rather than enhancing commitment.

Positive Incentives: Carrots

As we've discussed previously, one of the common, rationalist assumptions is that humans are rational, utility maximizers: we calculate the costs and benefits of available courses of action and choose the one that maximizes our desired outcomes at the lowest cost. This model of behavior is central to positive incentive-based performance management systems from Taylor's early time and motion studies with pig iron loaders to contemporary pay-for-performance programs being adopted across a wide range of public organizations. The central notion that first appeared with the adoption of piecework under the framework of scientific management is that if workers adhere to the processes and practices established by the industrial engineers, they will be able to maximize their productiveness, and because the compensation, or pay structure, is tied to outputs, increasing outputs increases individual rewards. Taylor believed that such arrangements were beneficial not only for the organization but for the worker as well. Because the organization structured work processes based on maximizing efficiency, the worker could then benefit himself by adjusting his behavior to conform with the identified best practices.

In more contemporary work, scholars and practitioners—especially those loosely oriented around ideas associated with new public management—have reinvigorated the discussions of incentives. David Osborne and Ted Gaebler, for example, give recurrent attention to the use of incentives for improving the performance of public organizations. In examining the use of incentives in new public management, it's important to distinguish between individual and institutional incentives. There are incentives that rational individuals will assess and take into consideration when determining individual courses of action. These can be distinguished from institutional incentives. For example, Osborne and Gaebler describe both types: individual, with examples from Phoenix, Sunnyvale, and Visalia of individuals who earn bonuses or base increases based on their performance against established indicators, and institutional—"we have argued throughout this book that the key to reinventing government is changing the incentives *that drive public institutions.*"[12, 13]

Techniques and Practices

Despite the appeal and widespread acceptance of the notion that employees respond to incentives, there was little effort to adopt incentive-based pay systems into the public service until relatively recently. For example, although the Pendleton Act created a merit-based system both for hiring and for promotion, it did not build incentive pay into the compensation system. It wasn't until the passage of the Civil Service Reform Act of 1978 that merit pay began to appear more consistently and regularly as a feature of federal, public sector employment. With respect to compensation, the 1978 act provided for performance awards for career executives, establishing limited Senior Executive Service Meritorious (career) executive awards of $10,000 for sustained accomplishment over a period of years and Distinguished (career) executive awards of $20,000 for sustained extraordinary accomplishment. It also put merit pay for supervisors and management officials in Grades GS 13–15 into place, with funding for merit increases limited to what agency would have paid as within-grade increases, quality step increases, and half of comparability adjustments. Since 1978, at least seven federal acts or significant performance regulations have been issued related to merit or pay-for-performance in the federal government.[14]

An argument can be made that there is a difference between those systems that provide pay or other sorts of incentives prior to one's work efforts in order to *induce* or lead to higher levels of performance and those that are designed to *reward* after the fact. Clearly, some federal and other performance management and compensation systems are consistent with the incentive and inducement logic described here, designed to prompt employees to perform more highly. For example, the Office of Personnel Management has reported on a US Postal Service program that emerged out of the 1993 Government Performance and Results Act that included explicit objectives to drive organizational behavior and continuous improvement.[15] And even though this distinction between inducements of behavior and rewards for behavior is an important one, there is also evidence to suggest that even in rewards-based systems, if those rewards are clearly articulated in advance and the metrics or standard measures for the assessing and making awards are well understood, then the rewards can operate prospectively, or in advance to induce higher levels of performance.

As widespread as merit and pay-for-performance programs have become, there are both conceptual and empirical critiques that warrant attention. For example, Alfie Kohn argues that above a minimum, equitable wage, monetary and other incentive schemes are ineffective, or worse, counterproductive as a means of managing individuals toward higher performance. For Kohn, it's not possible to consistently, let alone optimally, motivate people to perform. Instead, organizations should set the conditions under which individuals can self-motivate, including opportunities to make substantive work choices, to collaborate in authentic ways, and to engage in the content or essential work of the organization. The empirical research suggests a more nuanced picture, one in which context matters. For example, some studies have revealed that in positions that primarily require stable, routine, and repeated job tasks—those that bear some resemblance to the industrial production organizations described by Taylor and Gilbreth—metric-based pay-for-performance systems can improve performance. However, in those work settings characterized by variability, creativity, collaboration, and other inconstant factors, incentive pay systems not only fail to improve performance but they actually diminish performance.[16] At the very least, what this conceptual and empirical work reveals is that incentive systems function based on a relatively simple model of behavior. It is less and less clear that either that model of behavior or the variability of settings in which contemporary governance work is done shares such simplicity.

Structures

The use of incentives, both positive and negative, represents one line of rationalist thinking about the management of individual behavior. Another, dominant rational approach focuses less on what might be termed *obtrusive controls* of behavior—or techniques that focus directly on the individual and instead utilize less obtrusive controls. Keep in mind that we are not suggesting that structural strategies for managing individual behaviors are a mutually exclusive alternative to incentive systems but rather that it is another, categorical response that often exists in conjunction with other systems for managing individual behavior.

In this section we will primarily focus on the use of structures that are created out of a rational assessment and subsequent arrangement of resources, calculated to maximize their effectiveness.

Many of the classical management theorists looked to the establishment of rationally developed, formal structures as the basis of ensuring that the behavior of individuals complies with and advances the objectives of the organization. Weber, Henri Fayol, J. D. Mooney, Luther Gulick, and others identify a set of overlapping and complementary structures that serve to rationally shape and constrain the behavior of individuals toward organizational ends. All share an emphasis on rationalized authority and hierarchy—that is, individuals at the top of the organization have the formal right to establish the goals of the organization and to establish the systems and structures by which those goals are achieved.

There is also a set of complementary attributes of hierarchical structures including specialization, span of control, unity of command, and unity of direction. These attributes are, again, established rationally but more importantly for managing individual behavior, they establish a set of parameters that help establish behavioral expectations and coordinate task activities in complex work settings. They rationally organize the work to be done and ensure that individuals' behaviors are directed toward the correct ends.

Another set of structures can be found in the shared emphasis on rules, policies, and procedures among many of the classical management theorists. Like hierarchy and specialization, organizational rules are established rationally, in such a way that they contribute to the maximization of organizational performance. Moreover, they apply in a systematic way to everyone in the organization, supervisors and subordinates alike. Again, the result is clarity about behavioral expectations and continuity in directing behaviors to accomplishing work tasks.

Although, as we noted previously, Weber, Fayol, Mooney, Gulick, and other classical management theorists can be understood as rationally arranging organizational structures so as to maximize the efficiency and effectiveness of organizations, in Charles Perrow's assessment, Weber's focus on structures largely ignored individuals.[17] Perhaps more precisely, the classical structuralist management theorists retain an assumption about the wholly rational, thus stable and consistent behavior of individuals, obviating the need to give individuals specific attention. Simon, according to Perrow, recognizes a greater complexity of individual behavior, accounts for it in his theorizing and therefore, and adds muscle and flesh to Weber.[18]

As we described in Chapter 3, one of Simon's most critical contributions of social science is the development of his modified model of human behavior: bounded rationality. Although bounded rationality is, to some degree, an impediment to maximizing individual, and therefore organizational performance to a greater degree, bounded rationality not only makes structure possible but more importantly, increases organizational effectiveness. Simon argues that because human behavior is boundedly rational, members of an organization are able to, and in fact do, adapt their decisions to an organization's objectives. In other words, members of the organization don't conduct exhaustive searches of potential goals and pathways to accomplish those goals. Instead, they conduct limited searches based on the parameters established by the structures of the organization.

According to Simon, "Once the system of values which is to govern administrative choice has been specified, there is one and only one 'best decision'" in support of the organization's values and goals.[19] This approach places an emphasis and priority on organization variables such as the division of labor and communication systems. Simon, perhaps most famously in his essay *Proverbs of Administration,* denies that there is one best system to accomplish all organizational ends but rather that the best system is the one that is best able to lead to the best decisions.[20] Remembering that structure, for Simon and later James March and Simon, are those aspects and patterns of behavior that are stable and slow to change.[21] Such structures can be both formal and informal. A formal structure, like authority, is neither the bottom-up, cooperative authority of Barnard, nor the "do what you're told" authority of Taylor but rather is one wherein supervisors have the power and tools at their disposal that allow them to structure a workers environment and perceptions such that he functions in a way that contributes to the organizational ends established by leaders.

Communication is another critical, structural attribute. Communication for Simon has less to do with the clarity, speed, and precision of the delivery of orders than it does with the creation of recurrent channels and checkpoints, specialized vocabularies, and other attributes that highlight important organizational information and screen out information that is seen to be organizationally unimportant.

Not surprisingly, given the conditions of bounded rationality and the emphasis on structural attributes of organizations, decision making looks significantly different as well. Consistent with Simon's description of satisficing behavior, decisions utilize a sequential and limited search process and are extensively shaped by the specialization of activities and roles in such a way that the individual's attention is focused on organizational values. Rules, policies, and programs—all structures in and of themselves—limit the courses of action available to the decision maker and direct him toward organizational determined priorities. These structures are further informed by preestablished organizational vocabularies and are reinforced by training and indoctrination that allow the individual to make decisions without the need for obtrusive forms of control exercised by supervisors.

Perrow notes that while this structural model of managing individual behavior is clearly oriented to the benefit of the organization and organizational elites, the conditions of bounded rationality and organizational structures are not a completely inescapable iron cage.[22] Bounded rationality applies to elites as much as it does to workers, which means that their position and perspective is not totally secure. Their understandings and the information that inform them are never complete or fully rational. As a result, there is always the possibility of novelty— the possibility that new information, unexpected events, alternate values, and other variations from established structures creep into the organization. The consequence of these unanticipated occurrences is a space for resistance and change. Such a picture may be slightly less bleak than the wholly rationalized world that Weber was concerned about.

Case 5.1

Current Expressions: Classical and Rationalist Approaches at the US Department of Homeland Security

One of the aspects of public sector organizations that distinguish them from private, for-profit organizations is the political environment in which they operate. Public organizations face the challenge of having to be cognizant of, if not responsive to, multiple stakeholders and constituencies. One consequence of this highly complex political environment is that change initiatives seldom occur for a single reason. So while we present the following examples of structural attributes of organizations that have the effect of shaping individual behaviors, we also acknowledge that these structures changes are often initiative as much for political reasons, such as establishing greater influence for a political executive, or responding to partisan or electoral dynamics.

The creation of the US Department of Homeland Security (DHS) following the 9/11 attacks is the largest structural reorganization in the federal government in the last century. This initiative clearly reflects our previous acknowledgment that such initiatives are undertaken for many reasons, most of which have little if anything to do with practices designed to improve the management of individuals. The debate about the founding of the department, as well its own historical documents, reveal the extent to which politic dynamics and efforts to improve overall efficiencies were major drivers behind the creation of the department. The movement of agencies like the US Coast Guard and the Bureau of Alcohol, Tobacco, Firearms and Explosives (ATF) into the department, as well as the creation of a new or consolidated agencies such as US Immigration and Customs Enforcement (ICE) out of the older Immigration and Naturalization Service and US Customs Service, are examples of structural changes toward these ends. However, remembering Weber's, Gulick's, and especially Simon's descriptions of structural arrangements that are designed to configure search, decision, and communication processes, there is evidence in the debates and documents to indicate that management effectiveness was a consideration in the consolidation of agencies and the establishment of DHS.[23]

One of the major administrative problems that gained widespread attention following the attacks was the inability of agencies to share information and effectively coordinate their activities. Recall that one of Simon's significant contributions in this area is the idea and importance of uncertainty absorption. In order for organizations to not only overcome but in fact to take advantage of the bounded rationality of its members is the creation of communications and decision structures that absorb uncertainty about the environment and potential courses of action. The Homeland Security Act of 2002 includes four separate titles and at least seven sections of the act that deal specifically with structures and processes for information sharing and establishing specific requirements for coordination. More recently, others who have highlighted ongoing structural efforts in these same areas say, "The consolidation of DHS is necessary to facilitate communication, coordination and cooperation across the agency."[24]

Case Reflection Question

As you think about the political and social climate—the governance climate—at the time DHS was created, what influence do you think the climate had on the selection of management structures and practices?

In addition to the structural changes, the act and its subsequent implementation allowed for the establishment of a series of modifications to personnel practices that also embody classical and rationalist practices. For example, one of the central elements of the personnel reforms was the inclusion of a pay-for-performance compensation system that was intentionally designed to incent and reward higher levels of performance. The system, which was linked to measures of the wider labor market, linked annual compensation adjustments directly and proportionally to employee performance evaluations. The new systems also operate on the "stick" side, or negative incentive side, of the behavioral equation as well by giving managers greater flexibility and discretion in adverse personnel actions including sanctions and even termination for poor performance. In this case, personnel systems in DHS have been structured to limit and accelerate the involvement of the Merit Systems Protection Board (MSPB), which is the federal agency authorized to ensure federal employees' due process rights are protected during any personnel actions.[25] All of these reforms are situated within a set of structures that have shifted toward greater executive authority, or in other words, emphasizing presidential control over congressional oversight.[26]

Summary of Rationalist Approaches

Several themes should be recognizable in the preceding discussion. First, while the basic premise of rationalist approaches is relatively simple, the operationalized strategies used by organizations have become increasingly sophisticated. These approaches recognize and acknowledge new or emerging thinking about both human behavior and sociopolitical settings and institutions. Associated approaches encompass direct behavioral elements such as positive and negative incentives designed to shape performance. Rational and classical approaches also entail structural behavioral elements including Simon's admonitions regarding communications, goal setting, and decision structures. What unites this work over time and across organizations are the underlying epistemological and ontological assumptions, specifically its assumption of rationalism both in terms of the nature of individual behavior and the causal methods that should be used to optimize organizational performance.

Reflection Questions

As you think about organizations you are familiar with, what other practices have you encountered that work from rational or classical assumptions of behavior and performance?

As you reflect on the assumptions that underlie these practices, what are some of the strengths and weaknesses of the assumptions themselves? In other words, where do these assumptions seem to hold true, and where do they seem to fail?

Hawthorne Reprised: From Rationalism to Behavioralism

When Elton Mayo and Fritz Roethlisberger's Hawthorne studies, especially the bank wiring and relay assembly room experiments, emerged, they vastly complicated the picture of behavior and consequently the strategies that might be used to manage productivity. As management research further developed through the mid-twentieth century, more questions arose regarding other interactions and motivations that shape individual behavior in organizations. The narrow management principles developed in the classical period were simply not sufficient to explain nor effectively manage the behavior of individuals. Behavioralism, or *human relations theory (HRT)*, was a natural outgrowth of the limitations of rationalist or classical management theory. Behavioral theorists believe that a better understanding of motivation, conflict, expectations, and group dynamics in a work setting can reveal strategies to improve productivity. Individuals, from this perspective, are viewed as resources or assets that can be developed and support rather than decision machines or cogs in a larger machine. At the same time, the growth of public organizations first during the Great Depression and New Deal and subsequently during World War

II and the postwar period meant that the number, size, and complexity of those organizations grew. While the Hawthorne studies themselves revealed the presence of social and group dynamics as an influence on productivity, much of the behavioral, human relations work—especially that out of psychology—focuses on individual behavior patterns and influences. The breadth of the behavioralist research and theory is extraordinary, but despite the diversity of the work, the underlying assumptions shift from those of the classical, rationalist theories.

Assumptions

Driven both by normative perspectives that differ from rationalist perspectives and by the empirical research findings starting with the Hawthorne experiments, behavioralist theorists adopt a differing set of assumptions. Rather than starting with an economically rational model of individual behavior, Douglas McGregor posits the following:

- Work can be as natural as play and rest.
- People will be self-directed to meet their work objectives if they are committed to them.
- People will be committed to their objectives if rewards are in place that address higher needs such as self-fulfillment.
- Under these conditions, people will seek responsibility.
- Most have the capacity to be innovative and contribute to solutions.
- Most organizations utilize only a small portion of their employees' abilities.[27]

Abraham Maslow's theory of personality is based upon his understandings of human motivations toward action. Like McGregor, Maslow adopts a set of basic assumptions of behavior and motivation that also differ from the rationalist models described earlier in this chapter. Among these are the following assumptions:

- Motivation is usually complex: several sources can contribute to the eventual appearance of some behavior.
- People are universally motivated by the same basic needs.
- Additionally, certain motivations may be unconscious.
- People are continually motivated by one need or another. Satisfying one need only results in the individual trying to satisfy other needs.
- The whole person is motivated, requiring a holistic approach.

Maslow believes in the fundamental similarity of the human experience. Although we may achieve needs in a culturally specific (or culturally proscribed) manner that is idiosyncratic, the needs that must be satisfied are universal in nature.

Concepts

In the late 1960s, Clayton Alderfer took up and extended Maslow's hierarchy of needs in ways that both fit our intention of the complexity of behavior as well as give it further organizational application. Alderfer condenses Maslow's hierarchy from five levels to three: existence needs, relatedness needs, and growth needs. While Dennis O'Connor and Leodones Yballe and others interpret Maslow's theory such that as needs are satisfied, they no longer motivate behavior. Alderfer clearly indicates that all categories of needs can become more important as they are satisfied, that individuals can place more emphasis on one category than others, and that needs at different levels can be satisfied simultaneously.[28, 29] What Maslow's and Alderfer's work, as well as that of other motivational theory scholars including David McClelland, and Lyman Porter and Edward Lawler, reveals is a different set of assumptions about human behavior.[30, 31] Not only is human behavior not motivated narrowly by incentives or inducements but the breadth of motivational factors that do influence behavior are more wide, dynamic, and complex than rationalist organization and management theorists acknowledge. As a result, supervisors wishing to effectively manage individual behaviors need a more sophisticated understanding of that behavior and a wider, more nuanced set of strategies to do so.

One final variation in underlying assumptions that is important to note is revealed both in the results of the Hawthorne experiments and in Chester Barnard's claims about the nature of organizations—namely that they are cooperative. Barnard argues clearly that organizations are more than the sum of their parts and that members of organizations actually cooperate rather than merely work in parallel. Toward this end, he gives great importance to persuasion—much more than to economic incentives. He describes four general and four specific incentives. The specific incentives were as follows:

- money and other material inducements
- personal, nonmaterial opportunities for distinction
- desirable physical conditions of work
- ideal benefactions, such as pride of workmanship, etc.

Although there are many other behavioralist motivation and need theorists, what this brief review reveals is the degree to which the assumptions that underpin behavioralist approaches to management differ from those of the classical and rationalist management theorists. Core to these differences is the notion that motivation and need are key influences on individual behavior and, moreover, that need and motivation are complex in their shape and expression. The consequence is that strategies adopted to improve the productivity of individuals in organization settings must go beyond single dimensional incentives and inducements.

Leadership in Behavioralism

The first sections of this chapter focus on what managers and leaders do to ensure the greatest potential performance from their staff. This section shifts perspective and looks not at the techniques used by leaders but instead at the role and scope of leadership in activities associated with the management of individuals. The behavioralist leadership models described here are linked with the motivational management approaches previously described in part through their shared assumptions regarding the nature and capacity of the individual and thus linked to the motivational theories described previously by adopting an approach wherein leadership takes on less of a directive role and more of a motivational role.

In Chapter 3, we introduced Rensis Likert's four systems, or approaches, to leadership. Here, it is System 4 leadership that is advanced by Likert and others as a means of increasing the effectiveness of organizations. To reiterate the description from Chapter 3, in System 4 or participative group leadership approaches, responsibility for accomplishing goals is highly distributed across the entire organization. Supervisors have extensive trust and confidence in workers, and there is substantial communication across the breadth and height of the organization. While Likert does emphasize the importance of teamwork and substantive collaboration and engagement, one of the important attributes of leaders in System 4 organizations is their capacity to create an environment that motivates and engages employee contributions to the organization.

To that end, Likert and his colleagues also developed a set of seven process variables that were operationalized in order to determine where organizations fell in the broader model. The seven process variables are as follows:

- leadership processes
- motivational forces
- communication process
- interaction-influence process
- decision-making process
- goal setting or ordering
- control processes

Likert's empirical research reveals the potential benefits from adopting System 4 approaches via which one leads, motivates, communicates, and so forth in order to determine which of the four systems best characterized their overall management approach. Likert described organizations that adopt the practices and structures of System 4 organizations as being ones in which leaders would create an environment where groups would participate in the establishment and achievement of their own goals rather than simply imposing standards from the top. Extensive and multidirectional communication, support, and respect would be primary values of such organizations.[32]

Although Victor Vroom's research on leadership is primarily a *contingency model,* or one in which the particular leadership approach adopted is contingent on the circumstances and conditions present at that moment in time, Vroom and his fellow researchers extend the behavioralist leadership work present in Likert's work. Vroom studied the causes of people's decisions and actions in the workplace, and in his collaboration with Philip Yetton, he developed what became known as the Vroom-Yetton model of leadership decision making.[33] Theirs is a contingency model that identifies styles of leadership and their relative fit across different situations. Their work can be used by managers to determine the extent to which leaders should encourage people's participation in the decision-making process. In later work with Arthur Jago, Vroom further developed this model, culminating in the 1988 book, *The New Leadership: Managing Participation in Organizations.*[34]

In *Leadership and Decision-Making,* Vroom looked into the issue of leadership decision making and the role of participation in decisions by subordinates. Vroom and Yetton developed a set of rules for use by managers in determining the level and type of participation in decision making, which in turn renders the best solution in different problem-solving situations. The following list from Vroom and Yetton's work briefly describes the three categories and five total types of management decision methods for group problems:

Autocratic

Type 1 (AI)—The leader makes own decision using information that is readily available to you at the time. This type is completely autocratic.

Type 2 (AII)—The leader collects required information from followers, then makes decision alone. Problem or decision may or may not be informed to followers. Here, followers' involvement is just providing information.

Consultative

Type 1 (CI)—The leader shares problem to relevant followers individually and seeks their ideas and suggestions and makes decision alone. Here, followers do not meet each other and the leader's decision may or may not have followers' influence. So, here, followers' involvement is at the level of providing alternatives individually.

Type 2 (CII)—The leader shares problem to relevant followers as a group and seeks their ideas and suggestions and makes decisions alone. Here, followers meet each other, and through discussions they understand other alternatives. But the leader's decision may or may not have followers' influence. In this type, followers' involvement is at the level of helping as a group in decision making.

Group-based

Type 2(GII)—The leader discusses problems and situations with followers as a group and seeks their ideas and suggestions through brainstorming. In this type, the leader accepts any decision and does not try to force his idea. The decision accepted by the group is the final one.[35]

A manager's selection of one of these five types proceeds by means of a series of questions that require yes-no answers and that advance the manager along a decision tree path. The problem is ultimately defined as one of fourteen types, and Vroom and Yetton then recommend a contingent method for decision making (from methods AI to GII) based on the specific characteristics of each problem.

Techniques and Practices

In Chapter 3, we described the evolution of central elements of some of the key behavioralist management theorists. Here, we revisit those theories and focus instead in the applications, practices, and real-world expressions of those theories.

Of the various behavioralist approaches, Maslow's hierarchy of needs is perhaps the one that has been most extensively operationalized. Most working descriptions of the hierarchy suggest that the first level is fulfilled in an instrumental way. Salary, frequently assumed as a living or equitable salary, is the instrument by which basic physiological needs can be met. Progressing through higher levels of the hierarchy, work attributes such as job security, promotions, and salary are often means by which safety and security needs are met. The intentional creation of opportunity to associate with and discuss problems and projects with coworkers can be a response to social needs, and opportunities for and recognition of achievement, independence, and autonomy, as well as esteem factors like status, recognition, and attention, contribute to the satisfaction of esteem needs and potentially even actualization needs as well.

As organizations strive to create a climate that supports and motivates employees, administrators must first and foremost determine the existing levels of ability, skill, and interest as well as the scope of existing need. Additional strategies include efforts to engage participation in designing jobs, establish performance standards, and then measure that performance. Other efforts might include redesigning jobs to enrich them with variety and autonomy, creating task identity and task significance. Underlying many of these efforts is the development of formal and informal user or employee studies to assess status.[36] Absent some means of determining the standing of the organization's workforce, the potential to misallocate resources and opportunities is great.

Alderfer adds to Maslow's external needs satisfaction model of motivation the possibility of self-motivation and the dynamics of intergroup relations, changing the nature of people's jobs in being used as a motivational technique. Any of the alternatives to job specialization—job rotation, job enlargement, job enrichment, the job characteristics approach, autonomous work groups—could be used as part of a motivational program.

Moving away from a needs-based model, William Ouchi takes up and extends McGregor's descriptions of Theory X and Y and presented a Type Z organization that integrates aspects of the culture of Japanese organizations in compatible ways with American culture and experience. He emphasized the idea that employees who become involved and committed to the organization will be more highly motivated to improve their performance and productivity. Drawing from Japanese approaches, Type Z organizations provide rewards such as long-term employment, promotion opportunities within the organization, engaged or participatory management, and other techniques that motivate employees.[37]

A final, less direct approach to understanding the complexity of motivational factors in the workplace can be found in the use of employee surveys to determine the level of satisfaction staff have with job content, work environment, and organizational culture. Staff surveys can be a useful tool for applying behaviorist motivational theories such as Maslow's hierarchy of needs, Alderfer's existence, relatedness, and growth (ERG) theory or Porter and Lawler's expectancy theory. Unlike rationalist theories of motivation, which often assume to know in advance and in abstract universal terms and what incentive approaches will sufficiently motivate behavior—implementation of nonrational behavioralist theories in the workplace—employers need to understand what outcomes employees value and whether they perceive these outcomes as possible within the organizational culture. To get at such concerns, employee surveys assess employee perceptions of growth opportunities for career progression within the organization. If employee perceptions of such opportunities are low, then the organization might address its career development activities in order to improve the performance of employees who are motivated by the prospect of promotion.

As a practical matter, common interpretations of Maslow's hierarchy suggest that progression through the hierarchy occurs in a serial or stepwise way. As a need is met at one level, the individual progresses to the next or vice versa. The interpretation of Alderfer's ERG theory suggests that the "progress" through levels of need is more complicated and dynamic. It could be the case that needs at different levels are pursued and satisfied simultaneously or that higher level needs become more important than lower level needs—that is, the starving artist who pursues the self-actualization that results from the production of artistic works but foregoes basic needs or social relations. This possibility has particular resonance in public and nonprofit organizations where the perception, if not the reality, of lower compensation reveals that motivational factors other than pay are important.[38]

Frederick Herzberg recognizes that while there are attributes of organizational practice and experience that can serve as powerful positive motivators for individual performance, there are also job dissatisfiers, or hygiene factors, which define the job context and also have an impact of performance. For Herzberg, satisfiers or motivators follow closely with those that emerge from motivational theories described above. These include opportunities for development, achievement, recognition, and so forth. The addition of Herzberg's hygiene factors highlights the importance of organizational structures that are, to a large degree, outside the control of the individual but that nevertheless have a substantial impact how individual workers feel about and function within the organization. These hygiene factors, according to Herzberg's research, include things like company policies, working conditions, structural or authority relationships with supervisors and subordinates, and interestingly, salary. However, Herzberg's survey research found that unlike the position generally taken by rationalist management theorists, salary was a hygiene or dissatisfier factor rather than a motivator. When salary was an issue, it was associated with perceived unfairness or inequities in the salary system and its administration. In the cases where salary was mentioned in comments about motivation or satisfier factors, it was typically connected to factors of achievement and recognition rather than being a motivator in and of itself.[39]

Alternative models of motivation and the importance of motivation in public organizations is an ongoing concern where often the work is challenging in contextually very different ways. Additionally, sources of motivation are different, given that often the very work that one does in the public sector comes with inherent public perceptions (bureaucrat, number cruncher, law enforcer, Department of Motor Vehicles [DMV] employee, etc.). It is important to note that the dynamics of any specific setting can dramatically influence the dynamics of motivation. Working in a context where the very citizens you serve do not always readily appreciate the service you provide—for example, the Internal Revenue Service (IRS) or the DMV—can impact the dynamics of motivation. Such circumstances can affect and shift the ability and means to generate motivation.

The Role of Leadership

Likert's empirical research not only resulted in the development of a four-part model of leadership styles or systems but it found evidence that one particular system was likely to be associated with higher levels of organization performance.[40] In brief, System 4, or participative group leadership, sees responsibility for accomplishing goals as being highly distributed across the entire organization. Supervisors, consistent with McGregor's Theory Y, have extensive trust and confidence in workers and there is substantial communication, teamwork, and substantive engagement across the breadth and height of the organization.

In studying the organizations that lead to the development of this four-stage model, Likert and his colleagues also developed a set of seven process variables that could be used in a prescriptive way as administrators consider not *what* they do—all of these processes are organizational necessities—but rather *how* they are conducted. For example, linking Likert's findings about the effectiveness of System 4 approaches would suggest the selection of engaged or participatory processes not only with respect to leadership but also several of Likert's other processes including communication processes, routine interaction-influence processes, decision-making processes, goal setting or ordering processes, and finally, control processes.

In practical terms, work groups form the core of System 4 organizations, and such groups are characterized by several dynamics that clearly reflect the process variables that were previously noted. Members would have a well-developed capacity for both leadership and membership roles, which contribute to functional relationships and interaction. As a result, motivation is more likely to be intrinsic to the work and the process rather than an external motivator like merit pay. If the group can be maintained within the scheme of organizational priorities and activities, there is a greater likelihood that it will have developed relaxed and functional working relationships. In such settings, group members develop loyalty to both the group and to each other and will have built a high level of trust. The norms, values, and goals of the group will reflect the values and needs of its members and, again, influence which shape and determine individual behavior and performance will be intrinsic and social, rather than rationally calculated.[41]

Research has found that in organizations whose leaders adopt an approach that follows that of the Vroom and Yetton model have higher levels of employee satisfaction and productivity.[42] As previously noted, this is a contingency model of leadership, meaning that the underlying assumption is that no one of their styles fits in all situations. By studying the situation and understanding the problem based on time, team engagement, decision quality, and technical attributes of the decision, a conclusion about which style best fits the situation can be made. The model presents a very logical approach to which of the several styles to adopt. It is useful for managers and leaders who are trying to balance the benefits of participatory management with the need to make expedited decisions. Within this model, three criteria would merit examination as managers determine the level and form of participation:

Decision quality: How important is it to come up with the "right" solution? The higher the quality of the decision needed, the more you should involve other people in the decision.

Subordinate commitment: How important is it that your team and others buy into the decision? When teammates need to embrace the decision you should increase the participation levels.

Time constraints: How much time do you have to make the decision? The more time you have, the more you have the luxury of including others and of using the decision as an opportunity for teambuilding.

With these in mind, administrators would be in a position to select an approach that simultaneously yields decisions that are most beneficial to the organization and at the same time supports the social and motivational factors that enable to members of the organization to sustain their engagement and motivation.

With these generic, or abstracted, descriptions of practices and techniques in mind, the next section examines a small sample of organizations that have intentionally adopted elements of these behavioralist approaches to motivation and performance as way to push our efforts at operationalization further still.

Case 5.2

Current Expressions: Behaviorist Alternatives

Siemens

Private sector organizations like Siemens have adopted strategies for supporting individual and organizational performance that directly reflect both the assumptions and approaches of the behavioral management practices that were previously described. For example, Siemens provides the opportunity for employees to fulfill a range of their needs. Starting with lower order, Maslowian needs, the organization strives to provide a safe and secure working environment in addition to intentionally creating opportunities for socialization with friends and colleagues within the organization. For those engaged in creative and innovative activities, Siemens supports practices that contribute to the satisfaction of higher-order needs including programs in which suggestions and projects for organization improvement are rewarded. If self-actualization is understood as being concerned with the ability to reach one's fullest potential, Siemens supports such efforts by enabling, for example, engineers to take increasing responsibility for their jobs, making improvements and changes, and developing original ideas and solutions to the technological products that are core to the business. The organization further supports these activities by providing the resources and opportunities necessary for ongoing training and development such that employees can not only meet Maslow's higher-order needs but can do so in a way that supports Siemens' competitiveness in a competitive global market.

Siemens is also attuned to the possibility that it can not only support practices and processes that support and improve motivation among staff but hygiene factors or dissatisifers are present and must be managed as well. Administrators and Siemens work to strike a functional equilibrium between motivators and satisfiers, on the one hand, and hygiene factors or dissatisfiers, on the other. Toward that end, Siemens believes that one of the best strategies is to raise awareness of issues and encourage their involvement, which simultaneously supports a sense of achievement, recognition, and responsibility while at the same time identifies and potentially mitigates company policies and needless bureaucratic procedures that can be experienced as a barrier to the work of the organization.[43]

Herzberg and the Public Sector

Researchers including Alderfer have shown how behavioralist management theories including Maslow's hierarchy of needs, Alderfer's ERG, and Herzberg's two factor theories have been utilized in public sector and governance organizations at all levels and across sectors of government.[44] Brown and Lewinsohn describe an early municipal case in Kansas City, Missouri, that includes an emphasis on team on social or relatedness needs as described by Maslow and Alderfer.[45] Marvin Weisbord, Howard Lamb, and Allan Drexler present a case study that details the work of a local police department of 270 officers to improve problem-solving approaches by drawing on approaches will draw on social and relatedness dynamics as well as contributing to a sense of accomplishment as described by Herzberg.[46] Other work has examined the social dynamics and behavioral factors present in health care organizations and found the presence and importance of social-esteem or relational factors but also Herzberg's motivational factors—notably a sense of achievement and the importance or value of the work itself.

Miami-Dade College

Here is one example of the application of Likert's climate concepts across the various campuses of Miami-Dade College in Florida in 1986. An adapted version of the Likert profile of organizations was developed and used with Miami-Dade College, and the results of the study suggest that Likert's four-system theory worked well both for measuring climate and responses to leadership style and for describing ways leadership effectiveness and organizational climate could be improved within the institution.[47] From Likert's original studies, researchers at the National Initiative for Leadership and Institutional Effectiveness (NILIE) identified the four leadership models and organizational systems ranging from System 1 (coercion) to System 4 (collaboration). As was the case in other research, System 4 was generally seen as the ideal climate in that it produces higher levels of productivity, job satisfaction, communication, and overall organizational effectiveness.[48] The Miami-Dade project revealed the importance of factors related to leadership, including institutional structure, supervisory relationships, teamwork, and student focus.

Case Reflection Question

Given the variation in the examples in this case, what shared elements of behaviorism and HRT do you see across them?

Summary of Behaviorist Approaches

The shift from classical to behaviorist approaches to managing individual performance includes the adoption of different assumptions about the nature of and influences on behavior. The behaviorist models tend to be more complex in their recognition that there is a wider range of influences on behavior. For example, Maslow's hierarchy of need suggests that which level needs individuals are seeking to meet will determine the sorts of actions they're likely to take. In this regard, behavior is no longer understood as narrowly rational. Behavior is nonrational, as opposed to irrational, but it nevertheless remains discernable and understandable.

Beyond recognizing greater levels of complexity and variability in behavior—and correspondingly the development of strategies to manage that behavior—an argument can be made that this recognition of complexity fits better in governance settings. Because American political culture is characterized by a significant degree of political pluralism—the idea that plural sets of political values and goals are legitimately part of our discourse—then having workplace management practices that are more sensitive to multiple needs and interests may also be better for setting the tone, culture, and experience of working in settings also inclusive of multiple political needs, interests, and goals.

Reflection Questions

What elements of behaviorist theories do you see present in organizations you have worked in?

What do you think is the primary purpose of increased participation by workers in organizational decision making (e.g., Likert's System 4 or Vroom and Yetton's Type GII)? Stated differently, how democratic should public organizations in a democracy be? Why?

Foreshadows of Postmodernism

The material covered in this chapter reveals a chain of logic starting with autonomous, rational self-interested individuals of scientific management and trace its historical development concluding with a contemporary interpretation of a diffused, influenced, and embedded subject. This trajectory also reveals the extent to which we moved from notions of certainty and "one best way" to a more nuanced, contextual, and variable understanding of the organizational and broader social world. This approach not only lays some of the conceptual groundwork for Part III but is also intended to help make postmodernism far more accessible to students who may be unfamiliar with it and applicable for all readers by suggesting that it is not a radical departure from all else that is known, but is better seen as an extension of existing ideas.

Mary Parker Follett: Pragmatism and Antifoundationalism

In Chapter 2, we briefly described how some scholars view Mary Parker Follett's work as being of a substantially different type and approach than other management and OT work being done at that time.[49] According to this body of research, there are a number of attributes of her work that move it away from both the rationalist and behavioralist work we've described in this chapter. Her work includes significant antifoundational attributes. Rather than arguing for one best way or an empirically determined best way as rationalist management theorists do, or working from behavioralist assumptions about motivation, Follett suggests that the appropriate course of action is developed in a different way. Rather than retaining positivist notions about motivation and behavior, her antifoundationalist orientation suggests that no single "correct" understanding, or Truth of approach can be rationally, abstractly, or universally determined for *all* scenarios. A situationally dependent course of action emerges from the interaction of the individuals involved and the context, or as Follett termed it *the law of the situation,* and the social process by which knowledge and understanding develop. Further, her thinking tends to collapse the subject-object distinction, meaning that there is now a neutral position from which to observe or study a situation purely objectively. Rather, social actors are always and inherently in context or in the midst, and as such there is the possibility of new creativity and synergy beyond a sort of mechanical summation of forces. Similarly, her notion of interpenetration and the doctrine of the whole start with the notion that even if individuals can rationally calculate optimal courses of action and craft plans to pursue those courses, reveals Follett's interest in the synergies created when individuals engage in group processes where their individual perspectives are integrated synthetically such that individual's interest and the groups interest can coincide. Again, this process depends neither on an optimizing calculus nor psychological or social motivations. Instead, the process of determining the content of action is developed by the use of techniques including facilitated group problem identification or decision-making processes.

It's striking to note the prescience of Follett's in foreshadowing the poststructuralist work that emerged at the end of the twentieth century; we'll describe it in more detail in Part III.[50] What is important about Follett's work are the shifts in her ontological assumptions about the nature of the world broadly as well as organizations and human behavior within them more specifically. As a result, the contextual contingency her work highlights goes beyond the contingency theories of Vroom and others.[51] Moreover, Follett's work is particularly interesting in public sector settings where values and politics are inherent in decision processes, suggesting that Follett's notions are of value not only for participatory organizations but especially public affairs organizations wherein democratic values and practices are central.

Summary and Conclusions

ONE OF THE ISSUES WE RAISED in the Introduction to this book centered on the fact that much of the research in OT has historically been done by sociologists and business scholars in other places outside of public administration, and the recurring discourse regards the extent to which public organizations are essentially the same as or different from organizations in the private sector. As you will recall, we made reference to scholars like Graham Allison, who argue that there are environmental and structural factors in public organizations that make them fundamentally different than private, for-profit organizations. This question is worth returning to now while we are considering behavioralist theories that inform strategies for managing individual behavior and whether or to what extent these behavioralist theories apply to public organizations.

While Allison acknowledges that some aspects of the day-to-day work of public sector managers—what Selznick refers to as *routine decisions*—are not unlike that in the private sector, there are at least ten areas in which management between the two sectors differs significantly.[52] An exhaustive assessment of how all of Allison's attributes affect these behavioralist management approaches is unnecessary at this point, but it is worth noting that several of his attributes do appear to have a direct impact on how public sector staff members perceive their jobs and, consequently, how motivational approaches impact individual behavior. Those features include the following:

- *Measurement of performance:* In the public sector there is much less agreement about the standards and measurement of performance.
- *Equity and efficiency:* Equity and fairness of treatment amongst constituencies is the norm in the public sector while efficiency receives the preponderance of emphasis in the private sector.
- *Public processes versus private processes:* Public processes tend to be more open and transparent than private processes, where they are perceived to be closed, and more weight is given to demands for increased access in the public sector.
- *Persuasion and direction:* Despite Gulick's argument for a limited span of control and unified command, public officials generally feel responsive to the persuasion and direction of a wide range of stakeholders.
- *Bottom line:* Government seldom has a clear bottom line like that of profit in a private firm.[53]

Each of these public sector features, though each in slightly different ways, opens up the possibility that other factors are operative in public organizations and can therefore act as motivators or satisfiers as described by the behavioralist theories presented here. ∎

Discussion Questions

1. What similarities and differences might the two conceptual approaches described in this chapter (classical-rational and behavioral) imply for a manager responding to a low-performing employee?

2. What social and political changes impacted the shift toward the human relations perspective? What are the lingering impacts of these changes on today's organizations? What would organizations be like today if this shift had yet to take place?

3. Describe the importance of informal groups as they relate to an organization with which you have some familiarity. How do they impact behavior in organizations?

4. What do the differences between classical-rational and behavioral approaches imply for the techniques and strategies used by leaders?

5. Many contemporary organizations blend elements of both classical-rational and behavioral approaches in practice. Working from experience or case literature, how have these approaches been blended? What are the positive and negative effects of such blending of approaches?

6. How do you make a bureaucracy, which has a primary value of efficiency, work in a democracy that places the primary value on participation and responsiveness?

Notes

1. James Q. Wilson, *Bureaucracy: What Government Agencies Do and Why They Do It* (New York: Basic Books, 1989).
2. See the following for one model of how policies and procedures become decoupled from performance ends: John W. Meyer and Brian Rowan, "Institutional Organizations: Formal Structure as Myth and Ceremony," *American Journal of Sociology* 83 (1977): 340–363.
3. Frederick W. Taylor, *The Principles of Scientific Management* (New York: Easton Hive Publishing Company, 1985), 6.
4. Ibid., 45–46.
5. Julien Freund, *The Sociology of Max Weber* (New York: Vintage Books, 1968), 18.
6. Ibid.
7. While Weber doesn't write about organizational sanctions, or the performance and productivity of workers in bureaucracies, he does give some attention to psychological sanctions associated with the deviation from norms and accepted behaviors in community and cultural settings.
8. Frank Gilbreth, "Primer on Scientific Management," in *The Writings of the Gilbreths,* ed. William R. Spriegel and Clark E. Myers (Homewood, IL: Richard D. Irwin, 1953).
9. Amitai Etzioni, *A Comparative Analysis of Complex Organizations* (Glencoe, IL: The Free Press of Glencoe, 1961).
10. Jeffrey Pfeffer, *New Directions in Organization Theory: Problems and Prospects* (New York: Oxford University Press, 1997).
11. Although Pfeffer does explicitly identify sanctions as a mechanism of social control, it's important to note that he does so in the context of the presentation of ideas that are more consistent with

behavioralist concerns than rationalist approaches. Behavioral factors that influence individual behavior, like commitment and motivation, will be addressed in more detail later in Chapter 5.

12. David Osborne and Ted Gaebler, *Reinventing Government: How the Entrepreneurial Spirit Is Transforming the Public Sector* (Reading, MA: Addison-Wesley, 192), 156.

13. Ibid., 308.

14. US Office of Personnel Management, "Performance Management Overview & History: Historical Chronology," www.opm.gov/perform/chron.asp.

15. US Office of Personnel Management, "Performance Management Overview & History: Setting the Stage," www.opm.gov/perform/setting.asp.

16. Edward L. Deci, Richard M. Ryan, and Richard Koestner, "A Meta-Analytic Review of Experiments Examining the Effects of Extrinsic Rewards on Intrinsic Motivation," *Psychological Bulletin* 125, no. 6 (1999): 659.

17. Charles Perrow, *Complex Organizations: A Critical Essay* (New York: McGraw-Hill, 1986).

18. Ibid., 119–131.

19. Herbert A. Simon, *Administrative Behavior,* 3rd ed. (New York: Free Press, 1976), 204.

20. Herbert A. Simon, "Proverbs of Administration," *Public Administration Review* 6, no. 1 (Winter 1946): 53–67.

21. James G. March and Herbert A. Simon, *Organizations* (New York: Wiley, 1958), 170.

22. Perrow, *Complex Organizations,* 123.

23. US Department of Homeland Security, "Department Six-Point Agenda," www.dhs.gov/xabout/history/editorial_0646.shtm.

24. US General Services Administration, "St. Elizabeths and DHS Consolidation: Statement of Robert A. Peck, Commissioner Public Buildings Service, US General Services Administration before the Committee on Appropriations Subcommittee on Homeland Security March 25, 2010," para. 2, April 30, 2010, www.gsa.gov/portal/content/104271.

25. Norma Riccuci and Frank Thompson, "Reinventing Government," *Annual Review of Political Science* 1, no. 1 (1998): 231–257.

26. Donald P. Moynihan, "Homeland Security and the US Public Management Policy Agenda," *Governance* 18, no. 2 (2005): 171–196.

27. Douglas McGregor, *The Human Side of Enterprise* (New York: McGraw-Hill, 1960).

28. Dennis O'Connor and Leodones Yballe, "Maslow Revisited: Construction of a Road Map of Human Nature," *Journal of Management Education* 31, no. 6 (2007): 738–756.

29. Clayton Alderfer, "An Empirical Test of a New Theory of Human Needs," *Organizational Behavior and Human Performance* 4 (1969): 142–175.

30. David McClelland, *Human Motivation* (New York: Cambridge University Press, 1987).

31. Lyman Porter and Edward Lawler, *Managerial Attitudes and Performance* (Homewood, IL: Dorsey Press, 1968).

32. Rensis Likert, *New Patterns of Management* (New York: McGraw-Hill, 1961); Mark K. Smith, "Kurt Lewin: Groups, Experiential Learning and Action Research," *The Encyclopedia of Informal Education,* June 2001, www.infed.org/thinkers/et-lewin.htm.

33. Victor H. Vroom and Philip W. Yetton, *Leadership and Decision-Making* (Pittsburgh: University of Pittsburgh Press, 1973).

34. Victor H. Vroom and Arthur Jago, *The New Leadership: Managing Participation in Organizations* (Englewood Cliffs, NJ: Prentice Hall, 1988).

35. Victor H. Vroom, *Work and Motivation* (New York: Wiley, 1964).

36. Jay A. Conger and Rabindra N. Kanungo, "The Empowerment Process: Integrating Theory and Practice," *Academy of Management Review* 13, no. 3 (1988): 471–482; M. S. Sridhar, "Maslow's Theory and its Application to Librarianships," *IASLIC Bulletin* 26, no. 3 (1981): 135–139.

37. William G. Ouchi, *Theory Z: How American Business Can Meet the Japanese Challenge* (Reading, MA: Addison-Wesley, 1981).

38. The common conception that public sector employees categorically earn less than those in for-profit organizations is challenged by studies such as the following that indicate, at least in some cases, compensation levels are comparable, if not favorable, in the public sector: Congressional Budget Office, *Comparing the Compensation of Federal and Private-Sector Employees,* pub. no. 4403 (January 2012).

39. Frederick Herzberg, Bernard Mausner, and Barbara Bloch Snyderman, *The Motivation to Work* (New York: Wiley, 1959); Frederick Herzberg, "One More Time: How Do You Motivate Employees?" *Harvard Business Review* 65, no. 5 (2003): 109–120.

40. Rensis Likert, "System 4: A Resource from Improving Public Administration," *Public Administration Review* 41, no. 6 (1981): 674–678; Rensis Likert, *New Patterns of Management* (New York: McGraw-Hill, 1961); Rensis Likert, *The Human Organization: Its Management and Value* (New York: McGraw-Hill, 1967).

41. Smith, "Kurt Lewin."

42. Robert J. Paul and Yar M. Ebadi, "Leadership Decision Making in a Service Organization: A Field Test of the Vroom–Yetton Model," *Journal of Occupational Psychology* 62 (1989): 201–211.

43. The Times 100, "Siemens: Case Studies in The Times 100," http://businesscasestudies.co.uk/siemens.

44. Clayton Alderfer, "Organization Development," *Annual Review of Psychology* 28 (1977): 197–223.

45. Robert L. Brown and Thomas F. Lewinsohn, "Local Action—A Case Study," *American Review of Public Administration* 3 (1969): 32–35.

46. Marvin R. Weisbord, Howard E. Lamb, and Allan B. Drexler. *Improving Police Department Management Through Problem-Solving Task Forces—A Case Study In Organization Development* (Reading, MA: Addison-Wesley, 1974).

47. John Roueche and George Baker, *Access & Excellence: The Open Door College* (Alexandria, VA: The Community College Press, 1987).

48. Likert, *The Human Organization.*

49. O. C. McSwite, *Legitimacy in Public Administration: A Discourse Analysis* (Thousand Oaks, CA: Sage, 1997); Camilla Stivers, *Bureau Men, Settlement Women: Constructing Public Administration in the Progressive Era* (Lawrence: University Press of Kansas, 2000); Margaret Stout and Carrie M. Staton, "The Ontology of Process Philosophy in Follett's Administrative Theory," *Administrative Theory and Praxis* 33, no. 2 (2011): 268–292. These are examples of an interpretation of Follett's work as being fundamentally—ontologically—different than other social and organizational theorists of the time.

50. See Nitin Nohria, "Mary Parker Follett's View on Power, the Giving of Orders, and Authority: An Alternative to Hierarchy or a Utopian Idology?" *Mary Parker Follett: Prophet of Management* (Boston: Harvard Business School Press, 1995), 155–162.

51. This would include other contingency theorists like Burns and Stalker or Woodward. See Tom Burns and G. M. Stalker, *The Management of Innovation* (London: Tavistock, 1961). Or see Joan Woodward, *Industrial Organization: Theory and Practice* (New York: Oxford University Press, 1965).

52. Philip Selznick, *Leadership and Administration, A Sociological Interpretation* (Berkeley: University of California Press, 1957).

53. Graham Allison, "Public and Private Management: Are They Fundamentally Alike in All Unimportant Respects?" *Proceedings of the Public Management Research Conference November 19–20, 1979,* OPM Document 127-53-1 (Washington DC: Office of Personnel Management, 1980), 27–38.

Chapter 6

Understanding and Shaping Group Dynamics

The Management Attribute

The focus of the last chapter was on the theories and techniques of managing or shaping individual behavior. One of the most interesting attributes of organizations is that they are simultaneously comprised of individuals who are capable of exercising agency or free will independent of one another, and at the same time, organizations are collective entities that behave in systematic or collective ways. In this chapter, the central focus is on exploring the functionality and management of groups, or the *relationships* between individuals and groups, and the notion that in some organizational circumstances, the needs of the group—be it the organization or the unit—do rise above the individual.

The current focus on groups over individuals isn't new in organization studies. Dorwin Cartwright and Alvin Zander describe the focus as "a field of inquiry dedicated to advancing knowledge about the nature of groups, the laws of their development, and the interrelations with individuals and other groups and larger institutions."[1] From within this perspective, the claim that groups should become the unit of analysis is based on several observations about modern social and organizational settings. First, groups are inevitable and ubiquitous. Few, if any, human activities in modern society occur without direct group involvement or influence. This leads to the second observation: that groups mobilize power forces that produce effects of importance to individuals. These forces and effects are the factors that determine the effectiveness of organizational activities. Clearly, many of these forces and effects benefit individuals and society more broadly, and correspondingly the third observation that groups may produce both favorable and unfavorable consequences is of interest. However, these same forces and effects can also have negative effects on individuals, families, communities, and society broadly. It is these broader effects, positive and negative, that reinforce the importance of considering organizations from a perspective of public governance rather than just instrumental measures of effectiveness. Lastly, an accurate understanding of group dynamics enhances the likelihood that organizations can deliberatively achieve positive, functional performance.[2]

In addition to these observations about groups, we also assume and operate from a belief that organizations and the settings in which they operate are becoming increasingly complex. That growing complexity is due to factors that include an increasing diversity of the population public organizations serve, the growing size of many organizations (often under the transaction cost logic we described in Chapter 4), growing technological or environmental complexity, and many other factors. As increasingly large organizations face growing complexity, new challenges arise. No longer is productivity a matter of ensuring the coordination of individuals engaged in isolated tasks—the production line model where each individual has a discrete job is no longer the sole, or even predominant, model. More and more often, the success of contemporary organizations requires that groups of individuals work in collaboration to complete complicated, interrelated, and overlapping tasks.

As a practical or instrumental matter, groups and teams allow us to pull together multiple talents and skill sets in order to achieve synergistic results—results where the whole is greater than the simple sum of individual contributions. Among other factors, this brings to mind the social aspects of work, both formal and informal, and the shared beliefs that emerge as a result of the interplay or interrelations between individuals in the workplace. Further, there is evidence to suggest that not only are groups and group coordination central to the success of contemporary organizations but that groups are capable of accomplishing more collectively than individuals working in parallel with each other are able to.

At the beginning of the last chapter, we revisited the Hawthorne experiments in order to reveal how the findings of those experiments lead to new understandings of the variables that shape human behavior—that behavior is not exclusively rational—and that other assumptions and approaches to managing that behavior can be equally, if not more, effective. Here, we are returning to the Hawthorne experiments in order to highlight specific findings related to the development and behavior of group dynamics.

At least three particular portions of the Hawthorne experiments are worth highlighting in their focus on group dynamics—the relay assembly room study, the bank wiring study and the interview program carried out by researchers.[3] In an effort to better control the factors that confounded the lighting investigation, the Hawthorne researchers decided to move a group of workers into a separate room in the relay assembly room study. The relays being assembled were composed of about thirty-five small parts, and the study sought to determine the effects of fatigue on productivity and the extent to which rest periods and the duration of the workday affected productivity. After studying thirteen different combinations of rest periods and work-day lengths, the researchers concluded that productivity, measured as output per hour, was affected to some degree by fatigue. More importantly, however, the researchers also found that workers' attitudes toward each other, toward the group as a whole, and toward supervisors also influenced their productivity.

The bank wiring room portion of the study was designed to examine the social effects and the mechanics of small-group processes. Researchers endeavored "to obtain more exact information about social groups within the company" by using a methodology similar to the relay assembly room.[4] A small group was taken out of their regular work setting and relocated to a separate room in an effort to ensure that no other changes were made in the working conditions other than the location. In the bank wiring room, researchers first found that when workers reached what they felt was an acceptable or appropriate day's work, their individual productivity would decline. In other words, informal performance standards developed beyond the formal or explicit performance incentive systems developed by the organization. Further, the results of the bank wiring room also revealed that not only were group dynamics a factor in performance but that the emergence of informal social organizations could be a major limiting factor on performance. Over time, a common body of sentiments developed among the workers wherein pressure was brought to bear on high performance workers not to be a "rate buster." The relay assembly room experiment revealed, in part, that relationships between the workers and their supervisor had an effect on morale and productivity. Based on these findings, the researchers began the interview program, wherein a series of interviews were conducted with workers in an effort to better understand the nature of their concerns. In this portion of the studies, some 21,000 interviews with employees were conducted. Roethlisberger said the following:

> It became clear that many employee comments which had formerly been interpreted in terms of the interviewees' personal situation could be better understood if they were interpreted in light of the employee's existing social relations within the plant: the social organization of the group with which he worked and his position in that group.[5]

As with both the relay assembly and bank wiring rooms, the interviews demonstrated that social factors were a significant factor in worker productivity.

It's important to remember how confounding these results were at the time. The Hawthorne experiments were designed to follow the logic and behavioral assumptions of classical management theory and especially scientific management, and the results were largely inconsistent with those assumptions. Some years later, Eric Trist of the Tavistock Institute recalled the following:

> In our action research projects at that time, we and our organizational clients were baffled by the extent to which the wider social environment was moving in on their more immediate concerns, upsetting plans, preempting the achievement of operational goals, and causing additional stresses and severe internal conflict.[6]

The emerging question for researchers and practitioners was that if behavior is something much more complicated than narrow rational means-ends calculations and rationalized organizational structures were insufficient to maximize organizational behavior, what was the alternative? Or extending that logic further, how might we better describe and understand the factors that shape the behavior of work groups in organizations and the resulting effectiveness of the organization? Finally, and specifically for managers and supervisors, what strategies might be used to deal with what was apparently becoming a far more dynamic and complex environment?

Our treatment of the theoretical and practical responses that emerged following the Second World War is organized into three fairly distinct sections focused on human and group relations theories, systems theories, and organizational culture theories, respectively.

Human and Group Relations Theories

Human relations theory (HRT) and group relations theory (GRT) were introduced in Chapter 5, and rather than representing the complete intellectual and social context within which group relations thinking emerged, we will instead remind you that there is a large, diverse body of research that emerged over nearly sixty years, and it is one that includes a wide range of work. For the purposes of our presentation in this chapter, the focus of our summary will be on those aspects of HRT and GRT that emphasize the social and group dynamics of social and organizational settings. In the last chapter, we oriented our summary on emerging assumptions and their implications for organizational practices that focused on individuals. Here, the unit of analysis is the group rather than the individual. Obviously, one of the implications is that the same assumptions are in place here as they were in Chapter 5.

Assumptions

Driven both by normative perspectives that differ from rationalist perspectives and by the empirical research findings starting with the Hawthorne experiments, behavioralist theorists adopt a differing set of assumptions regarding human behavior. Rather than starting with an economically rational model of individual behavior, human and group relations researchers assume much greater complexity in the expressions of and the causes behind human behavior. One of the assumptions common to transitional thinkers like Chester Barnard—those linking classical rationalists theories and human and group relations—and shared by human and group relations theorists is a belief that the causes or motivations for human behavior are far more complex than is recognized by classical theorists. While blurring the important details of their thinking described earlier, both Maslow's theory of personality and McGregor's Theory Y adopt a set of basic assumptions of behavior and motivation that understands motivation as being highly complex and that any number of sources, including social and group relationships, can contribute to the eventual appearance of a given behavior. Moreover, the factors that shape behavior can be both formal and explicit, or informal and implicit. This assumption provides the basis for recognizing that in social environments—and for our purposes, organizations specifically—"perception is reality." Members of organizations are nearly as likely to recognize and respond to the perceived or inferred meaning of a manager's action, as they are to a formal, specifically articulated policy statement.

These emerging empirical findings and corresponding behavioral assumptions lead to an additional variation in underlying assumptions that is important to note. Chester Barnard's claims about the nature of organizations, namely that they are cooperative and shared understandings that become more developed later, assumes that organizations are more than the sum of their parts and that members of organizations actually cooperate rather than merely work in parallel. In the past chapter, we highlighted how this resulted in a shifted focus on motivation, moving away from a narrow use of money and other material inducements, and included other factors including personal, nonmaterial opportunities for recognition; favorable physical conditions of work; and others. In this chapter, we shift our attention from what motivates individuals to how collections of individuals interact with one another in a collective way.

Concepts

As we've noted before, the body of work in HRT and GRT is large and fairly diverse. Our description of concepts isn't intended to be exhaustive but does highlight a range of concepts that are recurrent in the literature and that are actionable—can be used to positively impact the performance of groups within organizations and organizations as a whole.

Factors Affecting Group Dynamics

Charles Perrow claims that the body of research from HRT is the most voluminous in the field of organization theory (OT).[7] Rather than attempt to summarize that work in any comprehensive way, the intent of this section is to discern from the research a useful set of empirical factors that researchers have identified that help us understand and more effectively manage the performance of groups.

Cohesiveness

To some degree, cohesiveness, or the extent to which the group is able to stick together and make mutually beneficial and reinforcing choices, is the core concept associated with groups. Without some level of functional cohesiveness, a group ceases to be a group. So, it makes intuitive sense that cohesiveness must therefore affect the performance of the group as a whole. Researchers have taken this as one of the important dynamics of organizational performance. Cohesiveness, in terms of the extent to which members are attracted or linked to one another, and importantly, the degree to which the group's goals align with the members' individual goals, speaks to the level of cohesiveness.

The existence or creation of stable relationships can improve cohesiveness and thereby improve performance, and vice versa. For example, Mayo and Lombard found that groups that were reorganized frequently had performance problems, including increased absenteeism and turnover.[8] Other research has revealed that the creation of communities of experience,[9] in addition to time spent engaged in shared tasks, also contributes to stronger intragroup cohesiveness.[10]

Similarly, Robert Blake and Jane Mouton studied intergroup competition and found that groups that had to compete with other groups increased cohesiveness.[11] Stephen Robbins also notes that in addition to competition, success, whether in a competitive environment or as measured against preestablished performance standards, has a positive effect on cohesiveness.[12] These findings are consistent with other research, which shows that threats or risks outside of the work unit can also contribute to cohesiveness and, correspondingly, the effectiveness of the group. The risk is that failures or losses, if not managed, can create divisiveness within the group. Another related body of research in this area found that high status can contribute to cohesiveness, but factors like performance, discretion, and organizational level can influence sense of status and, thereby, cohesiveness.[13]

Leadership

The work of Blake and Mouton begins from the notion that managers can build attitudes within a group that contribute to efficient performance and enhance creativity, innovation, and experimentation—and that this can happen through interaction with others.[14] The managerial grid, the concept that Blake and Mouton are perhaps best known for, presents a managerial framework based on the intersection of two continua—concern for production and concern for people (see Figure 6.1). The grid, and corresponding questionnaire that appears in their 1964 book of the same name, allows managers to locate themselves within the range of management styles and then assess the extent to which that style is likely to be effective. Blake and Mouton's notion of "concern for" is not narrowly instrumental and does not mean a narrow orientation toward task-specific targets but rather has to do with a more general approach to management that governs their actions. In other words, how do managers concern themselves with a range of, probably context-specific, considerations associated with the entire scope of production and the people who contribute to its generation?

Task leader (9,1—high production or task, low people or relationship)

Managers and administrators in this quadrant of the grid are very much task oriented and are demanding of their workers. There is little or no place for cooperation or collaboration. Highly task oriented people display traits including that they are very strong on schedules; expect people to do what they are told without question or debate; tend to focus on who is to blame rather than concentrate on exactly what is wrong and how to prevent it; are intolerant of what they see as dissent or conflict, leaving little room for workers to contribute or develop.

Figure 6.1   Blake and Mouton's Leadership Model: The Managerial Grid

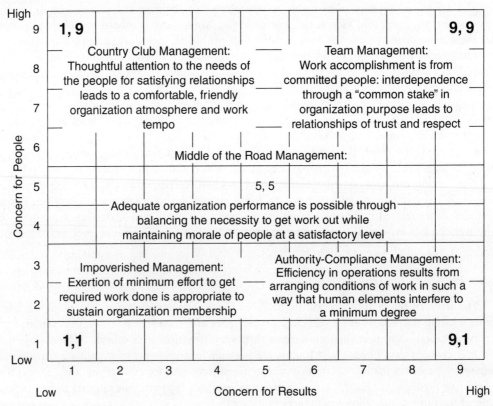

Source: Robert R. Blake, Herbert A. Shepard, and Jane S. Mouton, "Foundations and Dynamics of Intergroup Behavior," *Managing Intergroup Conflict in Industry* (Houston, TX: Gulf Publishing Company, 1964).

Team leader (9,9—high production or task, high people or relationship)

This type of administrator leads by positive example and strives to engender a cohesive and collaborative environment, in which all members of the unit can accomplish their highest potential both as team members and as people. They encourage a collaborative approach to achieve team goals as effectively as possible and at the same time strive to strengthen the bonds among work group members.

Country club leader (1,9—low production or task, high people or relationship)

Administrators falling into this quadrant tend to use rewards in order to maintain discipline and to encourage the team to accomplish its goals. Conversely, they are unlikely to use more punitive coercive powers. This tendency derives from concern that using overt authority could jeopardize relationships within the team.

Impoverished leader (1,1—low production or task, low people or relationship)

Leadership in this quadrant is characterized by a "delegate and disappear" management style. Such leaders are committed neither to task accomplishment nor group maintenance. As a consequence, they are likely to allow their team to do whatever it wishes and prefer to detach themselves from the group processes. One common result is that they allow the team to suffer from a series of internal power struggles.

Damped pendulum (5,5—moderate task, moderate relationship)

This last quadrant is characterized by leaders or administrators who seek to operate in a middle group where there is some push for production and some maintenance of group relations as well. The challenge here is whether this approach to leadership represents balance or too little focus on either dimension.

There are some who argue that it is possible that specific conditions could reasonably lead to the selection of one of the other three types to be used. For example, becoming an authoritarian leader within a unit that lacks focus or discipline may contribute to building a sense of discipline.[15] The notion advanced by this structured depiction of leadership orientations developed by Blake and Mouton is that by examining various management settings and circumstances, it is possible for an administrator to identify and select which points along the axis one needs to adopt in order to achieve the desired outcomes. However, Blake and Mouton reject a *contingency* approach to leadership, in which the selection of leadership styles is contingent upon the unique circumstances of the organization and it's particular context. For Blake and Mouton, the 9,9 team leadership style is always the most appropriate because of its positive effect on long-term relations of the group and the corresponding improvements on cohesiveness and performance.

Control and Compliance

Within the human and group dynamics literature, the focus shifts away from direct and authoritarian command structures and processes, as well as away from a narrow application of inducements. However, human and group relations theorists do continue to give attention to a means of establishing and maintaining control in the organization.

The group relations theorist who perhaps gives more attention than any other control is Arnold Tannenbaum. Tannenbaum pulls no punches when he says the following:

> Organization implies control. A social organization is an ordered arrangement of individual human interactions. Control processes help circumscribe idiosyncratic behaviors and keep them conformant to the rational plan of the organization. Organizations require a certain amount of conformity as well as the integration of diverse activities. It is the function of control to bring about conformance to organizational requirements and achievement of the ultimate purposes of the organization. The coordination and order created out of the diverse interests and potentially diffuse behaviors of members is largely a function of control.[16]

He also notes the following: "Hierarchy is divisive, it creates resentment, hostility and opposition. Participation reduces disaffection and increases the identification of members with the organization." Tannenbaum also points out that "paradoxically through participation, management increases its control by giving up some of its authority." Control, for Tannenbaum, has to do with ensuring or maximizing the "orderliness and predictability of organizational functioning and is predicated on the regulation of individual behavior in conformance with organizational purposes."[17] Control is expressed in processes by which individuals or groups determine the behavior of another individual or group.[18]

In order to understand the nature and distribution of power, Tannenbaum developed the control graph (see Figure 6.2). The graph, which is created using data gathered from a survey of members at all levels of the organization, depicts the perceived levels of control exercised at each level of the organization, as well as other respective levels—for example, managers, supervisors, and line workers. Respondents from each category of organizational members describe the degree of control they perceive themselves, and workers at other levels, to have. Control is measured using a five-point scale ranging from "little control" to "a very great deal of control." The data are then aggregated for workers at each level of the organization and plotted on a graph based on these categories.

At least two aspects of the resulting graph are important to recognize. First is the relative slope of the graph, which reveals respondents' perceptions of the relative distribution of power among categories of employee. While it is common for workers to perceive that managers and supervisors have greater power than frontline workers, changes in practices and processes can influence those perceptions. The perceived distribution of control within the organization isn't static or fixed; it can change in reaction to procedure and process changes. The second aspect of the graph that is particularly useful is the total amount of space under the curve. The more space under the curve, the greater the total amount of control is perceived to exist in the organization. The insight that the control graph reveals is that the total amount of control is not necessarily zero-sum. In other words, there is not a finite or fixed amount of control within any organization, and efforts by managers and supervisors to distribute authority more broadly do not inherently reduce the level of control they retain. The goal, therefore, is not simply to find the most effective distribution of control in the organization but rather to increase the total amount of control, thus giving more control to all members.

Other group relations theorists have also studied control as a critical variable in group performance. Richard Hackman, for example, looks to the use of norms as a means of controlling not just behaviors but also thoughts, feelings, and perceptions.[19] In his focus on establishing

Figure 6.2 Tannenbaum's Control Graph

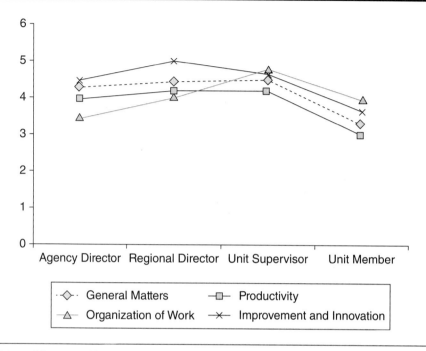

Source: Adapted from Arnold Tannenbaum, *Control in Organizations* (New York: McGraw-Hill, 1968).

social control, A. Paul Hare describes the process by which group members influenced individuals' behaviors. One set of approaches for establishing control and managing behavior is the use of formal and informal education. Ostracism and social sanctions form another set of approaches. The mechanism by which these approaches work is by increasing stability and continuity. Stability and continuity are critical to the ability of a group to function consistently over time, one of the key attributes of group performance. The downside of such stability and continuity is that it has the potential to reduce flexibility and adaptability. Moreover, self-control also becomes critical component of group stability and continuity as well. Self-control is expressed during the initial phase of the social act when the individual modifies his behavior as a result of *anticipation* of the other persons in the group's response.[20]

A number of conclusions and implications can be drawn from the wider collection of research on groups and control:

- Organizations in which the rank-and-file workers are influential can be as effective as those where workers have comparatively little control or influence (which is counter to bureaucratic theory).
- Organizations wherein workers and leaders are perceived as highly influential will be more effective than those in which either or both are less influential (area under the curve—total control).

- It may be more important to increase or maximize the total amount of influence and control than it is to equalize it across groups of members.
- More control and distributed control is linked to higher levels of effectiveness.
- Distribution of control is associated with greater effectiveness.

Interestingly, there are several points where these findings and implications overlap with other human relations research and confirm what we intuitively expect. For example, the research reveals that patterns of control have a direct effect on the human relations climate, which in turn impacts performance factors, such as group cohesiveness. Still focusing on control dynamics, we see that workers who have some control have more positive disposition toward their managers and supervisors and vice versa (supervisors toward workers).

Contingent Factors

Beyond the factors described so far, all of which speak to the nature and character of the relationships among workers and supervisors, researchers have also identified a set of contingent or nonsocial variables that have an impact on the behavior and performance of groups.

Task Factors. Charles Walker and Robert Guest's study of manufacturing operations found that physical or environmental characteristics of a task environment and operational features of the work affect the performance of the group. Factors, including physical separation, serve to reduce the interaction of the workforce, reducing cohesiveness and thus performance. The nature of the task, including repetitive, distinct, and nonoverlapping activities also served to disconnect workers with a corresponding effect on connectivity.[21]

Trist studied the shift from shortwall mining, where each miner was skilled at all of the tasks required for wall operations and all miners took turns at each of the tasks. In the move to longwall mining the miners operated in shifts with each shift being responsible for a single task. The researchers discovered that the longwall system failed—performed worse—as the cohesiveness of the group, which resulted directly from the task structure, disintegrated upon the disaggregation of the mining tasks.[22]

While the findings of both Walker and Guest's and Trist's work emerged from the context of industrial organizations, which, at least on the surface, share very little with contemporary public and service organizations, their findings do have implications. As we noted at the outset of the chapter, organizational settings and group activities within them are becoming increasingly complex. This corresponds with a growing level of inter- and intragroup interdependence. Given this independence, functional and sustained cohesiveness is, and will remain, important to achieving high performance organizations. Task settings where coworkers are physically or operationally dispersed and the task processes disaggregate work groups run the risk of reducing cohesiveness and, thus, performance.

Size. Not surprisingly, size affects group dynamics as well. As would be expected, cohesiveness declines as group size increases, but this is within small groups, up to about twenty members. Above that size, cohesiveness levels out. Size appears to be more important than traits of individual members, including age and education. This reflects other factors, including structure, in that communication and effective interaction are necessary for functional cohesive groups. As group size becomes larger, the number and possible places for breakdowns in communication also increases.[23]

Structure and Hierarchy. In his treatment of control, Tannenbaum argues that hierarchy is divisive. The paradox is that in organizations larger than a handful of employees, some sort of structure is natural, and necessary, as a feature of control and coordination of activities. Any such structure, when developed as a means of ensuring control and coordination, will also include attributes of hierarchy in support of control, communications, work flow, and other processes necessary to enhance the outputs of the organization. The paradox that results, if Tannenbaum is correct, is that the very structures that are necessary to support productive organizations are simultaneously detrimental to improving that productivity. The question that then emerges is the following: How might such a hierarchy be managed in a way as to retain the capacity to coordinate activities for the benefit of organizational goals, while at the same time minimizing the authoritarian attributes that diminish performance?

Techniques and Practices

If nothing else, one thing that should be clear by this point in our review of the research and theory on the management of groups is that it is diverse and quite broad. The factors and approaches to the management of groups and group dynamics are quite broad as well. As a result, our effort to present a set of techniques and practices that can be effectively used to manage groups is not exhaustive. However, the techniques and approaches we will describe emerge directly out of the research and theory we've presented thus far in both this chapter as well as the entire book. These techniques and approaches also reflect what we believe to be practices that are widely adaptable to the sorts of public and nonprofit sector organizations students of public administration are likely to find themselves a part of.

People and Relations—Cohesiveness

Intuitively and experientially, we tend to understand that all functional groups share some minimum degree of cohesiveness—connectedness between and among members that creates a measure of robustness and resilience. This, in turn, enables the group to work together effectively—even under some degree of stress. The prescriptive question is then what can managers do to develop the sort of cohesiveness that contributes to positive, functional group dynamics? Aronson and Mills find that the process and content of initiation into a group can affect the nature and strength of cohesiveness.[24] Specifically, they find that the more robust or severe the initiation into a group is, the more cohesive the group will be in the long run. Beyond a shared initiation experience, Edward Shils and Morris Janowitz's work on the disintegration of organizations indicates that building a broader shared community of experience and shared understandings, what they describe as *gemeinschaft,* contribute in important ways to sustain the coherence of a group, even under substantial duress.[25, 26] Moreover, this robustness emerges and exists in subunits of the organization in ways that both reflect the organization's mission and strategies but also develops in unique and specific ways within subunits.

In addition to the notion that shared experiences can contribute to the cohesiveness, and thereby the effectiveness of groups, other research suggests that the focus and perceptions of groups can also contribute to cohesiveness. A number of different studies have found that the nature, content, and achievement of goals all affect the cohesion of groups. For example,

William Scott's work reveals the extent to which group or organization goals influence the recruitment and retention of members.[27] Bertram Raven and Jan Rietsema's work found that the nature of group goals, including the formulation of them and the likelihood of success, impacts individual's engagement with a group and group cohesiveness more broadly.[28] While the coherence of goals and perceived status of groups within the organization can enhance cohesiveness, it can work against cohesiveness as well. J. R. P. French, for example, found that group members withdrew from participation in groups when agreement about means and methods diminished.[29] More broadly, the status of groups, including differences in organizational hierarchy, assessment of performance, perceptions of the work being done, or the amount of choice or influence granted to the group also impacts its cohesiveness.[30]

Blake and Mouton, in collaboration with Herbert Shepard, also give attention to the emergence of conflict within groups and describe means of enhancing not only managerial performance but also **intergroup and team development**. Organizational groups can take many different shapes and a wide range of sizes. For Blake, Mouton, and Shepard, what defines a group is less about size or structure but is better understood as a feature of their working relationships. In other words, a group is a number of individuals; it has a shared stake or investment of group outcomes, and it has a commitment to the survival of the group to attain a goal or purpose. The degree of group cohesion, or shared identity, varies around structure, management, and leadership approaches (i.e., location on the managerial grid), culture, normative attributes, and so forth. The stronger the group's shared identity is, the higher morale and cohesion will be. The reverse is true as well—the weaker that shared identity is, the greater the likelihood of conflict and the lower morale will be—all of which have an impact on organizational effectiveness. However, they also recognize that in intergroup conflict orientations: (1) disagreement is inevitable and permanent, (2) conflict is not inevitable and there is no agreement (group interdependency not necessary), and (3) conflict is inevitable, and agreement is possible.

Irving Janis' and Robbins' research indicates that some level of conflict is natural, necessary, and in fact beneficial to organizational success. In Janis' famous work on group dynamics and conflict, he finds that the presence of diverse perspectives and resulting conflict is necessary in order to avoid groupthink.[31] Groupthink represents the dysfunctional extreme of cohesiveness, wherein a group has such strong internal correspondence that alternative information or courses of action cannot be accepted, let alone even considered. Robbins' interactionist approach recognizes the importance of conflict by actively promoting some level of controlled conflict as a way of encouraging innovation and avoiding myopic decision making.[32]

In order to improve shared identity and reduce group conflict, the involved groups are separated and asked to generate two lists. On one they place thoughts, attitudes, perceptions, and feelings about the other group, and on the second list they predict what the other group will say about them. The groups then come together and share their lists for the purpose of creating clarity. The groups then reconvene separately to discuss their reactions to what they have learned about themselves from what the other group has said and identify issues that still need to be resolved between the two groups. The two groups come together a second time and share their lists, set priorities, and generate action steps for moving forward. A follow-up meeting is held to ensure that the implementation or follow-up steps have been taken. The method can be used with multiple groups where the conflict or tension between them may be lower. In this approach, each group separately develops several lists— positive feedback list, a bug list, and an empathy list. The two groups come together and share the lists. During this stage, there is no discussion except for asking questions for further clarification. The combined group then generates a list of major problems and unresolved issues between them. Then the groups rank issues in terms of importance. Subgroups are formed with members from each group, which then discusses and works through each item and reports back to the larger group. Based on the reports back and any other information collected, the large group develops final actions that might include efforts to generate action steps for resolving the conflict, assigns responsibilities for each step, and records a date by which the steps ought to have been carried out. The end result of this intensive interpersonal intergroup work is that the two groups can then more effectively work together.

Leadership

Intuitively and anecdotally, we have a sense that quality leadership contributes to the effectiveness of groups and of organizations more generally. In fact, research has shown that different leaders generate different levels of performance, even among the same group of workers.[33] We also have a sense that there must be some shared characteristics of successful or effective leadership. Unfortunately, the research suggests that the effective function of leadership is more complicated. So while there has been some effort to identify effective leadership traits, such research has been met with little success.[34] Lots of traits were identified across studies, but few were recurrent across those studies. The research seems to imply situational or contextual selection of traits. Following Cartwright and Zander's work, this suggests that the choice of leaders should take into account a person's suitability for the type of functions he or she is to perform within a specific context. Moreover, we should carefully consider the desirability of the selection of formal arrangements that maintain the responsibilities of leadership in the same person, regardless of the changes in the setting, task of the group, or the requirements of the leader.

However, this is not to suggest that the volumes of research have resulted in no actionable implications for leadership and its relation to group performance. Among the findings of the research described earlier in this chapter is that both the broader leadership activities and greater levels of delegation improve organizations' performance. First, the greater the level of role differentiation that leaders display—taking on activities including planning, acquisition, and distribution of resources; engaging in initiating efforts; and so forth—the better the performance of the group. Further, the more delegation of activities and responsibility the leader does, the better the group's performance. Similarly, the less direct supervision a manager is engaged in, and more support provided, the higher the level of performance of the group. Even so, context matters and other research has shown that in addition to focus and role differentiation, the complexity or difficulty of the task at hand also influences the shorts of leadership approaches that are likely to be effective. For example, group performance was higher in situations where leaders focused narrowly on tasks that were either highly difficult or of low difficulty. Performance was also high where organizations focused instead on relationships when the tasks were of moderate difficulty. The need to shift to a focus on relationships was supported by other findings that indicate the more the leader engaged in the development of cohesiveness among workers, the better the performance of the group.

Increasing Control

Tannenbaum and his colleagues found that organizations that expand participation increase the perception of control not only among line workers but also among managers and supervisors. The research indicates that managers do not view their control and influence diminishing as participation increases but just the opposite. Their perception is that managers in more participative organizations view themselves as having more influence.[35]

Simply adopting an unrefined mantra of "increasing participation" isn't necessarily sufficient to increase performance, however. The question remains of employee participation in what activities and to what end? In the context we are exploring here, control within a system of group dynamics, control, and control systems has to do with organizational processes of establishing and instituting performance objectives, standards, and practices of production, as well as the measurement of progress against those standards and the adjustment of those practices when or if necessary. Participation, then, has to do not necessarily with generating or shaping the mission and vision of the organization but rather is focused on employee engagement in the formulation of elements of the control systems in ways that reflect and take advantage of the contextualized knowledge of those individuals. In other words, it is those workers who are currently engaged in the specific work activities at various levels of the organization who are most likely to foresee the consequences of new or altered control systems or practices on the specific content of their work. Structuring participatory processes to elicit and include this sort of applied knowledge not only increases a perception of control and influence but is also likely to improve the performance of the system by helping to achieve the system objectives and minimize or avoid unintended consequences.

Contingent Factors: Environment and Task As Well as Size

Environment and Task. Trist and Ken Bamford's longwall and shortwall coal mining studies revealed an experiential limit to the concept that specialization can increase the performance and efficiency of some tasks. Specifically, they found that the effective performance of some tasks requires more subtle and complex interactions among work group members, but their and other research also exposes the possibility of managing the task and the environment to support group performance. This can include environmental factors such as variables like distance or noise that reduce communications effectiveness or the physical arrangement of the productive space, so as to enhance isolated but parallel work by comparison to engaged and collaborative work.[36] Similarly, Hackman suggests that it is also possible to structure the task in ways that support or enhance the work group's engagement with the task and each other in support of improved performance.[37]

Size. Although research does indicate a relationship between group size, cohesiveness, and ultimately performance, it is not merely a matter of reducing the size of work groups in order to increase cohesiveness, and therefore productiveness.[38] The coherence and clarity of the group's task, in conjunction with unit size, also effects cohesiveness. More concretely, this suggests that administrators seeking to improve performance by enhancing group coherence must be aware of the relative size of task groups, while also remaining attuned to the work of the group and the degree to which members share an understanding of, and can maintain a stable approach to, their tasks.

Case 6.1

Current Expressions: Control and Expanding the Area under the Curve at St. John's Health System

In their study of cost cutting strategies used in the St. John's Health System (SJHS), Rajiv Kohli and William Kettinger describe a series of approaches that had the effect of increasing and distributing perceived control among members of the organization.[39] Like many health care organizations, SJHS faced a variety of competing pressures to ensure the highest possible level of care outcomes to contain, if not reduce, overall costs for providing that care, while at the same time supporting physicians' ability to exercise processional discretion in provision of care. Classical management theories, and perhaps most famously in Frederick Taylor's "do what you're told" expression of managerial expertise, suggest that command and control approaches to decision making and implementation are likely to be most effective for organizations. Importantly, approaches driven by classical theories also imply that control is zero sum in the organization and that managers must retain and exercise that control in order to accomplish organizational ends in narrowly but rigorously calculated ways. Alternately, Tannenbaum suggests that control is not zero sum and that it can be distributed and grown, while at the same time effectively responding to the diverse pressures that develop within the organization.

Although there have been periods of slower and faster growth, the general trend in health care costs over the past thirty years has been one of consistent increase. SJHS faced the same demands as other hospitals, especially as reimbursement structures and cost caps have been established by both private insurers and public assistance programs. In their efforts to respond to these pressures, SJHS utilized a two-stage action research intervention that focused in large part on physician costs, which research shows can account for as much as 80 percent of hospital costs.[40] In the case of SJHS, the interventions involved a systematic process of engaging the breadth of the organization in the diagnosis of the issues, transparent planning of responses, implementation of response actions, evaluation, and systematic learning from the experiences. It's worth reiterating that the action research approach used for the interventions ensured that each stage of the initiative happened in an engaged way. One of the central features of the action taken was the utilization of an information system that provided systematic and objective information back to physicians for the reflection and use in care decisions. Moreover, this information was generally open to the entire organization, supporting the creation of dialogue not only among physicians regarding specific means of care provided to patients but also about the health outcomes and associated costs incurred. The effect was to more widely distribute control of information and correspondingly distribute control of care and cost decisions throughout the organization.

Although SJHS did not create control graphs to depict staff members' perceptions of control and its distribution, Kohli and Kettinger's report of the initiative does describe outcomes that suggest shifts in both behavior and perceptions. The authors report the expression of a range of different values emerging as factors that shape physician behaviors, including a sense of economic values, professional values, altruistic values, and status or ego values. Behaviorally, the report of the intervention reveals a range of alternative courses of action selected by physicians that had the effect of containing costs, while at the same time giving equal consideration to patient care standards and outcomes. Perceptually, physicians described, often based on the various expressed values, a range of reasons that drove their decision making. None of the expressed reasons described by the physicians had anything to do with classical command and control techniques, such as formal authority or adherence to policy. Instead, physicians were able to draw on a strong perception of distributed control, under which they were able to exercise their own rationale for decisions.

Human Relations Theory and Group Dynamics: Conclusion and Summary

Reflection Questions

Describe three factors that you think have a critical impact on group dynamics. How might these dynamics play out differently in public versus nonprofit versus for-profit organizations?

What do you see as the role of the leader in contributing to the effectiveness of groups? Describe a leader you've seen do this well/not so well. How has that leader exhibited (or not) the attributes of leadership described here?

Research (e.g., school leadership study) suggests that these factors, like the groups they apply to, are dynamic, mutually influential, and contextual. There is no single model of their relative priority or influence that holds in most, let alone all, settings. The consequence of this dynamism is that leaders and administrators must be skillfully attuned to many factors at once and be continuously prepared to engage in the active management of any number of these dynamics at the same moment. The notion of stable homeostasis may be more misleading than helpful in contemporary environments, where small changes can have significant impacts on the organization. Groups take on their own dynamics, which needs to be studied as a phenomenon rather than groups being studied as sets of individuals.

Systems Theories

In describing the notion of systems, Ludwig von Bertalanffy wrote the following:

> While in the past, science tried to explain observable phenomena by reducing them to an interplay of elementary units investigable independently of each other, conceptions appear in contemporary science that are concerned with what is somewhat vaguely termed "wholeness," i.e. problems of organization, phenomena not resolvable into local events, dynamic interactions manifest in difference of behavior of parts when isolated or in a higher configuration, etc.; in short, "systems" of various order not understandable by investigation of their respective parts in isolation. Conceptions and problems of this nature have appeared in all branches of science, irrespective of whether inanimate things, living organisms, or social phenomena are the object of study.[41]

From a systems theory perspective, groups are understood as more than mere collections of individuals but instead are studied as coherent phenomena that demonstrate distinct patterns of behavior. These patterns reveal something about the structure of relationships that exist, and these structures, in turn, suggest something about how to manage them so as to improve organizational performance. Systems thinking suggests that groups are more than just collections of individuals that develop social or organizational entanglements in their collective behaviors. Daniel Katz and Robert Kahn's system theory is basically concerned with problems of relationships, of structures, and interdependence rather than with the constant attributes of objects.[42]

Systems approaches start with the assumption that the system is the unit of analysis—"the system's the thing." Out of that assumption comes the recognition that the system's behavior is not just emergent from the collective actions of individuals that comprise the system but rather is a structure in and of itself. In assuming that the system is its own unit of analysis— and that moving beyond the individual human as the unit analysis, even when grouping humans together—theories of individual behavior are viewed as missing important functional attributes of the system as a whole.

Perhaps the easiest way to begin to untangle this claim is to identify other underlying assumptions of systems thinking. These assumptions help reveal the extent to which this approach to organization understands systems—stable, patterned groups—as not only the unit of analysis but more fundamentally as a coherent entity in and of itself.

There are a wide range of systems theories that have evolved from the preliminary thinking described here, including approaches that draw connections between organizations and even entire collections of organizations and biological systems. Partly because this body of literature is so large and heterodox but also to remain consistent with our organizing approach to the entire book to draw primarily on theories, which we believe to have practical applications for managers, we have chosen to narrow our focus on systems theories that emphasize quality and learning-based approaches.

Quality-Focused Systems

In the years following the end of the Second World War, Japan faced a long and arduous task of not only rebuilding its industrial sector but doing so in a way that could produce products of a quality that would be competitive in a world market. During the first two decades of their efforts, Japanese products were nearly universally seen as being cheap and inferior in quality to those produced in the United States, Europe, and elsewhere in the industrialized world. But during the 1970s and 1980s this reputation changed dramatically, and Japanese products went from being the butt of jokes to among the highest quality in the world. In Japan, several American engineers and statisticians are given extensive credit for having helped develop the approaches and processes that led to this massive turnaround in quality.

Assumptions

Complex, Mutual Causation

The nature of systems, as well as our knowledge about them, is characterized by circular causality rather than linear causality. This means that the causes of any given phenomenon are mutually influential throughout the system. The range of any possible behavior within the system is always simultaneously shaped and influenced by prior causes. Moreover, knowledge of *social* systems and the play of interconnected causes in such systems should be understood as an expression of constructivism rather than realism. In other words, while organizational systems may exhibit physical manifestations, they are best conceived as socially constructed entities composed of stable, repeating patterns of behavior.

Members of the system or organization system should be understood as being reflexive or knowing subjects rather than non-knowing. Members are more than mere cogs and can critically and self-reflectively make sense of and shape their activities in the system. Correspondingly, they can impact the system as a whole. Finally, and despite the existence of preestablished structures, systems are characterized by processes of self-organization. In other words, systems are capable of taking on a life of their own that extends beyond formal or designed structures.

Context Matters

Systems approaches understand the environment as being more than a neutral container for the behavior of the system. Rather, the environment is one of the critical, though often subtle, factors that shape the behavior of the organization. Because of the complexity and sensitivity of the system, it is best described as being indeterminate rather than predictable or deterministic, while it may be possible to successfully engage in probabilistic forecasting. Similarly, members of the organization as critical elements of the system should be understood and related to as being in a network of relationships, which is critical to the functionality of the system. Elements of the system are not simply entities that exist in preestablished, stable, or mechanical positions relative to each other. We are always already in the world and interconnected.

As a result, it's necessary to approach systems holistically rather than in a reductionist way so as to see all of the system elements as being inherently linked to the system as a whole.[43] One of the resulting criticisms of the open systems perspective is that while the concepts are intuitively attractive, the concepts are difficult to operationally define.[44] Because any system is conceived holistically, and factors that influence the system are diverse and complex, it is difficult to precisely define the boundaries of the system. Peter M. Senge attempts to address this criticism by focusing on operational learning, which allows for functional determination of organizational or boundaries.[45] As administrators engage in practices of assessing and understanding particular problems within the organization, a functional analysis of systems will see the boundaries differently depending on the nature of the circumstances. For example, questions about hiring and personnel management may see the organizational boundaries as being established by those who receive remuneration directly from the organization, while a problem associated with program delivery might include volunteers who deliver a program as a part of the system.

System Performance over Individual Performance

Quality-focused management approaches, including total quality management (TQM) and continuous quality improvement (CQI) also emphasize a focus on systems, though with a different approach than that of Senge and other advocates of a learning organization orientation. W. Edwards Deming, Joseph Juran, and other quality systems theorists seek to improve the performance of organizations by systematically assessing and identifying factors in the productive systems of organizations that lead to poor quality products or services. For Deming and Juran, the failure to meet performance and quality standards can often be attributed not to the individual but to the system. As a result, it's critical to have a precise understanding of the system and all of its interacting attributes in order to have any capacity to improve it. This also implies that managers can't hold individuals in isolation responsible for the system's performance. Requiring individuals to "do better," when their performance is likely driven by the system in which they operate, will have little, if any, impact on the overall performance of the system.

The focus on systems over individuals should not be assumed to ignore the possibility that individual employees can and sometimes fail to perform adequately. However, as Juran notes, quality systems approaches assume that many, though not all, problems are systems problems. Juran advocates the application of an 80/20 rule of thumb, which suggests that some 80 percent of the problems can be explained by 20 percent of the causes—which are likely to be systemic rather than individual problems.

Techniques and Practices

Research emerging out of systems approaches has led to a wide range of organizational approaches and techniques. In this section we describe two organizational approaches that draw extensively on systems theory to inform their content and strategies: Senge's learning organizations and Deming and Juran's TQM methods.

Senge argues that under complex conditions—typical of the political, economic, and social variability faced by contemporary public organizations—organizations must be able to learn how to cope with constant change. They must have the capacity to embody the art and practice of learning. Beyond the inherent difficulty of dealing with complex circumstances, most organizations, according to Senge, suffer from what amount to learning disabilities, including the following:

- *"I am my position."*—Excessive commitment of individuals to their own positions rather than understanding their responsibility in the results produced by all positions interacting.
- *"The enemy is out there."*—The external attribution of blame driven by a misunderstanding of how our own actions extend well beyond our own positions.
- *"The illusion of taking charge"*—The notion that we should step up and respond to organizational challenges and stop waiting for someone else to solve problems as a way of being proactive, which is really reactiveness in disguise.
- *"The fixation on events"*—A focus on immediate events and explanations for them rather than larger and longer-term patterns.
- *"The parable of the boiled frog"*[46]—A lack of awareness of how organizations dysfunctionally adapt to slow, gradual processes that are a greater threat than immediate events.
- *"The delusion of learning from experience"*—A failure to understand that our actions have consequences in the distant future or as a part of a larger system, which are nearly impossible to see, let alone learn from via direct experience.
- *"The myth of the management team"*—The fallacy that top management is in agreement and shares a united vision rather than recognizing that teams often spend more time fighting over turf and avoiding anything that makes individual members look bad.[47]

One of the key things to recognize in this list of organizational learning disabilities is the presence of systems-based assumptions that run throughout the collection of dysfunctions. Many of the problems outlined in this list are tied to a failure of the organization to understand itself and function as an integrated set of elements, all of which are nested within a larger system.

Moreover, because of the nature of the system, responsibility for causes and effects is simultaneously individual *and* collective. The individual actor and the system in which he acts are inherently and inseparably tied to each other.

The response Senge develops is the creation of a set of practices and habits that enable the system and its component members to learn and respond in a way that supports the robustness and resilience of the system. The five disciplines of the learning organization discussed in *The Fifth Discipline* are as follows:

- "Personal mastery" is the ability to continually clarify and deepen our personal vision, to focusing our energy, develop patience, and see reality based on available evidence rather than ideology.
- "Mental models" are deeply ingrained assumptions, generalizations, or even pictures of images, which influence how we understand the world and how we take action. These models are natural and unavoidable cognitive constructs that can be both valuable and problematic. The challenge Senge proposes is to craft organizational processes that enable us to recognize our models and use them to the system's benefit rather than assuming that interpretations yielded by these models is unquestionably true.
- "Building shared vision" entails practices by which we unearth shared pictures of the future that foster genuine commitment and enrollment rather than compliance.
- "Team learning" is related to both mental models and shared vision that occurs through dialogue and encompasses the capacity of members of a team to suspend assumptions and enter into genuine thinking together.
- "Systems thinking" is the last of the five disciplines and serves to integrate the other four. It is through the incorporation of all the disciplines via systems thinking that organizations realize their potential.[48]

The last of these, systems thinking, is the basis for organizational learning. It is essential to consider organizations from a systems perspective in order to move consideration of the dysfunctions away from the same old way of fixing problems. As with statistical quality control, it is necessary to understand the systems as a set of interactions. Senge identifies a number of systems laws that shape the consideration and understanding of organizations systems and their implications for organizational performance. One expression of this understanding is the realization that today's problems come from yesterday's solutions. Moreover, systems have a certain amount of elasticity and inertia. The result can be seen in a set of folk axiom, such as the harder you push, the harder the system pushes back, the easy way out usually leads back in, the cure can be worse than the disease, and finally behavior grows better before it gets worse.[49] The consequence of this shift is that it is possible for managers to see both the forest *and* the trees, highlighting the fact that typically managers are prompted to focus their attention on one or the other—typically the trees, or the details, to the detriment of recognizing broader relations and interactions that constitute the system.

Here again, it's important to realize the extent to which these are integrated and overlapping disciplines and that, from Senge's perspective, the effectiveness of the organization depends on the capacity of its members to embody all of these. In this regard, not only is the organization seen as a system of inherently integrated elements but the practices or disciplines of effective performance are similarly a system of inherently integrated elements.

The development and practice of these disciplines also occurs within the organization as a system rather than being a process of individual-level professional development. The process of collective or system development is encouraged, in part, via dialogue or discourse. Senge notes the following:

> In dialogue, a group explores complex and difficult issues from many points of view. Individuals suspend their assumptions but they communicate their assumptions freely. The result is a free exploration that brings to the surface the full depth of people's experience and thought, and yet can move beyond their individual views.[50]

Systematic Quality Improvement—The Plan-Do-Check-Act Cycle

Perhaps the most well-known approach to managed improvement of system performance from a quality systems orientation is the plan-do-check-act (PDCA) cycle described by Walter Shewhart and adopted by Deming. The purpose of the cycle is to focus quality improvement on processes rather than tasks. In part, this is a recognition that the work of organizations is done through interlinked and ongoing processes rather than discrete and finite, static task sets. Work is done in the context of systems. Moreover, this approach also recognizes that processes can't be solved but rather must be improved through systematic examination and assessment over time. To be clear, this approach is in stark contrast to Taylor and scientific management's use of time and motion studies to maximize the efficiencies of specific, discrete tasks in isolation. Continuous systems improvement requires a cyclical approach, and Deming proposes the following four-step cycle:

- *Plan*—Examine the process, and determine what limits exist and what changes might improve it. Doing so likely requires convening a team of sufficient diversity to minimize unintended consequences. The sorts of questions a quality improvement team may ask include the following: What happened? Who did it? How long will it take to fix the problem? More fruitful systems questions might include the following: What are possible system causes of the problem? What (specifically) are we trying to accomplish? How will we know that a change is an improvement?
- *Do*—This stage is focused on preliminary implementation of process changes, though the Shewhart cycle conceives of this stage in a fairly broad way of reducing the likelihood of ill-conceived or underdeveloped actions. Deming suggests that organizations should seek out existing data that can answer the systems or processes questions developed in the plan step. In the absence of such data, Deming suggests carrying out tests, preferably on a small scale.
- *Check or Study*—This stage entails methodically observing the effects of the changes or tests that have been implemented. When organizations examine the results of changes for improvement, a common practice is to observe day-to-day or month-to-month (such as point-to-point) differences based on the use of objective data, which indicate the extent to which change has taken place.
- *Act*—The scientific management approach tends to assume that when we are satisfied with the initial results of a change, further questions about it are unnecessary; the problem is "fixed." Within the PDCA cycle, after the organization studies the data collected from

the change or do stage, the organization must then consider what actions should be taken next. The process doesn't end. Depending on what we learn from ongoing analysis of the data, the organization can determine what is needed to sustain existing improvements and determine how those changes interact with the larger, or other, organizational systems.

Although Deming and Juran took TQM techniques to the Japanese industry in the 1960s and 1970s, it wasn't until Japan emerged as a real threat to US manufacturing dominance that it gained any traction in American firms. By the late 1980s, with the creation of the US Federal Quality Institute, the Baldridge Award for Quality, and later agency level units, such as the Total Quality Leadership Office in the Department of the Navy, TQM practices made their way into the public sector. The success of these initiatives have admittedly been mixed, as there is some indication that the limits of this success may be more political than conceptual or structural.[51, 52] The debates about TQM success aside, it is clear that quality processes, grounded in systems assumptions, have evolved in influential ways and continue to be influential in the form of programs, such as Six Sigma, which emerged from the same traditions and assumptions.

Case 6.2

Current Expressions: Total Quality Management and Local Government

The experience of the Columbus Consolidated Government is a recent example of how the practices and approaches of TQM continue to be relevant to the success of public organizations.[53] The Columbus, Georgia, Consolidated Government was created in 1971 by merging the activities and agencies of the City of Columbus with Muscogee County. The merger, no small feat itself, combined forty-four previously existing departments into twenty-two agencies and departments comprised of 2,700 employees, providing services to a population of nearly 200,000 citizens in 2005. Like all municipal governments, the Columbus Consolidated Government faced pressures to maintain and even expand essential services, as well as desired amenities to residents. These service expansions and cost containment pressures were compounded by the fact that the municipality had been working under a freeze in property taxes, which had been in place since the early 1980s. Beginning in the late 1990s, in response to both fiscal pressures and a court case focused on property tax structures, the city manager developed a quality management approach intended to help balance and respond to these pressures.

The system created includes a system of teams, including an oversight group tasked with sustaining and coordinating the vision of the initiative, a group of quality tool trainers who provided support and resources drawn directly on Deming's work and materials, and finally a range of project teams who first received training in quality techniques, including the plan-do-study-act (PDSA) cycle. They were then tasked to operationalize both the quality vision and approaches within various project areas. In addition to the PDSA cycle, all of the quality teams received training in and utilized other quality tools and techniques, including statistical control charts, cause and effect diagrams, run charts, systemic diagrams, and more.

An analysis of this particular case reveals both the promise and the challenges of TQM applications in the public sector. Lisa McNary notes that a major impetus of TQM—and more recently, Six Sigma initiatives—is their capacity to recognize significant cost savings. While reduced costs are an outcome that public and nonprofit agencies may well benefit from, the underlying benefit of system and quality approaches is the possibility of increasing the efficiency and effectiveness by making systems and processes leaner. This emphasis may miss or obscure other benefits of a quality approach, which is the potential for the resolution of citizen and employee problems. Given that the dollar savings for such initiatives in the public and nonprofit world are likely to be smaller, the benefit then is the potential impact on citizens and clients—that is, people rather than the bottom line. A further potential outcome of the adoption of systems and TQM approaches is a greater recognition and responsiveness to the complexity of organizational systems and organizational behaviors that account for and respond to that complexity. This is expressed in shifting understandings of nonlinear communications within and across units. It also appears as the potential for and responses to unintended consequences and ultimately the improvement of system performance.

Systems Theory: Conclusion

Although there are other specific organization theories that flow out of Bertalanffy's early thinking about systems, TQM and learning organization approaches are two of the most well-known, influential, and usable as administrators consider how to manage groups. One of the central features of these two, as well as many other systems approaches, is that they fundamentally understand human behavior as being intimately interconnected with others' behavior, as well as being hitched to nonhuman structures. From that starting assumption, all fruitful courses of action must give primary consideration to the interaction of the various elements of the system over narrower interpretations of human motivation and intentionality. Systems approaches to understanding and shaping these interactive dynamics, even with the two interrelated theories described here, run the gamut from harder, more technical approaches, such as statistical quality control within manufacturing firms, to softer more normative approaches used in collective problem solving efforts.[54] Given the recurrent attention given to these approaches both in the literature and practice, systems thinking is likely to be influential well into the future.

Reflection Questions

What are the strengths and weaknesses of TQM in governance organizations?

How does the move from production or manufacturing organizations to service organizations change or affect the implementation of TQM techniques?

Organizational Culture Theories

We briefly discussed organization culture in Chapter 4. There, we described the link between organizational culture and broader social culture, as well as the extent to which the latter shapes and informs the former. Organization theorists, such as William Ouchi, have used this aspect of literature to conduct cross-cultural or cross-national analyses of organizations to identify elements of social culture that may filter into and affect organization culture and performance.[55]

Here, we want to dig deeper into organization culture, a concept we all have some intuitive sense of but that tends to be a bit slippery when examined very closely. To paraphrase Supreme Court justice Potter Stewart, organization culture is hard to define, but we know it when we experience it.

One way of thinking about organization culture is to understand it as the patterned, stable expression of an organization's values, norms, working language, systems, symbols, and beliefs seen in the behavior of organizational members. Edgar Schein describes organization culture as the following:

> A pattern of shared basic assumptions invented, discovered, or developed by a given group as it learns to cope with its problems of external adaptation and internal integration that have worked well enough to be considered valid and therefore, to be taught to new members as the correct way to perceive, think and feel in relation to those problems.[56]

For our examination of culture, we will follow Linda Smircich's distinction between culture as something an organization is and something it has.[57] In focusing on the latter, culture as something that an organization has, we can tease out some of the functional aspects of culture, or those aspects that impact the performance of organizations and that can be affected so as to improve that performance.

Assumptions

The assumptions that underpin theories of organization culture differ from nearly all of those that we've examined thus far in Part II. Neal Ashkanasy, Celeste Wilderom, and Mark Peterson suggest that theories of organization culture fall into three ontological bodies, each of which work from slightly different sets of assumptions.[58] The first body of work operates from what can be described as a *structural realist* perspective, under which organizations are themselves structures—collections of stable patterns of behavior—that have a particular culture and climate associated with it. These structures operate but can be understood as being separate from the individuals in the organization. In this view, as we described in our discussion of structural functionalism in Chapter 4, culture is assumed to be largely independent of the members of the organization, and its presence serves or meets specific and particular ends or functions. So long as the structure continues to meet those needs or ends, it is likely to remain in place and operative.

A second ontology, one that is more *constructivist* in character, understands culture relative to the regularity of certain kinds of events and activities and defines culture based on the way stakeholders of the organization group these events together into coherent narratives representing the character or culture of the organization. Interpretations of experience based on this model of organization culture are crafted to explain and relate to these regularities. The relationship between patterns and interpretations becomes the core of the organization's culture. The expressions of these relationships can take more or less concrete forms in the organization and may be found in actual objects such as historical relics that express or make the culture manifest as well as less tangible elements of the organization such as values or belief sets.

Ashkanasy and his colleagues describe one further ontological approach to organization culture, which assumes culture and in fact organizations themselves to be *linguistic creations or contrivances* that serve as heuristics, or mental models that help us think about and make sense of the word and our place in it. Events and experiences, even encounters of material policies and procedures, are made meaningful or ignored based on how they are found to be useful or helpful by any given party or stakeholder within the organization. As such, culture shapes our understanding of the world, and that understanding then informs our behavior.

We will examine particular models of organization culture and their implications for administration further in the following pages, but for the moment, what is important is a recognition that what links all three of these ontological views—even the structuralist view—is a far more constructivist view of organizational reality than the theories we've discussed to this point in Part II. To be sure, culture can have discernable, possibly physical, and even measurable attributes. Nevertheless, it is created and maintained within and among those who are connected to the organization. Organization culture both reflects and is reflected in the formal and informal structures of the organization itself. It is malleable yet astonishingly stable and robust. These characteristics make organization culture both valuable and challenging to administrators.

Attributes of Organization Culture

Harrison Trice and Janice Beyer provide a conceptual model that is useful in order to operationalize organization culture into recognizable and actionable attributes.[59] They distinguish between the substance of culture and cultural forms. The substance of culture includes the values and beliefs held by members of the organization, whereas the forms are the observable aspects or expressions of that culture.

Values and Beliefs

There are any number of models of organization culture, each of which attempts to identify and organize the critical variables or indicators that comprise, more or less, a comprehensive picture of culture. The challenge, of course, is that while culture is a fairly compelling organizational and social concept, it's never actually present. What is present are the indicators, expressions, and consequences of culture, which means that when we attempt to understand culture, we are left having to do it indirectly—we have to look at those indicators, expressions, and consequences and infer what they reveal to us about the nature and function of culture. Moreover, while there are clear and real residuals or artifacts of culture, that culture exists and is expressed in the beliefs, values, and behaviors of organizational stakeholders. In this way, organization culture is socially constructed.

Despite these challenges—and the heterodox character of resulting theories of organization—there are some commonalities among these theories. One is the presence and importance of shared values and beliefs. Charles O'Reilly, Jennifer Chatman, and David Caldwell develop an organizational profile model that includes seven metrics that, in total, express the organization's culture.[60] Underlying these measures or metrics and what allows one culture to be distinguished from another are the values that are established and reinforced within the organization. The relation and parity between an employee's values and those of the organization then serve as the basis of understanding employee behavior, including longevity in the organization. Johnson's cultural web model describes a paradigm, or an underlying, shared sense of what the organization is about, specifically including its values.[61]

Schien's treatment of values within his model is perhaps most explicit in the description of values. For Schein, these aspects of culture are expressed in two distinct forms. First, espoused values include the stated strategies, goals, and philosophies of an organization. The espoused values of a group are the means of articulating what "ought to be as distinct from what is."[62] However, Schein argues that simply articulating a set of values is insufficient. It is not until the values of an organization are challenged under the pressures of the organization's operating world that they are found to really work or reflect what is true for the organization and its members. In this way, espoused values bring the group a measure of success in solving its problems.

Schein also recognizes a second, deeper expression of values and beliefs, which he describes as *underlying assumptions*. In simplest terms, these underlying assumptions are taken-for-granted assumptions about the way things are—the nature of the organization's reality. As assumptions, they are often held beyond awareness, below the level of consciousness, and provide cognitive stability for the members of an organization. Because they are held below the level of consciousness and reflect beliefs about the nature of organizational reality, and because underlying assumptions are taken for granted and are generally viewed as nonnegotiable, any attempt to challenge or confront, let alone change, a group's underlying assumptions creates strong resistance and potentially destabilizes the shared sense of reality that supports functionality in the organization. Leaders trying to change organizational culture must understand this point. It is here where the intrinsic power of culture resides.

Schein notes that "in analyzing values one must discriminate carefully between those that are congruent with underlying assumptions and those that are, in effect, either rationalizations or only aspirations for the future."[63] He recognizes that while there is likely to be continuity between espoused values and underlying assumptions, it is also possible that espoused values may be more easily challenged and may or may not reflect underlying assumptions. In other words, values may reflect what a group will say in a given scenario, but underlying assumptions operate in what they will do.

Structural and Behavioral Expressions of Culture

If values and beliefs are at the core of organizational culture and those values and beliefs cannot be seen or measured in and of themselves, then describing and defining indicators of those beliefs and values is critical to any useful theory of organizational culture. Here again, organization theories of culture are heterodox, but there are some commonalities.

Much of the classical and structural study of organizations that we have studied so far understands formal structures of authority and control as being established rationally to maximize the efficiency of the organization. While a cultural analysis doesn't deny or preclude the possibility of formal, intentionally crafted structures, it also reveals how formal, and especially informal, structures of control and distribution of power, can also even simultaneously be expressions of culture. Whether considering the acquisition and distribution of power; the determination of who makes decisions and how widely power is distributed; or the practices associated with monitoring, compliance, and feedback of rules, procedures, and other control systems, cultural researchers have found that structures of control and authority reflect evolving and developing belief and value systems, as well as rationalized structural decisions.[64, 65, 66] It's also important to recognize that these structural expressions operate in systems that are core to the functional capacity of the organization, decision structures, distribution of authority, and so on, as well as structures that have greater symbolic meaning but less productive value such as designated parking spaces, closed offices, and access to executive washrooms.

Beyond structural expressions, this approach to organizational analysis is also a behavioral indication of culture. For example, a number of cultural theorists note that rituals and routines adopted by the organization may reflect its culture as much or more than it does efficiency or effectiveness maximizing strategies. Such rites, rituals, or routines, or the collective behaviors, including myths and stories, give meaning and understanding to collective processes, such as management meetings, rewards distribution, or celebratory ceremonies. Moreover, these behaviors can also find expression in organizational artifacts. Artifacts that reveal culture include visual elements such as logos and recurrent imagery but also in more operational elements of organizational activity, such as policy and procedures manuals, performance evaluations, and board reports.[67] These artifacts have instrumental value but also express and exemplify aspects of culture.[68]

Techniques and Practices

Several areas of agreement emerge out of the breadth of work on organization culture. One is that an organization's culture can significantly influence the effectiveness of the organization in positive or negative ways. A second common issue that is consistent and is present in the research is that culture happens. All organizations have a culture, and while that culture can take many forms and have varying degrees of impact on the organization's performance, mere presence of a culture is a given. The question for administrators is, therefore, how can culture be actively and intentionally managed so as to increase the likelihood that it helps rather than hinders effectiveness? One approach for responding to this question is to frame it as a three-part approach, entailing first the measurement or assessment of culture, then the management or maintenance of culture, and finally strategies for cultural change when necessary.

Measurement

Part of measurement is selecting a model or theory of culture, articulating and operationalizing the variables in the model, and then examining the indicators as they are found in practice in the organization. Drawing on Schein's model, this would suggest examining observable attributes of culture, primarily at the level of artifacts, but potentially including espoused values, as expressed in mission and value statements as well.

The objective here is to identify facets of the organization and its culture that can be first measured, and in turn managed and changed, with a focus on assessable organizational variables, such as skills, strategy, structure, systems, style, and staff.[69] Smircich suggests that inquiry into culture should be focused on learning the consensus meanings developed by members of the organization in relationship to their experiences. This allows for a description of the thematic relationships, or attributes of culture, expressed in this meaning system to be identified.[70] Charles Handy, in his exploration of organizational phenomena that contribute to both the successes and downfalls of business organizations, identifies four cultures—*power, role, task,* and *person*—which provide an operationalized framework for assessing and understanding organizational culture.[71] Each of these cultures implies operationalized expressions of power distribution and function, role structures, and so forth.

Smircich develops an approach to studying organization culture driven by three forms of data collection and corresponding evidence.[72] These research strategies include direct observation of the organization and members' behaviors, reports directly from informants, and the researcher's direct participation in the organization. Other researchers suggest adding an examination of artifacts, such as reports, policies, and procedures. In total, these approaches provide researchers not with direct access to the culture of the organization but allow the researcher to infer something about the culture that is not directly measurable in and of itself.

Management

With a more systematic and structured assessment of the organization's culture in place, it's then possible to give explicit attention to the management of that culture in a way that will support the maintenance of a functional culture. Drawing on a wide range of cultural theorists, Lesley Willcoxson and Bruce Millett suggest that there is a range of organizational features that can be the focus of efforts to simultaneously manage performance and culture.[73] These features include the following:

- recruitment, selection, and replacement processes
- socialization practices
- performance management and rewards systems
- leadership and modeling approaches
- participation and engagement strategies
- interpersonal communications patterns
- formal structures, including policies, procedures, and resource allocation decisions

This list should make two things about culture and performance clear. One conceptual observation is that culture is its own measurable organizational attribute. It exists in and is expressed through other aspects of the organization. There is an inherent connection between functions and culture—that is, that culture, as understood via shared values and assumptions, is expressed in these and possibly other functional elements of organizations. This leads to the second observation, which is that the management of culture is not separate from management of instrumental processes—the two occur together. It may be possible to manage processes without attention to culture, but the reverse is not true. It's not possible to manage culture without giving attention to functional processes.

Change

The question and possibility of cultural change is an open one in the literature. There are theorists who suggest that some level of natural or evolutionary change does occur in culture; it cannot be consciously manipulated or changed.[74] Our approach, supported by empirical research conducted by Kurt Lewin and others, follows the line of thinking that culture can change. The challenge of doing so is not insignificant in that, for example, behavioral aspects of culture can become habitualized among most or all members of an organization. Anyone who has endeavored to change their own habits will understand the difficulty in changing the habitual behaviors of one person, let alone an entire organization. Nevertheless, we take the position that given strategically selected, sustained efforts, cultures can be changed for the better.

Case 6.3

Current Expressions: Organizational Culture and Management at Continental Airlines

In the mid-1990s, Continental Airlines was one of the lowest performing companies in the industry. In 1994, Continental lost some $200 million and had among the most demoralized workforces in the industry and an on-time rating that was the worst of the eleven carriers rated by the US Department of Transportation (DOT). It was into this setting that CEO Gordon Bethune and COO Greg Brenneman stepped and within two years were able to move the organization not only to financially break even but in 1996 Continental Airlines turned a profit of more than a half-billion dollars. This dramatic turnaround can partly be attributed to a very intentional and focused strategy to shift the culture of the organization to one that demanded, supported, and achieved high levels of performance across all areas of the organization's activities.[75]

Bethune and Brenneman adopted a set of strategies that clearly focused on outputs, such as on-time arrivals, as well as outcomes like perceptions of customer service but supported these efforts with deliberate attention to cultural attributes that supported and hindered change efforts. Such attributes included characteristics of the physical environment, practices, and behaviors codified in policies and procedure manuals, values and norms, myths, symbols, rituals, and ceremonies. In short, their attention to cultural attributes ranged across the expressions of culture described by Edgar Schein in his model of organizational culture.

Among the physical manifestations of culture that Continental addressed, attributes that Schein describes as artifacts, were a variety of changes and updates to both facilities and aircraft. Prior to Bethune and Brenneman's arrival, many of Continental's planes retained the color schemes from older airlines that Continental had acquired, with the Continental logo painted over the top of the prior scheme. When on-board seats needed to be changed, replacements were pulled from inventory or other planes, regardless of whether colors matched. The result was a sense of discontinuity and low quality. Some of the most obvious changes the new management team made included repainting planes and replacing carpets and furniture in boarding areas in a way that was consistent with and emphasized the organization's change in focus and strategy. Other artifacts that received attention were closer to the behavioral experience and processes within the organization. Perhaps the most famous of these was the replacement of a nearly 800-page human resources policy manual with a newer, streamlined 80-page document. What was most striking, however, was not just the replacement of one for the other but that the head of human resources collected several copies of the old manual and along with other members of the corporate leadership team burned those copies at an organizational celebration at the airline's headquarters as a clear sign that the sort of bureaucratic ponderousness embodied in the old manual had to go.

This powerful symbolic act also indicates that the organization gave conscious attention to making changes to the espoused values of the organization as well. The shift from rule-bound, bureaucratic approaches to a customer service oriented set of values was also embodied in a range of new messages and operating "mantras" about where the organization was going in concrete terms. These value statements were then expressed in corresponding practices from gain sharing or revenue sharing, to increases in employee discretion for problem solving and, importantly, in shifts to communication practices that placed greater emphasis on face-to-face interactions over asynchronous, and nonverbal communications.

Although operationalizing underlying beliefs—Schein's lowest level of organizational culture—is difficult, there are indications that Continental's underlying beliefs did undergo change. The pervasive adoption of new practices, language, perceptions, and orientation from top managers through mid-level administrators to, and including, line workers suggests the development of a shared understanding of what the organization was working toward and how it was doing so. This assessment is reinforced by the fact that there was substantial consistency in practice and perception across the organization and that this consistency occurred within an environment that granted employees greater discretion within a climate of fewer bureaucratic rules.

Organizational Culture: Conclusion

As we've noted before, organizational culture is a concept that we have an intuitive feel for. We recognize that different organizations "feel" different and that those differences play out in variations in expectations, practices, and in other ways as well. Organizational culture exists in all organizations, and at the very least, we understand that as administrators we ignore the presence of that culture at our peril. We can either hope that the culture of our organization develops in a way that happens to be functional and contributes in positive ways to operations and performance, or we can purposefully give attention to developing that culture in a way that helps the organization be effective. What should also be clear at this point is that Edgar Schein and other scholars of OT have developed operational models of organizational culture that allow us to move beyond our intuitional sense of culture and to systematically assess and manage that culture in a way that benefits the organization.

Reflection Questions

How would you define organizational culture for a new employee so that they would understand what it is and why it is important?

What strategies would you use to manage organizational culture in ways that improve group dynamics?

Foreshadows of Postmodernism

One of the most crucial findings from the Hawthorne experiments is that groups are complex. Groups can, and often should, be understood as their own unit of analysis. A group's behavior is different and more complicated than a set of individuals acting in parallel to one another. As a result, managing group dynamics requires different models than does managing individual behavior. The theories presented in this chapter embody a variety of different assumptions regarding cause and effect relationships, and the extent to which the social and organizational world is socially constructed. We want to conclude this chapter with a brief overview of one further theory of group dynamics that provides a bit of a preview of the assumptions and corresponding approaches to organizational administration that we'll be describing in Part III of this book.

In the mid-1990s, organizational psychologist Karl Weick published two different pieces in which he describes the processes of *sensemaking* and their consequences for understanding and operationalizing it in contemporary organizations. In the longer, book-length treatment, Weick presents an extensive depiction of the theory, its components, rationale, and operation.[76] In the shorter article-length piece, he applies the theory to a case study in which the capacity of an organizational group collapses with dire consequences.[77] This analysis not only presents an assessment of the events grounded in Weick's theory but it also suggests a series of approaches that can be adopted by administrators that enhance the robustness of organizations and make them less susceptible to collapses in sensemaking. Weick's work is presented here not only because of its contribution to organizational analysis and practice but also because it serves as a conceptual bridge to postmodern and poststructural theories that we'll explore in Part III.

Weick and the De-centered Self

In early August of 1949, a lightning-caused fire flared in the mountains not too far outside of Helena, Montana. Shortly after the fire was reported, a group of smoke jumpers, aircraft deployed fast-response firefighters, were sent into the area to suppress and control the fire. In the end, the fire overran the crew, killing thirteen men.

Weick's analysis of the events and decisions that led to the Mann Gulch disaster is generally understood as being interpretivist in its orientation.[78] The meaning of social situations is primarily a matter of subjective interpretation, or interpretation from the perspective and understandings of those in that setting. In this regard, social settings, like organizations, are constructed by those in and around the setting. Social structures—stable repeating patterns of behavior—like institutional norms, rituals, culture, and so forth, are created by group behavior and perception, and those within those settings are simultaneously created by those structures. For Weick and other interpretivists, those inside such structural settings can feel trapped or constrained, but recognizing those structures and viewing them from a new perspective can lead to new options and more effective courses of action.

In the case of Mann Gulch, members of the unit adopted roles and interpretations of their environment that were consistent with a particular way of making sense of the world but that were inconsistent with the empirical evidence available to them when assessing and confronting the fire. More specifically, they misread a series of clues, as well as disconnects and miscommunication between the formal and informal leaders of the unit, that led to a misunderstanding of the fire's behavior and ultimately the deaths of all but a few of the crew members. Weick argues that these misinterpretations and misunderstandings could have been averted based on shifts in group perceptions and group processes. Specifically, the adoption of approaches including virtual role systems and an attitude of wisdom rather than presumed knowledge, could have led to a different set of structural relations, as well as a different approach to data collection and decision making.

In terms of the theories and approaches to group dynamics discussed in this chapter, Weick's notion of group structures and the processes of sensemaking share assumptions

Reflection Question

If, according to Weick, the meaning of a social situation is primarily a matter of interpretation, and if perception is often seen as reality, what steps can administrators take to come to understand employee behavior in their organizations and then to manage that behavior in productive ways?

with both systems thinking and organizational culture. Further, the implications of Weick's thinking prefigures the postmodern notion of the *decentered self,* or the idea that the autonomous, largely rational subject from classical management theory isn't the most useful way of understanding social and group dynamics. Instead, the complexity of group dynamics decenters, or moves the individual out of the center of analysis, and instead emphasizes the structures (stable repeating patterns of behavior) as the center of social and organization analysis. Taken to its logical extreme, the reasoning of this line of thought leads to critical postmodern positions, like that of Jacques Derrida, who suggests that the subject or individual no longer has utility for us as an analytical concept, or that of Bruno Latour and actor network theory, which suggests that the individual is so tightly and intimately embedded in a network of social and technological relations that it is more useful to think of ourselves as cyborgs than as autonomous individuals. While these logical extremes seem just that—extreme—our point in this section is to reveal that there is a continuum of thinking that emerges with the theories of group dynamics in this chapter, which can be traced in incremental, logical steps to the post-traditional ideas we'll explore later.

Summary and Conclusions

SINCE AT LEAST THE HAWTHORN EXPERIMENTS, it's become clear that administrators who want to make positive contributions to their units' and organizations' performance, they have to pay attention to the formation and behaviors of these groups as groups. Organizational performance is not just the sum of the performance of the individuals that comprise it but that performance is at least, if not more, a factor of the interaction within and among groups. As such, the three overarching theories presented here—HRTs, systems theories, and cultural theories—represent a set of sophisticated, as well as actionable, theories for understanding and shaping group dynamics.

Models and corresponding approaches derived from HRT are among the most diverse and most extensively studied within the field of OT. Structures and processes of control, models of leadership, and contingency factors, such as size, are demonstrably and undoubtedly present in contemporary public organizations. There is also reason to believe that many of the factors explored by human relations researchers can be manipulated to positively contribute to organizational performance.

Similarly, systems and learning organization approaches recognize the extent to which individual performance is constrained by the organizational systems within which they operate. The potential for expressing some administrative discretion aside, systems and learning approaches highlight the degree to which our perceptions, and thereby our behaviors, are constrained by the systems we work in, as well as how those systems support some courses of action and preclude others.

Last among the group theories explored here, organizational culture is something we all have a sense of but often find difficult to articulate in a coherent way, let alone conceptualize in a way that administrators can actively and intentionally focus their actions on. Schein, Srivastava, and other cultural theorists have not only presented models that operationalize our intuitive sense of shared values and understandings but do so in a way that present potential courses of action focused on organizational manifestations or artifacts; shared and espoused values; and more subtle, underlying beliefs that can be shaped in a way that augments group—and therefore organizational—performance.

What we are left with is not necessarily an alternative to managing individual behavior as a means of enhancing organizational performance but instead a concurrent yet potentially paradoxical level of analysis and corresponding approaches. It's not so much that management and organization theorists who focus on individuals are wrong; as we noted at the outset of the book, all of these theories are wrong at some level and all have something to contribute to our thinking and responses to problems. Instead, it's more useful to realize that theories of group dynamics answer some organizational performance questions in a different way and starting from different assumptions, thereby yielding different strategies. It's also true that theories of group dynamics can answer different questions than those explored by theories of individual behavior. This returns us again to David Farmer's notion of epistemic pluralism and the value of conceptual and reflective flexibility. It may be that doing the same thing over and over again is a sign of insanity, or it may be a sign of tenacity. Knowing the difference may emerge out of the capacity for epistemic pluralism. ■

Discussion Questions

1. Describe three factors that you think have the most impact in group dynamics. What techniques can administrators use to effectively manage these factors?

2. Think back to the differences between public and private organizations as described by Graham Allison and Paul Appleby in Chapter 3. Do the factors affecting group dynamics play out differently in public organizations? Why?

3. If organizational performance is the sum of the performance of individuals within an organization, what is the benefit of individual performance evaluations? How might administrators usefully balance individual and group or system approaches?

Notes

1. Dorwin Cartwright and Alvin Zander, *Group Dynamics: Research and Theory,* 3rd ed. (New York: Harper & Row, 1968), 19.
2. Dorwin Cartwright in *Readings in Organization Theory: A Behavioral Approach,* ed. Walter Hill and Douglas Egan (Boston: Allyn & Bacon, 1967).
3. Gary Dessler, *Organization Theory: Integrating Structure and Behaviour,* 2nd ed. (Upper Saddle River, NJ: Prentice Hall, 1986).
4. Ibid., 385.
5. Ibid., 374.
6. Eric L. Trist, "The Evolution of Socio-Technical Systems: A Conceptual Framework and an Action Research Program" (Occasional Paper No. 2, Ontario Quality of Working Life Centre, Toronto, 1982).
7. Charles Perrow, *Complex Organizations: A Critical Essay* (New York: McGraw-Hill, 1986).
8. Elton Mayo and George Lombard, *Teamwork and Labor Turnover in the Aircraft Industry of Southern California* (Business Research Report #32, Graduate School of Business Administration, Harvard University, Boston, 1944).

9. Edward A. Shils and Morris Janowitz, "Cohesion and Disintegration in the Wehrmacht in World War II," in *Readings in Organization Theory: A Behavioral Approach,* ed. Walter Hill and Douglas Egan (Boston: Allyn & Bacon, 1967).

10. Stephen Robbins, *Essentials of Organization Behavior* (Englewood Cliffs, NJ: Prentice Hall, 1992).

11. Robert R. Blake and Jane Mouton, "Reactions to Intergroup Conflict Under Win-Lose Conditions," *Management Science* (1961): 432.

12. Robbins, *Essentials of Organization Behavior.*

13. John W. Tibaut, "An Experimental Study of Cohesiveness of Underprivileged Groups," *Human Relations* 3 (1950): 258–278.

14. Robert R. Blake, Herbert A. Shepard, and Jane S. Mouton, "Foundations and Dynamics of Intergroup Behavior," in *Managing Intergroup Conflict in Industry* (Houston, TX: Gulf Publishing Company, 1964).

15. In considering different leadership style options and choices, it's worth thinking back to some of the factors that contribute or inhibit individual motivation and behavior as described in Chapter 5.

16. Arnold Tannenbaum, *Control in Organizations* (New York: McGraw-Hill, 1968).

17. Ibid., 237.

18. Although he is often thought of as being an advocate of hierarchy and the control structures inherent in bureaucracy, Weber too recognized the divisive nature of bureaucratic control systems.

19. Richard Hackman, "Group Influences on Individuals," in *Handbook of Industrial and Organizational Psychology,* ed. Marvin Dunnette (New York: Rand McNally College Publishing, 1976), 1494–1497.

20. A. Paul Hare, *Handbook of Small Group Research* (New York: Free Press, 1962).

21. Charles R. Walker and Robert H. Guest, *The Man on the Assembly Line* (Cambridge, MA: Harvard University Press, 1952).

22. Trist, "The Evolution of Socio-Technical Systems."

23. Obviously, group size has an influence on the number and character of social relationships within a group. We have chosen to frame size as a structural, contingent factor because doing so is consistent with Gulick's examination of unit size and task diversity as structural factors related to span of control.

24. Elliot Aronson and Judson Mills, "The Effects of Severity of Initiation on Liking for a Group," *Journal of Abnormal and Social Psychology* 59 (1959): 177–181.

25. Edward Shils and Morris Janowitz, "Cohesion and Disintegration in the Vehrmacht in World War II," *Public Opinion Quarterly* 12, no. 2 (1948).

26. The notion of disintegration is particularly apt here in that cohesiveness and integration are closely connected and contribute to functionality of groups. Disintegration is not merely a collapse or failure of group performance; it is more accurately the pulling apart or disaggregation of the organization or unit, leading to diminishing or failed performance.

27. William A. Scott, *Values and Organizations* (Chicago: Rand McNally, 1965).

28. Bertram H. Raven and Jan Rietsema, "The Effect of Varied Clarity of Group Goal and Group Path upon the Individual and His Relation to His Group," *Human Relations* 10 (1957): 29–44.

29. J. R. P. French Jr. "The Disruption and Cohesion of Groups," *Journal of Abnormal and Social Psychology* 36 (1941): 361–377.

30. John W. Thibaut, "An Experimental Study of Cohesiveness of Underprivileged Groups," *Human Relations* 3 (1950): 251–278.

31. Irving Janis, *Groupthink: A Psychological Study of Policy Decisions and Fiascoes* (Boston: Houghton Mifflin Company, 1982).

32. Robbins, *Essentials of Organization Behavior.*

33. Cartwright and Zander, *Group Dynamics,* 3rd ed.

34. Ibid., 302–304.

35. Klaus Bartolke, Walter Eschweiler, Peter Flechsemberger, and Arnold Tannenbaum, "Worker Participation and the Distribution of Control as Perceived by Members of Ten German Companies," *Administrative Sciences Quarterly* 27, no. 3 (September 1982): 380–397.

36. Walker and Guest, *The Man on the Assembly Line.*

37. Hackman, "Group Influences on Individuals."

38. Edwin Thomas and Clinton Fink, "Effects of Group Size," *Psychological Bulletin* 60, no. 4 (1963): 371–384. Stanley Seashore, *Group Cohesiveness in the Industrial Work Group*, 5th ed. (Ann Arbor: University of Michigan Press, 1954), 90–95.

39. Rajiv Kohli and William J. Kettinger, "Informing the Clan: Controlling Physicians' Costs and Outcomes," *MIS Quarterly* 28, no. 3 (September 2004): 363–394.

40. *Action research* is a term used to describe a broad range of scholarly and practical approaches to studying and responding to organizational or community problems. All approaches to action research share some common features including the direct and immediate application of the findings back into the situation as a means of "fixing" the problem at hand. Action research also tends to have an emancipatory or empowering character in that it assumes that both the information necessary to understand and to fix a problem reside among those in the midst of the setting, not with outside experts. In this way, action research shares some common ground with Tannenbaum's notion that knowledge like control can be distributed widely around social and organizational settings.

41. Ludwig von Bertalanffy, *General System Theory: Foundations, Development, Applications* (New York: George Braziller, 1968).

42. Daniel Katz and Robert L. Kahn, *The Social Psychology of Organizations* (New York: Wiley, 1966).

43. Eric B. Dent and Stuart P. Umpleby, "Underlying Assumptions of Several Traditions in Systems Theory and Cybernetics," *Cybernetics and Systems '98*, ed. R. Trappl (Vienna: Austrian Society for Cybernetic Studies, 1998), 513–518.

44. J. Eugene Haas and Thomas E. Drabek, *Complex Organizations: A Sociological Perspective* (New York: MacMillan, 1973).

45. Peter M. Senge, *The Fifth Discipline: The Art and Practice of the Learning Organization* (New York: Doubleday, 1990).

46. The parable of the boiled frog suggests that if a frog is thrown into pot of boiling water, it will immediately recognize the threat and jump out. If, on the other hand, it is placed in a cool pot of water and then the temperature is slowly turned up, the frog won't notice that it is in danger until it's too late to escape. The parable reveals that we often don't recognize incremental changes until the negative consequences are quite significant.

47. Senge, *The Fifth Discipline*, 17–26.

48. Ibid., 7–10.

49. Ibid.

50. Ibid., 241.

51. George A. Boyne and Richard M. Walker, "Total Quality Management and Performance: An Evaluation of the Evidence and Lessons for Research on Public Organizations," *Public Performance and Management Review* 26, no. 2 (2002): 111–131.

52. Orion White and James Wolf, "Deming's Total Quality Management Movement and the Baskin Robbins Problem, Part I: Is it Time to Go Back to Vanilla?" *Administration and Society* 27, no. 2 (1995); Orion White and James Wolf, "Deming's Total Quality Management Movement and the Baskin Robbins Problem, Part II: Is This Ice Cream American?" *Administration and Society* 27, no. 3 (1995).

53. Lisa D. McNary, "Quality Management in the Public Sector: Applying Lean Concepts to Customer Service in a Consolidated Government Office," *Public Administration Quarterly* 32, no. 2 (Summer 2008) 282–301.

54. See Robert J. David and David Strang, "When Fashion Is Fleeting: Transitory Collective Beliefs and the Dynamics of TQM Consulting," *Academy of Management Journal* 49, no. 2 (2006), 215–233.

55. William G. Ouchi, *Theory Z* (New York: Avon Books, 1981).

56. Edgar Schein, *Organizational Culture and Leadership: A Dynamic Vies* (San Francisco, CA: Jossey-Bass, 1992), 9.

57. Linda Smircich, "Concepts of Culture and Organizational Analysis," *Administrative Science Quarterly* 28 (1983): 39.

58. Neal M. Ashkanasy, Celeste P. M. Wilderom, and Mark F. Peterson, *Handbook of Organizational Culture and Climate* (Thousand Oaks, CA: Sage, 2000), 7.

59. Harrison Trice and Janice Beyer, *The Cultures of Work Organizations* (Upper Saddle River, NJ: Prentice Hall, 1993).

60. Charles A. O'Reilly, Jennifer Chatman, and David F. Caldwell, "People and Organizational Culture: A Profile Comparison Approach to Assessing Person-Organization Fit," *Academy of Management Journal* 34 (1991): 487.

61. Gerry Johnson, "Rethinking Incrementalism," *Strategic Management Journal* 9 (1988): 75–91.

62. Schein, *Organizational Culture and Leadership,* 19.

63. Ibid., 21.

64. Geert Hofstede, *Culture's Consequences: International Differences in Work-Related Values* (Beverly Hills, CA: Sage, 1980); Mauk Mulder, *The Daily Power Game* (Leiden, The Netherlands: Martinus Nijhoff Social Sciences Division, 1977).

65. Johnson, "Rethinking Incrementalism."

66. Terrence E. Deal and Allan A. Kennedy, *Corporate Cultures: The Rites and Rituals of Corporate Life* (Harmondsworth, UK: Penguin Books, 1982).

67. For more on this notion of rites, rituals, myths, and symbols, also see the following: Gazi Islam and Michael Zyphur, "Rituals in Organizations: A Review and Expansion of Current Theory," *Group Organization Management* 34 (2009): 1140–1139.

68. Schein, *Organizational Culture and Leadership*; Johnson, "Rethinking Incrementalism."

69. Tom Peters and Robert H. Waterman, *In Search of Excellence* (Sydney: Harper & Row, 1982).

70. Smircich, "Concepts of Culture."

71. Charles Handy, *Understanding Organizations* (Harmondsworth, UK: Penguin, 1985).

72. Smircich, "Concepts of Culture." See also Linda Smircich, "Studying Organizations as Cultures" in *Beyond Method,* ed. Gareth Morgan (Newbury Park, CA: Sage, 1987), 160–172.

73. Lesley Willcoxson and Bruce Millett, "The Management of Organization Culture," *The Australian Journal of Management and Organizational Behaviour* 3, no. 2 (2000): 91–99.

74. See P. D. Anthony, "The Paradox of the Management of Culture or 'He Who Leads is Lost,'" *Personnel Review* 19, no. 4 (1990): 3–8; Stephen Ackroyd and Peter Crowdy, "Can Culture Be Managed? Working With 'Raw' Material: The Case of the English Slaughtermen," *Personnel Review* 19, no. 5 (1990): 3–13; David Knights and Hugh Willmott, "Organizational Culture as Management Strategy: A Critique and Illustration From the Financial Services Industry," *International Studies of Management and Organization* 17, no. 3 (1987): 40–63; Emmanuel Ogbonna and Lloyd C. Harris, "Organizational Culture: A Ten Year, Two-Phase Study of Change in the UK Food Retailing Sector," *Journal Of Management Studies* 39, no. 5 (2002): 673–706.

75. James M. Higgins and Graig McAllaster, "If You Want Strategic Change, Don't Forget to Change your Cultural Artifacts," *Journal of Change Management* 4, no. 1 (March 2004): 63–73.

76. Karl E. Weick, *Sensemaking in Organizations* (Thousand Oaks, CA: Sage, 1995).

77. Karl E. Weick, "The Collapse of Sensemaking in Organizations: The Mann Gulch Disaster," *Administrative Science Quarterly* 38 (1993): 628–652.

78. Gibson Burrell and Gareth Morgan, *Sociological Paradigms and Organizational Analysis* (Burlington, VT: Ashgate, 1998).

Chapter 7

Affecting Organization Change

The Management Attribute

Think about the following claim: "Every position exists to drive change." How does our perspective about public or nonprofit organizations change when we view them through the lenses of change? There is a paradox, especially in the public sector, wherein organizations simultaneously stay the same yet change. Public organizations are expected to stay true to certain values and traditions, but organizational life is not motionless. Change happens, and healthy organizations are ones that can adapt to changes.

Confucius once said, "What I hear, I forget, what I see, I remember, what I do, I understand." It is not enough to alter practice or action; we must alter behavior, which is action plus intention. To change an organization is to make something different, set a new goal, transform, transition, or strategically innovate in the name of organizational improvement. It is important to talk about change because everyone faces increasingly fragmented, evolving, and complex situations. Public administrators must be aware of the need for change and of various orientations toward reacting and adapting to it.

Change is part of individual and organizational life. It just occurs. Circumstances and attitudes impact the way we adjust to change. Do we see change as an opportunity or a negative event? Is it expected, so we can plan for it, or unexpected, so we cannot?

For purposes of this chapter, we must clarify that there are different kinds of changes: organization-wide versus departmental, strategic, procedural, incremental, sudden, or collaborative directed from above or others. The point of considering types of changes is not to develop an exhaustive or mutually exclusive list that allows for conclusive selection of strategies but rather to recognize that not all change is the same and that the differences may imply variations in change-management approaches. So while organization-wide change may be more about changing things like mission, structure, major processes, technology, partnerships, collaborations, mergers, or totally new administrations—things that impact and transform the way the entire organization works at a fundamental level—process change may focus on procedures for production of goods or services, practices of information dissemination, or methods of decision making. The strategies and approaches to accomplishing organization-wide change are likely to be quite different than managing procedure level change. Distinguishing between types of change enables us to think in more precise ways about what approaches to change are likely to be most effective in various settings.

Sometimes radical changes happen, and then it's about reacting and dealing with the aftermath in effective and well-planned ways. We will touch on that, but we are primarily talking about *planned* or anticipated change at the level of an entire organization. It is important to note that all change is not easy, anticipated, good, or bad. Change can be positive or negative—anticipated or unexpected—but change happens. It is the attitudes about and reactions to change that determine whether we sink or swim.

Organization theory (OT) has evolved over time to reflect changes in focus on the actual change agent. Thinking has gone from the manager as a change agent—reminiscent of Frederick Taylor's scientific management thinking in which change was done *to* individuals and organizations, to people as change agents—to thinking that is evident in work done by Mary Parker Follett and the Hawthorne studies, where change is done *with* individuals.

According to William Bridges, transition is the psychological process that accompanies change. How we adapt to change influences the outcome. Change requires transformation, which involves the following:

- *Ending*—loss of attachments, turf, structure, future, meaning, control
- *Neutral zone*—strategies, temporary policies and procedures and lines of authority in place. Do what is needed to create cohesion; old issues will resurface—don't choke them, be prepared for them. Keep reasons clear and at forefront of people's minds so that anxiety doesn't lead to escape.
- *New beginning*—new idea at heart of change? Who will make decisions? Vision? How? What? When? In what order? How will this fit? Training?[1]

Reactions to change are based either on feelings of threat or seeing the potential benefits of change. For any change, some may like it and some may not. Some want to stick to old habits and may feel threatened by the unknown. Some will anticipate the need for change and connect themselves to the idea proactively. Others might go along with the change rather than openly support it and wait out the settling of the dust before choosing a course. Others might sabotage change, resist, or undermine efforts. Not all resistance is bad either; sometimes it helps us to think about consequences we hadn't previously considered.

Lester Coch and John French, in a 1948 study of transition, found that the degree of participation in a change was directly related to resistance (the more involved, the less resistance).[2] Direct participation, rather than participation by representation, was more effective. They recommend open and ongoing communication in planning and in implementation of change. There is great power in just asking someone what he or she thinks. Let go of personal agendas. If you are the only one who stands to benefit then rethink.

According to John Kotter, a successful model for implementing change (and in some cases reacting to it) is as follows:

- Establish a sense of urgency.
- Create a guiding coalition.

- Develop a vision and a strategy.
- Communicate that vision.
- Empower employees to act.
- Generate short-term wins.
- Consolidate gains and produce more wins.
- Anchor new approaches in the culture.[3]

Among the variables that change theorists view as being critical for transformations to be successful are the following:

- *Training*—Do individuals understand their role? Have they been given clear expectations about their work? Do they have the tools or skills to be successful?
- *Information*—Has information about the change been presented to the individuals in a clear and effective way? Are we expecting them to act on issues without giving them all the information? How much information is too much information, and how much is too little? Significant organizational change may require input from employees because they know the whys and reasons for change before it occurs.
- *Participation*—Why are folks not participating? What would motivate them to participate more? Will engaging them in organizational issues actually increase their participation? If folks have limited amounts of time, what forms of participation would be most valuable to the department or organization? Group participation in planning change reduces their resistance to it, decreases turnover during and after changes, and accelerates relearning curves.
- *Support*—The minute a change is implemented, the gravity of old ways begins to pull against new behaviors. In the beginning, novelty can be an adequate source of energy, but over time a deeper and more sustainable force must be found. Once folks become motivated, how do we keep up the momentum? What can we do to continually support their efforts so they don't lapse into inactivity and disengagement again?

In the following sections we describe four distinct models of organizational change. We do so, as we have done with our examination of other organizational activities, by first examining the assumptions associated with the approach to change. Our examination of the assumptions imbedded in each approach serves two purposes. First, the theoretical assumptions allow us to demonstrate the explicit and implicit connections between these models and the theories we outlined in Part I. Second, by outlining the assumptions, we give you the opportunity to explore the extent of their validity, and the implications of that assessment on practice. In other words, if the assumptions on which an approach is grounded are valid, the likelihood of success would seem greater. If, however, the assumptions are dubious, at least in some contexts, then the efficacy of the approach bears closer examination. Beyond the outline of the assumptions of each approach, we also describe the core techniques advocated within each model as a way of providing a preliminary map of how administrators can implement these approaches in their current or future organizations. Finally, we conclude our exploration of each model with a description of expressions of the model in contemporary public affairs settings. We've attempted to identify and describe real, contemporary organizations that have intentionally or implicitly adopted the techniques we've described, and we have endeavored to describe these settings so that you can critically and contextually consider their use.

Reflection Question

What are some of the consequences of moving from an assumption that organizations are generally or typically static to an assumption that organizations are characterized by constant, ongoing change?

Key Theories of Change

As was the case with our approach to earlier management issues, there are many models and theories of organizational change. In the following pages, we examine four different models that are largely distinct from one another: business process reengineering (BPR), the Burke-Litwin change model, action research oriented organization development approaches, and chaos and complexity theory approaches to change. These are not the only theories of organizational change to be found in the literature, but they are among the most widely considered in practical and academic treatments of change, are used and considered widely, and offer interesting analytic and action possibilities.

One thing you should look for and give consideration to as you examine each of these models is the extent to which these models can be differentiated from one another both conceptually and in practice. As we have done in the previous chapters in Part II, we begin our examination of each model with a description of the assumptions, epistemological and ontological, that underpin each. We then present and examine some of the specific approaches and techniques that can be adopted by managers and administrators and conclude our treatment of each with a description of how these models appear.

Business Process Reengineering

BPR is a change management and performance improvement strategy, originally developed in the early 1990s, that focuses on the examination and redesign of work flows and work processes. BPR is intended to help organizations fundamentally rethink how they do their work as a means of substantially improving performance in areas of customer service, expenditures, or resource use as a means of becoming more competitive and more efficient.

In 1990, Michael Hammer authored an article in the *Harvard Business Review* titled "Reengineering Work: Don't Automate, Obliterate." A management and information technology (IT) consultant, Hammer argues that the emerge of powerful information management technologies afforded organizations the opportunity not to just speed up existing work processes but to radically rethink the way work was done. In his words, the idea was to "use the power of modern information technology to radically redesign our business processes in order to achieve dramatic improvements in their performance."[4] At its core, BPR entailed identifying and breaking away from fundamental assumptions and rules that have guided operations overtime. Anything less than an examination of these assumptions and the associated technologies (processes by which inputs are turned into outputs)—many of which had been in place for decades, if not to the Industrial Revolution itself, without being evaluated—was merely a "rearrangement of the deck chairs on the Titanic."

Within a few years of this first reengineering article, Hammer in collaboration with James Champy, Thomas Davenport, and others had built an extensive model for changing the core working processes of organizations not only in the United States but around the world.[5, 6] At the same time BPR was emerging, Osborne and Gaebler were advancing their work on the reinvention of government, and Al Gore was advocating for administrative and efficiency improvements in the federal government under the National Performance Review initiative and eventually the Government Performance and Results Act. The conceptual parallels between BPR and new public management will be described further after looking at the assumptions animating BPR.

Assumptions

The assumptions underlying BPR are rarely directly identified. Eliezer Geisler identifies a set of what he describes as critical beliefs that share by BPR initiatives in his book *Managing the Aftermath of Radical Corporate Change*.[7] Imbedded in Geisler's description of shared beliefs are a set of underlying assumptions about the core nature of organizations, actors within organizations, and what can be known. In other words, Geisler's description reveals a set of ontological and epistemological assumptions contained in BPR.

The first of several beliefs shared by BPR initiatives is that *vision proceeds obliteration*. Breaking that claim down in reverse order, a central premise of BPR since Hammer's first description of it in his *Harvard Business Review* article, is that "obliteration," or radical change in work processes, is required in order for dramatic performance improvements to occur. Here, vision, or a strategic "blueprint" of what the organization will be and how it will get there, is required for reengineering initiatives. With such a vision in place, obliteration of work processes will allow organizations to accomplish dramatic course changes. Geisler points out that imbedded in this conception of change is that a complete vision of both the critical and routine attributes of the organization, all the way down to basic work processes, is necessary for this sort of reengineering change to be possible and effective.

A second belief of BPR is that managers, as well as leaders, have a *full understanding of work processes*. In other words, accurate, timely, and adequate information—not even full or comprehensive information—can be acquired and transferred from line or operational levels of the organization, to mid-managers and ultimately to leaders.

BPR efforts also share a conviction in the need for and availability of *unabridged, unbiased, and definite evaluation criteria*. In order to assess and subsequently enact radical work process change, organizations mush have valid and definitive criteria by which to evaluate existing work processes. Organizations must know, with no uncertainty, what improvements result from which changes and what level of change.

The drive to obliterate also reveals a presumption about the *obsolescence of current logic*. As much as we may experience some organizational practices as being ridiculous under some conditions, the existence of those practices doesn't emerge without some motivating rationale. Organizational practices and policies emerge from experience, have intentional design attributes, and are developed with some instrumental function or purpose in mind. This is also not to say that, as John Meyer and Brian Rowan indicate, that organizational processes don't become decoupled form their original intent or function either.[8] However, BPR operates from the notion that whatever original logic existed, it is no longer valid. This presumption reinforces the assumption noted that the world operates in essentially positivist ways and that we can know those ways. Changes in the environment of an organization may be the driving force behind the need to abandon old logic for new, but underlying that causal force is a world that operates in stable ways and study of it can yield stable knowledge.

In the previous chapter, we described quality-based and continuous improvement management approaches like total quality management (TQM). BPR departs from these management theories in asserting that *improvements are no longer enough*. The claim that constant, systematic improvements are insufficient in current environment suggests a model of change in the environment that is characterized by punctuated equilibrium. If obliteration of old processes is necessary, but the new processes are assumed to be sufficient for some period of time, then the environment must have gone through significant turbulence followed by relative stability.

Finally, Geisler argues that BPR operates from a belief that the culture of organizations is relatively transferable or malleable. If change initiatives result in the abolition of old processes and the replacement of them with new and dramatically more efficient and effective ones, then the existing culture under the old processes—if functional and supportive of organizational objectives—must either be transferable into or sufficiently flexible to adapt to a new set of practices.[9]

Contained within these notions are at least two other deeper sets of assumptions. The first is more obvious but bears some scrutiny in its implications for the applicability of BPR in governance settings. BPR improves the performance of organizations by obliterating old work processes and replacing them with new ones that are substantially more efficient, allowing organizations to produce or accomplish more with the same investment of resources. In any situation where public resources are being expended, and particularly in tight or declining fiscal climates, enhancing efficiency is a reasonable strategy. In this way, BPR shares a perspective with new public management, and inefficient processes are assumed to have unacceptably high transaction costs. The question is, what are the transaction costs and why are they there? As noted previously, organizational processes and procedures evolve in order to serve some organizational function. BPR assumes that whatever that function may have been in the past, the environment has to change sufficiently to require its radical reexamination and reengineering. There are functions in public and nonprofit organizations operating in governance environments that encounter transaction costs that exist not because of shifts in the environment but because, as Graham Allison points out, we have different expectations of public sector activities in terms of transparency, equity, accountability, and other values. Reporting, oversight, review, and regulation activities that don't directly contribute to the output efficiency of the organization may be critical to the organization's function nonetheless.

There are also two other deeper and interrelated assumptions in BPR as well about the nature of organizations and what can be known of them. One is a belief that organizations and their work processes are objective and stable and that they operate in ways that comport with basic rules applicable in fairly universal ways. There are "laws" of governing the basic behavior of humans and thereby the organizations they population. The second assumption has to do with the nature of knowledge. In this case, that knowledge is objective and that conclusive knowledge exists and can be acquired by and acted upon by the organization. The claim reveals an extension of the assumption that was previously described—that the organization can be known in no uncertain terms not only by leaders but by staff at all levels of the hierarchy. Embedded in this assumption are claims. They are rooted and, correspondingly, they can be known in this way by leaders or change agents.

Assumptions about the nature of the world (ontology) and what can be known about it (epistemology) bear some interrogation. Geisler points out that BPR assumptions about knowledge for radical change, both in terms of quantity and quality, are problematic. The notion that a "full understanding" is possible, or that unabridged, unbiased, and definitive evaluation data be available is problematic given the complexity of organizations and their environments, the potential impact of small quantitative changes and the potential for distribution of that knowledge across the organization.[10] The notion of unity of comprehensive actionable knowledge is also in tension with the organizational reality that vision, even in the most coherent of organizations, rarely enjoys high levels of unity for long. Again, conditions of complexity and diversity of activities and personnel as well as limitations of comprehensive communication, all serve to challenge the possibility of complete or shared vision, let alone the knowledge require to evaluate let alone obliterate and reengineer new processes.

We noted previously that BPR and much of the early energy and thinking about reinvention, new public management, and BPR emerged at roughly the same time. Beyond timing, there are strong conceptual parallels as well. Christopher Pollitt identifies five core beliefs of managerialism, which on reflection are shared here too.

1. The main route to social progress now lies through the achievement of continuing increases in economically defined productivity.

2. Such productivity increases will mainly come from the application of ever-more-sophisticated technologies—communications, production technology. The larger, multidivisional form is now dominant.

3. The application of these technologies can only be achieved with a labor force disciplined in accordance with the productivity ideal.

4. Management is a separate and distinct organizational function and one that plays the crucial role in planning, implementing, and measuring the necessary improvements in productivity. Business success will depend increasingly on the quality and professionalism of managers.

5. To perform this crucial role, managers must be granted reasonable room to manage.

These beliefs and assumptions should be apparent in the techniques and practices associated with BPR.

Techniques and Practices

Because organizations are diverse and their work processes complex, there is no single turn-key or step stage approach to BPR. However, there are a set of common organization elements that tend to be the focus of BPR initiatives. Not surprisingly, the first element is the work processes of the organization themselves. BPR adopts any number of specific techniques or approaches to improve work processes by reducing duplication of activities or efforts, reduce unnecessary complexity, and eliminate unneeded transaction costs such as control or information management processes. For example, Hammer admonishes organizations to subsume information processing work into the real work that produces information in the first place and to capture information once and at the source.[11] Hammer and Champy advocate for efforts to ensure that unnecessary checks and controls are eliminated and that hand-offs and reconciliations are minimized to the greatest possible extent.

Reflection Questions

What are the assumptions of BPR?

What are the consequences of these assumptions for the processes—especially what factors are considered and which aren't or what's possible and what's not?

BPR initiatives also focus on shifting the attention of the organization from activities to outcomes. Hammer and Champy make this point explicitly in their argument that results rather than activities should be the focus of performance evaluation and compensation systems in the organization. They also advocate shifting both practices and culture in such a way as to emphasize production over protection. Hammer also makes this point in emphasizing the importance of organizing around outcome rather than tasks.

Consistent with efforts to streamline processes and focus on outcomes, BPR also expresses a shift in thinking about how and where decisions are made. Hammer advocates that organizations move to processes that place the decision points where the work is being done rather than locating it in a more centralized node with designated supervisors or "deciders." The logic of centralized decision has typically been linked to the importance of efficiency, consistency, and standardization. If decision making is decentralized, the likelihood of unnecessarily duplicated search processes, variation in criteria and approach, and general inconsistency increases. Hammer suggests that rather than vesting control for ensuring consistency and continuity with supervisors, control can be built into the processes.[12] Hammer and Champy later reiterate this notion that decision making should fall to workers and not managers, in no small part because those who do the work are in a better position to understand both the needs of the end user and the unique contextual factors that shape the potentially successful decisions.

This shift in decision making hints at another broad attribute of BPR initiatives with respect to personnel. In practical terms, Hammer and Champy describe the need to combine jobs in ways that support the integration of processes described previously. They also recognize the importance of formalizing work process shifts and point out that position descriptions need to be revised correspondingly to reflect broader and more multidimensional work. In no uncertain terms, Hammer and Champy encourage organizations to empower people rather than control them. Correspondingly, as decision making is distributed and empowerment increases, the locus of responsibility changes as well, being vested with those individuals. As the role of those doing the work expands and evolves, Hammer and Champy also see that the role of managers and supervisors must adapt as well. Rather than being control points, BPR suggests that supervisors and managers in the reengineered organization become facilitators and coaches.

In addition to these changes—the focus on work processes, a results orientation, decision points, and shifts in personnel responsibilities—BPR also gives attention to the structure of the organization. Hammer and Champy advocate flattening the organization. It's important to recognize that doing so is both a strategy in and of itself and a consequence of many of the other organizational attributes BPR seeks to improve. As a stand-alone objective, structural changes like reducing the hierarchy can be viewed as a way to reduce the overall complexity of the organization. Reducing the levels of hierarchy can have the effect of streamlining communication channels and decision cycles. And other BPR changes, such as streamlining working processes, expanding personnel responsibilities and position descriptions, and distributing decision-making authority all have the potential to result in a flatter organization as well.

In fact, this mutually reinforcing relationship between hierarchy and other focus elements of BPR is typical for each of those elements. For example, shifting personnel priorities, roles, and responsibilities is mutually reinforcing of decentralized decision-making systems. The evaluation and redesign of work processes, especially when driven by line-level knowledge held by workers, supports and bolsters both personnel and structural changes.

Case 7.1

Current Expressions: Business Process Reengineering at the Jefferson County Alabama Board of Personnel

In 1974 two separate class action suits were filed against the Jefferson County Alabama Board of Personnel alleging violations of the Civil Rights Act.[13] Through a series of rulings and negotiations among the parties to the suit, a consent degree was crafted that required the board to take certain actions to mitigate against the effects of the past and to ensure no future discriminatory practices would occur. In 2002, the US District Court in Alabama held the County Board of Personnel in contempt and appointed a receiver to take over the operations of the board. As a part of the ruling, the court also ordered other actions to be taken to update and ensure that the work processes used by the board would be brought into compliance with the Civil Rights Act.

In 2004, after the appointment of the receiver, the board began the implementation of a new human resource information management system (HRIMS) that was designed to respond to issues identified in the court's contempt ruling. The new HRIMS was designed to replace a legacy system. The legacy system was highly inefficient and left the board struggling to meet its mission, let alone the performance standards established by the court.

While these circumstances are not typical of most BPR initiatives—let alone those in the public sector—the focus, approach, and elements of the initiative are very much at the core of BPR processes. The design and implementation of the new HRIMS resulted in a phased approach, which embodies important elements of the BPR model described by Hammer and Champy, Davenport, and others. The five phases, according to Roger McCullough and Ronald Sims, are as follows:

1. visioning creation of a high-level business vision
2. scoping and planning—development of a detailed implementation plan
3. designing—development of detailed designs
4. constructing—building the new organization structure
5. implementing—validation of information and business processes

First, recognizing that the new system would present and require change not only for the board itself but also for all of the agencies and municipalities served by the board, a management plan articulating a *high-level business vision* was created. The plan was created in such a way as to keep the involved jurisdictions engaged in the design and development of the system throughout the project.

The scoping and planning phase focused on ensuring that the new system would meet several organizational objectives, including the following:

- radical efficiency gains including cycle time reduction
- improvements in high-impact areas, a reduction in manual or duplicative data collection and entry
- flexible and scalable IT infrastructure that could be more responsive to customer expectations and business requirements
- access to operational data in a way that approaches real time availability

These attributes reflect the efforts of the board to create systems that focus on results, subsume and integrate information processing, and move to a focus on production rather than process for the sake of process.

As the HRIMS was developed, detailed test scripts were crafted to confirm the software's support for *new business processes*. The design process was crafted to intentionally and carefully replace antiquated legacy systems that had been in place of decades and that had spawned countless high labor and low return processes and procedures. Initially much of the design was tested for validity and reliability in an isolated environment, but ultimately the system was crafted such that multiple data sources and processes could be effectively integrated and streamlined.

Finally, after systems options, parameters, tables, security roles, and authorizations were established in a test environment, *interfaces and integration strategies* needed for passing information between systems and for reporting processes were developed for implementation. In addition to supporting the integration of work processes at this stage, the validity of the strategies and processes were validated by external consultants, but the validation was done with significant, explicit support from top administrators and with awareness that the shifts in process had a short-term negative impact on productivity while the transition occurred but that as gaps were closed and processes became institutionalized, quality and efficiency would exceed old performance levels.

As we noted at the front end of this case, the impetus for this reengineering effort was a court order rather than changes in market demand or community need as would typically be the case in a BPR initiative. Nevertheless, this initiative does embody many of the attributes described in the conceptual literature developed by Hammer, Champy, Davenport, and other BPR advocates.

Business Process Reengineering: Summary and Conclusions

BPR is an approach to organizational change that has garnered fairly widespread attention in that it promises dramatic performance improvements. The apparent promise of BPR is couched in terms that are contained within a relatively simple set of principles and phases. The model does retain some elements of systems thinking in that BPR focuses awareness on how elements of the system function effectively together, but its promise seems greater than other systems theories like TQM in arguing that incremental improvement isn't enough. However, as we noted earlier in this section, there are assumptions within BPR that pose difficulties, specifically the possibility of having exhaustive knowledge or understanding of critical work processes in highly complex production, social, political, or other environments seems increasing challenging. Regardless, the language of change through BPR practices resonates well within the current administrative and political climate that seeks to dramatically improve performance and to do so while containing or reducing transaction costs. As a result, it seems likely that BPR will continue to be an important influence on change strategies into the future.

The Burke-Litwin Change Model

The Burke-Litwin change model is grounded in an open systems framework. As W. Warner Burke and George Litwin state, "We strongly believe in the open system framework, especially that represented by Katz and Kahn." As such, Burke and Litwin's model functions with a presumption that the organization is grounded in and open to the wider environment and that its relationship with that environment is characterized by a basic input-throughput-output-feed-back loop cycle.

The external environment, in open systems models, serves as the source of inputs, and indicial and organizational performance are the outputs. The other elements of the model are the central throughput features. In terms of thinking about the relationship between the organization and its environment, it's worth noting that the feedback loop includes a bidirectional arrow as a way of revealing that the relationship is mutually influential.[14] Change in environmental condition obviously has an impact on the organization, but the organization too, has the capacity to influence or impact the environment as it provides services, regulatory interactions, and so forth.

So to be clear, the factor that most likely triggers organizational change is the external environment. Within Burke and Litwin's model, the sort of change that receives attention is at the level of the mission, culture, leadership, and its operating strategies of the organization.

Their model of change centers on developing an understanding of the cause and effect relationship among twelve organizational dimensions that are key to organizational change. Let's take a look at how this change model can make the process easier.

All the affecting factors put together affect the motivation level of the individuals in an organization, which in turn impacts the overall performance.

Assumptions

Like BPR, the Burke-Litwin model adopts elements of a systems perspective on organizations and the mechanisms of change within organizations. For example, a key assumption is that the organization is open to its environment and receives direct and important feedback from the environment. The Burke-Litwin model also sees the organization in terms of a complex set of relations between critical attributes of the organization (see Figure 7.1). And finally, the model sees the relationships between these attributes as highly complex and variable and largely mechanically causal.

In describing the development of the model, Burke and Litwin acknowledge that while the model is informed by existing conceptual work, including open systems theory, the model largely emerged from their management consulting work.[15] As such, their model seeks to facilitate change and improvement of performance either in the organization as a whole or within subgroups of the organization by creating and improving various internal and external links—between and among throughput factors. This change model is based on assessing the organizational as well as environmental factors that can be affected in support of successful change.

Figure 7.1 Burke-Litwin Change Model

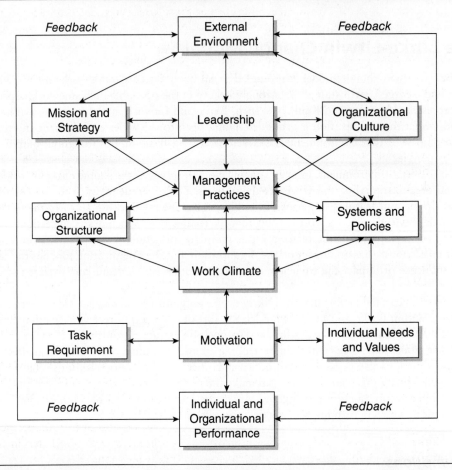

Source: Aaron L. De Smet, "Adaptive Models of Organization for Substance Abuse Treatment, Part I & II," National Institute on Drug Abuse, July 1998, http://archives.drugabuse.gov/about/organization/despr/hsr/da-tre/DeSmetAdaptiveModels.html.

Techniques and Practices

Before describing specific practices under this change model, it's important to understand the overall structure and operation of the model. Consistent with an open systems approach, the external environment box represents the source of inputs for the system, and the individual and organizational performance box represents the outputs of the system. The model also includes a feedback loop consistent with Daniel Katz and Robert Kahn's work as well. All of the other factors within the model represent the critical throughput aspects of organizations. Burke and Litwin subdivide the throughput portion of the model into two separate sets of factors. The first set, which they describe as *transformational* factors, includes leadership, mission and strategy, and organizational culture. Drawing on James McGreggor Burns' work, Burke and Litwin describe transformation leaders as those who bring about broader or more fundamental change in their situation, be that the organization, community, or some other setting.[16] This notion of leadership and change is also parallel to Abraham Zaleznik's work distinguishing between leaders and managers.[17] Leaders who focus on operations at this level tend to have a more fundamental impact on the nature of the organization, its mission, and its fit within a broader environment. In other words, this level of leadership and change is also parallel to Selznick's notion of critical decisions.

The second set, or *transactional* factors, includes management practices, organizational structure, systems and policies, work climate, task requirement, motivation, and individual needs and values. Burke and Litwin see operations at the transactional level as just that: a series of transactional if-then interactions with workers. If you, the worker, do X for me, I as the manager will do Y—likely provide reward or remuneration—for you. Burke points out that while change can occur at this level, that change is not likely to be at a deep level, or one fundamental to the organization.[18]

- *External environment*: This is the factor that generates the need for change in the organization. While not a homogeneous factor, the external environment is the source of energy or inputs that drive both regular operations and create the need for change within the organization, or at the level of throughputs.
- *Mission and strategy*: The vision, mission, and the strategy of the organization, as defined by the top management, provides a set of guiding and orienting claims about the central character and orientation of the organization.
- *Leadership*: As prior research has shown, leadership can have a significant impact on the performance of the organization and is closely linked to its mission and strategy, both in terms of establishing mission, visions, culture, strategy, and so on but also in terms of creating a climate where actions are consistent with stated directions.
- *Organizational culture*: While not working from Schein's model of culture specifically, Burke and Litwin's understanding of culture is consistent with a model that includes artifacts, espoused values, and underlying beliefs and assumptions.
- *Structure*: Consistent with our discussions of structure throughout the book, the study of structure should not be confined to formal or hierarchical structure but instead needs to be inclusive of other stable patterns of behavior within the organization.
- *Systems*: Systems include all types of policies, procedures, and organizational practices that involve both the people and the operations of the organization.
- *Management practices*: The management practices are the specific things that managers do to support the organization's activities to accomplish the mission. For example, this might include what managers do to encourage subordinates in their efforts.
- *Work climate*: Although somewhat abstract, climate is something we have a feel for and might best be articulated in terms of workers' perceptions of how well they feel they are managed, how they feel about how expectations are established and maintained, how they feel their performance is or is not recognized, and so forth.

- *Tasks and skills:* Most concisely or simply, this is the instrumental person-job match and is focused on the knowledge, skills, and abilities (KSAs) of employees to accomplish the duties of their positions.
- *Individual needs and values:* If tasks and skills have to do with the fit between the person and his or her ability to do the job, this factor has to do with the extent to which the job is able to fulfill needs and values of individuals. This and the last one (*tasks and skills*, and *individual needs and values*) represent two major influences on the subsequent factor: *motivation*.
- *Motivation level:* Motivation as well as climate and culture are concepts often discussed in organization settings but seldom defined with any precision. One useful way of thinking about motivation is to consider it in terms of arousal to engage in activities that enhance achievement, affiliation, and esteem.
- *Individual and overall performance:* This factor is the output of the system model and can include measures of individual and collective measures of productivity, quality, efficiency, budget performance, customer satisfaction, etc.

As we previously noted, Burke and Litwin acknowledge that their model is a simplification of the complex reactions that exist within and among all of the factors that they identify in their model. That model is also a simplification in that each one of the factors may well be exploded into further subsystems and greater complexity as well. When considering the systems factor, for example, it should be understood that the way that policies, practices, and procedures are operationalized in many organizations reveals both variation in implementation and use across large, diverse operational structures as well as the downstream effects of those systems. The way in which any unit operationalizes and then implements a given system reveals subsequent practices, which themselves become stabilized into structures and systems of their own.

Finally, in considering the techniques and approaches implied by the Burke-Litwin model it's also important to understand that the approach to change is not oriented toward a particular set of steps or menu of options. In other words, the Burke-Litwin model is not focused on how to change but rather helps leaders determine, based on new or evolving influences from the environment, what is in need of change. Rather than focusing on utilizing new technologies intended to dramatically reorganize work processes with the end of improved efficiency, or focusing on continuous improvement or flux, Burke and Litwin emphasize the importance of understanding the effect that variation in the external environment has on the broad structures of the organization and what new or different demands emerge from environmental conditions requiring change to one or more of the factors within the throughput elements of the organization. To that end, Burke's case examples describing the use of the model in change initiatives reveal a variety of techniques that provide benefits of improved diagnostic quality and guidance for change initiatives.[19] Those examples include collection of data, especially survey data, about the system performance and the collective understanding and perceptions of that performance. Table 7.1, then, is a propositional set of areas of inquiry that might be of use in such diagnostic and guidance inquiries. To be clear, the proposals in Table 7.1 are neither exhaustive nor comprehensive. They are merely provided as a starting point for considering the sorts of inquiry that might be useful to an organization as its leaders consider what is in need of change.

Table 7.1 Burke-Litwin Areas of Inquiry

Factor	Inquiry
Leadership	A study of the leadership structures and practices of the organization should be conducted with the purpose of identifying the central or shared role models in the organization.
Organizational culture	A study of organizational culture should collect and examine information on the explicit *and* implicit rules, policies, customs, principles, and values that shape organizational behavior.
Structure	Structure should be function-based, focusing on other core factors such as authority, communication, responsibility, decision making, and control mechanisms that exist between members of the organization.
Systems	Here, study involves the possibility of both quantitative and qualitative assessment of performance, perceptions, and experiences.
Management practices	Assessment of this factor might include a study of how well the managers conform to the organization's strategy when dealing with employees and the resources.
Work unit climate	This is a study of how the employees think, feel, and hope with respect to the kind of relationships they have with their team members and members of units.
Tasks and skills	Assessment in this area involves developing understanding about specific job positions and its demands as well as the kind of knowledge, skills, and abilities (KSAs) that an employee must have in order to fulfill the position responsibilities. This allows for an assessment of how well jobs and employees have been matched.
Individual needs and values	Study of this area seeks to understand the employee's attitude about their work in order to identify the quality factors that lead to job enrichment and better job satisfaction.
Motivation level	Identifying the motivation level of the employees will make it easier to determine how willingly they would put in their efforts to achieve organizational goals. This would also involve identifying motivational triggers.

Case 7.2

Current Expressions: Burke-Litwin in Texas Public Schools

In 1990, the US Immigration and Control Act was passed by the US Congress and among its provisions was the creation of a new visa category, the foreign professional specialty occupation, or H-1B visa. This visa was created for individuals who hold at least a bachelor's degree and qualify for a specialty occupation. Public school districts in Texas have been among the highest users of H-1B visas, and the 2010 study by Sergio Fernandez and Lois Wise seeks to understand this high use level as a change and innovation strategy adopted by Texas public school organizations. Fernandez and Wise's analysis reveals many striking attributes of Burke and Litwin's model and approaches to managing change.

At the very outset of their study, the authors acknowledge the external environment. In this particular case, changes in two sets of inputs—students and human capital—combined to prompt change in organizational practices among various school districts in Texas. Specifically, as the demands for multicultural and multilingual education have increased, and the availability of professionals to fill those needs has remained roughly constant, the use of H1-B visas has increased to the point where US Department of Homeland Security (DHS) reports have indicated that education is one of the leading professional fields recruited under the program.

After identifying the environmental factors that drove organizational change, Fernandez and Wise turn their attention to internal factors, or throughput factors that were instrumental in the adoption of change by the organizations they studied. Although their analysis does not reveal every element of the Burke-Litwin model, it does identify several, starting with leadership as a key transformational factor. Drawing directly on Burke's work, Fernandez and Wise point out the importance of leadership in both the theoretical and empirical literature. More specifically, by operationalizing leadership in part as being focused on perceptions of leadership being instrumental as a change agent, they place their work squarely within the transformational end of the Burke-Litwin model. The results of their study found that leadership, both in terms of the extent to which leaders saw themselves as change agents and the time on the job, which was used as a proxy for leadership experience, was related to the success of change.

Fernandez and Wise also give their conceptual and empirical attention to several transaction factors as well.[20] In discussing the conceptual framework and treatment of that framework in the literature they note several factors including *structure, systems and policies,* and *task requirements.* At the structural level, they include factors like organizational size and resulting structural attributes that allow effective coordination as the number and complexity of interactions and activities increase. With respect to systems and policies, Fernandez and Wise recognize administrative practices—in this case specifically in the area of human resources practices and corresponding policies that support change are critical to the success of innovation and change. Finally, task requirement attributes clearly and directly connect to the input characteristics that drive change in the first place. In this case, task attributes include the capacity to provide bilingual and vocational education as well as gifted classes within the districts being studied.

One other attribute identified by Fernandez and Wise bears mentioning here—namely the output factor of *organizational performance.* Obviously organization performance is the ultimate concern of leaders. Interestingly, however, Fernandez and Wise recognize that while this factor lies at the back end of the model, the factors do have a mutually influential character. Organization performance both influences the larger environment as Katz and Kahn's model indicates, but it also has a direct influence back on the throughput factors of the model, in this case on task requirements as well as *internal systems.*

Burke-Litwin: Summary and Conclusions

We noted at the outset of this section that it adopts elements of open systems theory and orientation shared with BPR approaches. One of the significant differences between Burke-Litwin and BPR is that the former is less mechanical in its approach to change. In acknowledging the complexity of the systems in which change is occurring, this model is less prescriptive about *what* should change and instead prompts administrators to think more about how to consider and approach change. In adopting this orientation, the model offers a range of proposition elements to consider. These elements aren't intended to be exhaustive, nor are they prioritized into a predetermined hierarchy but instead allow members of the organization to conduct their own context dependent assessment from which a change strategy can be developed.

Reflection Question

What strategies would you adopt to identify and prioritize critical system elements when approaching change using the Burke-Litwin model?

Organization Development

Of the theories of change presented in this chapter, organization development (OD) is the most conceptually diverse and heterodox of the four. OD is an ongoing, systematic process to effectively manage and facilitate change in an organization. OD is known as both a field of behavioral science having to do with understanding and managing organizational change and as a field of scientific study and inquiry drawing on disciplines including sociology, psychology, and theories of motivation, learning, and personality.

OD emerged as a self-identified approach in the mid-1960s as a way to manage organizational change. OD focuses on helping employees change as the organization changes, keeping in mind that it can take time to change basic patterns and assumptions. OD focuses on enhancing jobs by enhancing employees. The aim shifts from the specific job to the person's career and well-being and pays attention to life planning and intellectual motivations. OD is a form of planned change that includes the values of the OD perspective discussed in previous chapters. It assumes that change is purposeful and is concerned with how change is implemented and the situation in which it will be implemented. OD processes typically utilize outside facilitators (change agents) who diagnose, consult, team build, manage conflict, coach, help set goals, and design task forces to assist ongoing organizational improvement. It comes from the term *development group* and evolved through T-groups, to be called OD, meaning systemwide change effort. That system can function at any number of different scales including a single work site, multiwork site unit, department, work group, or entire organization.

> OD is a planned change process, managed from the top, taking into account both the technical and human sides of the organization and using inside or outside consultants in the planning and implementation of the changes to be made.
>
> —Edgar Schein

Organization development is a process by which behavioral science knowledge and practices are used to help organizations achieve greater effectiveness, including improved quality of work life and increased productivity.[21]

In the 1950s and 1960s a new, integrated approach originated known as OD: the systematic application of behavioral science knowledge at various levels (group, intergroup, and total organization) to bring about planned change.[22]

In the late 1960s OD was implemented in organizations via consultants, but was unknown in theory and relatively unclear in practice. Richard Beckhard, an expert in OD and change management, defined OD as "an effort, planned, organization-wide, and managed from the top, to increase organization effectiveness and health through planned interventions in the organization's processes, using behavioral-science knowledge."[23]

Throughout the 1970s and 1980s OD became a more developed area of study and practice, with courses and programs being offered in academic business, education, and administration programs. In the following decades, OD grew and evolved, and its influences could be seen in theories and strategies such as TQM, team building, job enrichment, and reengineering.

OD emerged through the National Training Laboratories' (NTL) development of training groups known as sensitivity training or T-groups. Work in this area began in 1946 when Kurt Lewin and his staff at the Research Center for Group Dynamics at MIT were asked by the Connect Interracial Commission and the Committee on Community Interrelations of the American Jewish Congress for help training leaders in the community. Initially, the researchers met at the end of each day of training to discuss privately the types of behaviors and group dynamics they had observed during the trainings. The group leaders subsequently asked for permission to sit in on these feedback sessions. Although they were reluctant to do so at first, the researchers finally agreed, and the first T-group was formed in which people reacted to information about their own behavior.[24]

A second line of OD that was critical to its development and evolution—and that we will focus on here—was the work in action research done by social scientists interested in applying empirical, contextual research to managing change. Kurt Lewin, whose work on leadership and participation we've explored already, was instrumental in early work in the development of T-groups and survey feedback and is credited for having coined the term *action research*.[25] As we noted before, OD is broad and heterodox both in terms of its influences and its expressions. In the following description of OD, we work from Lewin's approaches and follow that line of work and thinking into an area of OD developed subsequently by a practitioner and theorist, Neely Gardner, who extended the idea of OD in the public sector into an approach described as *action training and research (AT&R)*.

Assumptions

As with all of the theories and models we've explored, OD works from a series of assumptions about the world in which it operates, some of which are explicit and some not.

- *About individuals:* Gardner's approach to OD assumes people strive to grow and make a higher contribution to organizational goals.

- *About people in groups:* AT&R forms of OD assume that people wish to interact in groups and that work groups have great psychological impact on people. It assumes that suppressed attitudes have an adverse effect on the group. It also assumes level of trust and support is lower than it should be.
- *About leadership:* Leaders cannot be all things at all times so groups must assist each other.
- *About the nature of organizations:* Organizations are assumed to be socially constructed, and while there are manifest artifacts of organizations, their activities, and their effects in the world, the organizations themselves are constructed and constituted out of recurring patterns of behavior among members of the organization and those connected to it.

Further, development and change are not merely moments of punctuation. Although Lewin's initial model of change (unfreeze-move-refreeze) suggests otherwise, OD embraces the idea of the creation and subsequent reinforcement of change, and it explicitly moves beyond the implementation of a change initiative to a long term focus on stabilizing, institutionalizing, and augmenting new activities within the organization. The idea of *development* should be understood as ongoing.

- *About knowledge of organizations:* Within an AT&R approach to OD, knowledge too, is socially constructed. In other words, the important information about what the organization does, why it does it, and how it does it resides within and among those in and around the organization. One of the implications of this assumption is that the critical knowledge required to effectively manage change does not reside with single individuals. Instead, it resides among all those who are involved with the activities of the organization.
- *Inherent values:* People are important, valued, and can grow within organizations. Moreover, work and life are richer if feelings are allowed to be part of the culture. Doing so intentionally and with purpose can support processes to express feeling and emotion in a functional way. AT&R, as its name suggests, has an inherent commitment to *research* and *action*. AT&R is an ongoing and interactive process, based on data, goal setting, interaction, participation, and empowerment toward the improvement of the organization.

Several consequences flow from these assumptions and values. One consequence is that OD approaches that share AT&R orientation take the view that we don't live in a world where the pure bureaucratic machine organization can operate (nor have we ever), but it's increasingly difficult to make bureaucracy's component features operate. As such, we have to understand that information flows more widely and rapidly, due both to evolving technology and more open culture, than the bureaucratic model would suggest. We also live in a larger sociopolitical culture informed by political liberalism (legitimacy of multiple and varying interests). And finally, the organizational setting of our work, not just society broadly but of governance organizations specifically, is characterized by ongoing environmental change, both the political environment and the economic environment. Another consequence is that it seems increasingly unlikely that we're going to identify "one best way" to do the work of structuring and coordinating organizational operations.

Techniques and Practices

OD looks at how the organization and its constituents or employees function together. As a form of inquiry, it asks a range of questions that might include the following: Does the organization meet the needs of its employees? Do the employees work effectively to make the organization a success? How can the relationship between employee satisfaction and organizational success be facilitated? Based on such inquiry, OD looks carefully at the human factors and the performance data inherent in the observation organizational relationships. The results of inquiry lead to the selection of OD strategies that can be used to help employees become more committed and more adaptable, which ultimately improves the organization as a whole.

Organizations initiate the OD process when there is a need, gap, or dissatisfaction either at the upper management level or within the employees. Ideally, the OD process involves the entire organization, with explicit support and involvement from upper management and engagement in the effort by all members from all levels of the organization.

Lewin's model broke this process down into three discrete, distinct phases: unfreeze, move, and refreeze (see Figure 7.2).

- *Unfreeze*—This first step typically focuses on reducing those forces that maintain the organization's current behaviors or patterns of interaction. Unfreezing is often accomplished through a process of "psychological disconfirmation" or the presentation of information that reveals the inconsistencies, discrepancies, and even paradoxes between those behaviors and practices desired and espoused by the organization and those currently exhibited by its members.[26]
- *Move*—This step entails changing the behavior of the organization or some portion of the organization to a new pattern. This is the step that is often associated with a more or less formal intervention by an external or internal consultant who brings to bear some technique for engendering new behaviors, values, or attitudes and corresponding shifts in practices, processes, and structures.

Figure 7.2 Lewin's Model of Organization Development

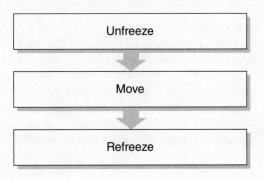

Source: Adapted from Thomas G. Cummings and Christopher G. Worley, *Organization Development and Change,* 9th ed. (Mason, OH: South-Western College Publishing, 2008).

- *Refreeze*—This final step stabilizes the new behavior. Early OD efforts and thinking viewed this stage as a return to equilibrium. Equilibrium is characterized by a new, more functional pattern of behavior but stable equilibrium nonetheless. Contemporary approaches to OD are more likely to view the new state as being more dynamic, as requiring continued focus, though perhaps not with the same investment of energy and resources as was required in the prior step.

Another important concept that Lewin contributed to our thinking about organization change is the idea of the force field analysis, or a systematic examination of the forces that support efforts toward organization change, and those that work to inhibit or constrain potential change. The simple model of a force field analysis (see Figure 7.3) includes several components. First, it includes a description of the current state or status quo as well as a concise articulation of the desired or future state that is the objective of change. The central feature of the force field analysis is a thorough listing of the driving forces and constraining forces. The driving forces are all of the major conditions and resources present that support the effort to move from the current state to the desired state. The constraining forces are those that present barriers of one form or another to the successful movement of the organization. It's also important to recognize that the articulation of driving and constraining forces is not merely a list of those factors but rather includes an effort to assign relative weights or strengths to both. Not all forces are created equal, and any effort to create successful change will need to take into consideration an assessment of the relative strengths of those forces. Within the model, the relative strength can be depicted in different ways, including visually—making arrows larger or smaller to depict strength or by assigning relative or absolute numerical weights to each force on both sides of the model.

To start the process, consultants with experience in OD and change management are often utilized. These consultants may be internal or external to the company, with the cautionary understanding that there are pros and cons to internal versus external consultants. Internal consultants might be too much a part of the existing company environment to effectively coordinate and enforce the action plans and solutions required for successful change. Outside consultants might not be around to see their work implemented and might not understand the culture. Also, they might run the risk of "going native," or making recommendations under pressure from leadership.

Thomas Cummings and Christopher Worley suggest that Lewin's original change model (see Figure 7.2 shown earlier) has evolved into at least two other action research models associated with OD (see Figure 7.4).

The third model, then, is Gardner's AT&R model (see Figure 7.5). Several similarities and differences should be recognized among the three models. First, all three make intentional and explicit use of empirical data collected from the organizations. That data—and this is true of all action research regardless of focus or setting—is problem and action oriented. It is collected with the intent of helping the organization respond to a particular problem. Data in action research OD is never collected in the abstract. Embedded in all three is a tendency to use survey or interview data as the basis of its empirical work. All three also have a cyclical feedback or evaluation component. While most OD practitioners recognize the iterative and ongoing nature of development work, Gardner's circular model most clearly embodies that character.

Figure 7.3 Lewin's Model of Force Field Analysis

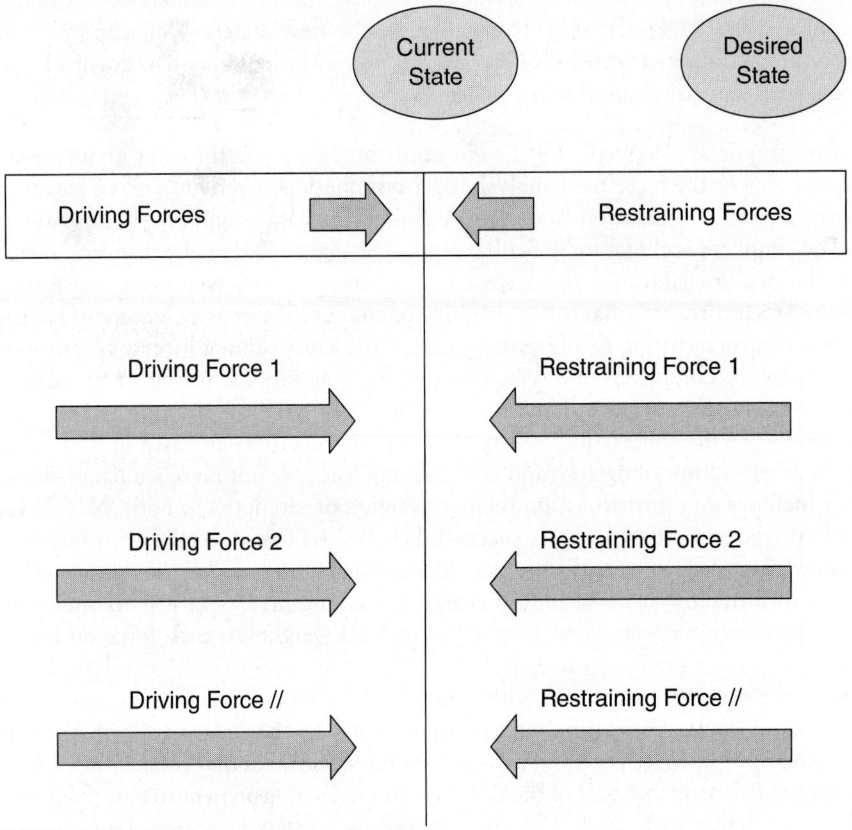

Source: Based on Kurt Lewin, "Defining the Field at a Given Time," *Psychological Review* 50, no. 3 (1943): 292–310, http://finntrack.co.uk/images/force_field_analysis1.gif.

Because Gardner's early work developed in a largely separate though parallel track from the scholarly research of Lewin and other pioneers in the field, we believe it is worth identifying the connections between those two lines of work as well as our rationale for reintroducing Gardner to the field. Many of the specific links between Gardner's working approach and those of Lewin, Chris Argyris, and other action research and OD scholars are described in the following section. Broadly, however, both action research and OD are derived from applied behavioral science and both share an action oriented, data driven, and practical problem-solving orientation. As Wendell French and Cecil Bell argue, "that is why we believe a sound organization development program rest on an action research model."[27] Moreover, in the AT&R model of Gardner, the *action* is undertaken by people in the organization in an effort to change themselves in terms of their work lives, experiences, and practices through a learning process supported by research of their own actions. This basic orientation links

Figure 7.4 Action Research and Contemporary Action Research Models

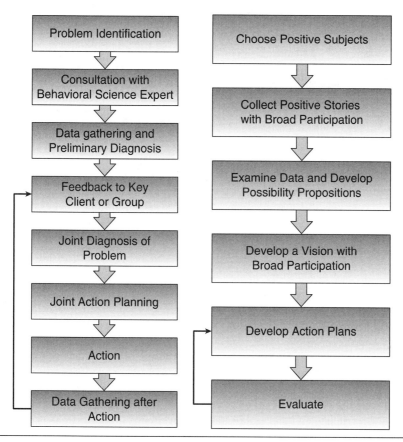

Source: Thomas G. Cummings and Christopher G. Worley, *Essentials of Organization Development and Change* (Cincinnati, OH: South-Western College Publishing, 2001).

action research and AT&R in a fundamental way. Finally, following the rationale of John Drummond and Markus Themessl-Huber, our reintroduction of Gardner is an effort not to contest existing work but rather to further enrich the thinking and practice of action research and OD.[28]

Gardner's thinking and practices, which he describes as AT&R, were not initially informed by the conceptual research being done by social and organizational scholars like Lewin and Argyris but were surprisingly consistent with them. For example, Michael McGill points out Gardner's move away from expert-based approaches and his oft-repeated claim, "I know very little."[29] Gardner worked in a profoundly participatory way. For Gardner, the responsibility and the knowledge necessary for effective OD permeates the organization rather than residing with an expert. In a directly parallel way, Robert Marshak and Loizos Heracleous advocate for an increasingly holistic understanding of organizational context.[30] Their advocacy is based, in part,

Figure 7.5 Gardner's Action Training and Research Model

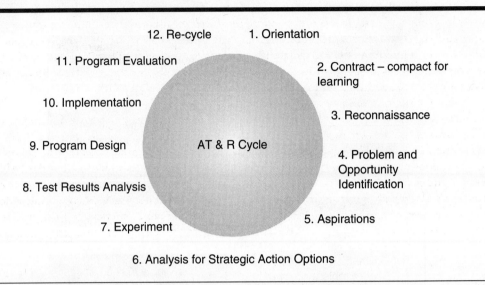

12. Re-cycle   1. Orientation

11. Program Evaluation

10. Implementation

9. Program Design

8. Test Results Analysis

7. Experiment

AT & R Cycle

2. Contract – compact for learning

3. Reconnaissance

4. Problem and Opportunity Identification

5. Aspirations

6. Analysis for Strategic Action Options

Source: Raymond Bruce and Sherman Wyman, *Changing Organizations: Practicing Action Training and Research* (Thousand Oaks, CA: Sage, 1998).

on Argyris and Donald Schon's, Lewin's, Schein's, and others' understandings of organization structure and culture.[31]

Leadership and development of organizational culture are recurrent concerns throughout the action research literature and are central concerns for organizational practice. One area that Gardner's work highlights is what he perceives to be the critical relationship between the role of leaders and the impact that role has on the construction of a culture that is imbued with the capacity to internalize and sustain a reflexive development orientation—that is, Gardner's approach to AT&R and development was essentially oriented toward putting himself out of a job. Through his approach, organizations developed the capacity, culture, and relationship with leadership wherein the reflexivity and robustness of engagement in ongoing practices of action research make OD a way of life rather than an intervention.[32]

While this orientation toward leadership is critical, it also moves sole responsibility and privilege for decisions away from the top of the organization and into a distributed leadership model. Like Lewin, Gardner and many researchers who follow his line of work point out that both responsibility for change and the requisite knowledge to make that change successful reside through the whole organization and not with elite individuals or roles at the top of the hierarchy.[33, 34] For example, John Hook describes the shift that occurs when moving from initial contracting stages in an intervention—when a manager is the sole client—to the point at which the whole organization becomes the client.[35]

The AT&R approach recognizes these attributes of contemporary organizations in several ways. First, like most action research–based approaches, it is participatory. It is participatory not because participation is inherently good, which it may or may not be, but because participation well managed can elicit critical information that makes the likelihood of success greater. It brings more information and data to the table, reduces the chances of unanticipated consequences, and it develops a shared understanding of the situation and in so doing helps avoid blocking behaviors. Along this line, it is also context driven, not ideologically driven. AT&R recognizes that each situation has important attributes that combine in unique ways. This emphasis on context implies that "improvement" is a functional consideration—negotiated and renegotiated—not predetermined, static, or immutable. Finally, it also means both the process and the desired outcomes are flexible and adhere to the notion that "what works" can change.

The AT&R is a process approach (not outcome approach) in that there are no prescribed outcomes resulting from the process. There are no particular authority or power or communication structures, no particular communications or decision processes, no prescribed policies or procedures. Also, as will be seen with the last stage in the cycle, the process is ongoing. It implies the continuous development of the capacity of the organization. It also means that the cycle is iterative and that while it's presented in a circle or cycle to demonstrate the looped nature of the process it's also possible to move backward or across the cycle if necessary. Finally, while it does have a bias toward participation over time—and that bias is more practical and the process is oriented toward data driven change—the position on participation is more practical than it is an ideological position (see Table 7.2).

Table 7.2 Stages of the Action Training and Research Process

Stage	Action Component	Training Component
Orientation	This is the opportunity to raise and answer questions that support the development of trust between parties. This is also the time to learn about the nature of the setting being studied and the manner in which the process will occur. All clients should come to understand that this process is highly participatory and tends to highlight the position of the individual and diffuse sources of power. Effectiveness is based on the perspectives of the individuals doing the work and the organization as a whole.	The implicit training that takes place at this stage is partially about participatory management, the establishment of trust, the action and training processes, the range of possible actions, and outcomes.
Contract setting	A contract need not be written, though a memorandum of understanding may be useful. Contracts from this action research perspective should be considered psychological agreements, derived through open and tough-minded interaction. During the contract-setting process, participation is made meaningful to the extent that the consultant is able to model and elicit effective and authentic communication. It should be a model and example of the sort of interaction that will be the basis of all future interaction.	Training is focused on process skills necessary for the process ahead—active listening, leveling or self-reflexive or other regarding speech (at the least, *I* statements—more sophisticated leveling would include recognition of how one's one assumptions appear in speech, reaction, etc.), values analysis.

(Continued)

(Continued)

Stage	Action Component	Training Component
Reconnaissance and exploration of the issues	Exploration is the action; this is not an exhaustive study of the situation and issues but is an estimate of the situation. It's based in data relevant to the change project and may evolve into a collection of perceived opportunities, problems, and potential solutions. Exploring issues can be understood as a sort of brainstorming. The idea is to examine what we see as issues in the organization without getting too deeply involved with identifying the problems, opportunities, or solutions.	Trainers can help client and researchers to become aware of their values and preconceptions in order to minimize the interference with the data collection. It is not essential that clients participate in the reconnaissance process, but it is useful. Clients appear to receive a fair amount of education by being involved in the data collection. The training impact here is a significant contribution to the cohesiveness of teams through participation and exploration of issues through processes including brainstorming techniques.
Identification of problems and opportunities	Activities at this stage are directed toward developing a "feel for the situation." Data collected from the reconnaissance stage is classified and tested for agreement and degree of importance. If the problem identification is occurring in a group that owns the information, the task is to develop agreement if not a consensus.	Training helps build skills and methods for ongoing problem identification and problem solving
Aspirations	In AT&R processes, aspiration refers to the issues that people would like to influence as they begin to solve their problems and exploit their opportunities. One approach that can work well is to organize the issues at this stage (now that problems and opportunities have been identified). The participants can convert the descriptions into "how to" statements or questions. This process (aspirations, data analysis, definition of strategic action steps, etc.) would typically be done in a workshop or retreat setting, though any venue that facilitates interaction could be used—groupware, Internet chat rooms, focus groups, etc.	Through the training function at this stage, the organization is developing the skills and capacities associated with setting goals, writing objectives, and creating vision scenarios.
Development of action options	Any number of analytical methods might be used to examine high-priority action options: force field analysis; strengths, weaknesses, opportunities, and threats (SWOT); assessment; and any systems or data analysis tools or problem-solving methods.	Training is focused on helping participants build the capacity to determine what significant action options seem attainable, which require further exploration, and which must be deferred until the critical constraining vector is removed or neutralized.
Experimentation	When clients agree to undertake a change, they are predicting success. Even though the change action is based on carefully	At this stage, participants test and further develop their ability to determine which assumptions about the

Stage	Action Component	Training Component
	developed data, the experimentation stage is a logical safeguard in a process in which all the action is considered conditional and subject to testing in a tentative and time-limited way before the change is fully operative. Research designs at this stage might include participative team building, group work dynamics, systems, and work flow analysis.	issue, problem, or opportunity are most critical to people and to the success of the changes envisioned.
Experimentation results analysis	The primary effort at this stage is the assessment and evaluation of the results of the prototype implementation. Efforts at this stage are directed toward answering questions such as the following:	Training at this point includes survey and feedback processes, and research methodologies.
	Are we doing what we said we would and as well as we said we would (formative and summative evaluation)? What new data do we need? Shall we go ahead with the change action? What can we do to adapt the change that will improve it further?	
Program design	The next step then is designing the continuing program for change following the analysis of the experiment.	Here, participants are learning program-project design and management methods.
Implementation	There are many ways to introduce and implement a program. By this stage in the AT&R approach, however, it is hoped that those affected know about and have participated in the decision to implement the change initiative. There is considerable merit in using the process known as the *risk approach* in disseminating information concerning change initiatives. In this process the affected persons are brought together and invited to contribute two types of feedback: critical comments and suggestions for overcoming the problems identified. It is called a risk approach because frequently changes are called for that are necessary or expedient and that ask for redesign or even abandonment of the proposed program.	This includes participative management, work group dynamics, project management, and research methods. Constantly cycle back through previous steps with the new knowledge learned from the current step. Document the process as you go along. One major research obligation for SEAR projects is to add to the body of knowledge about changing organizations. Each new action step is an opportunity for new knowledge. The first to benefit from this new knowledge should be the project participants themselves. Therefore, it is paramount to maintain this iterative approach at every step.

(Continued)

(Continued)

Stage	Action Component	Training Component
Program evaluation	Feedback implies some sort of evaluation. The opportunity exists to enrich the learning and to increase the effectiveness of operations when feedback occurs during and after each AT&R stage. In using this model, the idea is to develop a constant and automatic feedback system to be used to provide for readjustments as the change action operates.	Training and capacity development includes program evaluation, constructive critique, documentation, survey, and feedback.
Recycling	Begin the AT&R process again. Starting with the orientation stage, the processes retrace the AT&R path through the stages; though at this point, the thrust of the project should be quite different from the original project. New action options should develop into innovative and creative change options based on new data evolving from a changed environment to processes like strategic management and planning, program planning and evaluation, and human resources development.	

Having presented the "stages" or steps in the AT&R approach, one other critical aspect of this change should be recognized here. As Raymond Bruce and Sherman Wyman point out, and Gardner acknowledges as well, the AT&R process is best understood as a menu not a recipe. Because it's iterative and because organizations might start at any of the various stages of the process, the menu metaphor better captures the flexibility of the process.[36]

One of the key strengths can be found in the observation that organizations are collections of individuals and the entirety of the AT&R process works at that level. We have become increasingly aware, since the Hawthorne experiments, that organizations are complex compilations of individuals who interact in structured ways. Those structures are both formal and informal and range from highly productive patterns for the organization to highly dysfunctional patterns. But because they emerge from the interaction of individuals, crafting a change process that works from individuals to the organization creates a more robust set of outcomes that emerges from those dynamics rather than being overlaid on top of those dynamics. AR/OD, by embodying the variability and flexibility entailed in Gardner's model, has the potential to better engage the interactive character of organizational behavior.

Moreover, the process is flexible as well as being clearly oriented to the specific context of the organization. Within that context, it is also highly data driven. Empirical evidence indicates that experience works better than pure reason; if you experience the processes, if you experience the change, you're more likely to embody it in the future.

Case 7.3

Current Expressions: Organization Development in the Montana State University Research Library

In early 2008, library administration at Montana State University (MSU) began the process of acquiring compact shelving as a partial response to ongoing discussions about space constraints in the Renne Library Building. In a separate but parallel process, the dean of the library created the diverse group focused on leadership, professional development, and training, as a part of her efforts to generate greater engagement with library employees in support of organizational decisions and initiatives. The group was comprised of classified, professional, and faculty members from across the library's teams and was created to support the dean's efforts to enhance professional development opportunities within the organization.

In the spring of that year, the dean; the chair of the Leadership, Education Ability, and Potential (LEAP) group; and an outside consultant who is director of the MSU public administration program began a series of preliminary conversations about the possibilities for further developing the participatory culture of the library and its staff. During these discussions, two issues emerged. The first and primary issue was the library's need to do short-term strategic planning around the use of space and the acquisition of compact shelving. The relevance of space discussions was heightened in the summer of 2008 when a significant gift for the planned development of an "information commons" in the library was announced. Taken together, the addition of compact shelving and the conceptualization of an information commons created an opportunity for the library to consider a wider range of issues about physical space use, including the location of collections, the services provided, and how these are prioritized relative to the library's vision and mission within the larger university. A secondary discussion focused on the possibility of using a space-planning initiative to enhance the library's capacity for ongoing functional and cultural development. It was felt that discussions about the use of space provided a unique opportunity to build on the cultural development work already being done by LEAP.

The specifics of the process used here were heavily influenced by both Gardner and Bruce and Wyman.[37] This approach was used for the project because the intent of the project was to develop a change plan for the organization out of a minute and nuanced understanding in an effort to develop a rich or thick description of the relationships, processes, and activities of the organization that would both enhance the likelihood of success and reduce the chance that significant unanticipated consequences would emerge. The AT&R process encompassed two broad goals—to elicit relevant information about critical issues from across the entire organization and to model and experience an interactive and collaborative decision process that can be replicated in future initiatives.

The information gathered through this process revealed a detailed picture of the possibilities, risks, hopes, and concerns across the organization regarding potential changes. The research strategy developed by the AT&R team combined the use of extensive interviews with select individual members of the library organization, in conjunction with four additional focus groups of inter-team library employees. Between these two methods, every member of the organization was invited to participate. This approach was selected because it offered the greatest opportunity for participation from across the organization without the logistical difficulties of conducting one-on-one interviews with every faculty and staff member. Following the review of the findings from this project conducted in 2008, an analysis of the next four years following the study for examples of capacity building, including effective skills in change management and distributed leadership in the organization, is provided.

To some degree, this broader awareness set the stage for a second and slightly broader area of impact of the AT&R intervention, which has to do with the broader learnings and practices that emerged from the project. One result of the intervention was the emergence of a clear sense that the majority of faculty and staff members have the strong desire to be involved in some way. Further, there was a sense that members of the organization and those who are most likely to be affected by change should also be given intentional and due consideration both for normative reasons and because there was a growing awareness that those affected by decisions also had important information about the effects of those decisions on day-to-day work processes and their effectiveness.

In some ways, these impacts serve as a bridge from the short-term instrumental results of the project to the more fundamental and long-term impacts related to the organizational culture, capacity, and distributed leadership, which have had a longer and more substantial impact on how the organization functions. These cultural, capacity, and leadership shifts remain embodied in the work processes of the organization.

Organization Development: Summary

Of the three theories of change we've described so far, OD is perhaps the most open in that it is the least dogmatic or mechanistic in either its assumptions or its approaches. As a result, OD also runs the risk of being the most abstract and difficult to use in practical, instrumental ways. For this reason, OD tends to be much more process oriented, whether in the form of Lewin's early unfreeze-change-refreeze model, or Gardner's AT&R "menu." It is also the approach, especially in the case of AT&R, that has the most fluid understanding of organizations. OD is the most likely of the three approaches discussed so far to assume that change is a given and constant and that conceptions of organizations and change that assume the possibility of highly stable, let alone static, structures are inaccurate. AT&R suggests instead that organizations are always in flux, to a greater or lesser degree, and therefore administrators must be constantly attuned to that change lest it result in dysfunction. The promise of constant change, however, is the possibility of improvement in both instrumental performance and the human experience of the organization.

Reflection Questions

Given that OD and AT&R tend to view change as ongoing, what are the strengths and weaknesses in dealing with sudden and/or forced change?

What do you see as the major strengths and weaknesses of the AT&R cycle and approach?

New Sciences and Organizations

Of the theories we explore in this book, chaos and complexity theories are among the most difficult to apprehend both because the work, such as Ilya Prigogine's Nobel Prize–winning work in physical chemistry, is technically challenging and because these theories describe a world that is highly counterintuitive in many ways. In some respects, the application of new sciences, including chaos and complexity theories but also quantum theory and fractal geometry, makes little sense in that the collection of influences is so diverse as to make them unrelated or even unrelatable to organizational or other social settings. Considering the new sciences in terms of scale, from subatomic particles to cosmic equations, or scopes ranging from closed fluid systems to abstract mathematical equations, the work across these fields could scarcely be more diverse. Despite, or perhaps because of that diversity, there has been a great deal of interest in the application of the new sciences to OT, and the body of work does seem to reveal some important attributes of organizations and their behaviors.

Assumptions

The starting point for exploring the assumptions that are essentially shared across the new sciences has to do with a shared perspective on the nature of the world in which we live. As we'll describe in the following section, the new sciences diverge dramatically from early twentieth-century positivism that held out great hope for the precise predictive abilities of modern science and engineering; the new sciences see the world as being probabilistic rather than deterministic. Although there are variations across the new sciences with respect probabilities expressed, the new sciences don't make claims about the determinism of the systems they study.

While the new sciences break with modernist positivism on the issue of determinism, they do share with classical science the assumption that the causes of system behavior are real and can be empirically measured—that is, they are not socially constructed. Moreover, while causes in the new sciences don't function in a linear, causal way, if isolated they can be understood in ways that leave little if any uncertainty as to their effects. What makes systems complex is the interaction of variables but not their ambiguousness or constructed qualities.

Concepts and Insights

To this point we have focused on the techniques and approaches; here, the challenge is different. Partly because the application of ideas from the new sciences has emerged so recently and partly because the operationalization of the theories into social and organizational settings is both challenging and heterodox at this point, the literature does not reveal as much in the way of concrete techniques and applications as we have seen with other theories we've covered thus far. As a result, our strategy here is to describe what seems to be a coherent set of concepts with direct application to social and organizational settings and the corresponding insights and implications of those concepts. It's also important to recognize that we've broken out our treatment of the "new sciences" based on the natural sciences from which the concepts were derived. In part, we've done this to highlight the conceptual diversity that characterizes the new sciences and in part because we feel that some treatments of the new sciences in organizational applications mix concepts from different fields of science in ways that are scientifically inaccurate and that convolute their utility to organizational analysis and action.

Chaos and Complexity Theories

In our view, it's perhaps easiest to grasp the application of concepts from chaos and complexity theory by thinking about those concepts in terms of claims about preconditions that exist in the systems we're studying, implications of those conditions for the systems' behavior, and finally, the implications for administrative practice.

System Preconditions

There are several attributes and preconditions of chaotic systems that can be understood as a starting point for their use in organizational settings. First is that such systems should be understood as being nonlinear and sensitive to initial conditions. This means that chaotic or complex organizational settings don't change in direct, linear, or incremental ways. In linear systems, small changes in initial conditions result in correspondingly small changes in output conditions. In nonlinear systems, small quantitative changes in the inputs to systems—whether personnel, policy, budgetary, or otherwise—can have dramatic qualitative impacts on the outputs of those systems.

Moreover, these dynamic, nonlinear systems are also characterized by conditions of mutual causation. Unlike simple linear systems, where discrete and distinct independent variables cause some change or effect in dependent variables, in a dynamic, chaotic system, all variables are both dependent and independent simultaneously.

Chaotic and complex systems also have to be understood as being open, in some sense, to the wider environment. In a way not dissimilar to Katz and Kahn's description of open systems, which also draws on natural systems theory to understand organizational settings, chaotic and complex systems import energy. This importation of energy results in a certain level of dynamism. In other words, as dynamic systems continue to draw new energy from the wider environment, they may exhibit recurrent patterns of behavior, but they are not static.

One result of these preconditions is that the behavior of these systems is probabilistic rather than deterministic. Because organizational systems are dynamic, sensitive to initial conditions, and nonlinear, they function within a set of parameters; they are neither random nor are their behaviors totally unpredictable. However, our ability to predict their behavior falls within an identifiable set of parameters allowing us to predict their behavior within a range of likelihood rather than with deterministic certainty.

System Behaviors and Consequences

As a consequence of these conditions, chaotic or complex social systems can exist in states of relative equilibrium and in far-from-equilibrium states. Under relatively stable conditions, organizational systems can exist in equally stable states. However, when there are changes in the system's conditions, perhaps because of political, budgetary, or other crises or perturbations, the system can bifurcate, or move into a qualitatively different phase state in which the system is far from equilibrium. While these far-from-equilibrium conditions may appear on the surface, to be random, chaos theory suggests that there may be emergent patterns that are qualitatively different but patterned nevertheless.

Looking to another concept drawn from chaos theory, the idea of self-organization captures this idea of new patterns being revealed in different phase or behavioral states within a system. The patterns that reveal themselves in different phase states can sometimes be depicted by tracking different variables within the system. The butterfly fractal we presented in Chapter 4 is one such example. The three-winged bird attractor (see Figure 7.6) is another example of the patterns that can be revealed by tracking the status of the system over longer periods or iterations of the system.

Integrating these ideas into organizational and administrative settings has a number of potential implications. One is an explicit recognition of the complexity of organizational systems in that factors and variables are extensively interconnected and mutually influential. The consequence is something we intuitively and experientially know about organizational life: actions necessarily have unintended consequences. However, that shouldn't be understood as wholly unpredictable. We may not be able to predict, with high levels of confidence, but we should recognize that the consequence array themselves into new patterns, and those patterns may well fall within a set, probabilistic range.

Figure 7.6 Three-Winged Bird Attractor

Source: Mario Markus and Benno Hess, Max-Planck Institute, Dortmund.

Fractal Geometry

In the years just following the end of the First World War, mathematicians in Europe began studying and graphing complex number sets. The graphs revealed intricate, repeating patterns that appeared at many different scales. Although this work received little attention either inside or outside the field of mathematics initially, the work was picked up many years later by Benoit Mandelbrot and others who recognized that these complex geometric patterns were much closer to the complex patterns that appeared in clouds, plant leaves, and other natural structures. While this work would become critical for applications like computer animation, the appearance of the patterns or fractals also revealed something recognizable about social organization as well. Fractals reveal patterns of self-similarity in natural phenomena that we also see in social phenomena. For example, the idea of self-similarity appears in organizational attributes such as hierarchy. The patterns of hierarchy and breadth of span of control are replicated at different scales and in different forms across multidivisional agencies and organizations. Although it was developed from an entirely different application, the Sierpinski triangle (see Figure 7.7) reveals

Figure 7.7 The Sierpinski Triangle

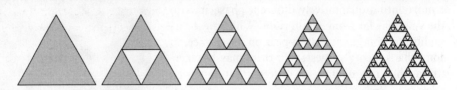

Source: Wereon, "File:Sierpinski triangle evolution.svg," Wikimedia Commons, http://commons.wikimedia
.org/wiki/File:Sierpinski_triangle_evolution.svg.

a pattern that very closely resembles many organizational charts. Importantly, the idea of self-similarity reveals informal as well as informal repeating structures or patterns. Not only can we find examples of self-similarity in organization structure but also in informal behaviors such as the patterns of social interaction across scales from nation, to region, to community, to family, to the individual. To be clear, the idea of self-similarity is limited to similarity and not sameness. There is no claim that the patterns or behaviors are identical across observational scales but only that they share some attributes.

Quantum Mechanics

The last example of the new sciences making its way into organizational settings we want to highlight is quantum mechanics, the behaviors of subatomic particles. One of the most famous and vexing analogies of quantum mechanics is that of Schrödinger's cat. Schrödinger's thought experiment is as follows: We place a living cat into a steel, windowless chamber, along with a device containing a vial of poison. There is also in the chamber a radioactive substance connected to a sensing device. If even a single atom of the radioactive substance decays during the test period, the device will release the poison and kill the cat. The thought experiment reveals that the observer cannot know whether or not an atom of the substance has decayed, and as such, we cannot know whether the vial has been broken, releasing the poison and killing the cat.[38] Since we cannot know, according to quantum law, the cat is therefore in the paradoxical condition of being both dead and alive—a so-called superposition of states. It is only when we open the box and empirically observe the condition of the cat that the superposition is lost, and the cat becomes either one or the other—dead or alive. This condition is described as *quantum indeterminacy* or *the observer's paradox*. The paradox is the bizarre situation, at least from a positivist perspective, in which the observation or measurement itself affects an outcome in such a way that the outcome as such does not exist unless or until the measurement is made.

In social and administrative settings, this paradox takes the form of theoretical indeterminacy. We have limited and incomplete information about what people do and why they do it. As soon as we select a theoretical lens by which to conduct our analysis, we find behaviors and conditions that comply with that lens. Paradoxically, we could simultaneously conduct the analysis through another, incommensurable lens, and corroborate that interpretation as well. This revelation is important not only in terms of interpretation of events but also in the communication and interaction related to the work of the organizations. If two or more members of the organization are operating from different theoretical or ideological perspectives without knowing it, the likelihood that the paradox will be made real is great.

New Sciences in Organizational Practice

Douglas Kiel and Euel Elliott's article "Budgets as Dynamic Systems" is among the most interesting and applied research efforts utilizing chaos theory and dynamic systems concepts.[39] Kiel and Elliott come to their use of chaos and dynamic systems via V. O. Key's call for a comprehensive theory of budgeting and suggest instead that given the nature of budget settings and conditions efforts and grand theory building are likely to be unproductive. Instead, they claim, scholars might be better served by developing more effective interpretive or heuristic tools useful in revealing and guiding work since theory building and testing is so problematic. Chaos theory and nonlinear dynamics, they suggest, is particularly well suited to this effort.

With that orientation in place, the authors dig further into the theory and its attributes consistent with our previously given descriptions and in Chapter 4. First, they recognize that budget systems are open and that they import resources from the wider environment. These resources are analogous to the energy that is imported and animates natural systems. These systems, according to Kiel and Elliott, oscillate between relative stability or equilibrium and unstable far-from-equilibrium conditions. In other words, the systems move between phase states. Moreover, their movement is characterized by nonlinear shifts in status. Linear changes in inputs do not result in linear output changes. The result of the characteristics appears to be random behavior but because their behavior is affected by prior conditions in the system are in fact chaotic.

Kiel and Elliott take this claim—that budget systems and their appearance are chaotic and not random—and examine in in the context of twenty-seven years of federal budget data. When percentage-change data for discretionary outlays and defense outlays are graphed with time, the change patterns do appear random. However, when those data are restructured in a way that reveals something about the history of the system, graphing time (T) by time minus one or change from the year prior ($T-1$) or $[T \times (T-1)]$, an apparent pattern does emerge (see Figures 7.8 through 7.11).

This pattern, or attractor, according to the authors, reveals something about the influential dimensions of the system and gives a qualitative assessment of the dynamism of the system as well. In this instance, this new approach to mapping the behavior of the system, especially as expressed in Figure 7.11, shows how the claim that incrementalism or incremental changes explain budget outcomes over time is insufficient. Kiel and Elliott also claim that the patterns in these new graphs also reveal the improbability of developing a comprehensive budget theory. From their perspective, subcategories of budgets may reveal quite distinct structures or patterns over time relative to the major budget category—for example, personnel expenditures by comparison to overall expenditures of an agency. Stated differently, the sensitivity and nonlinear nature of these systems are dynamic enough as to defy unifying or categorizing theory that would explain the variability across budget and budget systems.

Figure 7.8 Rates of Change in Total Domestic Discretionary Outlays, FY 1963–FY 1990

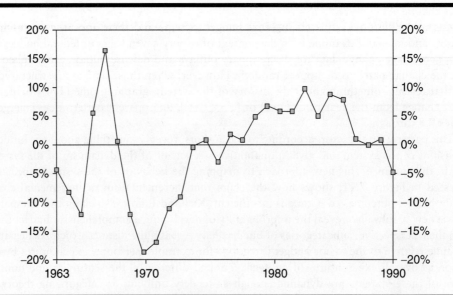

Source: L. Douglas Kiel and Euel Elliott, "Budgets as Dynamic Systems: Change, Variation, Time and Budgetary Heuristics," *Journal of Public Administration Research and Theory* 2, no. 2 (1992): 139–156.

Figure 7.9 Rates of Change in Total Defense Outlays, FY 1963–FY 1990

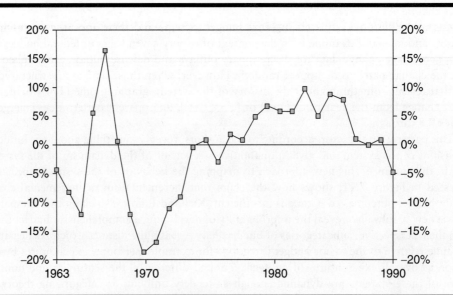

Source: L. Douglas Kiel and Euel Elliott, "Budgets as Dynamic Systems: Change, Variation, Time and Budgetary Heuristics," *Journal of Public Administration Research and Theory* 2, no. 2 (1992): 139–156.

Figure 7.10 Rates of Change in Total Domestic Discretionary Outlays, Excluding Defense, FY 1963–FY 1990

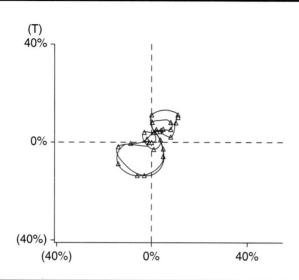

Source: L. Douglas Kiel and Euel Elliott, "Budgets as Dynamic Systems: Change, Variation, Time and Budgetary Heuristics," *Journal of Public Administration Research and Theory* 2, no. 2 (1992): 139–156.

Figure 7.11 Rates of Change in Total Defense Outlays, FY 1963–FY 1990

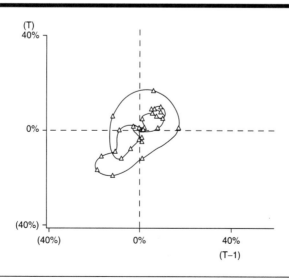

Source: L. Douglas Kiel and Euel Elliott, "Budgets as Dynamic Systems: Change, Variation, Time and Budgetary Heuristics," *Journal of Public Administration Research and Theory* 2, no. 2 (1992): 139–156.

The Challenge of the New Sciences

It's clear from the theoretical work in OT and public administration drawing from the new sciences since the 1990s that there is a great deal of energy and excitement about the possibilities presented by the adaptation of new sciences for organizational analysis. In an effort to adhere to our stated approach to this book—that a key criteria for a theory's inclusion is their applicability to addressing real administrative problems—we feel that there are some significant challenges to the use of the new sciences that we should explore. In part this exploration of the limitations is focused narrowly on this one theory. However, we also want to point out that we do think the central question—can these theories move beyond description to prescription?—is a worthwhile point of discussion.

With that caveat in place, there seem to be several central critiques that call the adaptation of the new sciences to organizational application into question. The first is the critique that the use of the new sciences here is essentially metaphorical.[40] The application of these theories symbolically compares attributes of natural systems to those of organizational systems in ways that highlight what may be important characteristics of the organizational systems but that these social and physical or natural systems are in fact not the same. Metaphorical comparisons, such as Forrest Gump's famous statement, "Life is like a box of chocolates," focus attention on an important attribute but ignore the myriad ways in which the entities are different. In the case of social systems, it may be that consideration of the social system as complex, self-organizing, probabilistic, or otherwise similar to chaotic, complex, or quantum systems does illuminate some interesting phenomena but defies the more empirical or analytical techniques of the original concepts.

There is also a second prescriptive concern related to the application of the new sciences, especially chaos and complexity theories. Although the theories are admittedly probabilistic rather than deterministic, that does not, in and of itself, preclude activities like forecasting. It may be that we have to exercise caution and reflectiveness in using such forecasts, but their availability would help us look and move into the future. However, the combination of sensitivity to initial conditions and the movement of systems between phase states seems to suggest that efforts to use the theory in social settings will be retrospective rather than prospective. Because social systems, and organization systems particularly, can be significantly affected by small changes in initial conditions, and their behavior is probabilistic, our ability to recognize the conditions that proceed, let alone cause a system to shift phase states, seems likely to be retrospective rather than prospective or predictive. The result is extreme difficulty in trying to anticipate, let alone leverage or respond to state changes.

Reflection Questions

How do chaos, complexity, fractal geometry, and quantum mechanics relate to change in public organizations?

What sorts of variables, indicators, and measures might be used in practice?

Finally, and from our perspective most problematically, none of the key variables in the systems studied in chaos theory, fractal geometry, or quantum theory exercise agency. A key feature, if not *the* key feature of social systems, is that people have the capacity to exercise agency or free will. While it is undoubtedly true that there are all sorts of system, social group, structure, psychological, and other influences on human behavior that are important for making sense of and improving organization performance, OT—and public administration more broadly—seem premised on the notion that we are capable of intentional action that can improve our share conditions. Working from a theory that has no mechanism for acknowledging human agency seems particularly problematic in applied, active fields such as ours.

Foreshadows of Postmodernism

While there are a variety of potential connections we could make between the theories in this chapter and postmodern and anti-essentialist ideas in Part III, we have chosen to focus on what we perceive to be particularly fruitful links that exist between the action research approach to OD we previously describe and attributes of postmodern theory (as much as they can be ascribed in generalizable ways).

The first link between OD and action research on the one hand and postmodernism on the other is a strong tendency toward anti-essentialism or antifoundationalism. Like other action research practitioners, Gardner pushes against the exclusive use of enlightenment reason and rationality.[41] Instead, Gardner recognizes the possibility of contextual, intuitional, and other forms of knowledge.[42] Others recognize diversity of knowledge and perspective as increasingly important to effective decision making in complex settings.[43]

A second link can be found in the action research approach to OD in that it places a strong emphasis on equity and emancipatory participation. In other words, both action research and postmodernism tend to stress fairly radical expressions of openness and engagement. It should be recognized that this openness and engagement is closely linked to its anti-essentialist character. The logic here is that the denial of privilege to any one, specific form of knowledge, discipline, or corresponding course of action is very parallel to the emancipatory denial of privilege of any particular individual or locus of authority in the organization or broader social system.

Summary and Conclusions

THERE IS A CONTINUUM of conceptions of change from the assumption that organizations and environments are relatively stable and need periodic but discrete and delineated change to more stark ontologies of change that suggest that organizations and the environments in which they operate are in constant, dramatic flux.

While the models of change are conceptually distinct, there are important links between them. These links include assumptions about the environment as being open and fluid as well as assumptions about internal and external connectivity and even mutual causality.

Not only are there links between and among the ideas here but also those presented in other chapters—for example, ideas of change presented here and those embedded in the systems and learning organization models presented in the last chapter (interconnectivity, mutual causality, learning-change).

Finally, we want to reiterate the questions we posed in assessing the new sciences. One, how applicable do theories need to be in order to be of practical use—descriptive and insight yielding or applied and action supporting? And two, what do current organizational conditions and climates mean for the idea of paradigmatic incommensurability? Part of our approach to the book thus far has been to illuminate the underlying assumptions of these theories in order to make more clear the consequences or opportunity costs (what's given up when one option is chosen over another) of adopting one theory over another. Or framed differently, and following David Farmer's admonition about epistemic pluralism, this awareness is not just an analytical tool but a very practical tool of both conceptual and strategic nimbleness. ■

Discussion Questions

1. What is the role of a leader in organizational change processes? How does that role vary across the theories in this chapter?

2. What are the potential reactions to organizational change? Think about a time when you observed organizational change and reactions to that change. How did the reactions impact the change or the management of change?

3. What are some factors considered when diagnosing the need for or approach to organizational changes? Compare and contrast those factors across the theories described in this chapter.

Notes

1. William Bridges and Susan Bridges, *Managing Transitions: Making the Most of Change* 3rd ed. (Philadelphia: Perseus Books, 2009).
2. Lester Coch and John R. P. French Jr., "Overcoming Resistance to Change" *Human Relations* (1948): 512–532.
3. John P. Kotter and Leonard A. Schlesinger, "Choosing Strategies for Change," *Harvard Business Review* (1979): 106–114.
4. Michael Hammer, "Reengineering Work: Don't Automate, Obliterate," *Harvard Business Review* (July/August, 1990): 104–112.
5. Michael Hammer and James Champy, *Reengineering the Corporation: A Manifesto for Business Revolution* (New York: Harper Business, 1993).
6. Thomas H. Davenport, *Process Innovation: Reengineering Work through Information Technology* (Boston: Harvard Business School Press, 1993).
7. Eliezer Giesler, *Managing the Aftermath of Radical Corporate Change: Reengineering, Restructuring and Reinvention* (Westport, CT: Quorum Books, 1997).
8. John W. Meyer and Brian Rowan, "Institutional Organizations: Formal Structure as Myth and Ceremony," *American Journal of Sociology* 83 (1977): 340–363.
9. It's worth noting that this element of culture is quite similar to what Edgar Schein would likely describe as artifacts.

10. Remember that this sort of information, according to BPR practices, should be available not just to supervisors but to managers and lower level workers as well—discretion to shift work processes should exist across the organization, not just in the hands of supervisors.

11. Hammer, "Reengineering Work."

12. It's worth noting that this sort of structural effort to ensure both control and efficiency is very consistent with the sort of structures and processes that Herbert Simon advocated and that we introduced in Chapter 4.

13. Unless noted otherwise, this description of a *Contemporary Example* of BPR is drawn from Roger McCullough and Ronald R. Sims, "Implementation of an HRIMS at the Personnel Board of Jefferson County, Alabama: A Case Study in Process Reengineering," *Public Personnel Management* 42, no. 4 (2012): 685–703.

14. Radha R. Sharma, *Change Management: Concepts and Applications* (New Delhi, India: Tata McGraw-Hill, 2006).

15. W. Warner Burke and George H. Litwin, "A Causal Model of Organizational Performance and Change," *Journal of Management* 18, no. 3 (1992): 523–545.

16. James McGreggor Burns, *Leadership* (New York: Harper & Row, 1978).

17. Abraham Zaleznik, "Managers and Leaders: Are They Different?" *Harvard Business Review* 55, no. 3 (1977): 67–78.

18. W. Warner Burke, *Organization Change: Theory and Practice*, 1st ed. (Thousand Oaks, CA: Sage, 2002).

19. Ibid.

20. Sergio Fernandez and Lois R. Wise, "In Exploration of Why Public Organizations 'Ingest' Innovations," *Public Administration* 88, no. 4 (2010): 979–998.

21. Thomas G. Cummings and Edgar F. Huse, *Organization Development and Change* (St. Paul, MN: West Publishers, 1989).

22. John Newstrom and Keith Davis, *Organization Behavior: Human Behavior at Work* (New York: McGraw-Hill, 1993).

23. Richard Beckhard, *Organization Development: Strategies and Models* (Reading, MA: Addison-Wesley, 1969).

24. Cummings and Huse, *Organization Development and Change*.

25. Thomas G. Cummings and Christopher G. Worley, *Essentials of Organization Development and Change* (Cincinnati, OH: South-Western College Publishing, 2001).

26. Edgar Schein, *Processes Consultation*, vols. 1 and 2 (Reading, MA: Addison-Wesley, 1987).

27. Wendell L. French and Cecil H. Bell,, *Organization Development* (Englewood Cliffs, NJ: Prentice Hall, 1995), 151.

28. John S. Drummond & Markus Themessl-Huber, "The Cyclical Process of Action Research: The Contribution of Gilles Deleuze," *Action Research* 5, no. 4 (2007): 430–448.

29. Michael McGill and Neely D. Gardner, "Od Orienteer," *Public Administration Quarterly* 6, no. 2 (1992): 190.

30. Robert J. Marshak and Loizos Heracleaous, "A Discoursive Approach to Organization Development," *Action Research* 3, no. 1 (2005): 69–88.

31. Chris Argyris and Donald Schön, *Organizational Learning: A Theory of Action Perspective* (Reading, MA: Addison-Wesley, 1978); Kurt Lewin, *Resolving Social Conflicts. Selected Papers on Group Dynamics* (New York: Harper and Row, 1948); Edgar H. Schein, *Process Consultation: Its Role in Organization Development* (Reading, MA: Addison-Wesley, 1969).

32. Neely Gardner, "Action Training and Research: Something Old and Something New," *Public Administration Review* 32, no. 2 (March 1974): 103–112; Neely Gardner, *Group Leadership*

(Washington, DC: National Training and Development Service Press, 1974); Camille Gates Barnett, "Leadership: Arranging the Chairs—Reflections on the Lessons of Neely Gardner," *Public Administration Quarterly* 16, no. 2 (1992): 180–188

33. Kurt Lewin, "Conduct, Knowledge and Acceptance of New Values," in *Resolving Social Conflicts,* ed. G. W. Lewin (New York: Harper & Row, 1948), 56–70; Kurt Lewin, "Action Research and Minority Problems," in *Resolving Social Conflicts,* ed. G. W. Lewin (New York: Harper & Row, 1948), 201–216; David Bargal, "Personal and Intellectual Influences Leading to Lewin's Paradigm of Action Research," *Action Research* 4, no. 4 (2006): 367–388.

34. Norman R. King, "Managing Values at City Hall (with a Lot of Help from Neely)," *Public Administration Quarterly* 16, no. 2 (Summer 1992): 235–253; Frank Sherwood, "Institutionalizing Training: Another Gardner Legacy," *Public Administration Quarterly* 16, no. 2 (1992): 164–179.

35. John R. Hook, "Neely Gardner: An Interpretation of His Approach to Organization Development," *Public Administration Quarterly* 15, no. 4 (Winter 1992): 451–456.

36. Raymond Bruce and Sherman Wyman, *Changing Organizations: Practicing Action Training and Research* (Thousand Oaks, CA: Sage, 1998).

37. Gardner, "Action Training and Research"; Gardner, *Group Leadership*; Bruce and Wyman, *Changing Organizations.*

38. This system, like chaotic systems, is probabilistic, so we cannot determine or predict with any level of certainty what the state of the atom, or the poison, or the cat is.

39. L. Douglas Kiel & Euel Elliott, "Budgets as Dynamic Systems: Change, Variation, Time and Budgetary Heuristics," *Journal of Public Administration Research and Theory* 2, no. 2 (1992): 139–156.

40. Darryl Hunter, "Chaos Theory and Educational Administration: Imaginative Foil or Useful Framework?" *EAF Journal* 11, no. 2 (1996): 9; Frank A. Dubinskas, "On the Edge of Chaos: A Metaphor for Transformative Change," *Journal of Management Inquiry* 3, no. 4 (December 1994): 355–366.

41. V. J. Friedman and T. Rogers, "There Is Nothing So Theoretical as Good Action Research," *Action Research* 7:1, 31–77.

42. James F. Wolf, "Neely Gardner and Deming's Total Quality Management: Parallels and Connections," *Public Administration Quarterly* 16, no. 2 (1992); McGill and Gardner, "Od Orienteer."

43. James Suroweicki, *The Wisdom of Crowds* (New York: Anchor, 2005); Mary Schmidt, "Grout: Alternative Kinds of Knowledge and Why They Are Ignored," *Public Administration Review* 53, no. 6 (1993): 525–530.

Chapter 8

Managing Organization-Environment Relations

The Management Attribute

In this final chapter of Part II, we are moving our level of analysis to another, broader level. Here, we are turning our attention to theories of organization that help us understand and affect the relationship between the organization and the wider environment in which it operates. In his exploration of institutional leadership, Philip Selznick remarks the following:

> When institutional leadership fails, it is perhaps more often by default than by positive error or sin; and the institution drifts, exposed to vagrant pressures, readily influenced by short-run opportunistic trends.[1]

In part, the rationale for including this topic is reflected in Selznick's attention to "critical" or strategic decisions that are related to the extent to which the "vagrant pressures" he refers to—and that affect institutional character of the organization—are many instances pressures from the organization's environment. As Selznick reveals in *TVA and the Grass Roots,* the composition of the institutional character of an organization is shaped by the organization's relationship with its environmental field—that set of entities, including customers or clients, oversight or regulator organizations, suppliers, and other stakeholders.[2] Or more instrumentally, those decisions that drive the *strategic* orientation and effectiveness of the organization are directly about the environment.

As a way of working our way into a discussion and developing understanding of organization-environment relations, let's start by revisiting the closed system image of organizations we explored way back in Chapter 2. Although some early organization theorists, especially Weber, did recognize the existence of an environment outside the organization, within a closed system perspective, the key focus of organization theory (OT) has to do with structures, relations, and dynamics solely within the organization.

The difficulties of that model emerge nearly immediately. For example, how do we determine who is included as being "in the organization"? From one perspective, the answer is fairly straightforward: whoever receives a paycheck. The difficulty, of course, is how do we categorize volunteers, especially in volunteer-based organizations? They directly contribute to the mission of the organization, they commit significant portions of time to delivering services or producing goods, shouldn't they be considered in the organization? There is a similar ambiguity with respect to roles like board members of nonprofit organizations. From one perspective they contribute directly to the strategies and mission of the organization—maybe even directly to the resource development and planning efforts of the organization. From another perspective, however, they likely earn their livelihood from a different organization and the nature of their role is to retain some independence for the purposes of neutral, objective decision making.

It wasn't until the introduction of open systems theory, drawing on the work of Ludwig von Bertalanffy from the natural sciences and organization theorists like Daniel Katz and Robert Kahn, that there was preliminary attention given to the influence of the environment on the organization. From this first recognition of the relationship with, and influence of the wider environment, increasingly sophisticated and nuanced models of that relationship have emerged. As we noted in earlier chapters, the open systems model articulated by Katz and Kahn largely conceives of the external environment as a source of inputs and a recipient of outputs.

Similarly, contingency theory, especially the work of Paul Lawrence and Jay Lorsch, recognizes not only the existence of a wider environment but that environment has a specific, assessable impact on the organization. In the case of contingency theory, that impact is expressed in that it influences tasks differentially across organizations and even among different units of the same organization.

Before working too far into particular characterizations of organization-environment relations or models in the literature, it's worth taking a moment to explore a few preliminary depictions of the nature and conception of the relationship between organization and environment. Mary Jo Hatch's description of three different levels or models of organization-environment relations is useful here.[3]

Hatch's first model, shown in Figure 8.1, is perhaps the simplest and most common way of thinking about organization-environment relations. It depicts the organization as a sort of bubble, or relatively isolated entity that exists discretely within a larger environment. In this model, that larger environment is comparatively undifferentiated—that is, the model does not depict any particular attributes in the environment that are of particular concern.

A second model, one in which the organization is situated within a network of other organizations, presents a richer conceptualization of attributes of the environment that may demand awareness and response. This network of other organizations are ones in which the central organization has some direct and ongoing relationship. Such organizations might include oversight or regulatory organizations, partner organizations, special interests, labor organizations, and while not a formal organization, citizens, clients, or customers might be a part of the network environment as well. A simple depiction of the network environment might be similar to the one shown in Figure 8.2.

Hatch also presents an alternative, perhaps richer depiction of that same network environment, similar to the one shown in Figure 8.3. Here, the model of the environment includes representation of the relative importance of other organizations to the central organization being studied—in this case represented by relative size of each node within the network. This model also recognizes that not every organization in the network is directly connected to every other

Figure 8.1 Simple Organization-Environment Model

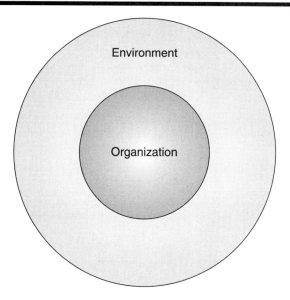

Source: Adapted from Mary Jo Hatch, *Organization Theory: Modern, Symbolic and Postmodern Perspectives* (New York: Oxford University Press, 1997).

Figure 8.2 Organization-Network Environment Model

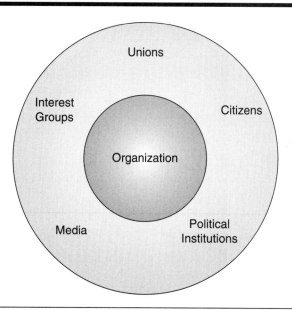

Source: Adapted from Mary Jo Hatch, *Organization Theory: Modern, Symbolic and Postmodern Perspectives* (New York: Oxford University Press, 1997).

Figure 8.3 Complex Organization-Environment Model

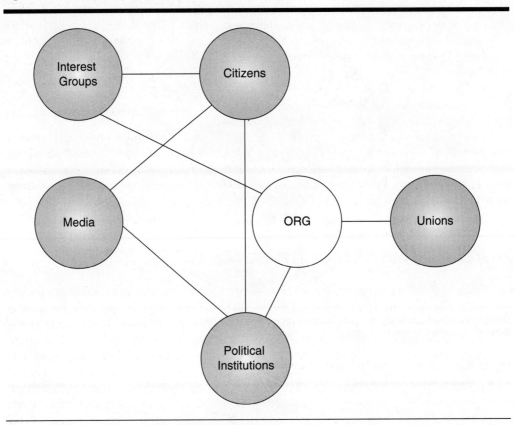

Source: Adapted from Mary Jo Hatch, *Organization Theory: Modern, Symbolic and Postmodern Perspectives* (New York: Oxford University Press, 1997).

organization. Such a model could easily be developed further to represent greater detail about the nature of the relationships by adding arrows or lines of different types to indicate direction of the relationship or other attributes such as collaboration, conflict, or competition. Regardless of the detail included, these two models highlight one particular attribute of the larger environment that networks can and should be aware of in order to manage its performance.

Hatch's third model adds an additional layer—one that she describes as the "general environment." This general environment, according to Hatch, includes political, legal, economic, social, and other dynamics that have the potential to affect the work and effectiveness of the organization. The elements of Hatch's model—whether the second model that identifies other entities within the organizational network or the third model that highlights specific attributes of the working climate of the organization—tend to be oriented around the factors of production that are critical to private sector organizations. The applicability of a direct conversion of those elements into a public or governance setting may be problematic. For example, using

Graham Allison's assessment of the differences between public and private sectors, such as the inclusion and relationship with the media, suggests the need to adapt Hatch's work in ways unique to public and governance settings. Nevertheless, it's clear that a general environment does exist and can be described.

In the remainder of the chapter, we look at three particular organizational theories—*resource dependence theory (RDT), network theory,* and *neoinstitutionalism.* Each of these theories highlight and focus on particular aspects of the environment and an organization's relationship to it. In doing so, the three theories reveal different but important understandings of the factors that affect their relationships with their environments and also suggest possible strategies that might be crafted by organizations to respond to and endeavor to be more effective within those settings.

> ## Reflection Questions
>
> How do Hatch's depictions help us understand the relationship between organizations and their environment?
>
> What do they highlight, and what do they miss?

Resource Dependence Theory

By the late 1970s, the development of organization theories that directly or metaphorically draw on attributes of natural systems had become quite diverse, ranging from the open systems approaches we've described already to population ecology theory that seeks to understand the commonalities in the behavior of groups of similar organizations as they seek to secure a niche for their success.[4] In 1978, Jeffrey Pfeffer and Gerald Salancik published their classic work *The External Control of Organizations: A Resource Dependence Perspective,* in which they present the core ideas of RDT.[5] RDT takes as a starting axiom, that organizations are dependent on the environment for resources necessary for their ongoing activities, and at the most basic level, their survival. These dependencies are usually manifest as a relationship between themselves and other organizations in their environment.

Assumptions

The assumptions in RDT can be thought of as emerging out of two distinct perspectives: ecological and rational-behavioral.

Out of the ecological perspective, one important assumption of the theory is that the *unit of analysis* for RDT is the organization and, more specifically, the relationship between the organization and its broader environment. Rather than focusing its analysis on the behavior of particular individuals or roles in the organizations, or structures in the organization, RDT seeks to show how the organization and its relationship to the environment can be the basis for understanding and explaining its behavior.

Coupled with this ecological perspective, a further key assumption of RDT, one that we've seen with other theories explored thus far, is *bounded rationality.* Recall from our early discussion of Herbert Simon that bounded rationality is the condition—because of limited information and limited analytical capacity, humans act in bounded or satisficing ways. The notion of bounded rationality here suggests that organizations neither have perfect information about the resources they need to acquire for their continuing success, nor do they have the information processing capacity and cannot accurately and precisely assess the information they do have about requisite resources. The result of these conditions is some level of uncertainty. A related behavioral concept that applies here is the notion of *intended rationality*. Organizations are assumed to work toward two related objectives: acquiring control over resources that minimize their dependence on other organizations and acquiring control over resources that maximize the dependence of other organizations on themselves. Attaining either objective is thought to affect the exchange between organizations, thereby affecting an organization's power. Here, the notion of intended rationality suggests that organizations intentionally seek to maximize these two ends based on calculations regarding the information they have available to them—that is, they intend to be rational and utility maximizing, though problems of information availability and quality impede that capacity.

Simon's work suggests that through the development of standardized routines and vocabularies, as well as the creation stable structures and practices in the pursuit of organizational goals, organizations can overcome information gaps and analysis limitations. Despite these limitations and the instrumental responses to them, the ontological assumption embedded in RDT, both in how organizations operate and how researchers following the theory operate, is a high degree of positivist empiricism—that is, the theory and its sense of how organizations function assumes that while the organization and actors within it behave based on bounded rationality, the broader world still operates in a functionalist, causal fashion. As such if there are empirical factors that causally contribute to the behavior of organizations, these factors can conceivably be identified and analyzed, even if individual actors don't recognize or account for them in determining courses of action.

Functionally, the environment is assumed to contain scarce and valued resources essential to organizational survival. As a result, the environment poses the problem of organizations facing uncertainty in resource acquisition. A further assumption about organizations and their capacity within the theory is some degree of *intentional action or agency*. Organizations in RDT are assumed to be able to act with intentionality or agency, and while that intentionality may be affected by conditions of bounded rationality, they do have the ability to undertake courses of action that are likely to achieve intended outcomes (because of the functionalist-empiricist causal character of the world).[6]

Operation of the Theory

The starting point for RDT is that organizations look to their environment for resources that are required for their survival. Similar to Hatch's depiction shown in Figure 8.2, the environment that RDT assumes organizations to operate within is largely comprised of other organizations. This is a crucial shift away from a strictly natural metaphor that compares biological organisms to organizations. That metaphor infers that resources necessary for organizations' operations exist in a natural environment and can be collected, perhaps competitively with other organisms, but that another organism in the environment does not control those resources. The organizational environment under RDT is different in that necessary resources are a sort of "loose ball" that competing organizations seek out and jostle for. Instead, necessary resources are likely to be controlled by some other organization in the environment.

The result is that interdependencies between organizations develop as each individual organization seeks to maximize the stability and reduce the certainty associated with the availability of their required resources. Organizations that become reliant on other organizations for their continued success may build "behavioral dependencies" with them to reduce risk. The resulting "coordination and mutual control over each other's resources" has the effect of both reducing organizational risks associated with the stability and uncertainty of resource availability and at the same time creating interdependency among organizations. Such interdependencies have become increasingly common in contemporary settings as organizations become more specialized. This occurs because although specialization does potentially increase the efficiency of organizations' productive activity, it can also reduce their flexibility and adaptability. One consequence then, is "the fact of the organization's dependence on the environment that makes the external constraint and control of organizational behavior both possible and almost inevitable."[7]

Although organizations are likely to take steps to strategically balance any dependencies they develop, requisite resources are unlikely to be equally distributed throughout an organizational environment, and inequities or asymmetries are likely to develop in that environment. Such dependence asymmetry between organizations creates power differences. Pfeffer's subsequent work pushes the idea that organizational success in RDT is linked to organizations' ability to maximize their power.[8] Control over resource access and allocation is an important basis of power and can be derived from several obvious strategies including control of, positioning of, or ownership of a necessary resource. Politically, the ability to control the use of the resource, or being able to control the rules that regulate resources, also become tools of power in the RDT environment.

While some theories of the environment, such as population ecology, assume that organizations are unable to respond and adapt to changes because of the inertia they develop over time, RDT holds to the possibility that organizations do have the capacity to adapt to changes in the environment as a means of overcoming uncertainty regarding sustained access to necessary resources. RDT, then, is interested in how organizations manage their resources, the movement of those resources, and the interdependencies that are created with other organizations in the wider environment.

Hatch sketches out a preliminary outline of an RDT analysis in which organizations first identify the resources they need and trace them to their sources. Subsequently, the organization examines the structure of actors in the environment to determine which organization-environment relationships either help or hinder the organizations resource access and exchanges.[9] This analysis includes an assessment of inputs, such as necessary raw materials and customers, as well as of competitors, regulatory agencies, and interests. This analysis gives the organization the information in needs to determine the *criticality* or an assessment of the importance and scarcity of resources.

From a governance perspective, it's also important to understand that the theory as developed, focused centrally on private, for-profit firms rather than public or nonprofit service or philanthropic organizations.

Figure 8.4 depicts an adaptation of the relationships and features of a resource dependence model reflecting some of the similarities and differences that governance organizations might need to take into consideration. In the simplest depiction, all organizations have inputs and outputs. More specifically, all organizations share inputs, such as the need for information

Figure 8.4 Resource-Dependence Model

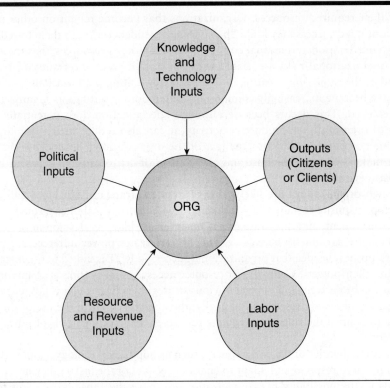

Source: Adapted from Mary Jo Hatch, *Organization Theory: Modern, Symbolic and Postmodern Perspectives* (New York: Oxford University Press, 1997), 79.

and knowledge, and all organizations require some form of equipment that allows them to convert inputs into outputs. Another common resource, regardless of sector, is that all organizations require some level of labor to do the work of the organization. However, public and nonprofit organizations are unlikely to have capital inputs or investors in the same way that for-profit organizations will. Nor are they likely to require raw materials in the way that producers of physical products will. While still being finite or scarce, a public organization's access to funding through a legislative appropriations process, or a nonprofit's access to grant funding, is likely to be different than a for-profit's pursuit of capital investment or market share. Moreover, a public organization is likely to have a different relationship with citizens, or a nonprofit will interact differently with clients, than a for-profit organization will with customers.

Recently, RDT has been under scrutiny in several review and meta-analytic studies—all of which indicate and discuss the importance of this theory in explaining the actions of organizations by forming interlocks, alliances, joint ventures, and mergers and acquisitions in striving to overcome dependencies and improve organizational autonomy and legitimacy.

Case 8.1

Current Expressions: Resource Dependence Theory at Brigham Young University

Throughout the book, we have made the case that the application of OT in the public sector has broadened beyond traditional public agencies at the local, state, and federal levels. We've used the idea of *governance* to suggest that different organizational arrangements and organizational types, including nonprofit organizations and other nonpublic entities have a role, even a central role, in governance activities. Kaplan and other scholars have made the case that museums and other cultural organizations play an important role in helping communities of different sorts establish and maintain their identities and therefore fall well within the scope of what we would describe as governance.[10] The following description of theory in practice examines the way a single museum, the Brigham Young University (BYU) Museum of Art, dealt with two exhibits that placed the museum in a contentious relationship with other entities in its environment.

BYU was created in 1903 by the Church of Jesus Christ of Latter-day Saints with the intent of creating a leading institution of higher education that could blend cutting edge secular learning with the teachings of the church.[11] In 1993, the university opened the Museum of Art, which at the time was the largest such museum between Denver and San Francisco. Not long after the museum opened, museum administrators learned of a traveling Rodin exhibition organized by the Iris and B. Gerald Cantor Foundations and began efforts to bring it to the museum in Provo, Utah. In the time between the initiation of efforts to bring the exhibit to the museum and its opening at the museum in October 1997, the university, Cantor Foundation, and the museum all underwent changes in leadership. Importantly, the museum appointed Campbell Gray, an individual with extensive experience in the field but who was not intimately familiar with the administration of the university or the church, as its new director. At the same time, B. Gerald Cantor passed away, leaving his wife to take over the leadership of the foundation. In tribute to her husband, the decision was made to add several other renowned works to the Rodin exhibit, including a nude sculpture titled *The Kiss.*

As these changes were occurring and arrangements for the exhibition were being made, issues of nudity and pornography were coming to a head in Provo. In this context, museum and university administrators in concert decided not to display three works they felt might stir controversy, including *The Kiss.* However, the decision was conveyed to the Cantor Foundation just days before the exhibit was to open and was shared in an incomplete way with the media. Because of the high profile of the exhibition—and the poor communication with the media and public—the withdrawal of the works quickly garnered first local and ultimately national and international media attention as well as protests by hundreds of BYU students.

Several years after the Rodin controversy, the museum learned of a traveling exhibition of works from ancient Egypt, Greece, and Rome and by the spring of 2003 began to assess whether or not to bring the works to Provo. Not surprisingly, the exhibit did include a small number of Greek nude sculptures, which the staff assessed as important to the character of the exhibit. Given the nature of these works, and the controversy over the Rodin exhibit, museum staff also realized that inclusion of the Greek sculptures posed a potential risk.

In response, the education staff at the museum reached out to the Utah State Office of Education as well as university administration to get feedback about the exhibit. While not doing so immediately or without debate, the university did eventually approve the exhibit. Museum staff then crafted a set of strategies related to how they would interact with different groups of visitors, the media, and other constituent groups. Ultimately, the exhibit opened to positive reviews and ran without any of the controversy associated with the Rodin events six years prior.

The Rodin case reveals the consequences of an organization's failure to recognize the structure of formal and informal resource dependence relations. While the museum's administrators did understand the importance of the relationship with its parent institution, the university, and what it believed to be its social environment, the physical community from which most museum visitors came, it did not recognize that a series of structural relationships had developed with other entities in the environment such as students, media organizations, and artistic foundations, upon which the museum relied for exhibits beyond its own collection. Moreover, the relationships did in fact develop elements of power that expose the presence of both power and agency on the part of other entities in the environment.

Christopher Wilson, Brad Rawlins, and Kevin Stoker's analysis of the two scenarios suggests that the relative youth of the museum, changes in leadership at the museum as well as the other involved organizations, and a lack of reflexivity on the part of museum decision makers were critical limits hindering administrative strategies in this case. These limits led the museum to underestimate the complexity of structured relations between the museum and other actors in the environment and to fail to recognize the relative distribution of power among those relations the Rodin case.

In the years following the Rodin case, the museum appears to have developed a more sophisticated understanding of the structure of relationships with other entities in its environment, which positioned the organization to rebuild and renew some of those relationships and to craft more effective courses of action prior to the opportunity to display the later Art of the Ancient Mediterranean World items. The later case demonstrates a more strategic understanding of the structure of relationships and reflexive effort to balance relative power of other entities in the environment in both direct and indirect ways. These efforts included the museum's engagement directly with schools and the media as well as efforts to reach out to the state education department. Together, these efforts suggest a broader, resource-based understanding of the environment.

Reflection Questions

How is the environment for governance organizations similar or different than that of for-profit organizations from an RDT perspective?

What are some specific resources administrators in governance organizations might look to in their environment to enhance organizational success?

Summary Reflections on Resource Dependence Theory

In some ways, RDT represents an important conceptual link with several other essentially rational theories we've explored in previous chapters. RDT understands the environment as being a complex but more or less comprehensible set of relationships that are shaped by fairly clear intentionality in pursuit of identifiable and measureable resources. Those resources may be quite concrete, in the form of revenues or clientele needed by an organization, or more symbolic, such as the image and reputation of the organization. Regardless of the form, however, organizations can identify and effectively and accurately calculate the distribution of those resources among organizations in the environment and strategies to gain stable access to those resources. RDT moves the unit of analysis from the level of the individual or a structure within the organization to the organization itself. However, like the individual manager in classical management and economic theories, the organization in RDT exercises agency under conditions of intended or bounded rationality. In taking these positions, RDT expands organizational awareness to the environment in useful ways and does so in ways consistent with assumptions we see in other organization theories.

Network Theory

Administrators and managers forget at their own peril that they must consistently pay attention to their organization's access to the resources necessary to undertake actions that enable the organization to accomplish its mission. To some degree, maps of relationships within RDT look a bit like networks comprised of key "nodes" or locations that are important relative to the flow and distribution of resources.[12]

Having acknowledged that this is the case, it is also true that governance settings are unlike the market where resource allocation is a central focus in some important ways. One critical difference is the absence of a profit motive. Public choice theorists argue that public and non-profit organizations do act based on self-interest and that they purse their own self-interest expressed in forms of expanding access to resources, augmenting personal or organizational power, expanding organizational influence, or enacting other outcomes. For public and rational choice theorists, all of these are clear and direct manifestations of self-interest, and any organizational analysis should proceed accordingly. Outside of public and other rational choice theorists, the majority of organization theorists acknowledge that the absence of a profit motive opens a space for organizations to be more expansive and potentially innovative in crafting a mission that aims toward different ends and need not focus organizational structures to most efficiently meet those ends. In other words, the shift away from a profit motive allows organizations to engage in politics as the pursuit of the good life in a wide variety of ways. This move also means that the presence of multiple organizations in any given community is shaped and determined by something other than uncontested resource niches and the establishment of a competitive edge. Such conditions both open up the possibility of new and different sorts of relationships between and among organizations in any given environment but at the same time make the interorganizational dynamics more complicated.

A second important difference is that identifying, let alone meeting, needs and niches in a governance environment is likely to be more complex than in a for-profit setting. Because governance and politics go hand-in-hand, the determination and fulfillment of needs in a governance environment is going to be as potentially contentious as the community is diverse. The more ideas that exist regarding the form and content of the good life, as well as about how that life is to be achieved, the more challenging the environment is likely to be for the organizations that populate it.

Assumptions

These observations about the character of the environment lead directly to some of the suppositions that underpin the development of network theory as it applies to public administration and governance. Consequently, there are three assumptions about the world and organizational operations within that world that we want to highlight here. The first is the presence of so-called *wicked problems* in networked environments. As we noted in Chapter 4, wicked problems are those difficulties that are characterized by a wide range of political, economic, and social attributes.[13] Horst Rittel and Melvin Webber, who coined the term, suggest that such problems are integrally interconnected with other problems. To make responding to wicked problems still more difficult, they are characterized by conflicts in which stakeholders bring significantly different perspectives to the table, meaning that developing a common understanding of the situation—let alone crafting a common or coordinated response—is itself problematic. As a consequence, any governance level responses to wicked problems are neither right nor wrong but instead are better or worse within a specific context. Moreover, wicked problems are not solved as a rational-comprehensive model might suggest but are improved or worsened by iterative initiatives that shape and create new dynamics to be addressed.[14]

Content and Techniques

Keith Provan and Brinton Milward propose an approach for evaluating networks of organizations and is useful in and of itself. They point out that in circumstances where resources are scarce that problems are complex, service providers are narrowly focused functionally and financially, and constituent outcome evaluation isn't adequate.[15] Beyond the practical benefit of having an approach for evaluating networks, Provan and Milward's model is also useful for conceiving of a practical set of concerns that can be considered when crafting strategies for maximizing the effectiveness of the network and its constituent organizations.

Provan and Milward begin the description of their model by describing three different levels at which networks can be considered: a community level perspective, a network level perspective, and an organizational level perspective. Consideration of the community level, or that local area that is served by network, prompts attention to factors such as aggregate outcomes for the populations of clients. Because networks are particularly useful in circumstances where problems and solutions, as well as causes and effects, are complicated and highly interconnected, populations of clients may be broad and impacts of programmatic interventions may be both narrowly and broadly recognized; aggregate measures that both discern individual programmatic impacts and recognize cumulative or collective impacts is important.

Another factor that emerges as important at the community level is the status of stakeholders and the satisfaction of needs within these groups. The diversity and interrelatedness of stakeholder groups derives from and reflects the nature of problems in wicked environments. Giving attention to these stakeholder groups and the satisfaction of their needs is important from an evaluative perspective in terms of understanding the impact of programming efforts but also from an operational perspective. At the very least, there may be variation in expectations regarding service levels or content between and among these groups. To some degree the operational approach at this level may be more about minimizing problems rather than elimination or avoidance of negatives, or even instead of positive outcomes. In part this is because outcomes, at this larger scale, are difficult to measure let alone attribute in a valid and reliable way, to programmatic efforts. One other operational factor that is potentially important with respect to stakeholders is that it is also likely that these groups have critical information necessary for effectively working in the given setting. Considering and including their status and satisfaction can contribute to the effectiveness of the network in highly complex settings.

The second level Provan and Milward focus on is the network itself. At this level, questions shift from a focus on dynamics and impacts across the community to one of coordination and interaction among working members of the network. While the study of coordination within networks is not new, one of the important contributions Provan and Milward make, again for evaluative and operational purposes, is the attention, awareness, and focus on the establishment of a network administrative organization (NAO).[16] As Laurence O'Toole recognized in his early work, networks are not hierarchies.[17] While hierarchies may have their own weaknesses, they are effective in establishing a structure to support the coordination of complex activities.[18] In the absence of a hierarchical structure for coordination of complex activities, an NAO can serve as the locus of efforts to coordinate efforts between and among members of the network. As was the case with community level evaluation measures, Provan and Milward identify network level evaluation criteria including the following:

- the growth and retention of member organizations
- the comprehensive and coordinated provision of services actually needed by clients
- the effectiveness of an NAO in coordination and diversification of services and ties
- the maintenance of effective relationships between and among members
- the "multiplexity" of the network, or the existence of multiple ties between organizations as an indication of greater strength and robustness of the network
- the existence of and administrative structure within the network that would be indicative of how active and powerful the NAO is in its coordinating activities

As revealing as these measures are of the potential effectiveness of the network, they are also valuable for providing a set of working factors to help guide the efforts of an organization serving in the role of the NAO, or for a network, more broadly, that has chosen to coordinate efforts without the formal establishment of an NAO.

The last level identified by Provan and Milward has to do with factors related to individual organizations and their mission and activities within the network—that is, while we are focused here on networks, it is important to remember that organizations are created individually to fulfill a particular mission that their founders and members identify. Regardless of the potential impact and value of network membership for particular communities or populations, organizations do function more or less autonomously. As a result, there are a set of individual level concerns for organizations that merit attention. One question for individual organizations has to do with resource acquisition and the extent to which network membership supports or hinders organizational efforts to acquire resources. Another factor is organizational legitimacy. The concern with legitimacy has to do with how membership in the network or a relationship with specific NAOs adds or diminishes legitimacy of the individual organization with its stakeholders and constituents. Network membership can also have costs for constituent organizations. For example, organizations must consider the cost of network membership in terms of losing identity or focus. A final factor that requires individual organizational attention has to do with client outcomes. The question for individual organizations here may turn, for example, on whether there is any synergy of benefits for clients who have new access to other services. Network membership may allow for focused or targeted services to the neediest of clients. However, as individual organizations assess their participation and consider how participation impacts their mission, the extent to which the organization's participation in the network affects their clients' outcomes is another important factor.

While not necessarily focused at any of the three levels described so far, Provan and Milward also identify a set of issues related to integration across the three levels—that is, network success is at least in part contingent on success and integration across all three levels. Effectiveness at any single level or on any single outcome factor won't be a good predictor or indicator of success (or survival) of the network as a whole. Moreover, network outcomes may evolve so as to be counter to individual organizational outcomes. For example, it is possible that individual organization's missions—and therefore their success and survival—may evolve in a way that is counter to the success of the entire network. Tensions like this reveal a critical question for organizations to consider with respect to examining network arrangements across these three levels—namely, what sorts of tensions exist for our organization between and across these levels? And how do we prioritize our objectives such that we can resolve any emergent tensions? While potential conflicts with mission and organizational identity will undoubtedly be key factors in resolving tensions, it's less clear what other factors might be considered and prioritized when such tensions arise. The result, it would seem, would be contextualized efforts by organizations to weigh and balance any emergent tensions and standing concerns or objectives.

Box 8.1 Operational Questions for Network Coordination

Community Level

- Who are the client populations?
- What are the stakeholder groups (direct and indirect members of the network)?
- What are the characteristics of the community?
  - for example, via demographic assessment or strengths, weaknesses, opportunities, and threats (SWOT) analysis

Network Level

- Is there an NAO?
- What is the size of the network growth rate?
- What are the network's activities and services? Extent of services?
- How strong and complex are the relationships?
- What is the nature of the network's structure (remember that structures are repeating, stable patterns of behavior)?

Organizational Level

- What resources are available in the system?
- What sort of standing or legitimacy do members have?
- What are the costs of membership for the organizations? What are the risks of membership?
  - Where do client outcomes fit?

Case 8.2

Current Expressions: Networks and Municipal Housing in the Phoenix-Mesa Area

Network theory has emerged as a major theme in the organizational literature, and there have been a significant number of studies examining the function, structure, and other attributes of functioning networks. Moreover, the studies appearing in the academic literature represent just the tip of the iceberg in terms of the actual number of operating networks engaged in more-or-less coordinated responses to various community and other complex problems. As such, the question we want to examine through this case is not the mere existence or functionality of networks but rather the extent to which Provan and Milward's framework and measures of network effectiveness are potentially present in a sample case and the degree to which that framework and set of measures can be used as the basis to craft strategies that enhance effectiveness across levels.

The Phoenix-Mesa metropolitan area is one of several regions in the nation that has received extensive attention because of the degree to which the region experienced the greatest extremes of the housing bubble and bust late in the first decade of the twenty-first century.[19] Between 2000 and 2006 housing prices soared 74 percent while median income grew by 15 percent.[20] Some counties in the region, such as Maricopa, saw even more dramatic price increases paired with similarly disparate income changes. Not surprisingly, these drastic price and income gaps left many potential homebuyers effectively locked out of the market and led to the creation of many programs to assist homebuyers.

The difficulty associated with responsibly supporting potential homebuyers was complicated further when the housing bubble began to deflate. Rather than just needing to counsel low income buyers into sustainably affordable homes, the shift in the housing market meant that the challenge of getting buyers at all income levels into vacant homes, acquiring financing in drastically tightened credit markets, while simultaneously dealing with broader fallout of the housing and wider economic crisis resulted in the makings of a wicked problem. The emergence of what would become a networked response included the creation of regional housing task forces, the development of public-sector-driven housing plans, private sector initiatives to support employer side strategies, as well as other nonprofit and private efforts.

One of the confounding characteristics of affordable housing in the greater Phoenix area is the presence of multiple municipalities, making the need for an NAO greater. The emergence of two task forces, one privately driven and the other convened by then governor Janet Napolitano, indicates the organic emergence of entities positioned to take on the tasks of the NAO. These two entities—one because of its private sector orientation and origin and one because of its state level creation—were situated to serve in the needed role and capacity.[21]

The presence of these entities also reveals something of the attention given to community level outcomes. One example of this community level awareness driven by the two task forces was their use of macro or community-wide indicators of the health and vitality of the housing markets, including regional rather than municipal housing status and income data. These task forces drove efforts to bring together diverse stakeholders who would collectively have the capacity to impact the system at that level.[22] Joanna Lucio and Edgar Ramirez de la

Cruz also recognize that there are social and cultural dynamics at the community level that impact housing programing, including "not in my backyard," or NIMBY, concerns that can affect housing programming.[23]

Drawing on Kenneth Meier and O'Toole's work to extend their network level analysis, Lucio and de la Cruz recognize both the structure and practices of networks as being critical aspects of network behavior and performance.[24] The makeup of the network included several cities; nonprofit organizations involved in a variety of programmatic activities including advocates, counselors, and developers; private organizations including for-profit developers; and larger industry associations. Lucio and de la Cruz examine two structural measures, *closeness* and *betweenness,* as a way of depicting the nature of relationships within the network.[25] Their findings indicate that at least in this network, public organizations are not situated at a central location within the structure of the network and that nonprofit organizations have evolved into that role and location.[26] Although Provan and Milward don't make an argument that NAOs should be exclusively public organizations, O'Toole and others do infer that public organizations are uniquely positioned in both practical and normative-democratic terms to take such a position. Lucio and de la Cruz suggest that public agencies have the potential to serve in such a role and that they have a unique position in the community to fulfill a normative-democratic role in creating discourses to respond—for example, to NIMBY-ism. The researchers' findings also indicate the importance of closeness and betweenness within the network, in supporting the creation of critical contacts that enhance the coordination within the network.

Because network theory tends to be more focused on the relationships between member organizations and the impacts of those member organizations on the community level problems, impacts at the level of individual organizations tend to get little attention. Provan and Milward point out the importance of this level in that regardless of the potential for improving community level conditions around wicked problems, if membership in a network negatively affects an organization's ability to meet its own mission, membership in the network is, at the least, likely to be short lived. As a result, organizational level effectiveness relative to that organization's mission is relevant.

Although organizational level measures are not core to Lucio and de la Cruz' study, they do provide some indication of how organizations seek to be a part of networks that support their missions and how networks can simultaneously meet different organizations goals. The researchers note two specific examples of how this might play out. One is the extent to which housing programs support developers' objectives. During the housing crisis developers held unsustainably high levels of housing stock and membership in the network supported their ability to reduce available surpluses. Similarly, these same conditions enable nonprofit service providers to leverage opportunities for more of their clients who were seeking housing. While some of this symbiosis resulted from the unique circumstances of the collapse of the housing market, it is possible that other sorts of arrangements and incentives might emerge during more normal market conditions. Moreover, the establishment of effective working relationships between members of the network would likely support the identification of such incentives.

Lucio and de la Cruz' research contributes directly to the work on network theory and governance by developing a specific model for understanding and analyzing the structure of the network with measures of closeness and betweenness. More importantly for our purposes, their research both corroborates the model developed for evaluation purposes by Provan and Milward and provide indications that this model can be used prescriptively by specific organizations as they consider whether and how to engage with network efforts to respond to wicked problems.

Network Theory: Summary and Conclusion

O'Toole introduces his treatment of networks in governance settings by arguing that these organizational arrangements are increasingly common and useful in settings characterized by wicked problems. As we've hinted at thus far, and will make more explicit in Part III, our assessment is that social, economic, and technological conditions are becoming more complex, suggesting O'Toole's prediction may just be the tip of the iceberg. This presents all sorts of challenges for democratic governance but poses particular quandaries for administrators as they strive to balance the decisions necessary to meet their own mission with the external pressures of a network that may not fit perfectly with that mission. In identifying the need for an NAO, and presenting a framework for the assessment of performance at different levels of analysis, Provan and Milward provide a framework for organizations to assess how to maximize the impact of the network in responding to wicked problems at the community level, the performance of the network, and how these first two levels fit with organization level questions of mission fit.

Reflection Questions

How might an examination of networks change when viewed from different levels—for example, local, state, or federal?

How would this affect strategies adopted by organizations at these different levels?

Neoinstitutionalism

In Chapter 4 we introduced institutional theory, which gives us the analytical tools to begin to understand how and why organizations, and structures within those organizations, often take on a life of their own and become valued for more than just their instrumental purposes. Philip Selznick developed many of the central ideas of institutionalism beginning with his work in *TVA and the Grass Roots*.[27]

In the late 1970s and early 1980s, institutional theorists, including John Meyer and Brian Rowan, Ronald Jepperson, and Walter Powell and Paul DiMaggio, took what some believe to be a substantively new approach to institutional analysis.[28] Although Selznick has argued that there is little substantial difference between this body of new or neoinstitionalist work, and that which he first introduced with the Tennessee Valley Authority (TVA), others point out the importance of the appearance of Peter Berger and Thomas Luckmann's *The Social Construction of Reality* in the intervening years.[29] In the extreme, it may be that neoinstitutionalism should be understood as a postmodern approach to OT. This claim is driven by the recognition that many of those writing in this area have made the *linguistic turn*. We'll briefly revisit this idea at the end of the current chapter and delve into it much further in Part III of the book, but for the moment it is enough to think about the linguistic turn as a recognition that although ideas like organizational efficiency, efficacy, and equity are manifest in real, concrete ways in our organizations, the definitions of these concepts, as well as our understandings of them, are not grounded in some indisputable, transcendent way. Such concepts may well be, in postmodern terms, free-floating and self-referential.

Powell and DiMaggio essentially accept Selznick and other institutional theorists' work that organizations and many of the practices within those organizations take on a life of their own. They then extend that work by seeking to develop a better understanding of the dynamics that shape the institutionalization of organizations. Specifically, they are interested in what they describe as isomorphic relations and pressures. More simply, they explore questions of how the structures of different organizations evolve to look increasingly similar to one another over time.

Assumptions

As with the theories we've covered thus far, we begin our examination of Powell and DiMaggio's development of neoinstitutional theory by first examining some of the assumptions embedded in the theory as a way of understanding both how the theory operates and the premises on which it rests. For our purposes, we highlight three core assumptions: a structural functionalist orientation, constructivism, and collectivism.

Like "old" or Selznick's and other early treatments of institutionalism, Powell and DiMaggio recognize that structures and functions in organizations are related not only through the instrumental purposes for which structures were intended to support but the functions that those structures take on over time. It is important to recognize in this assumption that the link between structures and functions is not merely an instrumental let alone intuitional one. The functions of any given structure should be understood as potentially having noninstrumental, social, symbolic, or other purposes. Moreover, the function of any given structure can change over time so that even those structures that are created with a particular instrumental purpose in mind can evolve and change over time so as to serve other purposes as well. To complicate matters further, it's also possible for structures to serve more than one purpose at a time, meaning that functions can be both instrumental and noninstrumental simultaneously.

This perspective moves the theory out of a rational objectivist perspective to one taking on an assumption of social constructivism. To recap our description from Chapter 4, constructivism takes the position that individuals and groups construct knowledge for one another—collaboratively and through their ongoing interactions with each other in the same or similar settings. Through collaborative efforts (both intentional and unintentional) to make sense of and effectively navigate the world around them, social groups construct or create a set of shared beliefs and understandings and subsequently act and interact with each other and the wider world based on these constructed artifacts with shared meanings. While these constructed belief systems are stable, they are not inflexible, meaning that when one is immersed within a socially constructed setting, one is learning all the time about how to be a part of that setting.[30]

A final, related assumption that we want to highlight here is a sense of collectivism. Collectivist orientations emphasize the importance of group or social cohesiveness within groups. As a prescriptive theory, collectivism can be used to argue, in some cases, for the priority of group goals over individual goals. Jean-Jacques Rousseau, for example, in *The Social Contract* argues that the individual finds true freedom only in submission to the "general will" of the community. For Rousseau, we give up a small portion of our natural liberties that are enforceable only through individual might so that we might gain civil liberties that are enforceable through the will of the whole community. In other words, we give up our ability to speed through residential neighborhoods in our cars or to have chicken farms in our suburban backyards, but we gain greater collective benefits like safety and sustained quality of life.

While Rousseau and other political theorists highlight a constitutive political aspect of collectivism that is interesting in public governance settings, the point in raising collectivism here is descriptive rather than prescriptive. The structural functionalist and constructivist aspects of neoinstitutionalism imply the degree to which the behavior and performance of organizations is not merely a matter of individual decisions and actions but also emerges clearly and extensively from collective social interactions.

Content of the Theory

We begin our description of the content of neoinstitutionalism by pointing out two important aspects of the theory: its link to institutionalism and why the work of Powell and DiMaggio fits within a chapter on organization-environment relations.

First, this form neoinstitutionalism is connected to and is an extension of institutionalism because it retains its focus on processes of *institutionalization,* or the extent to which organizations and their structures take on non-instrumental characteristics. Selznick's work on the TVA and other institutions helps us understand how and why organizations, and their practices, take on a life of their own and how they become valued for more than their instrumental purposes. In this expression of neoinstitutionalism, certain structures of the organization that may or may not be necessary requirements of production processes become the central focus instead because of how they provide legitimacy rather than improving performance. The structures and behaviors are both constructed and institutionalized in that they fall beyond efforts to maximize efficiency and instrumentality. Powell and DiMaggio's work looks at a particular set of dynamics that emerge in a particular relationship that can develop between organizations. To a large degree, these dynamics are processes of change. We place them in this chapter rather than Chapter 7 because the mechanism of change, and the possibility of managing that change, has to do specifically with the relation between the organization and its environment.[31]

It is that last institutional attribute that leads this form of neoinstitutionalism to be placed here in this chapter on the environment. In examining the relationship between organizations, in the impact those relationships have on institutionalization, the focus is primarily on the environment—or in institutionalist terms, the *organizational field*. The notion of an organizational field suggests that while the unit of analysis remains at the level of single organizations (not individuals or structures within organizations), the influential variable is comprised of a wider set organizations that constitute a recognized area of institutional life. These organizations—whether they are key suppliers, resource and product consumers, and regulatory agencies—constitute the organizational field. The field idea is interesting and useful because it captures both the ways in which these organizations are connected and allows for the assessment of how they are structurally similar or equivalent.

As we previously noted, the concept of isomorphism has to do with changes in organizational structure such that one organization begins to appear more like other organizations in the same field. Powell and DiMaggio identify three mechanisms of institutional isomorphic change.

The first form that institutional isomorphism takes is coercive. Here, influences, both formal and informal, from other organizations in their field or in society force the organization to take on structures that it would be unlikely to absent those influences. More specifically, those influences may include legal processes, generally accepted practices, and regulatory processes. The coercive effect of legal processes might be expressed in personnel actions like hiring and performance management, where laws or legal rulings have established parameters that all organizations in a given environmental field must comply with. Less formal, but no less influential, factors might include the adoption of generally accepted practices, such as accounting principles. Another coercive isomorphic influence can be found in the regulatory or oversight processes required of many organizations.

Powell and DiMaggio suggest that the greater the dependence of an organization on another, the more similar it will become to that organization in structure climate and behavioral focus. For example, the greater the centralization of an organization's resources supply, the greater the extent to which that organization will change isomorphically to resemble the organizations on which it depends for those resources. Beyond the acquisition of resources, Powell and DiMaggio also suggest that the more interaction an organization has with the state— whether that occurs through regulatory or oversight processes—the more isomorphic similarities will exist between organizations.

To be clear, in order for the adoption of any of these practices or processes to rise to the level of coercive isomorphism, their adoption must be essentially forced on the organization. For example, nonprofit organizations that take on specific reporting, evaluating, or accounting practices in order to become or retail eligibility for particular funding streams could be considered subject to isomorphic pressures. The more organizations seek out these same revenue sources, the more these organizations will begin to structurally resemble one another.

Historically, and even now to a great degree, organizations have been understood as adapting and changing in order to meet machine, or productive and instrumental, needs. An argument can be mounted that such technical constrains are less at play today as organizations, especially in governance environments where equifinality—the ability to get to the same ends by different paths—better characterizes the conditions associated with the provision of services and administrative activities in a complex environment. As a result, structure may be imposed by membership in credentialing groups, and professional mandates have growing coercive influences. For example, the National Association of Schools of Public Affairs and Administration (NASPAA), the organization responsible for accrediting Master of Public Administration (MPA) programs, has established a set of criteria for curriculum content, faculty composition, outcome reporting, and other factors that must be met in order to attain or retain accreditation. These standards, while establishing a high and consistent quality across accredited programs, simultaneously have a coercive isomorphic affect on NASPAA affiliated programs.

Normative isomorphism constitutes a second set of pressures that influences the shape and structure of organizations. Normative, or value-oriented, pressure can include several expressions as well. One form, professionalization, can include the processes of education and legitimization of a particular cognitive base that subsequently shapes the processes and structures of organizations. Professional norms and standards can also be enhanced and extend through the strength and influence of professional networks. Such networks provide a means of adaptation and evolution as well, through the quick diffusion of new models, practices, and forms of work. Another manifestation of normative isomorphism can occur via the filtering of personnel to ensure continuity of values, assumptions, and perspectives as well as corresponding practices.

Personnel filtering can occur by selecting staff from similar firms in the industry or field, hiring out specific schools, or developing internal training and promotion tracks.

As a bit of an aside, normative isomorphism may also shed light on the phenomenon of *agency capture,* or the notion that regulatory agencies can become captured or unduly influenced by the industries they are charged with overseeing. The US Forest Service, for example, has been charged with being captured by the timber and forest products industry, resulting in a much higher likelihood that the agency will render decisions favorable for timber harvesting over other uses of the national forests. Using the normative mechanism of education, training, and professional norms as an analytical lens, the notion that the Forest Service was simply corrupted or captured by the timber industry becomes a bit more murky. Credit for the creation of the Forest Service is often given to Gifford Pinchot, an early twentieth-century conservationist and associate of Theodore Roosevelt. Pinchot, who trained in forestry in France, also created the first school of forestry in the United States at Yale. The Yale program subsequently became a model for many of the forestry programs around the country. Returning to the normative lens of education, training, and professional values, an admittedly speculative thought experiment would suggest that the close parallels between the views on forest management held by the Forest Service and the timber industry might be a result of the fact that their staffs have similar education and training and as a result have the same, or at least similar, norms and values when it comes to making forest management decisions. The result is that normative isomorphism rather than conspiratorial strategy may explain that pattern.

The final form of isomorphism, mimetic, occurs when organizations choose to mimic, or copy, one another. Of the three forms, mimetic is likely the least common and least strategic. Mimicry as a strategy seems to emerge in circumstances where the criteria for the selection of processes and structures are unclear or undeveloped. In other words, if you don't know what to do and you don't have a clear means of figuring out what to do, copy someone else. At times when there is significant ambiguity about what should be done, mimic organizations that are successful in their own right. The potential for this to be a successful strategy follows at least two lines of logic. One line would suggest that if the organization can copy the right instrumental structures that will directly contribute to the capacity of the organization to be successful. The second, less instrumental line of logic suggests that if nothing else, symbolic mimicry may have the effect of enhancing an organization's legitimacy if not its objective effectiveness. While not a maximizing strategy, mimicry is a way to take action under conditions where there is more uncertainty about the relationship between means and ends. Similarly, the more ambiguous the goals of an organization, the greater the extent to which the organization will model itself after organizations that it perceives as successful.

The theory of isomorphism may help explain the observation that organizations are becoming more alike. Perhaps more importantly, neoinstitutionalism broadly and organizational institutionalism specifically explain why there are tendencies in organizations to be nonrational and resistant to applications of power as well as fail to innovate. The theory also adds to the perspective that focuses on the struggle for symbolic attributes and expressions of organizational power and survival that is not merely a part of ecological or resource models of organization. Finally, neoinstitutional isomorphism may have implications for policy and governance in those areas that the state contracts or collaborates with private organizations—that is, in governance settings. It has the potential to help find mechanisms that maintain diversity and pluralism (may mean resisting or overcoming isomorphism).

At least two last observations about isomorphic dynamics are worth noting here. One is that all of these isomorphic elements allow organizations to become active and passive models within their fields. A second observation is that regardless of gains to organizational efficiency and effectiveness, structural changes may be, or are even likely due to their becoming preferred within the field. These observations reinforce the assumptions we noted at the outset of this section. The notion that organizations are active and passive models, that they are potentially both models for other organizations, and that they also seek out models for themselves to replicate highlights the extent to which neoinstitutionalism adopts a structural functionalist, constructivist, and collectivist set of assumptions.

Case 8.3

Current Expressions: Isomorphic and Governance Organizations

Research on institutionalization since Selznick's initial work with the TVA has continued to show that that these processes have an impact on public and governance organizations.[32] Others have found that public organizations may actually be more susceptible to institutional pressures than private organizations.[33] Given the relationship between hospitals and the communities in which they operate, it's not surprising that they become institutionalized. Margarete Arndt and Barbara Bigelow studied private, not-for-profit hospitals throughout Massachusetts to determine the extent to which isomorphic pressures from the organizations' environment affected structures and the strategies used by those organizations to function within that setting.[34]

Consistent with Powell and DiMaggio's theory, Arndt and Bigelow found that hospitals were attuned to all three forms of isomorphic pressure from the environmental field. Moreover, these pressures resulted in structural changes that had as much to do with establishing and maintaining perceptual legitimacy within the community—both geographic and professional— as with improving the effectiveness of the organization.

However, their findings also suggest a more complicated organizational response to isomorphic pressures. The hospitals in this study did not simply submit to the pressures but instead exercised some level of strategic agency in both resisting and taking advantage of those pressures. For example, Arndt and Bigelow's research found that rather than merely responding to or complying with coercive pressures, the hospitals they studied invoked coercive pressures as justification for innovation. Following a similar strategy with respect to mimetic pressures, hospitals referenced mimetic pressures to validate innovations by indicating that such innovations were common or standard within the industry. Finally, the researchers found evidence that the hospitals retroactively presented their actions in ways that show responsiveness to normative pressures as a way of softening the impression of organizational agency and independence.

More interestingly and importantly from the perspective of practitioners, these findings are clear indications that administrators with these hospitals used their understanding of isomorphic pressures both to manage their relationship with the environmental field and to frame the structural changes that were adopted by their organizations. Specifically, Arndt and Bigelow's findings show that organizations appealed to both coercive and mimetic iso-morphic pressures to explain and justify new structural arrangements. Their findings were also somewhat more complex in that they found that not only were these hospitals' structures subject to isomorphic pressures but that administrators used their awareness of the pressures to legitimate structural innovation and change. In other words, administrators were able to enact innovative structural changes and subsequently justify those changes, even when they resulted in differentiation rather than isomorphism.

Neoinstitutional Isomorphism: Summary and Conclusion

In some ways, neoinstitutional isomorphism is the ideal theory to end this chapter as well as this section of the book. It combines many of the factors that we've discussed to this point. In examining how organizations come to look like each other, it assesses structural attributes of one organization in comparison to the next to understand how similarities develop. As we noted previously, it is also a theory of change—change that is largely driven by factors outside the organization, by other organizations in the environment.

Not only does neoinstitutionalism combine many of the attributes of the study of organiza-tion that we've examined so far but the theory provides a nice segue to the last major section of the book as well. The theory's claim that these attributes can become disconnected from the instrumental purposes of the organization highlights the symbolic character of organiza-tions and their behavior. The idea that organizations act for symbolic reasons—for example, to enhance their legitimacy within a given community—moves our interpretation of organizational behavior toward constructivism if not post-modernism.

And still, the concept of isomorphism can be a valu-able perspective from which administrators can consider the extent to which they can or should strive to organizational independence on its own. Selznick's early depictions of how organizations take on a life of their own via the strategic and critical decisions they make point out how organizations can exercise agency in establishing an identify and relationship within their communities of operation. Powell and DiMaggio extend that notion by describing particular ways the environment can push to shape the identity in various ways. This leaves administrators with some, though not total, discretion in determining where and how to resist isomorphic pressures and where those pressures should or must be accepted.

> ## Reflection Questions
>
> What are some of the normative isomorphic pressures that affect public and governance organizations?
>
> In what ways are governance organizations more or less susceptible to normative isomorphic pressures than are for-profit organizations?

Links to Post-traditionalism and Postmodernism

In her discussion of postmodernism and OT, Hatch draws an analogy from the 1980 cult film *The Gods Must Be Crazy*. In the film, a Coca-Cola bottle is tossed from a plane and accidentally falls into a remote African village, where such a thing has never been seen before. Believing it to be a gift from the gods, and not knowing its instrumental purpose, members of the village contrive all sorts of uses and values for it, all of which are entirely unrelated to the purpose for which it was originally manufactured. These contrivances, Hatch points out, are social constructions. As such, Hatch argues, the villagers have made a shift from a positivist or functionalist paradigm, to a constructed or even postmodern paradigm.

We noted earlier in the book that institutional theory, for example in Selznick and others' studies of how organizations take on a life of their own, makes a similar shift. In fact, within institutional theory, there is some debate as to whether or how far the theory has to move toward a constructivist paradigm. For our part, what seems important to recognize is that the symbolic importance of organizations to communities, as well as the normative and mimetic relationships between organizations, are not purely instrumental and do take on socially constructed attributes. Our ability to give meaning and description to this phenomena is tie to the concept of the linguistic turn that we noted earlier in this chapter.

We want to point out a further link between the theories presented here and the postmodern approaches we'll describe in the next chapter. In popular discourse, anarchy is typically associated with social chaos. However, in political theory, the notion of anarchy—society without formal government—has a longer, richer, and more developed body of thinking. Although most of the formal theorizing of anarchy disappeared during the Cold War, there has been a small reemergence of the anarchist theory since the end of the Cold War. For example, anarchocapitalism, which can be thought of as an extreme form of libertarianism in which markets are the sole basis of social coordination and organization and no formal government is necessary, has received renewed attention in recent years. Setting aside that specific line of thinking, there is also a link between anarchic theory, networks, and OT.

The illumination of that link requires several conceptual steps. As a political theory, anarchy might well de described as the development of "political and organizational systems (that) might successfully elevate individual liberty to the highest importance, doing away with all government but self-government and all management but self-management."[35] Interorganizational networks fit this description to the extent that member organizations are likely to be beholden to a central decision authority. Linda deLeon reminds us that the derivation of the term *anarchy* is the Greek *anarchos,* or "without a ruler," a notion that is consistent with the challenges posed by networks. DeLeon continues by drawing on James Thompson and Arthur Tuden's decision strategies and structures model and suggests that under particular circumstances and conditions—namely the level of certainty that exists regarding both goals and outcomes and cause and effect relations—networks fall into a realm of decision making described as *anomic,* or lacking centralized direction and authority. The more a network tips toward conditions in which relationships are flatter and nonhierarchical, power is decentralized, and relationships are not characterized by high levels of trust or shared values, the more likely that network to run anarchically. The consequence from deLeon's perspective is a organizational motto of "live and let live," encapsulating the expression of choice, flexibility, creativity, and accommodation.

Political and social theorists have taken up the concepts of anarchy and brought specific attributes of postmodern theory to bear as a way of conceiving of rulerlessness in contemporary conditions.[36] The important tie to postmodern theory here is the lack of certainty relating to cause-effect relationships. As we've described in previous sections, one of the common attributes of postmodern and antifoundational theory is the ontological claim that the social world is not characterized by clear, discernable cause-effect relationships. Moreover, because of the variations in epistemic communities, the information and knowledge used to drive decisions can vary, creating knowledge assumptions, what constitutes knowledge, and how that knowledge can be compiled to craft courses of action. There is the importance of contextual knowledge and understandings of how the setting behaves, variations in goals and objectives that are derived in each social setting, the power of symbolic or normative elements of the setting, and the potential for creativity and flexibility. As we'll explore further in the Part III of the book, it is these attributes that we believe postmodernism can reveal and develop in new ways.

Summary and Conclusions

THE ORGANIZATION-ENVIRONMENT RELATIONSHIP is the highest level of analysis we examine in this book. While W. Richard Scott suggests that there are two further levels, the behavior of groups or populations of organizations and the impacts of organizations on society, these two levels move beyond where managers and administrators are likely to have a direct impact. At this level, managers and administrators continue to have the capacity to impact the activities of the organization as well as the effects that the organization has in the communities where it operates.

The three theories we've focused on here all function in ways that create opportunities for managers to conceive of the organization in some actionable relationship to the environment. So, in RDT, the theory focuses on the structure or patterns of relationships as shaped by resource availability and allocation. These structures and patterns create a space for power dynamics that administrators can recognize and respond to either proactively or reactively. Network theory examines the establishment of coordinated or even cooperative relationships among organizations in an effort to impact large and complex problems. In doing so, it conceives of a window in which managers can conceive of objectives that strategically enhance community conditions, network performance, and organizations' individual missions. In doing so, Provan and Milward's model allows administrators to give consideration to all three outcome levels and then some. Moreover, their model provides a means for managers to assess and act in ways that enhance conditions at all three levels while at the same time maintaining a clear sense of how network and community performance is tied to organizational performance—the level that administrators are ultimately responsible for. Finally, neoinstitutionalism, in its focus on the structure of organizations as they compare to other, related organizations in their environment, highlights both direct as well as indirect and informal factors like normative or cultural value–based influences and in doing so opens a space for administrators not only to assess their organization's circumstances but a perspective from which to respond.

It's also worth noting here that there are conceptual links between the theories. For example, RDT and isomorphism in neoinstitutionalism both give consideration to the development of power and influence in the relationship between organizations. In the case of RDT, that power and influence comes from the distribution of necessary resources. Resources may be the basis of coercive isomorphism, but normative and mimetic forms extend beyond concrete sources of influence into more symbolic or socially constructed forms. Further, network theory and RDT are both focused on the patterns and structures of relationships. While RDT examines those structures from the perspective of resources needed for organizational survival, network theory looks at relationships based on how they support the capacity to have an impact on community problems. ■

Discussion Questions

1. What are the major environmental factors considered by each of the three theories described in this chapter? Compare and contrast the strengths and weaknesses of the approaches.

2. What positions, or roles, in the organization are responsible for thinking about organization-environment relations? How do differences in these roles affect how each considers organization-environment relations?

3. Thinking again about Allison, Appleby, or others' comparisons of public and for-profit organizations, how do the differences or similarities impact administrators' efforts to manage organization-environment relations?

Notes

1. Philip Selznick, *Leadership in Administration: A Sociological Perspective* (Berkeley: University of California Press, 1984).

2. Philip Selznick, *TVA and The Grass Roots* (Berkeley: University of California Press, 1949).

3. Mary Jo Hatch, *Organization Theory: Modern, Symbolic and Postmodern Perspectives* (New York: Oxford University Press, 1997).

4. See Michael T. Hannan and John H. Freeman, "The Population Ecology of Organizations," *American Journal of Sociology* 82 (1977): 929–964; John Betton and Gregory Dess, "The Application of Population Ecology Models to the Study of Organizations," *Academy of Management Review* 10 (1985): 750–757.

5. Jeffrey Pfeffer and Gerald Salancik, *The External Control of Organizations: A Resource Dependence Perspective* (Redwood City, CA: Stanford University Press, 2003).

6. Daniel W. Greening and Barbara Gray, "Testing a Model of Organizational Response to Social and Political Issues," *Academy of Management Journal* 37 (1994): 467–498; Christine Oliver, "Strategic Responses to Institutional Processes," *The Academy of Management Review* 16, no. 1 (1991): 145–179.

7. Pfeffer and Salancik, *The External Control of Organizations,* 43.

8. Jeffery Pfeffer, *Power in Organizations* (Marshfield, MA: Pitman, 1981).

9. Hatch, *Organization Theory,* 79.

10. Elisabeth Kaplan, "We Are What We Collect, We Collect What We Are: Archives and the Construction of Identity," *The American Archivist,* 65 (Spring/Summer 2000): 126–151; Annie E. Coombes, "Museums and the Formation of National and Cultural Identities," *Oxford Art Journal* 11, no. 2 (1988): 57–68.

11. Unless otherwise noted, the description of this theory in practice case is drawn from the following: Christopher Wilson, Brad L. Rawlins, and Kevin Stoker, "Public Relations Paradox on Display: A Comparative Case Study Analysis of the Autonomy-Dependency Paradox at a University Art Museum," *Public Relations Journal* 7, no. 1 (2012): 1–52.

12. Edward O. Laumann, Joseph Galaskiewicz, and Peter V. Marsden, "Community Structures as Interorganizational Linkages," *Annual Review of Sociology* 4 (1978): 455–484.

13. Horst W. J. Rittel and Melvin M. Webber, "Dilemmas in a General Theory of Planning," *Policy Sciences* 4, no. 2 (1973): 155–169.

14. Jeff Conklin, *Dialogue Mapping: Building Shared Understanding of Wicked Problems* (West Sussex, UK: Wiley, 2006).

15. Keith Provan and Brinton Milward, "Do Networks Really Work? A Framework for Evaluating Public-Sector Organizational Networks," *Public Administration Review* 61, no. 4 (2001): 414–423.

16. Edward H. Lorenz, "Trust, Community, and Co-operation: Toward a Theory of Industrial Districts," in *Pathways to Industrialization and Regional Development,* ed. Allen J. Scott and Michael Storper (London: Routledge, 1992).

17. Laurence J. O'Toole, "Treating Networks Seriously: Practical and Research-based Agendas in Public Administration," *Public Administration Review* 57, no. 1 (1997): 45–51.

18. Charles Perrow, "A Society of Organizations," *Theory and Society* 20, no. 6 (1991): 725–762; Charles Perrow, "Organizational Theorists in a Society of Organizations," *International Sociology* 7 (1992): 371–380.

19. Unless noted otherwise, the details of this case are drawn from the following: Joanna Lucio and Edgar Ramirez de la Cruz, "Affordable Housing Networks: A Case Study in the Phoenix Metropolitan Area," *Housing Policy Debate* 22, no. 2 (2012): 219–240.

20. Ronald J. Gunderson, "Housing Affordability," *Economic Development Journal* 6, no. 2 (2007): 39–46.

21. Lucio and de la Cruz, "Affordable Housing Networks," 222.

22. Ibid.

23. Ibid., 224.

24. Kenneth J. Meier and Laurence J. O'Toole, "Managerial Strategies and Behavior in Networks: A Model with Evidence from US Public Education," *Journal of Public Administration Research and Theory* 11, no. 3 (2001): 271–294; Kenneth J. Meier and Laurence J. O'Toole, "Public Management and Educational Performance: The Impact of Managerial Networking," *Public Administration Review* 63, no. 6 (2003): 689–699.

25. *Betweenness* is a term used by Lucio and de la Cruz in their analysis. For a more extensive description of the concept, see Lucio and de la Cruz, "Affordable Housing Networks," 223.

26. The importance of the role of an NAO and it being located in organizations other than public agencies reinforces our argument about the importance of considering governance more broadly than traditional public entities.

27. Philip Selznick, *TVA and The Grass Roots.*

28. Ronald L. Jepperson, "Institutions, Institutional Effects, and Institutionalism," in *The New Institutionalism in Organizational Analysis,* ed. Walter W. Powell and Paul J. DiMaggio (Chicago: University of Chicago Press, 1991), 143–163; John W. Meyer and Brian Rowan, "Institutionalized Organizations: Formal Structure as Myth and Ceremony," *American Journal of Sociology* 83, no. 2 (1977): 340–363; Paul DiMaggio and Walter W. Powell, "The Iron Cage Revisited: Institutional Isomorphism and Collective Rationality in Organizational Fields," *American Sociological Review* 48, no. 2 (1983): 147–160.

29. Philip Selznick, "Institutionalism 'Old' and 'New,'" *Administrative Science Quarterly* 41, no. 2 (1996): 270–277.

30. Peter L. Berger and Thomas Luckmann, *The Social Construction of Reality: A Treatise in the Sociology of Knowledge* (Garden City, NY: Anchor Books, 1966).

31. See also W. Richard Scott, "The Adolescence of Institutional Theory," *Administrative Science Quarterly* 32 (1987): 493–511; Talcott Parsons, *Talcott Parsons on Institutions and Social Evolution* (Chicago: The University of Chicago Press, 1982), 189–209.

32. Scott Helfstein, "Governance of Terror: New Institutionalism and the Evolution of Terrorist Organizations," *Public Administration Review* 69, no. 4 (2009): 727–739.

33. Peter Frumkin and Joseph Galaskiewicz, "Institutional Isomorphism and Public Sector Organizations," *Journal of Public Administration Research and Theory* 14, no. 3 (2004): 283–307.

34. Margarete Arndt and Barbara Bigelow, "Presenting Structural Innovation in an Institutional Environment: Hospitals' Use of Impression Management," *Administrative Science Quarterly* 45 (2000): 494–522.

35. Linda deLeon, "Embracing Anarchy: Network Organizations and Interorganizational Networks," *Administrative Theory & Praxis* 16, no. 2 (1994): 234–253.

36. Lewis Call, *Postmodern Anarchism* (Lanham, MD: Lexington Books, 2002).

Part III

Toward Post-Positivist Organizations

At the close of each episode of the 1950s TV program *The George Burns and Gracie Allen Show,* George would turn to Gracie and say, "Say good night, Gracie" and Gracie would reply, "Good night Gracie." In one interpretation, this is merely a grammatical misunderstanding of where the comma is placed: "Say good night, Gracie" or "Say, good night, Gracie." In another interpretation, it's an indicator of a different feature of language, one that suggests language not only evolves and changes over time but also that at any given time language may not be as stable or grounded as we tend to believe. In this example we see a shift from what is assumed to be a clear, shared, stable understanding of meaning to a varied, less stable set of equally grammatically valid meanings. If the shared meaning and understanding of critical political concepts become unstable and fluid—for example values that are part of our shared political culture like liberty and equity—the consequences for our communities may be tragic rather than comic. As such, it is this question of stability and groundedness that we take up as a central theme, both in organization theory (OT) and effective practice, across the two chapters of Part III.

The final part of the book shifts its attention to post-positive thinking and applications. This final section introduces many of the affirmative aspects of postmodern or post-positive thinking and explores ways to apply these aspects in real settings of contemporary organizations.[1]

We spend a significant portion of Chapter 9 introducing concepts, describing terms and vocabulary, and exploring their expression in public and governance organizations. At this point, we want to begin to ease into these ideas both because they are likely to be new to many readers and because the literature in this area of theory is diverse, complex, and often contested. For the moment, there are a handful of terms we need to describe (note that we did not say "define"—an issue that we explore in Chapter 9). The title of this part of the book is Toward Post-Positivist Organizations. We are using *post-positivist* as a fairly broad umbrella term that is inclusive of an array of theories including postmodernism, poststructuralism, and antifoundationalism. To be sure, there are variations and important differences among these three and other related concepts we explore, but we are choosing to group them together because what they share is a rejection of many or even all of the ontological and epistemological assumptions of the modernist or positivist theories we've explored in the prior parts of this book.

Our objectives in including this material in the book are severalfold. As an academic endeavor, the body of research and theory that falls under this umbrella of post-positivism is quite large and continues to grow. Although it is not the predominant theoretical line of inquiry in the field, it is substantial and its introduction in a primer text like this one is important in order to understand the broad themes and approaches in the field.

More important, in our view, is the potential these theories offer for understanding complex governance organizations in a new way and alternative courses of action the theories may yield. Early on in the book, we played with the colloquial definition of insanity as doing the same thing over and over again and expecting a different outcome. One rationale for exploring this material is to investigate the possibility doing something different, either in our analysis of organizations or in our actions in organizations.

In terms of analysis, it is our belief, supported by a growing body of evidence, that the world of organizations is qualitatively different now than it was 100 years ago and perhaps even 30 years ago. These differences include highly complex political and economic dynamics, like organizations that have become too big to fail or too integrated to fail. If this is true, then the exploration of theories that help illuminate what those qualitative differences are and how they matter is a useful enterprise. If an exploration of these theories yields new ways to craft strategies of action, or at the least new ways of conceptualizing and adapting old strategies, then the theories can help make administrators more effective. Helping administrators find new ways to be effective was a key criterion we have used throughout the book to select and include ideas. We feel that the theories and concepts that follow in Chapter 9 meet that criteria, and Chapter 10 then describes how that looks.

Chapter 9

Escaping the Void

History of Post-Positivism

This chapter presents a brief introduction and overview of the history and heterodox body of thinking that has emerged in the last decades of the twentieth century, a body of work we're describing as post-positivist. Our emphasis is on the appearance and application of these ideas in public and governance organizations. Chapter 9 also connects back to Chapter 1 in demonstrating how elements of the "other voices" identified in the first part of the book can be traced to post-positive theory.

For our purposes, post-positivism should be understood as including postmodern, post-structural, and antifoundational theories. Our approach to introducing the concepts and ideas associated with postmodernism or post-positivism is to describe them as discrete and distinct.[2]

One of the difficulties posed by postmodernism is that it tends to reject the notion that the world—ontologically and epistemologically—fits into a mutually exclusive and exhaustive taxonomy. In other words, for most postmodernists, the world is not either-or but both-and. The consequence is that the concepts we want to describe are better understood as overlapping, mutually influential and in some cases even contradictory and paradoxical. For this reason, post-positive theory has always been and continues to be intellectually controversial. Some critics argue, for example, that postmodern theory, in its tendency to reject reductionist logic and truth claims, is so relativist that it precludes the ability to exercise reasoned judgment about the comparative value or effectiveness of different courses of action. In the extreme, the logic of this critique would suggest that acceptance of postmodern claims can lead only to nihilism—the belief in nothing.[3] Our position is that rather than leading to nihilism, postmodernism, and post-positivism—more broadly—resolve to a recognition that the social world is diverse and complex and that value pluralism and epistemic pluralism are central to that diversity. As individuals and groups, we believe in a wide range of things, and we exercise a variety of forms of judgment in selecting among courses of individual and collective action shaped by those beliefs. Within groups and communities that by extension are characterized by value and political pluralism, that process of judgment and selection can and should be democratic.

In such an environment, the acceptance of both-and and the possibility of paradox is more than a claim that the social and organizational world is highly complex. Bear in mind that in modernism—especially logical positivism—paradox, or the simultaneous existence of two mutually exclusive conditions should be logically impossible. We've seen throughout the first three sections of the book ways in which organizations and the individuals who populate them behaving based on the influence of other individuals, on formal and informal structures, elements in the environment, and so forth. As we move into postmodernism, we begin to accept and come to terms with the possibility that coming to understand behavior is not just a matter of adding more independent variables to an increasingly complicated causal model. Instead of finding new, albeit more complex, order, David Farmer describes postmodernism as "a rough and tumble disorder/order of ideas/non-ideas."[4] In the postmodernist view, "an orderly and true account of reality is not what we should expect, nor should we expect a disorderly and untrue account."[5] What we should expect is an account that reflects the variation, complexity, and even paradoxical nature of our experiences in organizations. The practical consequence of this description is that while we do present concepts and ideas from postmodernism in a fairly discrete, somewhat linear framework, the concepts should not always be understood as functioning in that way.

One other structural item should be mentioned before we proceed. In this chapter, we have selected five broad concepts from post-positivist theory—all of which have been utilized to both analyze and inform action in contemporary organizations. In order to provide a practical reference point to consider how organization theorists use post-positivist theory, we've included what we describe as *analytical uses* examples, or illustrations, of how these concepts are used in actual studies to examine and understand concrete organizations. We will give more detailed attention to the practices and actions that emerge from these concepts in Chapter 10.

History and Genealogy

We've indicated in previous passages of the book the importance of understanding that theories and ideas don't emerge in isolation. They develop and evolve in a complex context of prior intellectual work as well as social, political, economic, and technological influences. For example, Dadaism, the artistic and literary movement that includes works like *The Scream*, emerged in Europe following the First World War. The movement's rejection of traditional notions of beauty and embrace of cynicism and incongruity were a direct response to the horrors of the war.

Similarly, there are a variety of conditions and experiences out of and then following the Second World War that similarly shape and contribute to the emergence of postmodernism. Some of the intellectual and social dynamics that precede, inform, and contribute to (note that we don't attribute "cause" here) post-positive theory have already been outlined in Chapter 4. In short, these include political changes like decolonization in Asia, Africa, and Central America, the emergence of nationalist movements in those areas, technological events like the use of the atomic bomb at the end of the war as well as the emergence of analog and later digital media and communication technologies, and also economic changes including the emerge of complex interrelationships between industries and government even in market economies like the United States.[6]

Interpretation of these trends embraces the paradox of promise and peril—energy and apocalypse in the atom, freedom, and tyranny in nationalist movements; efficiency and globalization; or oligopoly and consolidation in economic trends. As a result of these qualitative shifts in the size, complexity, diversity, and impacts of these shifts, some philosophers and social theorists began to suggest that existing theories were no longer sufficient to explain and describe the dynamics.

Intellectual Development

In Chapter 4 we also described how the intellectual diversity and shifts that we're interested in, and that developed over several decades and many disciplines, were exemplified most clearly in Peter Berger and Thomas Luckmann's *The Social Construction of Reality.*[7] Berger and Luckmann take up the notion of social construction to describe how people and groups interacting in a social system over time establish concepts or mental representations of each other's behaviors as a way of understanding and fitting themselves into those behaviors. These mental concepts and representations eventually become habituated into mutually reinforcing roles played by the individuals in relation to each other. When these roles are made available to other members of society, the reciprocal interactions are said to be *institutionalized.* In the process of this institutionalization, meaning—which allows for the understanding of and relating to others' behaviors—becomes dispersed throughout society. Meaning, knowledge, and people's understanding of reality becomes embedded in the institutional fabric of society. As such, reality—at least social reality—can be understood as being socially constructed and, moreover, not formally constructed by official actors or institutions.

In philosophy, postmodern thought is often traced back to the work of Friedrich Nietzsche, who is given credit for first challenging assumptions about the nature of the world and what can be known about it. In contrast to claims by other European philosophers, especially Immanuel Kant, Nietzsche suggests that truth claims, claims about the fundamental nature of the world, are not common, universal, or accessible to all people but are illusory and driven by contextualized perceptions and experiences. In other words, the nature of the world is not a given, that can then be known in precise ways by all, regardless of background, experience, or perception. Nietzsche also challenges Rene Descartes' notion of the *cogito,* or one who can know. Famous for his statement "Cogito, ergo sum," or "I think, therefore I am," Descartes sought to build a body of knowledge from an indisputable first claim, "I am," or I exist. The question for Descartes and much of Western philosophy from that point forward was what else can we deduce and know about the world that can be derived from that first claim and the use of rationality? Nietzsche rejects the self as the center of observed reality and opens the door to challenging the possibility knowledge and truth claims, and the nature of a rational knowing individual.

Several decades later, Martin Heidegger takes up similar challenges and seeks not only to refute the system of philosophy that extends from Descartes' work but also to build an alternative system that better adheres to and describes the experience of humans in the world. In phenomenology, a body of philosophy first developed by Edmund Husserl, Heidegger seeks to show how *Dasein,* a term Heidegger uses rather than subject or agent or individual, exists in a world that functions not because of the interaction of universal traits that are inherent in objects but because of quality as attributes we perceive and utilize. In a famous example of a hammer, Heidegger points out that what makes a hammer a useful tool is not some property that is inherent to the hammer and shared by all hammers and not shared by tools which are not hammers. Rather, what makes a hammer a hammer is its experiential utility to do a job. As such, Heidegger distinguishes between the *world,* which is inhabited by *Dasein,* who interacts with it via perceptions and interactions shaped by experience, and a *universe,* which might be understood as the abstracted setting where we study abstracted, nonexperienced objects like black holes (on the cosmic scale) and quarks (on the subatomic scale). The former of these two, the world, begins to resemble the socially constructed world described in earlier sections of this book. Post-traditionalism pushes the exploration of social constructivism further, and poststructuralists, particularly, push the logic to limits.

It is in the context of these social, political, economic, and intellectual trends that post-positivism emerges in the humanities and subsequently in the social and behavioral sciences. To some degree, post-positivism can be understood as a critique of modernist theory and practice, and the perceived tendency for modernism and positivism to lead to oppression of minority ideas and populations, and to have unintended or ignored negative consequences. The ideas associated with post-positivism can also be understood as the logical extension of ideas that emerge directly out of modernism and the precise, logical forms of inquiry and intellectual criticism that is central to enlightenment thinking.

Assumptions

Ontological

As a reminder, ontology is the study of the nature of the world, and ontological positions or commitments are belief sets about the nature of the world. Although we are admittedly setting up a bit of a straw man of positivism in order to make distinctions clear, the attributes of positivist or high-modern ontological positions we're describing are ones that have in the past been claimed and defended by natural and social scientists. The contemporary ontological reality is more nuanced and complicated, with empirical and theoretical researchers falling along a wide continuum of assumptions from logical positivism to what Pauline Marie Rosenau describes as critical postmodernism.[8]

With that caveat in mind, we'll start by suggesting that positivists are arch-scientists and view the world as being real and existing independently from the human existence. The world is seen as an ordered, structured place that is governed by physical laws. The social world, correspondingly, is simply an extension of the physical world. The laws that govern behavior in the social world are not the same as those in the physical world, but they are internally consistent with them. Moreover, it may be possible to derive social laws by directly extending physical laws. This would suggest then, that the utilization of Ludwig von Bertalanffy's systems theory is not a *metaphorical* extension of the theory from natural to social world but a *direct application* of the theory in a new setting. In other words, social settings are not *like* natural settings; they *are* natural settings and function essentially identically. More commonly, however, contemporary organization and social theorists apply concepts from the natural sciences in metaphorical ways. So organizations share behavioral commonalities with biological or ecological systems, and we can use our understandings of the natural systems to gain new insight into the corresponding social systems.

As we indicated in the introduction of precursor concepts developed by Nietzsche and Heidegger, post-positivist ontologies understand our perception of the world as being socially and internally constructed. We create reality from our individual and collective experience with and interpretation of the world. As we do so, we make sense of and set the stage for future experiences at the same time. As we've seen, for example, in Heidegger's distinction between the world and the universe—and will encounter again with Jacques Lacan's three registers—the claim here isn't necessarily that *everything* is socially created but that at the very least social and political phenomena like fairness, liberty, justice, and democracy are constructed in this way.

Epistemological

Another way to think about post-positivist assumptions is to consider the relationship between ontology and epistemology and to examine the implications of the assumptions from each perspective. From a functionalist-positivist perspective, ontology (nature of the world) precedes and determines what can be known. Because the world is out there and is independent of human experience and perceptions, the acquisition of knowledge proceeds from the positive or real character of the world—that is, all knowledge comes from positive information of observable experience, and empirical, scientific methods are the best way of achieving this. While humans can have an impact on the world, we cannot change its fundamental character and operation. The nature and function of that world and the way our own sense organs and the technologies we use to augment our senses comply with the laws of that world and help us learn about it. In a postmodern world, that may not be the case. Instead, what can be known may determine what we think the world is like. The analogy is wavelengths of light—what we can see versus what's out there. In a constructed world, all we can do is study the semiotic world, or the system of signs and symbols, and what people report about their perceptions and inner worlds. While we can attempt to be systematic and rigorous, what we have is a set of informed guesses about experience based on the clues they give us.

> ## Reflection Questions
>
> What other social (including political, scientific, and economic) events or trends contribute to the emergence of post-positivist thinking?
>
> To what degree does post-positivist thinking represent a dramatic shift from previous organization theory (OT) or an extension or continuation of that thinking? What evidence can you point to in the literature to support your answers?

Post-Positive Concepts Appearing in the Social Sciences

The following ideas are drawn from among the myriad concepts explored and exploded by post-positive thinkers coming from a variety of perspectives and traditions. The set of concepts we've chosen to explore have been selected because they are extensions of ideas we've already examined in previous chapters and also because they appear in varying forms in the public administration literature.

The descriptions we present here should be considered as both a preliminary and incomplete depiction as well as one among many possible understandings of these ideas. Our strategy in describing these ideas is to give a starting place, or a "touchstone," understanding that can be returned to in order to make sense of ideas you find elsewhere in the literature and in your experience rather than a definitive depiction that requires no augmentation or variation. What we mean by this odd caveat should become more apparent as we explore the first concept of this subsection—language.

Language

The ability to communicate and the development of language as the means of communication are necessary conditions for social coordination, whether at the level of the earliest hunter-gatherer clan-based communities or the most sophisticated technical activities like putting humans into space and having them safely return. Without the ability to communicate, the capacity to coordinate activities, especially in complex activities, is impossible. Our ability to communicate effectively depends, at least in part, on the stability and shared character of language. If the meaning of language isn't shared, or isn't stable, that language would cease to serve as a mechanism of coordination. One conception of language that meets these conditions views it as largely or entirely *denotative*; words denote or represent reality in a direct, precise and objective way. Most philosophers of language—up until the early twentieth century—argued that language can and does function this way. And this belief is consistent with our general experience with and use of language. When we use terms like *rock* or *tree,* those words convey an objective representation of those entities to the recipient of the statement. Moreover, not only do individual words have a direct and complete capacity to represent individual things in the world but language systems as a whole can be an exhaustive representation of the world as a whole—that is, language systems can comprehensively represent the entirety of the world.

Ludwig Wittgenstein, an Austrian-born British philosopher, published his work *Tractatus Logico-Philoshophicus* in 1921, which essentially supports this understanding of the function of language.[9] Later in his career, however, he began to rethink this question, asking whether language can, in fact, objectively describe truth. Wittgenstein changed his position, concluding that language cannot objectively describe truth, arguing instead that all language is socially constructed and conditioned. Our interaction and understanding of the world is shaped in and through constructed and ultimately unstable uses of language. In making this case, Wittgenstein introduced the notion of **language games**.[10] Language games is a sort of metaphor Wittgenstein uses to describe various ways the same language can be used in different ways, each of which is stable, but follows different rules linked to different language games.

Although language is socially constructed and has countless possible uses, *our experience* is that its actual uses are reasonably stable and are linked to actions in specific contexts.[11] Think, for example, of our "Say goodnight, Gracie" example at the beginning of Part III. In the action context of the end of that TV program, the statement, "Say goodnight, Gracie" operates within a specific context and with a generally known and understood set of expectations or rules of the game—that is, we know what the game is, we know what the rules of that game are, and we act correspondingly. Gracie, however, chooses to act within the confines of a different language game and by a different set of rules.

Charles Fox and Hugh Miller present a concise overview of how language moves beyond Wittgenstein's characterization of language games and slips from and simultaneously retains its coherence and some of its denotative character. Drawing on postmodernists including Jean

Baudrillard, Fredric Jameson, and Matei Calinescu, Fox and Miller point out that "words, signs and symbols have become increasingly divorced from 'reality.'"[12] Our very language, especially in charged sociopolitical settings, has become increasingly unstable.

We have moved from conditions under which language directly refers to or denotes objects in the world. The fairly direct denotative and still stable use of language to represent objects continues to be functional in many instances. Fox and Miller present this arc of language in a sort of historical thought experiment, but it should be understood as being present in contemporary settings. The character and function of language, following post-positive thought, is another both-and instance of paradox. So there clearly continue to be terms—*rock, tree, desk,* and so forth—that clearly denote corresponding entities in the real world.

At the same time, we also find instances where language connotes characteristics or has the ability to represent characteristics that are not beyond the object itself. To use an example from Fox and Miller that we quite like, a snake is not just a reptile that fits within a discrete taxonomy of species, genus, and so forth. "Snake" may come to represent physical danger, evil, or even lunch. The snake has multiple connotations, all of which are present in the experiential world in different circumstances.

As we move into modern societies, and especially late-modern settings, language is used to represent things that do not exist at all in our physical reality. Concepts like social equity or equality, justice, and democracy do not exist in and of themselves in reality. They may be expressed to greater or lesser degrees in experiences we can describe and share, but the things themselves don't exist as entities. As such, the possibility that language can be purely or directly denotative becomes increasingly problematic.

It's also important to understand that language, text, or discourse are not just written or spoken for post-positive or postmodern thought. Meanings can be expressed and shared in many forms, including images and sounds, all of which can make more or less direct reference to the things being represented. One familiar setting where we can easily find the interplay of texts as explicit language as well as implicit image, symbol, and sound is contemporary advertisements. Messages are presented in multiple, overlapping forms and convey information that can be more or less representative of some objective reality. We know them to be incomplete and indicative of any of a range of language games. Yet they are nevertheless treated as real in that we act on them as such.

Think, for example, about the phenomenon of individuals' personal images being stolen from personal, social media sites by commercial entities and then used to tell other stories in Internet advertising of products that may be of dubious quality. Despite sometimes fantastical claims about these products, the advertising, supported by stolen images, is convincing enough to generate substantial sales volumes. The meaning of the narrative embodied by these stolen images is at once about selling a product (for the advertiser), improving life dramatically (the consumer), and sharing a personal experience (the individual whose likeness was stolen). To make things more difficult in an increasingly diverse, fast-paced contemporary environment, the pace at which the meanings of signs and symbols changes is so rapid as to become disconnected from reality yielding conditions of **hyperreality**.[13] Hyperreality, or as Jameson describes it, the free and random play of signifiers, might be understood as conditions in which it becomes increasingly difficult if not impossible to distinguish between what is real and what is fictional. Such conditions reverse the tagline from the old Sprite advertisement from "Taste is everything, image is nothing" to "Image is everything, taste is nothing."

One outcome of the emergence of hyperreality or the postmodern condition is that subcultures or small pockets where robust, stable signs and language exist begin to emerge—perhaps tied to a particular ethnicity or religion or political community. The difficulty is that a sort of incommensurability of language games develops across these pockets of robust meaning. So if Fox and Miller and Farmer and others who see our contemporary experiences as being characterized in terms of the postmodern condition are right, then simply having more discourse or better discourse won't overcome the incommensurability of language games. It won't enable the contenting perspectives to come to agreement about the fundamental values associated with the sorts of wicked problems we face. Stated differently, if the political discourse of rights, justice, equity-equality, freedom, and so forth become incommensurable between communities, more and better discourse in and of itself is not enough.

Baudrillard describes the phenomenon that nonreferential signs take charge of and determine the real. The result is a uniquely post-positive phenomenon, the emergence of simulacra, or copies for which there is no original.[14] Simulacra are a bit like caricatures that come to represent a real entity—one that is widely recognized as depicting a particular idea or entity but one that never existed in anything resembling its current form.

Turning again to Fox and Miller's description of the postmodern condition and simulacra, they describe the appearance of the character Mr. T from the 1980s TV program *The A-Team*. Mr. T represented a gruff, tough Vietnam War veteran who while perhaps was frightening in reality had a heart of gold. That caricature, a recognizable copy of something that never existed in that form, was then copied into a Saturday morning cartoon, a movie character (in *Rocky II*), and more than twenty years later, a different movie character with a slightly different but more contemporary backstory. This image, which we recognize and resonates with us as portraying a certain set of traits and features, is one that never existed in reality. It is a copy of a copy of a copy for which there is no original.[15]

The common thread that emerges from the linguistic phenomenon of language games, hyperreality, and simulacra is the recognition that language, while retaining significant stability, increasingly takes on a free-floating character. Meanings and uses of any given piece of language are increasingly variable. This poses both opportunities and challenges as we seek strategies to coordinate activities in and outside of organizations. In the following section, we take up another model of language—one that suggests a different relationship between language, ontology, and epistemology.

Lacan and Language

Trained initially as a Freudian psychoanalyst, Lacan developed a different theory of language that he used in his efforts to work with individual patients suffering various forms of mental illness. This theory has subsequently been moved into other social and behavioral disciplines, and it reveals a different set of interesting and useful insights related to organizations and governance. Lacan's ontological commitments break dramatically with that of mainstream organization and public administration theory and in doing so provide an opportunity to further shift our exploration of regarding the recurrent questions about the politics-administration dichotomy and legitimacy and, for our purposes, OT.[16] Lacan provides us with another means of understanding of how the world is constructed in language and how organizational processes reflect that construction.

For Lacan, human cognitive development occurs in a series of identifiable steps as the individual or subject acquires language and matures from infancy into adulthood. This process of language acquisition and maturation constitutes both the individual's personality and gives structure to the individual's means of interacting with the socially constructed world. In Lacan's model, consciousness and our interpretation of the world—rational or otherwise—is entirely constituted through language. This is opposed to the conceptions developed by John Locke and other Enlightenment thinkers who argued that we were born into a comprehensible world as fully constituted, rational individuals.

The Lacanian Registers—The Real, Imaginary, and Symbolic

Lacan theorizes the existence of three "registers": *real, imaginary,* and *symbolic.* The *real* is, in fact, just that—the real world that exists in some physical form. However, for Lacan, we have no direct or unmediated experience of the real. Our connection to the real is always mediated through the other two registers, the imaginary and the symbolic. As a result, the real is that which cannot be described or symbolized. It is that which fits none of the dimensions of consciousness and stands outside our experience of the world around us. The *imaginary* is the world that we experience and tend to consider as being "real." Imaginary, as Lacan describes it, should be understood not as unreal but instead as a collection of images. As such, the imaginary is the mental construction that results from the interplay of images and subjects with one another. The *symbolic* order is that which overwrites the imaginary, and imposes categories, structure, and apparent stability and order onto the imaginary world. The symbolic order includes but is not limited to constructs such as language, culture, and law.

In short, the real exists and is what our connotation of the world would suggest, but we have no direct, unmediated experience with or understanding of it. The imaginary is the mediated, familiar experience of the world, and the imaginary is organized, structured, and stabilized through the symbolic. The symbolic is that which bounds and limits our expectations and experiences of the imaginary. The symbolic operates according to a structured dynamic. While Lacan does not use Baudrillard's terminology, it may be useful to think about the symbolic relative to the stable familiar rules of language games as we described them earlier. There is a pattern to the symbolic and this pattern, when it is stable and robust, has the ability to configure a stable imaginary.[17] When this condition exists, our experience of the world is comprehensible and understandable. However, when the symbolic becomes unstable and loses its integrity, the imaginary and our experience of it loses its consistency and no longer makes sense.

Although this depiction of the world may seem quite alien, it is not dissimilar to Karl Weick's description of the collapse of sensemaking. While our perceptions of the world around us are consistent with the perceptual feedback and language we have to interpret that feedback, the world is stable and understandable. In those conditions, it is relatively easy to craft effective strategies and actions. In circumstances that are novel, highly complex, rapidly evolving, or otherwise unstable, there is likely to be growing volatility and discord in both individual perceptions of the situation as well as in collective efforts to respond. In this way, the collapse of sensemaking is consistent with the destabilization of the symbolic order. This destabilization will be discussed further in the next section in terms of Lacan's four discourses. For the moment, however, we want to point out Lacan's model of language; its place in this ontological model has the potential to help us understand organizational and political experience and also suggests possible means of retaining or reconstructing the integrity of the symbolic order in useful ways.

The Four Discourses

In addition to Lacan's notion of a stable symbolic order and its importance to functional social relationships, Lacan identifies a set of four discourses and understanding of which that can be useful to public administrators. It is possible through the use of the four discourses to account for the structural differences among discourses and their use allows us to understand the ways in which different discourses function in a distinct ways.[18] For our purposes, we'll be considering the four discourses in terms of rough but recognizable sketches of social discourse rather than the more specific application of the mathemes (roughly mathematical formulae) Lacan developed to describe the discourses at the level of the individual subject. As such, the discourses can be understood analogically as types of societies that have historically and to some extent still exist. The first is traditional society, which is represented or described by the discourse of the *master*. In the discourse of the master or traditional society, there is a single authority—one who imposes the law so that he can live in the way that he chooses. The people see in the master what they lack. The representation is so strong that the people believe he is, in fact, complete. The symbolic order in traditional society is quite robust and maintains stability and social order. The discourse of the master begins to break down when it is recognized that the master's authority is not based on a fundamental truth, like divine right, or in Lacanian terms, when it is recognized that the master is a nonsensical signifier that refers to nothing. In the example of rule by divine right, if the fundamental truth of God's power comes into question, rule based on God-given rights becomes nonsensical.

This break in the authority and power of the discourse of the master brings forth the second discourse, that of the *university*. In the discourse of the university, knowledge stands in for or attempts to hide the lack in the master or nonsensical signifier; the discourse of the university tries to hide the fact that the authority of the master is based on nothing by using knowledge as the basis for legitimizing the master's role and hiding what he lacks. The university discourse can be understood as linked to modern society, where knowledge and science rule. The discourse of the university accurately describes the dominant ontological position of public administration and its long tradition of neutral or technical competence and reliance on social and physical sciences as a basis of action.[19] Think here, for example, of Frederick Taylor's scientific management, Woodrow Wilson's call for the systematic, or scientific, study of administration, and later behavioralist scientific studies of individual and social conduct in an effort to understand and reveal the natural or "real" causes of human comportment.

What manifests itself in the discourse of the university is a sort of slippery slope. The promise of science and the Enlightenment project is to describe the world, or the real, in ever-increasing detail. Its failing is twofold. On the one hand, if one tries to trace the "chain of evidence" or "logic of science" back to a single, stable point, it cannot be done. What we find is that the basis upon which knowledge and the discourse of the university is built is a nonsensical or is perhaps the same signifier that the discourse of the master is built on—that is, the discourse of the university acts to hide the true nature and lack of the master and attempts to prop up or sustain the discourse of the master.

The second failing is that in an effort to describe the real in ever-increasing detail, contradictions in knowledge emerge. This plays out in public lands management in the inconsistencies that can and have developed between various sciences—for example, forest ecology and wildlife biology and the contradictory knowledge and subsequent courses of action proposed by each.

The emergence of such contradictions leads to the third discourse: the discourse of the *hysteric*. This can be understood as the discourse that characterizes the postmodern condition or as the discourse of the market. The hysteric interrogates the master or the established order to find out exactly what the master desires—or more importantly, what the basis of the master's rule is. In terms of the postmodern condition, the discourse plays out in a different way. We—all of us who are confused by contradictory demands placed on us in modern society—begin to interrogate the master (established order) to find out what we must do to become the object of desire, to fit in, and to do what is right. For a public manager, that may translate to a question of the following: "Do I embrace the newest management fad, or do I continue to follow older management doctrines?" Or even more specifically, which science is *the* science to follow behavioralism, economics, psychology, neurobiology, or something else still? This question isn't intended as a blanket rejection of empirical science, as there is valid scientific research emerging from each of these positions. But the question Lacan's work illuminates is that as we learn more and embrace the possibility that there are still other forms of valid knowledge, which "truth" does the manager follow in order to garner approval or legitimacy or, in Lacanian terms, to be desired?[20]

What, then, is the alternative? What do we do that is not simply a replacement of one master or one set of knowledge for another? The final discourse, the discourse of the *analyst*, seems to offer promise in that it rejects the ontological universalism of the master and university discourses and yet allows for the possibility of positive agency not possible under the discourse of the hysteric. In other words, the discourse of the analyst moves away from the universal truth claims of both the discourses of the master and university and instead grounds actionable knowledge in situational contexts. Moreover, the hierarchical or authoritarian social bonds based on the discourse of the master or the university are dissolved, allowing for alternate sources of knowledge to enter the discourse. The discourse of the analyst responds to the demands of the discourse of the hysteric through the development of genuine social process and relationship. It simultaneously reveals and mitigates the discourse of the hysteric by merging the demands of the hysteric into alternate social processes. In short, what we find in the discourse of the analyst is the opportunity for social interaction and social discourse grounded in group processes and situational context rather than psychodynamic abstraction. We'll take up more specific applications of Lacan and the discourse of the hysteric in Chapter 10, but for the moment, the takeaway from our description of Lacan's model is that it identifies a set of recognizable patterns that we see in organizational and management discourse, and it depicts those patterns such that we might be able to craft responses that are effective and subtly different from those we've examined to this point in the book.

Reflection Question

What other manifestations of these ideas can you identify in contemporary uses of language, perhaps in the media, pop culture, politics, or other areas?

Box 9.1   Analytical Uses

Language

We have described some of the attributes of language from a post-positivist perspective. We've highlighted Jacques Lacan's depiction of how language shapes individual behavior and configures broader social structures or discourses. Kate Kenny takes up Lacan's understanding of language and examines how the function of language both informs our grasp of organization change but also reveals alternatives when enacting change. Her analysis recognizes the extent to which assumptions about the world are embedded in our language rather than emerging empirically from objective characterizations of the world. These linguistic artifacts include aspects central to organization behavior and change, including the extent to which control and coherence are illusory, and yet remain crucial to our individual and collective sense of stability and efficacy—that is, the emergence and maintenance of a stable symbolic order is necessary to sustain organizational effectiveness, yet the basis of that stability is essentially imagined. Kenny's analysis understanding of the operation of the symbolic and other Lacanian orders as a psychological dynamic reveals something about not only the basis of the symbolic order's robustness and its resistance to chance but also the means by which change in the symbolic order is possible. Kenny draws on Michel Foucault to describe the political character of language and how it reveals expressions of power both in the organization and in Lacanian thought itself. In other words, she reminds us that Lacan's use of language is as instilled with assumptions of power as our organizational language is. As such, she acknowledges the sorts of paradox endemic to post-positivist theories and depictions of our experience. Nevertheless, Kenny concludes that recognition of this paradox allows us to consider *how* we want to use Lacanian insights rather than *whether* we want to use them because they are incomplete or imperfect. Beyond Lacan and language, that stance is consistent with the broader epistemic and ontologic openness we've described in post-positivist work.

Structures

We described in Chapter 4 a preliminary means of conceptualizing structural functionalism as an approach to studying structures, or stable repeating patterns or systems of behavior, in such a way that structures are intimately linked to the functions they serve, both formal and informal—that is, if one wants to study and understand, let alone change existing structures or patterns, the most fruitful approach is to determine what function they serve. Structures may take many different forms and provide for a wide array of functions ranging from formal decision systems to informal authority patterns and serve functions that range from supporting the accomplishment of ends to enhancing rituals that build symbolic identity.[21]

As we come back to structures in this chapter, we are going to broaden our conception of structuralism to describe a general approach used in various disciplines in the social and behavioral sciences as well as the humanities. A working notion of structures that starts with the idea that they are stable, repeating patterns or systems of behavior will continue to be a good starting point. Adding to that idea, structuralism is a social or behavioral framework that explores the relationships between fundamental elements, from which broader and more general mental, linguistic, social, cultural, or other "structures" or patterned systems are built. For structuralist social scientists, whether studying organizations, political systems, cultures, or other social settings, it is through these structures that meaning is produced, and thereby, stable social behavior is established and maintained.

The advent of structuralism is often attributed to the work of Ferdinand de Saussure on linguistics. Saussure's structural linguistics propounded three related concepts.[22] First, Saussure argued the need to distinguish between *langue,* or an ideal form of language, and *parole,* or the way language is actually used in daily life. He introduced a terminology and corresponding three-element framework that structuralists and poststructuralists still refer to, a *sign, signifier,* and *signified.* The sign is a concept that has shared meaning in a social setting and is composed of both a signified, an abstract concept or idea, and a signifier, a sound or image that represents the idea. Figure 9.1 shows the relationship using a common example of a tree.

This basic model reveals the beginnings of a set of linguistic structures, or stable repeating patterns or systems of language that allow not only for shared understanding and knowledge development but subsequently for the emergence of stable patterns of behavior that are derived from shared language and understanding.

Saussure pushes this framework further and points out that because each unique language has different words to describe the same objects or concepts, we have to conclude that there is no inherent reason why a specific sign is used to express a given signifier. The selection is therefore "arbitrary" and, more importantly, socially constructed. Signs gain their meaning from their use, and in that use, stable relationships form that both link and contrast with other signs. Saussure indicates that "in language, there are only differences 'without positive terms.'" Positive terms, for Saussure, are those that would have inherent, or grounded, meaning. His claim that linguistic structures lack positive, or grounded terms, sets the stage for a move into the post-positivist ontological and epistemological assumptions we've already set out and is consistent with the linguistic turn we described earlier in this chapter.

Figure 9.1 Saussure's Structural Linguistics Model

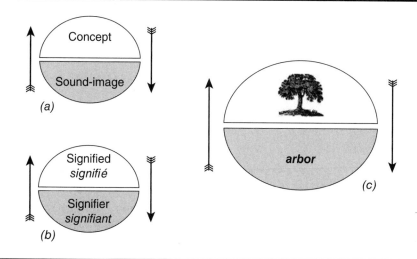

Source: Wendell Piez.

Structuralism moves from linguistics into other disciplines first in psychology in the 1800s and then in the latter part of the twentieth century in sociology, anthropology, and political science. The move into poststructuralism takes place with thinkers like Foucault, who more categorically reject the possibility of grounded, or positive, foundations; they reject the possibility of a so-called *master signifier*.[23] The master signifier is thought to be one that has the capacity to stop the slippage of meaning in a chain of signification. For example, in liberal political and economic theory, we might engage in a conversation about political or economic decision making that includes concepts such as justice, democracy, and utility. While we might be able to develop agreement about whether certain life experiences or examples are just, democratic, or utility generating, developing a positive definition of these concepts, either *a priori* or *a posteriori*, is not possible. However, if we could develop a natural, positive definition of the individual, something like *homo economicus*, the rational model of man, this could serve as a sort of master signifier that could stop the slippage in the chain of signification, or the slippage due to the ambiguity of things like justice, democracy, and utility. In other words, the positively defined individual as rational and utility maximizing provides a stable foundation from which to develop the logic and rationale of popular sovereignty and subsequently of both the concept of and forms of democracy. However, as we'll see in a subsequent section of this chapter, post-positive theory problematizes the notion of the individual too.

One other important attribute of structuralism is that it rejects the concept of an unchanging and universal human subject, or of an underlying human nature. Structuralism discards both rational and behavioralist models as being the basis of action in society and argues that individualism should not be the foundation for our understandings history, existence, or meaning. Where Foucault and other poststructuralists diverge from structuralist thinking is their rejection of the ahistorical formalism, or the idea that there are formal processes of structuration that function outside historical context and influence. For Foucault particularly, his genealogical analyses look to history as a way of finding the nonlinear, subtle, but still critical influences and catalysts that contribute to contemporary structural expressions.

Reflection Questions

What other examples of master signifiers can you identify in our political, economic, social, or scientific discourses?

What sorts of "cracks," or limits, are starting to emerge in these master signifiers?

Box 9.2 Analytic Uses

Structure

As we described in Chapter 8, theories that describe and enable organizational change operate at different levels of analysis, from individual behavior to the relationship between the organization and its environment. David Dent's study of a change initiative at a teaching hospital utilizes post-traditional notions of structure to assess the degree to which constructivist and antifoundational concepts can be useful both methodologically in the study of the organization and practically in understanding the change. Methodologically, Dent adopts an antifoundational approach that recognizes the presence of multiple, simultaneously present perceptions of the organization and its circumstances. As such, his case study adopts an open orientation toward what constitutes data and where those data reside. Practically, he finds that members of the organization have multiple, phenomenological—or deeply contextualized—narratives. Dent concludes first that polyphony, or the simultaneous presence of two or more independent narrative realities, and ambiguity are operational realities in organizations.[24] Dent's second conclusion is that researchers, and managers in their role of seeking to understand their operational circumstances, are faced with either being the arbiter of what is the accurate or valid narrative reality, or the less comfortable and more challenging role of exposing the existing tensions, contradictions and inconsistencies. The managerial extension of this conclusion implies that supervisors, rather than being the source of repository of "true" knowledge, have the role of reconciling these tensions.

Of Agents, Individuals, and Subjects

We've noted periodically throughout the book that one of the central criteria that we use to select theories for inclusion is that they must be explicitly or implicitly actionable. Theories have to allow managers to apply them not just to understand their circumstances but to take intentional actions that are likely to improve their circumstances. Whether that manager works from classical management theories informed by scientific management, economic theories informed by principal-agent theory, behavioralist theories informed by social psychology, or others, we've crafted the book around the notion that those who read it are or will be working in settings where effective action must be taken by someone.

Embedded in that criterion is an assumption that there are *agents*, individuals who are capable of exercising some degree of autonomous decision making and more or less independent action. At one level, this assumption seems so self-evident as to defy any other possibility and is deeply imbedded in philosophy, politics, economics, psychology, and beyond.

Post-positive theory, working out of literary theory, contemporary continental philosophy, and other disciplines, picks up several reasonable ideas and traces the logic of those ideas to a point where the self-evidence of the agent or Cartesian cogito, the autonomous agent who thinks and acts, is called into question. This logical inquiry is more than an intriguing thought experiment and potentially has implications for how we think about public administration and governance.

The deconstruction of the agent or subject can easily begin from any number of different starting points, some of which we've already introduced in the book and others you are likely already familiar with. For example, structuralist approaches to examining culture and institutionalization that we examined in Chapters 4, 7, and earlier in this chapter do not deny the existence of the autonomous agent but do suggest that structures—inside and outside organizations—are a more useful basis for understanding social phenomenon. Moreover, this structuralist analysis suggests that the autonomous individual isn't even necessary to understand social organization and social phenomenon.

Although homo economicus, the economic model of man, continues to shape our thinking and discussion of human behavior, economic and other treatments of human behavior after Herbert Simon's introduction of bounded rationality have moved away from a wholly rational depiction of behavior.[25] Economic and psychological models, including the Lacanian model described in this chapter, suggest that many factors in our history, experience, habit, and perceptions shape our behavior, suggesting that our autonomy and independent of action may be significantly constrained. Behavioral research has shown how, regardless of our self-perceptions of autonomy and independence, our actual behavior is highly patterned and quite constrained in the exercise of creative or variable actions.[26] These attributes of human behavior, which are not terribly unfamiliar to us, suggest that the wholly rational, autonomous agent is at best an incomplete model of human behavior and at worst an unnecessary fallacy. Post-positive theory takes up different variations of these observations and extends these implications to their logical limits and suggests alternative models.

One such model is the notion of the *decentered self,* or a depiction of the subject that is not the ultimate source of knowing—from this perspective, the *cogito,* or our egos and thinking minds are not at the center of things as autonomous knowers. Instead, what we *know*—or better, what we believe we know—exists only in relation to other people and within social systems. Discursive practices, the complex forms of verbal, nonverbal, symbolic, explicit, and implicit interactions, create "subject positions" or nodes rather than an empirical subject or agent.[27] The practical issues that emerge here for our purposes include questions such as the following: Can there be "deciders" without the modern subject? What does leadership look like without the modern subject?

One implication of this decentering is that it shifts attention beyond or away from the subject as both a linguistic (i.e., subject-object) and empirical focal point and opens a space to examine other structural arrangements. One manifestation of this is the concept of *alterity*. In simplest terms, alterity simply means the other or the other as one who is not the subject or the center of perception and understanding in a modernist frame of reference. Alterity implies the ability to distinguish between self and not-self and consequently to assume the existence of an alternative viewpoint. Philosophers like Emmanuel Levinas and Baudrillard extend the notion of alterity to give a sense of the other both in contrast to the knowing self but also as the entity in contrast to which a positive, stable identity is constructed.[28] Alterity points us to the other not only as different and separate from ourselves but also in contrast to the identity that is constructed for the other. Alterity reveals that there is more to the other than what we believe we know.

In public administration, Farmer takes up the notion of alterity and its tendency to reveal not just the other but the complexity and variation of otherness and suggests some very specific implications for the both the practices and the normative orientation of public administration.[29]

Reflection Questions

What are other examples of organizational practices that assume the atomistic, autonomous individual?

What are some possible implications for shifting to organization practices and procedures that function based on a post-positivist understanding of the individual or agent?

Farmer embraces the implosion of the politics-administration dichotomy and argues, following Baudrillard, Foucault, and implicitly the ethical claims of Levinas, that public administration practice would be reflexive about and critical toward authoritarian, closed, or homogenized routines and procedures. We'll explore the expressions and implications of Farmer's argument more in Chapter 10.

Jerry Frug takes the notion of the decentered self in a different direction. Extending the idea that the self is a constructed phenomenon, he extends the decentered self to analyze the operations of municipal governments in their attempts to deal with the kinds of issues that we've previously described as wicked problems.[30] Frug suggests that both municipal policy and local agency behavior reveals the degree to which municipalities conceive themselves as autonomous selves and have constructed extensive bodies of beliefs and corresponding practices that follow from the assumption of local or municipal identity—selfhood. Although these practices have become deeply institutionalized, and thereby habitualized in action and in perception, Frug's analysis does provide a conceptual framework and corresponding language from which we can engage differently in efforts to respond to those conditions we feel should be changed.

Box 9.3 Analytical Uses

Agents

Our discussion of agents, subjects, and actors shows some degree of the breadth of post-positivist thinking about the nature of what is sometimes called *methodological individualism*, or the idea that the individual is the primary actor and unit of analysis in social science. David Nel and Jan Kroeze push this line of logic even further than we've described so far by positing that information technology (IT) might well be considered an agent of postmodernism. Nel and Kroeze begin by identifying key themes in both the literature on technology and postmodernism, which reveal a new form of innovation and evolution in contemporary IT, a form not present in earlier uses of technology. With that literature as background, they examine the role of IT in contemporary settings and argue that its effects, in terms of displacement of space and time; its support of conditions of hyperreality; and its tendency to undermine the stability of both tradition and identity make IT a post-positivist phenomenon. But more importantly, because IT *acts* to extend or exacerbate these trends, rather than just being a reflection of these trends, IT has become an agent. Moving beyond the decentering of the self, or intensified understanding of the other, Nel and Kroeze suggest that in post-positivist conditions we should consider the possibility of nonhuman agents. As odd as this position sounds, Nel and Kroeze have company in pursuing this line of logic. Science and technology theorists including Bruno Lator and Michel Callon advance a parallel idea in their work on actor network theory, and Kevin Kelly describes a similar momentum in his depiction of the *techonomy*, a sort of evolutionary drive in technology.

Representation as More Than a Constitutional Structure

In political science and public administration, the treatment of representation tends to be focused on the strategies and mechanisms adopted by different constitutionally based political systems in order to deal with the difficulties of a large republic. The use and structure of representational arrangements were one of the core arguments over the framing and ratification of the US Constitution and have been an ongoing theme in political science ever sense.[31] A significant theme in the treatment of political representation explores the weaknesses of representation in political communities that are growing in size and diversity. Such treatments argue, for example, that the 435 members of the House of Representatives in Congress cannot adequately represent a nation of 300 million citizens, either descriptively or substantively. They can neither descriptively represent the ethnic, racial, gender, sexual orientation, or other forms present in the population of the United States nor can they effectively, substantively advocate for the breadth and growing diversity of those interests.[32] Just as a modern theory of language assumes that it is possible for the language system to capture and represent the entirety of the world it denotes, it is assumed that a system of political representation can do the same thing.

Post-positive theory starts its exploration of representation as an issue of ontology and epistemology and then traces the consequences for political representation. As we noted in our treatment of language in post-positive theory earlier in this chapter, a modern understanding of language assumes that words can directly denote or represent the thing the word refers to. In doing so, that understanding of language adopts important assumptions about the nature of the world and what can be known about it—namely, that all of the critical aspects of a thing can be known and represented, or re-presented, in the word. Moreover, the system of language is also assumed to have the capacity to be comprehensive and exhaustive in that all of the attributes of the world can be known and represented in the system of language. Post-positive theory challenges the notion of both ontological and epistemological claims.

Thomas Catlaw's genealogy of the ontology of representation and illumination of the legitimacy problem makes this case and the consequences of it even more forcefully.[33] Catlaw points out that from the time of Greek political thought until today, the logic of democratic political authority requires some form of categorical exclusion. For the Greeks this is philosophically embodied in the distinction between *zoë* (bare life) and *bios* (political life). The necessities of bare life and physical survival were excluded from political discourse. In the practice of Greek political experience, the exclusion was women, slaves, and any others barred from political life. Today, the demos of democracy, or the people of "We the People" are purportedly a universal category or unity but are actually empty if any positive content. So in order for it to have functionality, it must do so by establishing an exclusion—that which is *not* the people.[34]

The logic of the categorical exclusion remains in place throughout the development of modern political systems but is obscured and convoluted by political liberalism and the advent of the notion of popular sovereignty. The difficulty in the United States, both theoretically since the founding, and increasingly in practice, is that the exclusion has been brought into the system. More specifically, the notion of a sovereign people from whom political authority is drawn implies unity. Despite the impossibility of this unity, the system remained functional in the structural limits on power built into the Constitution, which recognize the inevitability of divisions within the people. Moreover, many practical difficulties of any extant diversity were further obscured by the categorical exclusion of larger portions of the population from political life. The notion of a unified people decays further as the logic of liberalism and inclusion has increasingly brought those who were excluded in practice into political life, therefore increasing the diversity of political discourse and further eroding the notion of a unified people. What remains is an irresolvable paradox in which the logic of representation is simultaneously comprehensive and exhaustive and at the same time must retain some form of categorical exclusion in order to function.

The effect of these trends that obscure or erode the distinction between zoë and bios is at least threefold. One effect relates to the difficulty of representation in that this erosion also has the effect of highlighting the tension over another exclusion from the political—that is, who is in and who is out expressed, among other ways, in terms of the contentiousness of immigration. Catlaw's analysis reveals this to be an issue of political ontology and epistemology rather than one contending rights of sovereign states and members of, for example, migrant populations and others who seek representation.[35]

A second effect is also one we're familiar with in contemporary American political culture. Here the effect is experienced as a breakdown in the boundaries between public and private life. Increasingly, the private is seen as public. This trajectory sheds new light on the cynicism about the legitimacy of public administration in that it reveals an interpretation wherein questions of legitimacy derive from the perception that the government is increasingly encroaching into the private sphere. But legitimacy is not the only casualty of the collapse of zoë and bios. The effect of this collapse for Foucault is to subordinate human existence (bios) to biological existence (zoë).

A final casualty, one that is more important in terms for questions of ethics that we will take up in Chapter 11, is the liberated subject—the subject free from endless self-decipherment and from subjugation to psychological norms.[36] Sigmund Freud, according to Foucault, relentlessly pursues the *truth* of the identity of the subject, a truth that is hidden far from his conscious awareness.[37] In other words, Freud seeks to create a positive definition of the subject, which as we have seen now in several different interpretations is, at the very least, intensely problematic in post-positivist thinking. A positive definition of the individual, one who thinks and acts such that responsibility can be attributed as a consequence, seems to be evaporated in this analysis of politics. Instead, we will have to think differently about the sources and causes of ethical and corrupt behaviors, their causes, and solutions.

It is perhaps worth working through Catlaw's analysis of the political ontology of the people and the corresponding epistemological problem of representation, political or otherwise. The starting place to understand the problem of representation can be found in what Catlaw describes as the *myth of the given,* which is the assumption that something exists outside of the objective observations of science—i.e., the language of science—that there is something real to which the science refers. Classification schemes (and representational choices) are claimed to be and, moreover, are generally assumed to be natural. In both the social and natural sciences, taxonomies emerge based on natural and organic distinctions and are manifest in organic structures. Discourse under this set of assumptions appeals to facts as an appeal to the natural world. To the general-abstract model copy we add the following:

> [The model-copy relation] is not merely the position from which representation can be judged, but in its objectivity, [is] also that which makes representations possible. It is by virtue of the fact that there is a natural, content-emitting "real" that allows for representational copies that there is thought plausibility to be a stable and objective position from which to array, distribute and decide upon representations.[38]

In the discourse of politics and representation, a major focus has been on the minimal distance, on closing the gap between referent and represented. The concern with minimal distance is evident from the founding debates to the representative bureaucracy literature to redistricting controversies in contemporary political settings.

Literature, as well as practice, has the possibility of turning on itself and becoming an infinite critique of the gaps and holes. However, Catlaw points out that the distance between representative and represented cannot be closed in this way. As a result, two different courses of action become apparent. First, Catlaw suggests that we should develop a wider reconceptualization of the critique of representation at the level of ontology. We should become more aware of the extent to which we use this representational logic in practice. Second, we need to better understand the processes by which the artifacts are created, maintained, and changed.

Foucault's work in the *History of Sexuality* seems to do exactly this with respect to the creation of, or the technologies of, the self.[39]

Catlaw notes several consequences of these claims that bear on the question of immigration. One is that no quantity or quality of representation can ever add up to one or a unity. Representation and representatives are thus "always running a deficit." The sociocognitive response is to manage the deficit—"the materialization of the exclusion materializes the impossibility of the posited unity," for example, in the identification of the "other."

Working from McSwite, Catlaw highlights another outcome of this set of dynamics—that is, that the other, for McSwite, is manifested in woman, who symbolically becomes a source of both attraction and loathing.[40] This tension creates a paradox that reveals tendencies toward either annihilation or integration. For example, Zygmunt Bauman sees a similar tendency in the late modern, or what he calls liquid modern, immigration debates in the United States and elsewhere, in the simultaneous attraction and loathing of the foreigner and those things that are foreign. The foreign and foreigner are at once exotic and bizarre, an opportunity and a threat. Bauman describes the current conditions in which strangers, aliens, foreigners, and people of different forms of life are nowadays the one case in which you can say that we are going to meet tomorrow, the day after tomorrow, next year, and as far in the future as our fantasy may reach. And so, as always in such situations, we have to work out the ways of reconciling natural attraction with natural repulsion—the mode of coexisting.[41]

Reflection Question

How might representative institutions and practices be realigned without assuming the possibility of positivist forms of representation?

Broadly, Catlaw prompts us to become attuned to our perceptions, connotations, and expectations of how these model-copy relations are formed and function. Doing so allows us to see where representations have become unchallenged or untested mental shortcuts that preclude other understandings and other courses of action. Said differently, the mental constructs expressed in the various model-copy relations we work from constitute the box we are challenged to think outside of.

Box 9.4 Analytical Uses

Knowledge

The role of information systems (IS) and IT is often orientated toward knowledge management, or the acquisition, analysis, and access to that knowledge as an instrumental means to improving decision making. John Pillay and Ray Hackney's case study of mission statements and their relationship to the role of IS-IT functions shifts the organizational understanding of knowledge, or the epistemology of organizations, into a post-positivist or antifoundational orientation. Pillay and Hackney's case study draws on antifoundationalist philosophy and considers mission statements to be ontological claims rather than instrumental positions. The implication is that what constitutes knowledge for the organization is inherently tied to particular cultural contexts, which are themselves socially constructed. In other words, mission statements should be understood as claims about the nature of reality that emerge from a particular concrete setting rather than being instrumental, or ends-oriented, statements. As such, the narratives in these concrete contexts are polyphonic, suggesting not just multiple voices but multiple knowledges—all of which inform the actions of the organization. Granting legitimacy to these knowledges and crafting different processes of analysis and reflection that the researchers describe as textual and deconstructive allows different forms and types of knowledge to be present in functional and constructive ways.

Postmodern Governance

The last post-positive concept we'll explore is a bit broader and is inclusive of several different ideas. It also draws on the descriptions of language and representation that we've already presented. As a way of working into an understanding of postmodern or post-positive governance, it might be helpful to think about a historical heuristic of organizations and public administration.[42] This heuristic suggests an incremental, conceptual development of public administration. Early theories of organization and public administration—those associated with classical management—saw all organizations, public and private, as essentially alike. That understanding and interpretation evolves with interpretations like that of Graham Allison and Paul Appleby, such that we can find important differences between public and private. Our use of the idea of governance to this point in the text has been slightly different still. We have suggested that governance organizations can't be understood as just public or private but instead should be thought of in terms of what sorts of organizations are engaged in delivery of services or goods associated with democratic politics. As such, governance organizations may well be public but likely include many service-providing nonprofit organizations and conceivably some for-profit organizations that, for example, provide services either to the public sector or even directly to citizens. What they share is a role in politics as the pursuit of the good life.

The move into post-positive governance shifts our understanding again by arguing that governance may be better understood as functioning in a different way and that within that understanding we also need to reexamine ideas like power, and knowledge. In this section's discussion, we're drawing primarily on the ideas of Foucault, though his work and ideas have been taken up and extended and applied by many others.

Perhaps the easiest entry into these ideas is through the notion of *governmentality*.[43] Foucault's briefest pronouncements about governmentality are described in terms such as "the art of government" or "the conduct of conduct." While not particularly robust or illuminating, these do give some indication that Foucault does have something different in mind than Wilson's notion of the science of administration or Luther Gulick's POSDCoRB.

Foucault does provide a more detailed treatment in one of his later essays, which focuses directly on the notion of governmentality. In it, he describes it in three fairly different but related ways.

1. Governmentality can be understood as the arrangements formed by the institutions, procedures, analyses and reflections, the calculations, and tactics that allow the exercise of this very specific and complex form of power. Governmentality explores this form of power through its various target populations, its principal forms of knowledge political economy, and its core technical means of security.[44]

2. Governmentality is also the tendency that has, over a time, inexorably led toward the preeminence of this form of power over all other forms (sovereignty, discipline, etc.). These forms result, on the one hand, in formation of a whole series of specific governmental apparatuses, and, on the other, in the development of a whole complex of *saviors* or knowledges that allow and encourage self-control and self-governance. This is a sort of variation of the axiom that knowledge implies action. Here, self-knowledge implies self-disciplined action.

3. Governmentality is concerned with the processes—or better, the result of the processes—by which the state of justice in the modern age is transformed into the administrative state.[45]

Colin Gordon boils these three down to what he views as a central question Foucault pursues along these lines—namely, what are "the different ways in which an activity or art called government has been made thinkable and practicable"?[46] This statement makes plain a largely hidden paradox in our intuition about government and governance as it operates at levels running from the nation-state down to the management of individual behavior. That paradox is that we simultaneously believe that governance and sovereign authority is at once crafted in a rational way through the development of the Constitution or any other political document and is at the same time so pervasive and embedded in our everyday experience as to seem as if it's an almost natural structure. Foucault reveals to us, or at least reminds us, that administration in all its forms is a development that had to be invented. This has at least two implications. One is that the invention and development of governance required and continues to require a rationale supporting it. Its invented character also implies that because it isn't somehow a natural entity that its adoption was at least in part a political choice and that there can be alternative political choices as well.

From these observations, Foucault focuses not on questions of sovereignty or legitimacy but rather turns his attention to the "manifold forms of domination" that exist and operate "among subjects in their mutual relations."[47, 48] More explicitly, Foucault claims the following:

> Government resides in the things it *manages* and in the pursuit of the perfection and intensification of the processes which it directs; and the instruments of government, instead of being laws, now come to be a range of multiform tactics. Within the perspective of government, law is not what is important.[49]

One reading of this passage, especially the last sentence, is a logical extension of Wilson's observation in his essay—that it has become harder to run a constitution than it is to frame one. Moreover, Foucault's move in this direction also recognizes that governmentality, or governance, has to do with the management of behavior across all levels of society. And for our purposes, Foucault's work certainly applies to behavior in and outside organizational settings.

To be sure, Foucault doesn't reject the importance of the state but instead traces the relations of power as it is expressed in the tactics of governmentality beyond the state or that "fly below the radar of sovereignty and law."[50] Foucault's analysis of an emergent tension in political theory and American—and to some degree European—political culture is revealing of such tactics. The theoretical and practical move from understanding a political state as a collection of individuals or monads to a *population* that can be measured, statistically categorized, and re-presented, and as a result can be made subject to administrated action is, for Foucault, more important that the examination of legislative or executive politics. This understanding of the population makes the application of "technique," or governance, possible—that is, thinkable and practicable.

R. McGreggor Cawley and William Chaloupka's analysis of American public administration and American governmentality make the link more explicit still. Wilson, they point out, recognized that changing social, economic, and political conditions required giving attention to administration, running the Constitution, and, more importantly for a Foucaultian analysis, using specialized tactics. His call for both the politics-administration dichotomy and the development of specialized training and skills for public administrators becomes an expression of governmentality. Similarly, Cawley and Chaloupka find in Taylor's development of the practices or tactics of scientific management a parallel focus on the multiform tactics of governmentality emerging out of his call for time and motion studies in that such empirical approaches have the effect of creating particular arrangements of knowledge and discipline. Perhaps most interestingly they turn also to Mary Parker Follett's notion of the law of the situation. They argue that Follett's attention to context and the emergence of specific attributes of context that are critical to effective decision making and action is in fact parallel to Taylor's critiques of (then) contemporary workplaces and his presentation of scientific management as an alternative. Cawley and Chaloupka's interpretation of Follett is clearly different than the one we presented in Chapter 2, largely because we are working from an examination of her ontological and epistemological assumptions, and they are examining manifestations of her practices in relation to manifestations of Taylor's work.[51] Nevertheless, Cawley and Chaloupka's assessment finds support in how Follett's contemporaries, including Elliot Fox and Lyndall Urwick, understood her work and attempted to both operationalize and link it to Taylor.

Power-Knowledge

One common definition of power indicates that it is the capacity to get people to do things that they wouldn't otherwise do. Following this definition, we often narrow our consideration of power to forms of coercion and persuasion. Foucault pushes his thinking about governance further in his analysis of power expressed in a different form. Unlike most liberal and Enlightenment political philosophers, Foucault does not attempt to develop a logic of authority and power derived from and then extended from theories of sovereignty. He argues that by working from sovereignty, especially liberal notions of popular sovereignty, explorations of power tend to obscure the profound and pervasive expressions of power as manifest in discipline. Discipline, like governmentality, appears in multiform variations. Foucault's studies of prisons, mental health, medicine, and sexuality reveal variants of this form of power or, more accurately, discipline, which is intimately linked to particular, politicized (in that it supports particular visions of the *good life*) expressions. These variants of power foster particular and stable patterns of knowledge as well as corresponding behaviors. The combination of power-knowledge is a technique of control that combines hierarchical, purportedly objective, scientific, or natural observation with normalizing judgment. It determines what "is: and correspondingly, what we can do. This dynamic links power/knowledge in that it combines into a unified system both discipline as a coercive force shaping behavior with the establishment of truth."[52] Power-knowledge both establishes the truth about those who undergo examination and controls their behavior by forcing them to follow a particular, ostensibly objective but ultimately political course of action.

It is worth reflection on the relation of Foucault's depiction of power and knowledge in comparing the familiar axiom that power is knowledge. This conception suggests that knowledge is an instrument of power, especially in situations of information asymmetry. Foucault's point differs in that he points out that in social settings, the utilization of power to accomplish certain ends and the utilization of knowledge for certainty cannot be separated such that "in knowing we control and in controlling we know."[53]

Foucault's study of Jeremy Bentham's Panopticon is perhaps the most well known of his disciplinary analyses. For Foucault, the Panopticon is a prime manifestation of disciplinary power. The Panopticon is a prison architecture arranged so that each inmate is separated from and invisible to all the others. However, every inmate can, at any time, be seen by the guards who are located in a central tower. Those guards will actually not always see each inmate but because they *could* at any time, prisoners act as if they are always objects of observation. As a result, control is achieved more by the internal monitoring of those controlled than by physical coercion by the guard—the one who controls.

The principle linking knowing and controlling as expressed in the Panopticon can be found not only to prisons but across practices in society. As such, principle of power-knowledge as expressed by the Panopticon has come to pervade every aspect of modern society, resulting in *societies of discipline*. Discipline and knowledge used for control and largely expressed by self-application has become the primary instrument through which control and stability functions and is maintained. Governmentality through discipline and power-knowledge, from a Foucaultian perspective, has replaced premodern forms of sovereignty, such as kings and patriarchs, and modern forms of authority, such as Weberian rational-legal, as the fundamental forms power relation.

As we previously noted, Foucault pursued variations of these same structural dynamics through mental health systems and the medical profession. Other studies have looked at the emergence of these configurations as diverse as the American penal system, systems of online securities trading, and human resources systems.[54]

Image 9.1   Foucault's Panopticon

Source: Library of Congress.

Within the realm of study here, organizations can be understood as quintessential systems of disciplinary power. Weberian bureaucracy and rational-legal authority continues to be the dominant model of organization regardless of alternative approaches that might be grafted onto or synthesized into contemporary organizations. Weberian bureaucracy is premised on knowing what is to be done, how it is to be done, the techniques needed to get the thing done, and so forth. Taylor, too, focuses on knowledge and control in this way; though now, because we all know— not just the engineer or expert—we submit to self-control rather than external coercion or persuasion. Moreover, the development of modern IT and management approaches (also known as *knowledge management*) continues to take on a greater importance for the coordination (i.e., governance) of organizational activities. These techniques are becoming their own disciplines (fields of study) and simultaneously become knowledge-driven mechanisms for conducting conduct.

In private sector organizations, where normative questions of democracy and equity are less central to the work of the organization, such structures may be less of a concern in that we want humane organizations, but because "business is business" we have fewer concerns about manifestations of power internally and externally. In public organizations, where these normative questions are more central, the move from practices and questions of sovereignty, to governance, discipline, and power/knowledge are more important. Legitimacy questions, whether focused on constitutional institutions (Congress, the president, and the Supreme Court) or on public administration, tend to obscure the extent to which mechanisms and techniques of control and coercion have moved. As liberalism moves power and sovereignty away from centralized institutions and appears to diminish the use of that power for domination, modern liberal analyses miss the extent to which power and domination appear instead of disciplinary settings both inside organizations and to questions of power-knowledge outside organizations but still in governance settings like public policy.

Reflection Question

As you think about organizations you've worked in or are interested in, what are some examples of post-positivist governance and power in the practices and structures (whether physical, behavioral, linguistic, or otherwise) of contemporary organizations?

Box 9.5 Analytical Uses

Power-Knowledge

The analysis of power and control, both formal and informal, is pervasive in the OT literature. As we've described, Foucault significantly shifts the conceptualization of how power functions and is manifest in organizations and elsewhere. Christopher Cowton and Sue Dopson take up Foucault's notion of power,

(Continued)

(Continued)

governmentality, and discipline in their analysis of an automotive parts distributor. Their inquiry is driven by a concern with how management control really operates rather than how it is purported to function based on what they describe as the "canonical texts." In order to do that, they draw on and operationalize Foucaultian concepts such as power-knowledge, surveillance, and discipline and then utilize this framework in a case study of a large—more than 200 outlets—auto parts distributor. Their case study entails a detailed examination of managers' behaviors with respect to sources and uses of power, in conjunction with structures of oversight and surveillance to assess the presence of wider patterns of behavior consistent with Foucault's depiction of panoptic structures. For example, they found evidence that formal control systems served to create stable forms of discipline that shaped individual behavior. The "gaze," or surveillance of managers and supervisors, was a key mechanism that drove these control systems. The researchers conclude that Foucault's ideas required some adaptation using the constructivist work of Anthony Giddens.

Summary and Conclusions

THE CONCEPTS FROM POST-POSITIVE THEORY that we've explored here are, in many ways, just the tip of the proverbial iceberg. The literature that can be linked to the assumptions we identified at the beginning of the chapter is diverse and continues to grow. The concepts are, to some degree, difficult to wrap one's head around. We hope to have presented them in a way that is fairly approachable and that grounds them in material and ideas with which you're already familiar. Our sense—after working with this material for the past two decades for our own research and having presented elements of these ideas in many classrooms and to many students—is that these ideas and their use are clearly iterative. The material does become easier and clearer with repeated use, consideration, and even application. Although repeated, subsequent work with complex ideas is valuable with just about any material, post-positive theory isn't something that can be mastered after a short introduction like the one we've presented here. To shift metaphors, coming to grips with these ideas will likely require some mental marination; they will probably make more sense once they've rattled around in your head for a while.[55]

Nevertheless, we hope to have accomplished several outcomes with this chapter. First, we've introduced a set of post-positive concepts in this chapter that extend ideas including alternative understandings of language, agency, the subject, structures, and governance. While we haven't approached these concepts in a rigorously post-positivist way in previous chapters, we have placed them in a historical and conceptual context. As such they should not feel entirely alien or unfamiliar. Second, because they shouldn't appear to have dropped out of thin air as overly abstract, distinctly different, or inapplicable in real governance settings, some sense of their implications and potential uses should also be taking shape. In the next chapter, we'll take up these ideas again and explore how administrative and organizational theorists are endeavoring to operationalize these concepts in ways that are not only concrete but improve both organizational means and organizational ends. ∎

Discussion Questions

1. As you think about the range of concepts we've described, what are some ways that they overlap, link, or reinforce one another in contemporary governance organizations?

2. What are some ways or places that suggest that these concepts are in tension or incommensurable with one another?

Notes

1. See Pauline Marie Rosenau, *Post-Modernism and the Social Sciences: Insights, Inroads and Intrusion* (Princeton, NJ: Princeton University Press, 1992). Rosenau distinguishes between critical postmodernists—and a more nihilistic and radically relativist set of positions that they tend to hold—and affirmative postmodernists, who adopt many of the same assumptions but tend to be more positive with respect to the possibility of action and improvement in social, political, economic, and other conditions.

2. See, for example, Göktuğ Morçöl, *A New Mind for Policy Analysis: Toward a Post-Newtonian and Postpositivist Epistemology and Methodology* (Westport, CT: Praeger, 2002). While Morçöl suggests that chaos and complexity theories embrace assumptions such as probabilism rather than determinism, which are distinct from high-modern or positivist (especially *logical positivist*) ontological thought, our focus on social constructivism and the linguistic turn is quite distinct from his approach.

3. The "void" in the chapter title is a reference to nihilism and the logical consequence of radical relativism.

4. David John Farmer, *The Language of Public Administration: Bureaucracy, Modernism and Postmodernism* (Tuscaloosa: University of Alabama Press, 1995), 145.

5. Ibid.

6. This was exemplified in Eisenhower's comments about the threat posed by the "military-industrial complex."

7. Peter L. Berger and Thomas Luckmann, *The Social Construction of Reality: A Treatise in the Sociology of Knowledge* (Garden City, NY: Anchor Books, 1966).

8. Rosenau, *Post-Modernism and the Social Sciences.*

9. Ludwig Wittgenstein, *Tractatus Logico-Philoshophicus,* trans. D. F. Pears and B. F. McGuinness (New York: Humanities Press, 1961).

10. Ludwig Wittgenstein, *Philosophical Investigations* (London: Blackwell, 1953).

11. In an early draft of this book, this passage read as follows: "The reality is that its actual uses are reasonably stable, and importantly are linked to actions in specific contexts." The original terms reveal the extent to which a modern, denotative tendency is built into common use language. This is a useful reflection in confronting the difficulty we sometimes have making sense of post-positivist thought—it is counter to our uses and connotations, which both reveal and reinforce the way we think about things.

12. Charles J. Fox and Hugh T. Miller, *Postmodern Public Administration: Towards Discourse* (Thousand Oaks, CA: Sage, 1996), 45.

13. John Tiffin and Terashima Nobuyoshi, *Hyperreality: Paradigm for the Third Millennium* (London: Routledge, 2001).

14. Jean Baudrillard, *Simulacra and Simulation,* trans. Sheila Faria Glaser (Ann Arbor: University of Michigan Press, 1994).

15. Just to reinforce the description of how the chain of simulacra develops, a version of Mr. T recently began appearing in a series of local television ads featuring the "E-Team," a set of characters based on the A-Team used to advertise for a business in the community where one of the authors of this book lives. A Mr. T-like character is featured prominently in the ads, which are targeted to a fairly young audience—most of whom have never seen the original show but know the characters and their personalities nonetheless.

16. O. C. McSwite, "Jacques Lacan and the Human Subject: How Psychoanalysis Can Help Public Administration," *American Behavioral Scientist* 41, no. 1 (1997): 43–63.

17. Bruce Fink, *The Lacanian Subject* (Princeton, NJ: Princeton University Press, 1995).

18. Fink, *The Lacanian Subject*; Bruce Fink, *A Clinical Introduction to Lacanian Psychoanalytic Theory and Technique* (Cambridge, MA: Harvard University Press, 1997).

19. O. C. McSwite, "Jacques Lacan and the Human Subject."

20. For a description of multiple forms of knowledge, see Mary Schmidt, "Grout: Alternative Kinds of Knowledge and Why They are Ignored," *Public Administration Review* 53, no. 6 (1993): 525–530.

21. Symbolic identity might, for example, be the institutional or cultural character of an organization.

22. Simon Blackburn, *Oxford Dictionary of Philosophy*, 2nd ed. (Oxford, UK: Oxford University Press, 2008).

23. Complicating efforts to "wrap our heads around" these ideas, those theorists who are generally associated with structuralism, and even more so with poststructuralism, reject the title category and deny their association with it.

24. Mike Dent, "The New National Health Service: A Case of Postmodernism?" *Organization Studies* 16, no. 5 (1995): 875–899.

25. Freud's depiction of the bicameral, conscious-unconscious mind, provides a quite developed and sophisticated model of nonrational behavior.

26. Chaoming Song et al., "Limits of Predictability in Human Mobility," *Science* 327, no. 5968 (2010): 1018–1021.

27. Alan Sheridan, *Michel Foucault: The Will to Truth* (New York: Tavistock Publications, 1980).

28. See Jean Baudrillard, *The Ecstasy of Communication*, trans. Bernard Schutze and Caroline Schutze (New York: Semiotext(e), 1988); Jean Baudrillard and Marc Guillaume, *Radical Alterity*, trans. Ames Hodges (New York: Semiotext(e), 2008); Emmanuel Levinas, *Alterity and Transcendence*, trans. Michael B. Smith (Columbia University Press, 1999).

29. Farmer, *The Language of Public Administration*.

30. Jerry Frug, "Decentralizing Decentralization," *The University of Chicago Law Review* 60, no. 2 (1993): 253–338.

31. For examples of variations of this research, see Hannah F. Pitkin, *The Concept of Representation* (Berkeley: University of California Press, 1967); J. D. Kingsley, *Representative Bureaucracy: An Interpretation of the British Civil Service* (Yellow Springs, OH: The Antioch Press, 1944).

32. Prior to ratification of the Seventeenth Amendment to the Constitution in 1913, which established direct election of members, the US Senate was better understood as a body intended to represent the states, not citizens. The original structure and responsibilities of the Senate established in Article II of the Constitution, including ratification of international treaties, executive activities such as the confirmation of Cabinet appointees, and the judicial responsibility to try presidential impeachments indicate that the Senate was not created to be a representative body nor is it entirely a representative body even in its current form.

33. Thomas Catlaw, "Constitution as Executive Order: The Administrative State and the Political Ontology of 'We the People,'" *Administration and Society* 37, no. 4 (2005): 445–482.

34. See also Thomas Catlaw, *Fabricating the People: Politics and Administration in the Biopolitical State* (Tuscaloosa: University of Alabama Press, 2007), 11–13.

35. Ibid.

36. James W. Bernauer and Michael Mahon, "Michel Foucault's Ethical Imagination," in *The Cambridge Companion to Foucault*, ed. Gary Gutting (New York: Cambridge University Press, 2003).

37. Michel Foucault, "Governmentality" in *The Foucault Effect: Studies in Governmentality*, ed. Graham Burchell, Colin Gordon, and Peter Miller (Chicago: University of Chicago Press, 1991), 87–104; Michel Foucault, "The Birth of Biopolitics," in *Ethics: Subjectivity and Truth*, ed. Paul Rabinow (New York: New Press, 1997), 73–79.

38. Catlaw, *Fabricating the People*, 71.

39. Michel Foucault, *The History of Sexuality: The Use of Pleasure*, trans. Robert Hurley (New York: Vintage Random House, 1990).

40. O. C. McSwite, *Legitimacy in Public Administration: A Discourse Analysis* (Thousand Oaks, CA: Sage, 1997).

41. Zygmunt Bauman as quoted in Adrian Franklin, "The Tourist Syndrome: An Interview with Zygmunt Bauman," *Tourist Studies* 3, no. 2 (2003): 215.

42. Heuristics can be understood as frameworks, or models, used as the basis of interpretation.

43. Before describing what governmentality is, keep in mind that Foucault adopts, as do we, a post-positive understanding of language as being nonrepresentational. This means that our descriptions of these concepts should be a starting point to support your understanding, not a concrete, denotative definition. We're attempting to present the "shape" of the idea, but you will have to work with it; push on it; and develop the details, content, and features of if through your own discussions, use, and consideration of the ideas.

44. Political economy for Foucault is the broader set of relations and patterns of exchange of not just goods and services but of power-knowledge in all its forms.

45. Foucault, "Governmentality," 102–103.

46. Graham Burchell, Colin Gordon, and Peter Miller, *The Foucault Effect: Studies in Governmentality* (Chicago: University of Chicago Press, 1991), 9.

47. Bear in mind that the legitimacy question is a central and recurrent concern in public administration. Essays such as Wilson's 1887 article, and to some degree even Weber and Gulick's treatments of organizational form and management practice, can be read as serving as founding documents in public administration.

48. Michel Foucault, *Power/Knowledge: Selected Interviews and Other Writings 1972–1977*, ed. Colin Gordon (Hemel Hempstead, UK: Harvester Wheatsheaf, 1980), 95.

49. Ibid.

50. R. McGreggor Cawley and William Chaloupka, "American Governmentality: Michel Foucault and Public Administration," *American Behavioral Scientist* 41, no. 1 (1997): 28–42.

51. Although it's not an idea we're exploring in our treatment of post-positive thought, there is a concept out of postmodern literary theory known as *the death of the author*, which suggests that once a text is complete any interpretation should proceed as if the author is dead. In other words, it doesn't matter what the author intended but merely what is revealed in any subsequent reading of the text. This may well be a post-positive way of making sense of the widely diverging understandings of Follett's work.

52. Michel Foucault, *Discipline and Punish: The Birth of the Prison*, trans. Alan Sheridan (New York: Vintage, 1977), 184.

53. Gary Gutting, "Michel Foucault," *The Stanford Encyclopedia of Philosophy* (Summer 2013), ed. Edward N. Zalta, http://plato.stanford.edu/archives/sum2013/entries/foucault.

54. Thomas L. Dumm, *Democracy and Punishment: Disciplinary Origins of the United States* (Madison: University of Wisconsin Press, 1987); Annette D. Beresford, "Foucault's Theory of Governance and the Deterrence of Internet Fraud," *Administration and Society* 35, no. 1 (2003): 82–103; Barbara Townley, "Foucault, Power/Knowledge, and its Relevance for Human Resource Management," *American Management Review* 18, no. 3 (1993): 518–545.

55. As conceptually challenging as this material is in and of itself, some theorists have adopted explanatory approaches that make understanding even more difficult. For example, Heidegger's phenomenology is in large part a critique of Cartesian philosophy. Heidegger believed that Descartes' philosophy had so pervaded Western philosophy that he invented a whole new set of terms that he believed would be less likely to fall into or be captured by Cartesian assumptions. Lacan, as a psychoanalytic theorist, wrote in a way that he believed wouldn't be apprehended by the conscious mind but would instead work its way into the unconscious such that it would reappear as new understanding at some later date. While these approaches may be consistent with the views of the theorists who develop them, they also make understanding and using the ideas more difficult for the rest of us.

Chapter 10

Learning to Fly

Applying Post-Positivist Theory

The second chapter in Part III turns its attention to an exploration of how post-positivist theories can be and in some cases already are being applied in organizations involved in governance. There are several issues that we need to note about our approach in this chapter before diving into applications. First, it demonstrates that post-positivist theory is applicable in useful rather than narrowly esoteric ways. Next, it reveals how the theory and application may not constitute a radical departure from existing practice but still differs in subtle but important ways. Finally, it suggests new and emerging opportunities to further apply post-positivist theory in ways that support governance organizations and broader democratic society.

Chapter 9 presents a brief introduction to the history and heterodox thinking that has emerged in the past twenty years. Chapter 9 also connects back to the chapters in Part I in demonstrating how elements of the *other voices* identified in the first part of the book can be traced to contemporary theory.

Chapter 10 turns its attention to praxis, or the intersection of theory and practice, and in doing so connects to the applications of earlier organization theories we explored in Part II. Throughout the book, we have made the case that theory matters—at the very least because it helps us make sense of the complexity of our experience. Moreover, the possibility of exercising some level of theoretical flexibility enables us to "think outside the box," so to speak, and thereby craft new and different ways of acting. However, post-positivist theory has a reputation, sometimes deservedly, of being very difficult to understand, let alone apply. We believe that based on the material we've covered so far there are inroads to its application.

We've endeavored to show through the *other voices* in Part I and through the presentation of theory and literature links in Part II that there are conceptual and practical connections from existing and more mainstream literature to post-positivist theory. Here, we will work the other way and show how the post-positivist concepts we described in more detail in Chapter 9 can be applied and how those applications link back to existing and mainstream practice. In other words, this chapter also reveals how the theory and application may not constitute a radical departure from existing practice but may differ in subtle but important ways, suggesting new and emerging opportunities to further apply theory.

One caveat about our approach needs to be mentioned here as well. Part of our treatment of the theory we've described has been to articulate what we view to be the assumptions underlying each concept. As should be clear at this point, a central assumption of post-positivist theory is a high degree of antifoundationalism. Post-positivist theory eschews the notion that there are universal foundations or universal truth claims that can serve as the basis of knowledge and action. This stance leads directly to the conclusion that there are many courses of action that might be developed, which can be quite consistent with the theory. The consequence for this chapter is that the approaches, practices, and techniques we describe here must be understood as being both propositional and incomplete. Conceivably, there are many other courses of action that might be pursued and that are equally consistent with the assumptions and ideas we've presented. What follows is a starting point to consider application, not an ending point.

There is a related point about prescriptive use of post-positivist theory. That is, in its antifoundationalism and rejection of universal truth claims, it is, at the very least, highly skeptical of claims of "one best way." Many of the post-positivist theories are not just skeptical of such claims but are in fact hostile to them to the degree that such claims tend to reify and privilege some assumptions and marginalize others. As a result, there is debate within the literature about the extent to which it is possible to even speculate about prescriptive strategies and courses of action.[1] While we are sensitive to this conceptual argument, our position is that it's neither helpful nor reasonable to merely describe the theory and then expect practitioners to simply embrace and apply ideas that are quite challenging. For this reason, we feel it is important to reiterate that what follows is a prospective starting point. What we describe here is one among many avenues into the consideration of application.

Lastly, because our treatment of post-positivist theory in Chapter 9 was organized around ideas that have implications across many of the activity areas we used as the basis of organizing Part II (i.e., managing individuals, group dynamics, change, and environmental relations), we're structuring our approach to this chapter differently. In this chapter, we've started with a small number of broad categories of practices, and within each, we'll narrow our discussion to specific topics where we find a confluence of post-positivist theory and day-to-day practices. To reiterate the point we made in the previous paragraph—these confluences and practices are a propositional starting point, not a best practice end point. Moreover, the categories we've selected as a way of organizing application of theory are admittedly incomplete and overlapping. Here, too, we are trying to find a balance between the need for some sort of framework to organize our thinking and speculation about practice but to do so in a way that isn't so concrete as to tend toward reification.

Organizational Activities

We've selected three broad categories of activities that roughly overlap with many of the practices we covered in Part II: information and knowledge activities; people-oriented activities including leadership, supervision, and coordination; and finally, structurally focused activities. To these, we've added one new category: organizational ethics. We feel that these broader groupings have sufficient continuity from which to think about applicable arrangements and recurrent patterns and also to frame conceptual interconnections where different areas of theory are mutually supportive across activities and levels of organization.

Information and Knowledge Activities

One of the recurrent concerns of organization theory (OT) throughout the literature and across many theories is the acquisition and use of information in support of a range of activities including managing performance, allocating resources, making routine decisions as well as selecting strategic directions. It should be clear at this point that post-positivist theory conceives of information in a different way. Modernist conceptions of knowledge and information focus largely on efforts to improve individual rationality, organizational rationality, or both and to do so for instrumental purposes. In a post-positivist understanding of the world, information is conceived of differently. Post-positivist approaches to information and knowledge don't reject the possibility of improving access to and analysis of information. However, post-positivist theory intentionally expands our thinking about what counts as useful information and extends how such information is collected and the uses to which it can be put. To make the case that these broader conceptions of information and knowledge can be practically useful, we want to focus on two attributes of information and knowledge in particular: the nature of knowledge and the sources or locations of that knowledge.

Way back in Chapter 1, we introduced the concept of **epistemic pluralism** as described by David Farmer.[2] Farmer argues that in the current governance environment—one that is characterized by high levels of technical complexity, political divineness, value diversity, and other features of contemporary organizations—adhering to single epistemic or knowledge ideology is unlikely to bring much success. Instead, the orientation public administrators might most effectively adopt is one that gives them greater sensitivity to and awareness of the variety of factors that influence governance settings. In doing so, they improve the likelihood of crafting strategies that will be effective.

For Farmer, epistemic pluralism, or the acceptance and embrace of multiple forms of knowledge, includes a variety of orientations, some of which we're already familiar with and others that extend beyond our coverage in this book. He includes knowledge frames or lenses that include classical, economic, political, and poststructural. To these he adds ways of knowing that those shaped by feminist and critical theory, neurosciences, and others. His consistent point is that by developing basic understandings of these orientations, as well as the intellectual flexibility and reflexiveness to move between them, we gain understanding and the capacity to, as he describes it, synthesize them toward useful forms of praxis—the interaction of theory and practice. Farmer's movement of these ideas into practice includes not only mundane but critical activities like planning. Farmer explores the sorts of questions each of these epistemic orientations might ask about management practice and then considers the sort of practices and approaches an epistemically pluralist manager might adopt. In the case of management practices, Farmer highlights the importance of visioning as a theme that emerges across the lenses he utilizes and then shows how visioning manifests in the United States as well as other places in the world.

The flexibility and reflexiveness required by epistemic pluralism also suggests the need to consider how we might orient ourselves to these different lenses or forms of knowledge. In Chapter 9, we described Martin Heidegger's critiques of the Cartesian individual or *cogito* as a part of his phenomenological approach to philosophy. Heidegger instead presents an alternative model of the subject—Dasein—or literally "there being." Rather than describing Dasein as a Cartesian, rational actor, Heidegger looks at the Greek notion of *phronesis* and the *phronimos*.[3]

Phronesis can be understood as *wisdom,* distinct from knowledge. Where knowledge, especially positivist knowledge, is universal, phronesis (or wisdom) is contextual and variable. Wisdom is also different than knowledge in that rather than being observed and revealed from an outside, universalistic perspective, it is disclosed in and operates within the specifics of a situation. The phronimos, or one who acts from wisdom, is embedded in the concrete situation. This means that the wise actor seeks information or wisdom not for its universal, empirical, or logical accuracy and preciseness but for its applicability and benefit to the task at hand. Heidegger says that Dasein's "resoluteness does not first take cognizance of the Situation and put the Situation before itself; it has put itself into the Situation already. As resolute, [Dasien] is already *taking action.*"[4]

This depiction of wisdom as distinct from knowledge—especially as it emerges in the context of a situation, particularly in complex or novel situations—should harken back to Karl Weick's analysis of the Mann Gulch fire. To reiterate the relevant attribute of his argument, Weick takes up the notion of wisdom and suggests this form of wisdom can be a key organizational attribute that can enhance the robustness and resilience of organizations in the face of a potential collapse of sensemaking. Susan Gilbertz and her coauthors take up the idea of wisdom and explore its expression in conditions where actors are unlikely to have the sorts of knowledge purportedly necessary to "good" decision making in the complex conditions of contemporary organizations. They find that forms of wisdom, which are informed by multiple forms of knowledge, can develop and support the cultivation of effective action strategies.[5]

Hubert Dreyfus draws on a post-positivist understanding of knowledge, and a phenomenological notion of how the subject interacts with the world in order to describe how we might conceptualize actually working under these theories.[6] Dreyfus describes a four-stage phenomenological framework of skill acquisition that begins with the "novice" who learns and applies what are supposed to be an exhaustive, discrete set of rules. The rule sets are purported essentially increasingly complex if-then assessments, grounded in modernist forms of knowledge. The larger process of skill acquisition proceeds through stages in which the actor recognizes limits in rule sets and acts in ever more sophisticated ways. This framework of skills acquisition culminates with the "expert" or virtuoso, whose behaviors exceed the constrictions of rule-oriented choices. The virtuoso, with sufficient experience across a variety of situations and all seen from the same perspective but requiring different specific choices, or "the competent performer seems gradually to decompose this class of situations into subclasses, each of which share the same decision, single action, or tactic. This allows an immediate intuitive response to each situation."[7] The virtuoso, generally without paying attention to the explicit rules or their violation, not only feels or senses the important attributes or information about a situation but also knows how to select and execute the appropriate action without formally or rationally calculating, comparing, and selecting alternatives.[8] Further, this virtuoso use of wisdom is embedded not just in a physical world but also in a sociocultural awareness as well. Virtuosity results from "the gradual refinement of responses that grow out of long experience acting within the shared cultural practices" and is necessarily active rather than mentalistic.[9, 10] The very fact that these are cultural practices reminds us that Dasein is always already in a world that is constituted as those things that are present-at-hand (those things that generally are available to us but not part of our immediate consciousness), ready-to-hand (those things that are immediately useful to us and that we give direct attention to), and other *Daseins.*

In Chapter 2, we placed Mary Parker Follett's work into what we referred to as a set of other voices—theories that diverged from the predominant approaches to organizational thought, suggested alternative practices, or both. Here, we come back full circle to reiterate some of the core elements of her work that aligns with the descriptions of "knowledge" we're developing here and how Follett and contemporary thinkers utilize those elements. Several key elements of Follett's work bear most directly here. One is the importance of experience. First, Follett emphasizes the importance of experience as the basis of governance processes. The *law of the situation* is the expression of the relevant knowledge that both emerges from what is and subsequently shapes what might be. That law of the situation—as constructed in and from experience and both personal and shared, past and current—drives the particulars of our interactions. Our knowledge of the world, as well as what we know of it, emerges from process.[11] A second attribute that links Follett to our post-positivist narrative is her description of the subject or individual. Just as Heidegger's Dasein is active, engaged, and attuned to the world, Follett sees the individual not as an atomistic and rational entity ontologically separate from the world. Both the virtuoso and one who follows the law of the situation sense that situation from past and current experiences that shape interactions in ways that help us develop and exercise wisdom over time. Follett's individual materializes from the complex interactions and convergences with the world and those in it. She says, "Life is not a move for us; you can never watch life because you are always in life."[12] Knowledge and information, then, are emergent, contextual, and social. They are a process.

One of the consequences of this shift is both a reconceptualization of what constitutes wisdom and an expansion of our understanding of where that wisdom resides. We described Neely Gardner's concepts of action training and research (AT&R) and its links to mainstream organizational scholars like Kurt Lewin and Chris Argyris in Chapter 7. We also highlighted how Gardner moves away from expert-based approaches and his claim: "I know very little."[13] The participatory techniques he develops assume that wisdom required for effective organization development (OD) resides throughout the organization. For Gardner's approach to OD, there are many forms and locations for wisdom. Eliciting and aggregating that wisdom, through the use of processes of participation and engagement, contributes to better decisions and strategies. For example, obtaining operational wisdom from line-level workers reduces the likelihood that changes in work processes have unintended consequences. As we also noted in Chapter 7, Lewin, Gardner, and others who study change along these lines argue that the knowledge needed for change and the responsibility and support for that change are distributed across the organization rather than residing with elite individuals or positions at the pinnacle of the hierarchy.[14, 15] It's also worth noting that this notion of change deviates quite distinctly from classical management approaches that imply that change, if needed at all, is driven by top-down decision making based on indisputable and universal forms of objective knowledge.

While the practices and techniques utilized here are already familiar and anything but radical, our point here is that Gardner and other action research practitioners push against the exclusive use of Enlightenment reason and rationality.[16] Instead, Gardner recognizes the possibility of contextual, intuitional, and other forms of knowledge.[17] Others, including Mary Schmidt, recognize diverse forms of knowledge and perspective as increasingly important to effective decision making in complex settings.[18] Schmidt's examination of the forms of information and knowledge used to inform management decisions that led to the collapse of the Teton

Dam in Idaho reveals several forms of knowledge that were available to decision makers during the construction of the dam but that were obscured by assumptions privileging only expert forms of knowledge. Moreover, Schmidt points out how the set of assumptions manifest in the Teton Dam project are indicative of knowledge structures and assumptions widely embedded in public administration practice.

Margaret Stout and Carrie Stanton extend these ontological depictions into the articulation of a process-based ontology that can be operationalized in governance settings.[19] This thinking about ontology implies a shift from "re-presentation."[20] Representation, again, is not just a political question of pluralism and how it can be included in representative practices. It revisit's Thomas Catlaw's critique of a political ontology of representation in which interests are re-presented in setting. This impossibility of re-presentation reveals a paradox of inclusion and unity. Stout and Stanton point out the following:

> Together, these concepts negate the notion of representation, because while there is similarity based on relatedness, each expression of becoming, each individual within society, is unique and cannot be replicated. No particular configuration can be held up as the right or proper expression of pure potentiality.[21]

The result is that knowledge is far from universalizable. Moreover, paradox within and across bodies of information is the norm and not, by itself, an indication of bad information or bad methodologies.

The link between the antifoundationalism of Follett's work and its expression in post-positivist theory is not just inferred. David Schlosberg looks to Michel Foucault as well as Gilles Deleuze and Felix Guattari in order to craft and argument that the pragmatism of William James and Follett share a rejection of the "one form," or a single ontological framework and corresponding epistemology.[22] The alternative for the pragmatists early in the twentieth century and today is multiplicity. Multiplicity inheres sources, forms, and expressions of wisdom. Deleuze and Guattari use the metaphor of a rhizome (see Figure 10.1) to express the extent to which there can be multiple paths and forms and interactions that are interconnected, for which the direction of relationship is unclear, yet nevertheless hangs together in a recognizable form. The rhizome is at once diverse and complicated but also exhibits a kind of unity.

As a practical matter, this shift might play out in a wide range of different ways. The following two examples are intended be suggestive and illustrative rather than any sort of limit cases. Ann Webster-Wright argues for a shift from professional development approaches, which implies deficiencies, and the need for "authoritative shepherding" and a modernist and paternalistic expertise-based response.[23] Knowing, in a post-positivist approach to learning as opposed to development, moves to a contextual, embedded, or situated response grounded in practice. Learning and the choices that ultimately result, occurs through practice, experience, and reflective action within contexts. In making this case, Webster-Wright draws explicitly on Foucault's characterization of knowledge and John Dewey's pragmatic antifoundationalism. The practical implications of this shift, according to Webster-Wright, start from a recognition that targets of educational efforts cannot be *made* to learn. Instead, professional learning (and by logical implication, all forms of learning) would be better supported by taking into consideration learners' expectations of their working or other applied contexts. This requires mechanisms of social construction such that meaning can be made for the learner. Extending this idea, learning as meaning-making might permeate organizations as the organization seeks to continuously build and rebuild a shared understand of the organization's status and trajectory. Webster-Wright looks to action research as one approach that embodies these attributes.[24]

As should be clear, beyond the questions about what constitutes information in this setting, where it resides, and how to collect it, another practical

Figure 10.1 Rhizome

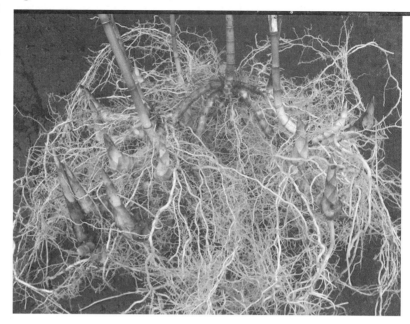

Source: Noah Bell, Bamboo Garden, www.bamboogarden.com.

question has to do with how such diverse bodies of information are synthesized into use by organizations. Milorad Novicevic and his colleagues reveal one possibility in their exploration of communities of creative practice.[25] Communities of practice take on a pluralism and diversity of reciprocal relationships based on a wide range of different activities and lead to social inclusion of multiple different individual experiences. The effect is the creation of an enlarged space of social intersubjectivity in which members are linked by solidarity. This solidarity, or unity, develops such as to allow diverse groups of individuals to adjust in building novel, creative experiences. The multiplicity of actionable ideas and issues links diverse groups into larger alliances of creation and communities of practice. In this respect, Follett's concept of unity without uniformity suggests how groups coevolve and support integration of differences and the nurturing of human relations. Such practices model many contemporary ideas on pluralist forms of organizing. One expression of this is the broadly oriented *life model practice* in social work. This model utilizes a situational approach as an alternative to an authority, exchange, negotiation, bargaining, power, and decision-making model that emphasizes modernist self-interest and rationality as the basis of social engagement and change. The alternative begins with the provision of service but ends with both attention and capacity to support engagement at a whole community level.[26]

One practical consequence of these dynamics can be found in various forms of internal and external decision making by organizations. Internal activities such as performance appraisal

Reflection Questions

As you think about organizations that you are familiar with or interested in, what forms or sources of knowledge and wisdom might traditional organizational processes ignore?

How might these sources be accessed?

By whom?

What effect might these new sources have on the organization's activities?

How might these sources differ by comparison to other types or sizes of organization?

and program evaluation and bridging activities such as policy analysis that bring external analysis into internal, strategic decisions all require information. Unlike Herbert Simon, who views information systems (IS) as a means of enhancing the rationality of organizations and their decisions, post-positivist theory recognizes the constructed nature of both data collection and the data themselves.

There is another level of consequence that this conceptual shift regarding knowledge and information suggests—one that can be accessed by thinking about governance rather than organizational effectiveness. Catlaw's assessment of public administration, or better, governance, beyond a three-sector society describes a scenario that we're probably personally familiar with and that is certainly reflected in opinion and approval polling on all levels and institutions of government. Clearly there has been a dramatic decline in the perception of the legitimacy of government and how it functions. While our experience and the polling results aren't monolithic—we have more favorable views of our representatives and of public agencies we're more directly connected to—the trend is clear and consistent. With respect to governance and politics, public administration is in a unique position to not just support the pursuit of good life but also to help craft a shared vision and unity of direction. In short, governance organizations are at the heart of politics, and politics are at the heart of governance organizations. In adopting a post-positivist orientation toward the collection of information and about the legitimacy of multiple forms and expressions of knowledge or wisdom, organizations become positioned to embody a democratic ethos because the values that inform our notion of the good life are more likely to be present in constitutive ways.

People-Oriented Activities

In Part II, we organized our exploration of how theory can be applied into a collection of more-or-less distinct sets of activities. Clearly the boundaries between those activities are blurrier in our presentation than they are in practice and to some degree than they are in the literature. Here, we want to push that blurriness even further. We want to consider activities that have people as their unit of analysis or the focal point of the theory—that is, rather than other variables like information or structure. These people-oriented activities include practices that we're familiar with such as management activities; leadership; and broadly, coordination of groups of people toward a common end—in other words, activities that are at the heart of organizations and their efforts. We want to consider these as overlapping, indistinct, circularly related, and nonlinear.

We've described, starting in Chapter 4, a set of theoretical perspectives that view organizations as socially constructed entities, which, while they have physical manifestations and leave empirically measurable traces, are collections of people. As a manager or administrator, a central activity in organizations will always be about the interaction with and coordination of the activities of people toward the ends of the organization. Whether we work in a way that's consistent with positivist or post-positivist theory, coordination of activities remains a central issue.

The depiction of knowledge and information, or wisdom, in the preceding section does have implications for how we conceive of and approach coordination efforts. For example, if we reject the notion that there is a finite body of knowledge that can be compiled and acted upon by authoritative or knowing figures in organizations, then it may be necessary to shift to alternative conceptualizations of activities like coordinating and deciding.

O. C. McSwite, drawing on Gardner as well as Herbert Marcuse's thinking, describes the concept of *refusal* in organizational settings. To be clear, this is not a "take my ball and go home" sort of refusal that results in apathy or disengagement. McSwite's notion is, instead, a refusal to grant deference or privilege solely to formal expertise or authority derived from position, while at the same time remaining fully engaged in organizational processes and activities. This form of refusal is the recognition that there are structural or role necessities associated with coordination of productive activities along with a simultaneous refusal to allow authority or knowledge to rise to the level where it precludes alternate forms of wisdom or other collaborative contributions to organization processes. So it is in the deprivileging of various structural elements, like hierarchy and privileged knowledge, that action research retains its liberation values in an organizational setting. Structurally and procedurally, this shift may result in little change beyond being more attuned to opportunities for engagement and participation. However, the changes in orientation and stance with respect to the interpersonal and epistemic views of organizational members may be dramatic.

McSwite argues, based in Lacanian psychoanalytic theory, that one of the key ways in which the symbolic universe structures our experience is in its treatment of leadership.[27] Our culture and ideology assumes, and repeatedly reinforces, the importance of having a leader, a man of reason, or one who both knows and is in control—be it a president, king, or CEO.[28] The problem, of course, is that control is an illusion. If knowing in absolute terms is undermined, then control based on the ability to act from knowledge collapses as well.

Remember our introduction of Jacques Lacan's discourses in the last chapter: that the discourses of the master and university support the need for the man of reason. The difficulty is that leaders who know represent the discourse of the university and from that orientation, try to cover the lack—the fact that they don't have all the knowledge. If they individually cannot obtain or act from knowledge, the ideal that they represent, the man of reason, is supposed to be able to so.

At one level, the belief that leaders have *the* answers is decaying generally and concretely in some of our organizations. We've already explored the difficulty with scientific knowledge and reason in the last chapter, so when this lack becomes apparent, there are three response options. First, we can attempt to find a new paradigm to constitute our beliefs. This drive to find a new and comprehensive paradigm is one explanation of the tendency of organizations to "management flavors/theories of the month." While management fads undoubtedly have useful attributes or insights, we intuitively understand that none of these "next big things" are likely to be the end-all approach that stops the flow and slip of management theory. Moreover, the breadth and pace of change across theories suggests that our beliefs are becoming more fragmented, compounding the difficulty of finding a new, comprehensive paradigm. It is worth reiterating that part of what this book seeks to accomplish is to show the importance of many theories and to recognize that each has its value but not necessarily as a replacement to the one that came before or as a be-all-end-all but, rather, as one tool in the toolbox.

A second option is that leaders will fight to retain authority by arguing that they do, in fact, have critical knowledge that all others lack. This is one way of understanding the rationale behind justification of salaries demanded by Wall Street CEOs, which are so radically out of sync with the average workers in their firms. The claim has been that these firms are so complicated that effectively leading them justifies massive compensation packages. But we find the collapse of this option is present in these same organizations. The excuses many of these same CEOs gave when explaining the failure of their organizations in 2008 and 2009 was that these enterprises are large and highly complex so they couldn't possibly know all that was going on—that is, they couldn't possibly manage the enterprise. On this point, David Weidner of the *Wall Street Journal* acknowledges that "their firms have grown so complex and unwieldy they can't be conquered from the executive suite."[29] Daniel Mudd, former CEO at Fannie Mae, earned compensation of $11.6 million dollars in 2007 before saying balancing the mission and business was "impossible" in the aftermath of the organization's 2008 implosion.[30] At the very least, the claim of authority grounded in exclusively held knowledge seems problematic in highly complex and tightly coupled settings. One reading of the partial government shutdown in the fall of 2013 reveals an expression of electoral politics and changes in campaign finance law. However, the shutdown can also be read as revealing the political consequences that occur when stakeholders or decision makers view themselves as being undeniably correct in their knowledge and resulting position.

The final response is one of refusal, a sort of deconstructive refusal from a position that stays within the same organization. It entails a choice to see the organization for what it is; refuse to grant deference to constructed loci of knowledge, authority, and claims thereby developed; and yet remain entirely engaged with the organization. This form of refusal is not expressed in a destructive way that undermines the capacity of the organization and neither is it a call to take a symbolic stand in opposition to the organization; this isn't a call for Don Quixote–like tilting at windmills.

Because the symbolic order is socially constructed, refusal also prompts us to begin to recognize that we are not radically autonomous, atomistic individuals. We are mutually created by one another in relationship to each other and to the symbolic order. This is the decentered or embedded subject we described in the last chapter. It is also a paradoxical subject who is simultaneously responsible for his actions and at the same time is unavoidably a product of his circumstances.

In order to come to terms with these conditions, the individual goes through psychoanalysis to recognize how those circumstances shape his behavior and how both function within and at the same time stand apart from them. Psychoanalysis is a means of deconstructing identity and allows for the possibility of identifying what Freud referred to as *das Ding*—the thing that animates or energizes behavior. At the level of nationalities, it might be the king, the flag, or "the People." At the organizational level, it might be the mission of an organization, its institutional identity, or the myths and rituals that give stability and distinction. In deconstructing these things, they disintegrate or "dis-integrate" Their inherent hollowness or contradictions become apparent. There is no stable foundation on which these were constructed. But as we pointed out in our discussion of structural functionalism, these things have functions—they serve to give meaning, stability, and identity to the organization. In other words, they provide a shared reality. But they do so in ways that are often internally dysfunctional or ignore pressing external dynamics. Stable, shared reality is necessary for the organization to operate effectively. In the end, we may choose to retain or reject existing practices, but we do so reflectively.

More concretely, the organization can go through a social emergent action research of the sort described by Gardner. Through the collective or interactive process of acquiring data, reviewing that data, and identifying courses of action, the organization can deconstruct its identity, identify and make sense of the underlying symbolic structures, and begin to affect them. As such, refusal is more than and in fact an alternative to cynicism—or the loss of belief that exists in so many settings.

The next step is to acknowledge and retain the role of leaders in the organization. This acknowledgment won't be in traditional, hierarchical ways, nor in unreflexive ways but rather in truly collaborative ways that acknowledge that the unifying symbolic order (under a mission, etc.) is unstable and not permanent. If the ends of the organization are to be furthered, the way forward is to collaborate with leaders and others to that end.

There are other practical implications of making this move. For example, those who refuse in this way are necessarily leery of abstraction. Abstraction is anathema to the refuser in that there is no possibility of collaboration under conditions where abstract, overarching symbolics exist. Effective, pragmatic collaboration is possible only in concrete or contextualized settings where it is possible for actors to build a shared understanding of the setting and important factors therein. Abstractions such as universal categorical schemes and taxonomies of knowledge and patterns of authority that pull participants out of context make collaboration more difficult, if not impossible. This does not mean that categories are useless and shouldn't be utilized but rather that they are tentative and propositional. They are developed and used in ways that are helpful but not reified into universals. In data and information analysis, the sort of long table sorting or thematic analysis of data that is used in qualitative and action research would be typical. In management and coordination interactions, it also implies a shift in the sort of interaction that takes place. Post-positivist interaction emphasizes listening and understanding over reasoned arguing and convincing.

Barry Schwartz, Timothy Wilson, and Gerd Gigerenzer each examine and describe the variations and deviations from rational comprehensive decision making.[31] A recognition and embrace of nonrational decision making would seem to move us toward a perspective on both knowledge and the nature and interplay of subjects that is more consistent with post-positivist thought. We've discussed already that alternative thinking about where information for wise action resides, and in Chapter 9 we explored the nature of the subject from the perspective of alterity and the other. Here we want to combine the two in thinking about the possibility of both coordination and decision making.

Information and alterity depictions suggest that management is about direction, and frankly, Foucault's depiction of poststructural discipline in a panoptic world suggests that Frederick Taylor's world of "do what you're told from morning until night" is a vastly incomplete picture. Our normative expectations of organizations privilege those approaches to management that don't rely on direct coercion as a means of ensuring coordination. As much of the research from human relations theories (HRTs) suggests, more humane approaches that build shared direction through culture and vision help organizations become more effective. And who wouldn't prefer working in an organization that is more humane and more productive? But Foucault's assessment of the manifestation of discipline, governmentality, and power-knowledge remains operative—perhaps even more so in late modern, postindustrial organizations than in earlier industrial age, Taylor-esque organizations.

At the level of management practice, Peter Kobrak and Gardner's portrayals of *caveman management* reveal the modernist power gambits we've experienced or at least seen in

The Office and *Office Space*. These are forms of power politics and psychological warfare in the most petty of ways. Whether it's a manager like Lumbergh in *Office Space*'s superficially friendly request to work on the weekend or *The Office*'s Dwight and his simultaneously crucial and petty personal and professional initiatives at Dunder Mifflin. McSwite's proposal of refusal suggests a different orientation that moves away from attentiveness to the real but nevertheless misfocused efforts of power and psychology and to the more authentic and robust engagement in discussions. Organizations are not Hobbesian states of nature but rather settings where we come to understand that at the end of the day we are all in this together. Refusal moves us from misaligned attention to shared vision and coordinated efforts. It is no longer about managing as manipulation—however humane and enlightened that might be—to the creation of a space and context for collaboration and coordination.

Farmer describes this orientation as *practice as art* in which administrators engage in discourse about and action within a concrete and pragmatic realm of practice.[32] It is for Farmer one that works toward concrete, directed, and reflexive actions. It also holds open the possibility of alternatives.

James Suroweicki describes a set of problem types and conditions within which collaboration can yield much better decisions. The necessary conditions include decentralization, independence, and diversity. Maintaining decentralization and diversity in conditions of refusal may, in fact, be easier than it is in traditional organizations, because there is an inherent openness to the other and other forms of knowledge or wisdom. This reflection leads also to an understanding that diversity, the inclusion of the other, and alternative forms of knowledge are far different from the superficial forms of diversity through political correctness that has received significant criticism. Diversity here implies more than tolerance but sustained engagement, if not acceptance.

These notions apply to the ties between both management and coordination as well as leadership and coordination. Earlier in this chapter we described Dreyfus' depiction of phenomenological skills acquisition, in which individuals move through a series of stages. Starting with the novice, who entails a strict adherence to rules, actors can progress all the way to the expert, or virtuoso, for whom the rules are no longer present and action is guided by deep experiential wisdom, contextual awareness, and situational engagement. Dreyfus' depiction of the jazz musician who has the capacity to solo within a larger musical group parallels nicely with the conceptualization of leadership advanced by Robert and Janet Dehardt.[33] Based on years of observations and interviews with dozens of organizational and community leaders, as well as dancers and dance educators, they describe leadership as a dance. They acknowledge that there are leaders who operate from intellectual expertise, or from the quality of their ideas, but they argue that "effective leaders more often lead through the kinds of emotional connection" that can be produced through artistic performance. Lest we think the artistic reference is too touchy-feely or soft to be of value in complex technical and political environments, they emphasize concrete skill sets—soft skills to be sure—that contribute to leadership effectiveness, including active listening and vigorous communication, successful collaboration, and critical self-reflection. They are attuned to variables like time and context as well as the use of space—both psychic and physical. What emerges is a depiction of the virtuoso—one who through practice and observation, creativity and context develops the ability to at the same moment both navigate and set the path for others to engage and contribute in parallel ways.

One further aspect of coordination warrants some attention at this point. Farmer, Gardner, Schmidt, and others explore in various ways alternative forms of knowledge that reside in and around organizations as well as the processes by which that knowledge can be acquired and aggregate in ways that improve the capacity of organizations to function. This understanding of knowledge and the processes that operate out of that understanding orbit around practices that link coordination and collaboration. They require the engagement of a diverse, independent, and decentralized set of actors to function in a coordinated way.

This understanding of organizational processes has a political and governance analog. In the organization, the central focus of these practices is the improvement of the organization's effectiveness. In the relationship between the organization and the wider environment, especially the relationship between governance organizations and the environment, there is also a question of how the organization fits with and contributes to functional democratic practices.[34] Collaboration between organizations and their constituencies, which is structured such that the will of the people can be directly expressed in the actions of the organization, can be considered an answer to that question.[35] McSwite and Eric Austin argue that governance organizations have the capacity, and are uniquely positioned, to support the emergence of the social bond.[36] That social bond, a rudimentary connection between members of a community, is necessary for basic communication, let alone effective organizational or community action. Moreover, this social bond may well be an effective mechanism to overcome or end-run the sorts of incommensurable language games that develop in conditions of postmodernism.[37] Lest we believe this is some new age, touchy-feely idea, it may be worth recognizing that Alexis de Tocqueville's identification of the importance of community and civic organizations to American democracy can be read as the venue in which the social bond was generated and maintained at the turn of the nineteenth century.

> ## Reflection Questions
>
> As you think about various organizational roles and responsibilities in different types and levels of governance organization, what changes in interpersonal and authority relations might result from these sorts of practices?
>
> What other changes in practice might result from adopting a new orientation or stance in your organization or one you're familiar with?

Structures for Coordination and Cooperation

Our exploration of structure has taken on several different forms to this point in the book. One notion of structure that we're fairly familiar and comfortable with has to do with formal and rational structures, which serve as a sort of skeleton, or framework, to give shape and order to organizations. The clearest expression of this notion of structure is Weber's bureaucratic organization and its emphasis on hierarchy and specialization and the resulting pyramid structure we find in organization charts. Another notion of structure, drawing from, for example, behavioral and institutional theories, emphasizes informal and emergent structures that are expressions of stable, repeating patterns of behavior. We recognized such structures first in the relay assembly and bank wiring experiments at the Hawthorne plant, and subsequent research and theory has explored their appearance in a wide range of other settings. We explored a third approach to structural, or more accurately poststructural, analysis in Chapter 9 and Foucault's studies of power-knowledge, discipline, and governmentality. The Foucaultian poststructural analysis extends the institutionalist and behavioralist understanding of structures to reveal how structures aren't grounded in natural or transcendent models of human nature or social relationship, but rather are socially constructed and free-floating.

Stewart Clegg argues that modernism can be understood not just as a being a paradigm that embraces a realist or empiricist set of epistemological assumptions but also as a social and political trajectory driven by a logic of structural differentiation.[38] In other words, modernism might be understood not based on its epistemic or ontological assumptions but by its omnipresent emphasis on differentiation into formal taxonomies. In organizational settings, this is most apparent in the focus on the division of labor and specialization.

This poses an interesting challenge to those who would take up post-positivist theory in that such differentiation—forms of which include specialization, division of labor, categorized hierarchy, and others—is both a result *of* and necessary *to* the quality of life and standard of living widely enjoyed in the developed world. The availability of the diverse, plentiful, and high-quality services and goods that we all enjoy and benefit from could not have come about or be maintained without the efficiencies and coordination that result from these forms of differentiation.[39] To paraphrase the well-known bumper sticker, structure happens.

Given the scale, scope, and complexity of modern goods and services, division of labor, specialization, and hierarchical systems of coordination necessitate the emergence of some form of structure—stable, repeating patterns of behavior. Post-positivist theory that is at once critical of the negative and unintended consequences of this ethos of modernist emphasis on bureaucratic organization and that purports to offer better outcomes than modernist organizational forms faces the significant challenge of figuring out how to mitigate the negative consequences without abandoning the substantial and real benefits.

One path forward can be found in Clegg's move from ontology and epistemology to differentiation in conjunction with, for example, Farmer's notion of *anti-administration*. Introduced first in his book *The Language of Public Administration,* Farmer describes anti-administration as an understanding of public administration—rather than a theory of public administration—that exhibits radical openness in both thinking and in action.[40, 41] Anti-administration is intentionally attentive to and seeks out the *other,* or those people or ideas that are traditionally excluded and subordinated, and in doing so does not reject the mainstream. In a subsequent work, Farmer describes anti-administration as taking on a gadfly orientation, which intentionally and reflexively takes on different perspectives in order to describe and redescribe the scenarios administrators find themselves a part of.[42] Others take on this notion of anti-administration and suggest that such perspectives might include but certainly are not limited to Lacanian, value pluralist, ecological, critical theory, or multigendered perspectives.[43] Such perspectives offer varied understandings that encompass substantially different frameworks of differentiation—any of which in turn offer the possibility of revealing critical information that results in both instrumentally and normatively better outcomes.

Moreover, because these and other potentially emerging perspectives come out of the setting in question—that is, they are contextually grounded—they are also instrumentally and normatively grounded in ways that both generate and maintain stability and routines. They become structures of intentionality.

Though intentional, anti-administrative structures do not purport to be *the* way to do the work. Farmer's notion of anti-administration is also informed by the notion of refusal such that privilege and deference are not granted in ways that become "fire and forget." That is, anti-administration resists claims of any structural or procedural arrangements to be *the* way. Whether classical forms like that of Taylor and Luther Gulick or more contemporary approaches like total quality management (TQM) or Six Sigma, anti-administration's gadfly and reflexive ethos avoids the impulse to rationally create the *right* structures and then trust and forget them. As a result, structural and procedural choices are less likely to creep or evolve in unnoticed, unintended ways, becoming the sorts of myths and rituals neoinstitutionalists study and that may well function in dysfunctional ways.

On the one hand, this shift is perhaps comforting in that, again, the move into a post-positivist world and post-positivist OT and practice does not necessarily result in radical departure from familiar and indeed tested practices and the adoption of something heretofore unknown and unfamiliar. On the other hand, it does open the possibility that we may choose to make radical departures nonetheless. This also means that we have to do the hard work of creating and sustaining these new practices. These will not be replacement "fire and forget" processes or practices that can run on autopilot and which we can trust to function effectively well into the future without reflection.

This leaves this daunting question: How do we, in concrete ways, proceed in the absence of the reliance of what we believe to be best practices and procedures (we are, after all, a procedural republic)? McSwite's depiction of public administration as the new carrier of the social bond gives some hints about what such a world might look like.[44]

McSwite's description of moving into global economic markets, increasing diversity, and growing discord and uncertainty is reminiscent of Jean-François Lyotard, Jean Baudrillard, and Jacques Derrida's portrayal of the postmodern condition. The coherence of processes or institutions as the basis of the social bond—the basic connection between humans that makes stable social interaction, let alone complex forms of coordination possible—has already significantly disintegrated and will continue to do so. Again drawing on Lacanian psychoanalytic theory, McSwite argues that public administration is in a unique position to use sociopolitical process to create a space for that bond to be built and sustained.

That process would then be the mechanism by which any number of different structural arrangements and coordinative processes might be selected and intentionally adapted over time. Traditional concerns of uncertainty mitigation, organizational responsiveness, efficiency, and so forth are resolved not by the creation and selection of any one turnkey system that optimizes the balance of instrumental and normative objectives but instead by providing a shared sense of what to do next.

McSwite points out that this requires a sort of personal reorientation on the part of administrators across levels of governance organizations. This reorientation includes being attuned not just to the knowledge, skills, and abilities (KSAs) requisite for any specialized job but also to the internal and external circumstances of the organization in an ongoing way. This attunement should be reminiscent of several practices we've described already. Let's look all the way back to Chapter 4: Weick's description of structures that support resilience and robustness as mechanisms for avoiding collapses of sensemaking.[45] Weick's structures, which again are first and foremost stable repeating patterns of behavior rather than formal hierarchical or other formal arrangements, mitigate uncertainty and provide for the necessary stability through which effective action can occur. The ability to enact such structures is both consistent with and supported by Dreyfus' virtuoso. Finally, these orientations and practices occur in a context entirely consistent with Gardner's developing organization and Stout and Stanton's process ontology, which considers the organization and the setting as always in some state of change, whether gradual or radical. The result is fluid organization wherein the structures we've traditionally looked to for coordination—whether hierarchies, webs, matrixes, networks, or otherwise—are artifacts of intentional, open, and reflexive processes rather than the cause of those processes.

Reflection Question

Based on this discussion of structures, what similarities and differences in structures might be identified across various types of governance organizations? Think, for example, about differences of size, level, sector, and mission differences.

Ethics

A radio story recently aired in which a former homicide detective describes a case he worked and on which he and several of his colleagues, all of whom were responsible, well-trained investigators, inadvertently extracted a false confession from a murder suspect.[46] While the suspect was ultimately determined to be not just innocent of but entirely uninvolved in the crime, the original investigation as well as wider administrative involvement had substantial negative personal and professional consequences for the suspect. The criminal investigation, which tarnished the suspect's personal and professional reputation, triggered the involvement of other agencies including Child Protective Services. To be sure, cross-agency and cross-system coordination is important in this and similar circumstances in that we don't want coordination problems to result in children or others to "fall through the cracks." However, in this case, the result was that despite her innocence, the suspect lost custody of her children and as of the airing of the story still had not regained it.

There are several ethical issues manifest in this case. One is that although the detectives made a number of mistakes of practice, they did not violate—willfully or otherwise—the ethical codes or standards of the agency or their profession. For example, during the course of the detectives' interview with the suspect, they engaged in the common practice of showing the suspect the weight of the evidence against her in hopes of garnering a confession. However, the suspect was working on the belief that if she said what the detectives wanted to hear, she could go home. So although she was in fact innocent, what the detectives inadvertently did was give her enough information about the crime for her to craft a story that made it sound like she had firsthand knowledge of it. The detectives then used the story she told, using information they fed to her, to indict her for a crime she didn't commit.

So while they did nothing *wrong* in terms of the policies, practices, and standards of the organization, their actions resulted in substantial *harm* to an innocent person. Similarly, the operation of the systems that reasonably and legitimately were established to ensure the safety of both involved children and the wider community functioned in ways that did no wrong but also resulted in significant harm.

The modernist response to such problems would require institutional and perhaps personal or individual reforms. While such reforms are important, a post-positivist analysis of systems—their creation and function—reveals how such a program of reform can never be complete or comprehensive. That is, because the "letter of the reform"—like the "letter of the law"—cannot, from a post-positivist perspective, ever be compressive or exhaustive.

Beyond what a post-positivist analysis reveals about the nature of behaviors and systems, there is conceptual work out of post-positivist theory that suggests alternative practices and processes that while not precluding the doing of harm create a space where there is intentional reflection on behaviors and potential or actual harms; there is hopefully a better ability to avoid doing harm in the first place. In order to get at that alternative, some additional background is necessary.

In their study of the legitimacy question in public administration McSwite poses two simple but profound questions. The first question is as follows: How do we create the world (or at least our organizations)? The question is a variation of a central concern throughout OT. We've spent the entirety of this and the previous chapter—and in fact most of this book, if you include our examination of constructivist approaches to understanding institutions, culture, and other elements of organizations—answering this question.

The second question McSwite poses is the following: How do we treat each other? This question makes ethics in organizations explicit. Ethics has not really been explicit or even implicit in our treatment of the organizational literature so far. To be sure, there is a robust and expanding body of work on corporate social responsibility and organizational ethics. There is also an extensive and sophisticated body of literature on administrative ethics. Although we do see a move in contemporary research and practice to treat ethics as an integrated element of organizations and public administration more broadly, there has historically been, and we think to a great degree, a tendency to think about the normative and ethical aspects of organizations and governance as being separate from the technical and instrumental studies and practices.

Tackling ethics from a post-positivist perspective poses a bit of a challenge. An often used, and at least partially accurate criticism of post-positivism, is that it tends toward nihilism. That is, if there is no universal truth and everything is relative, then there is nothing to believe in: we are at the edge of the abyss of nihilism. We've addressed this issue already, but it is worth recognizing that in some ways post-positivist ethics faces this critique very acutely. If the description of the current social environment is correct and postmodernity does offer an image of our current experience, we are left with the considerable challenge of formulating an alternate ethical framework that is not as vulnerable to postmodern criticisms while at the same time is not nihilistic.

A first post-positivist, ethical insight can be drawn from Derrida's notion of deconstruction and its consequences. The term *deconstruction* was originally coined by Derrida and is used as a means of analyzing literature. It has since been used to assess all types of texts rather than just literary ones. Pauline Marie Rosenau defines deconstruction as the tearing apart of texts in order to reveal its contradictions and assumptions. Its intent is not the improvement or revision of text or to offer a better version of the text.[47] It should be noted that Derrida argues that deconstruction is neither a method nor an operation. Moreover, it is neither a simple means of analysis nor a critique. It is a singular event, like an idiom or a signature.[48] For our purposes however, Farmer's description of deconstruction is most useful.[49] Deconstruction can be understood as a good reading of any text—a text, here again, including a wide range of discourses and narratives, written or otherwise. Deconstruction can be oriented toward the identification of differences rather than understanding intents, transcendent meanings, or foundational identities. It discovers the blind spots and ironies in a text and illuminates the author's epistemological and ontological assumptions. Deconstruction investigates the work of the metaphysical oppositions in their arguments and the ways in which textual figures and relations produce a double, aporetic logic, or in other words, a logical argument in which the individual propositions are plausible but are collectively inconsistent.[50] It is, in many ways, consistent with the idea of the gadfly described earlier in this chapter.

The result of the act of deconstruction is the insight of undecidability and responsibility. For Derrida, deconstruction leads to the understanding that there is no universal or transcendent basis on which to make a decision, which he describes as the condition of undecidability. It is because actors make choices and act under the condition of undecidability that they bare infinite responsibility. In other words, because there is no universal basis on which to justify decisions, the one who decides and acts bears the ultimate responsibility for the consequences. If, according to Derrida, there were an empirical basis from which to make decisions, some of the responsibility for the decision would shift away from the decision maker to the basis or rationale for the decision. If that basis or rationale does not exist, then the decision maker bears infinite responsibility. This, according to Derrida, "is the infinitude that inscribes itself within responsibility; otherwise there would be no ethical problems or decisions."[51] While Derrida does acknowledge that one cannot live up to the infinite responsibility resulting from undecidability and decision, one must be aware of and take the other into account when making decisions.

In addition to the radical responsibility described by Derrida, there are a growing number of what have been described as affirmative postmodernists who are building a different concept of public administrators that while not invulnerable is sensitive to the postmodern critiques. Administrators in a postmodern world strive for "foresight, initiative, flexibility, sensitivity and new forms of knowledge," which are not grounded in grand truth claims nor are they based in technical or procedural knowledge. Instead, they are based in interaction and synergy.[52]

Our entry into post-positivist ethics thus far has focused on reconceptualizing how we think about our actions in relation to others. It suggests an analysis different than one driven by utilitarian or deontological rationale. The second issue has to do with what course of action to actually select in conditions of undecidability.

Zygmunt Bauman argues that modernity and the relentlessness of economic progress has the effect of producing "human waste," or collections of wasted lives.[53] These wasted lives are the superfluous populations of migrants, refugees, and other outcasts—exactly the other we most fear. These are, for example, the excluded others depicted in popular sci-fi movies like *Total Recall* and *Elysium*. For Bauman, this is an unavoidable side effect of economic progress and the quest for order, which is characteristic of modernity. In the past, so long as portions of the planet were outside, or largely unaffected by the processes of modernization, those areas were treated by modernizing societies as sinks that could take in the excess of population produced by development.

However, as modernization has increasingly become a global phenomenon, the creation of human waste occurs everywhere. The global spread of modernity has resulted in ever-increasing numbers of humans who are excluded from access to basic survival needs, and at the same time, the planet is fast running out of places to put them. The logic here is subtle but important. The logic of the market as applied to globalization is exemplified in the aphorism "a rising tide floats all boats." Development, globalization, and modernization should benefit all, so if some have been left behind and don't have access to the benefits *so far,* be patient and the benefits will eventually arrive. Bauman argues that the conditions now are different and that some portions of the world's population have been categorically excluded from globalization's benefits and are in fact the fodder for globalization. The result, according to Bauman, are the growing anxieties about immigrants and "asylum seekers" and the increasing resonance garnered by abstracted security fears, be they criminal or economic, within our political discourse.

The same operational logic that Bauman identifies has been identified in critiques of a host of other modernist bureaucratic procedures that result in human waste by-products—harm without wrong. Assessments of the impact's eminent domain on property owners and communities following the US Supreme Court's decision in the *Kelo v. City of New London* case, examinations of criminal justice systems like the example at the beginning of this section, and appraisals of what has been described as environmental racism all function by this logic of exclusion, which results in harm but not wrong.

One possible post-positivist response can be found by returning to the collapse of *zoë* and *bios*, the distinction between bare, or biological life, and political life. Foucault suggests that ethics is associated with the task of detaching ourselves from those technologies of the self that subordinate human existence to biological life—or better, the science of life. Foucault's ethics is a style of life, or "'an esthetics of existence' that resists a 'science of life.'"[54] If one milestone of the movement into postmodernism is Friedrich Nietzsche's admonition that God is dead, Foucault extends that trajectory in his ethics with the possibility that man, at least the modernist subject or agent, is dead too. Foucault also observes from his genealogical studies of Greek and Roman morality that there is no Cartesian, or even Augustinian, self in the ancient conception of the individual. As such, the Cartesian/Freudian self is neither a transcendent figure, nor a necessary one.

If this is the case, then ethics for Foucault is something quite different than a code of conduct or a set of prescriptive rules that determined what one—the agent—should or should not do. James Bernauer and Michael Mahon summarize Foucault's position as having no universally applicable principles, no normative standards, "no order of human life, or way we are or human nature that one can appeal to in order to judge or evaluate between ways of life."[55] The consequence is that Foucault's notion of ethics does not depend on the modern understanding of subjectivity, nor does it entail narrowing the domain of ethics. The post-positivist self's relationship to itself has to do with the proper way of life. Moreover, the study of the history of codes of moral behavior is insufficient to resolve problems under a fragmented epistemology. We must also examine the history and forms of moral subjectivation—that is, to how we constitute ourselves as moral subjects.

So ethics for Foucault is "that component of morality that concerns the self's relationship to itself."[56] As such, Foucault outlines four aspects of ethics. First is ethical substance, or that part of the self that is the relevant province of ethical judgment. The second aspect is the mode of subjugation, or the way the subject orients himself or herself to moral rules and duties. Next is work one does to transform or make oneself an ethical subject. And finally is the *teleos,* or mode of being one strives for through appropriate or ethical behavior. It is worth noting the link that this conceptualization and study of ethics as the self's relation to itself and the corresponding technologies of the self has with two dominant themes in Foucault's work— namely the history of subjectivity and governmentality.

From this conceptualization of ethics, ethical problems are not resolved by reference to a list of required or prohibited acts but are centered around one's attitude to oneself and so to others and the world. The resolution of such problems has to do with one's style or mode of life. In Arnold Davidson's interpretation of Foucault, "each particular conceptual combination of ethical substance, mode of subjection, self-forming activity, and telos as representing a style of life."[57] One's style of life gives expression to the self's relation to itself. Here, Foucault introduces the notion of *askesis,* or a style of practice of relating to ourselves that allows us to invent (not discover) a new manner of being. Foucault's study of both ancient and modern practices of sexuality, as well as ancient philosophy, are efforts to understand the style of life and the corresponding art of life in which the activities are a part. A connection of both the ancient and modern practices is that both require an ethics or ascetics of the self-connected to not only a particular style of life but a particularly threatening style of life. Care of the self, for conversion of the self is a precondition of the transformation that constitutes philosophy. This transformation, however, is neither the psychologization or estheticization that "shrinks the world to the size of oneself."[58]

Here, *parrhesia,* another element of Foucault's thinking about ethics, becomes operative. Parrhesia is sometimes described as a form of speaking candidly or asking forgiveness for so speaking. Most literally it means "to speak everything" and by extension "to speak freely," "to speak boldly," or "boldness." It implies not only freedom *of* speech but the obligation *to* speak the truth for the common good, even at personal risk. It entails speaking frankly and with radical, even courageous, frankness. Parrhesia does not entail confessional attributes, nor confidence in ideas, but is, according to Arnold Davidson's reading of Foucault, grounded in love. Rather than romantic love, what Foucault has in mind is a form of love wherein the relationship is characterized by a robustness, authenticity, and resilience that when shared has the ability to build personal community. Foucault's ethics, then, is the practice of an intellectual freedom that is transgressive of knowledge-power-subjectivity relations. "Foucault's ethics is an invitation to a practice of liberty, to struggle and transgression, which seeks to open possibilities for new relations to self and events of the world."[59] Taken together, this transgressive style of life, embodying askesis and parrhesia, has, for Foucault, the potential to stand against the fascism in us all—the tendency to act oppressively when working from ethical frames grounded narrowly in either deontological or utilitarian frames.

Any answer to the question of what a move toward post-positivist ethics means for organizational and governance settings is complicated given Foucault's criticisms of moral codes and related efforts to prescribe behaviors. It may be the case that moral codes and the use of well-established ethical formulae are useful to us in revealing different aspects, or attributes, of moral dilemmas. It may also be that the sort of discourse ethics associated with McSwite's notion of collaborative pragmatism and Michael Harmon and McSwite's work on an ethics of relationship in that all three projects reveal something of the orientation toward the other and social process by which we might proceed.[60]

Collapsing assumptions associated with a representational ontology might prompt us to think and view migrants differently from the start. If we think differently about the *other,* it may be that the artifacts and structures that form the basis of our assumptions will have less power over us and open the possibility of something different occurring. Giving attention to styles of life and askesis or practices may similarly diminish their constituted power but also give rise to new practices and new styles that can more easily or effectively transgress existing power-knowledge relations. Finally, parrhesia—authentic and perhaps risky discourse to and in the face of power, especially when emerging from models and practices of subjectivity different from the ego or self-interest conception of subjectivity—opens the possibility of something different as well.

The implications of this conception of ethics are severalfold. First, it reorients our thinking such that the possibility of the "human waste" that Bauman identifies is much less likely because askesis and parrhesia, within an ethos or worldview grounded in undecidability and responsibility, places us in an orientation where the possibility of waste can't simply be ignored. It leverages individual awareness and political discourse in such a way that those consequences that economists describe as negative externalities are more likely to be front and center in are perceptions and limits our ability to abdicate or duck the individual and systemic responsibility for them.

However, this does not require us to upend the processes and decision criteria that we are familiar with and that have resulted in real and substantial benefits to our quality of life. For example, it does not necessarily replace the current use of reasoned assessment, analysis, and action. Rather, it legitimizes the inclusion of other decision influencing factors. Further, anti-administration provides an alternative that is more defensible to postmodern critique than the administrative model based on grand purposive administrative action.

This results in two important changes to planning and practice. First, it emphasizes concreteness and context in ways that can more fully recognize and include the complexity of the socially constructed individuals and environments. Second, activities like strategic planning must recognize and embody an understanding of the rapidity of change in the post-positivist world and as such must be a fluid process that acknowledges that a static end state does not exist. Planning, management, leadership, and decision-making processes then focus on the immediate steps moving toward an ever-changing target.

A final advantage of this conception of ethics is that it provides an alternative to current organizational processes that have been characterized as undemocratic because of their lack of citizen input and their domination by interest group politics. Anti-administration, in conjunction with the decentralization detailed previously, allows for greater opportunities for individuals to participate in the decision-making procedures. While it's true that such processes increase levels of democratic action, a more important result is that these processes yield more effective results.

Summary and Conclusions

As a doctoral student, one of the authors of this book made an early attempt to use post-positivist theory in a journal manuscript exploring alternative approaches to public policy development that might be less susceptible to the limitations of interest group liberalism. The faculty supervisor of the project, as a part of some early feedback on the manuscript, indicated that the key objective of any effort to use post-positivist should be to demonstrate that the theory was more than "old wine in new bottles." His argument was that for post-positivist theory to be of value, it had to do more than the same old thing under the auspices of new packaging. A related implication in his comment was that if post-positivist theory was really a new, purportedly radical body of theory, it should provide an equally radical departure in practice.

In the time since receiving that feedback, we've come to believe that the maxim should be reversed when applied to post-positivism. Rather than being old wine in new bottles, it's more like new wine in old bottles. As such, by all appearances from the outside, practices may look pretty much as they have in the past. But on closer, more subtle inspection, there is something significantly different going on. That difference exists largely in the attitudes and orientations—the assumptions and ideologies—of those who embrace the theories as a way of making sense of and then making the reality of their organizations and environments.

We've argued that conditions are changing qualitatively. Whether that's true or not, the basic issue for organizations is the same: coordinating the activities of increasingly diverse workforces and doing increasingly complex tasks in increasingly interconnected and mutually dependent settings. We still need structures to support efforts at coordination and will get (regardless of efforts to do away with it) structure in one form or another. We still have to manage relationships in order to coordinate and support achievement of organization goals. We still strive to build—socially construct—organizations and their practices, and we need to get into and reflexively interact with others around us.

In organizing our treatment of practices and applications of post-positivist theory around activities that are focused on knowledge and information, people, and structures, but showing also that these categories are overlapping and incomplete, we are endeavoring to retain the post-positive ambivalence toward category yet at the same time give some sense of how applications can be organized.

The addition of ethics is important in part because while there is a literature on organizational ethics and social responsibility, most OT does not directly address ethics. We believe that given the size and influence of public and governance organization, questions of ethics—how we make decisions and the consequences of those decisions for how people are treated by these organizations—are quite important. In our teaching and research, for example, we've encountered women's advocacy and support services organizations that don't provide maternity leave for their staff and disability services offices housed in facilities that aren't Americans with Disabilities Act (ADA) accessible. Other organizational behaviors and their effects, like criminal justice organizations that produce false confessions, slip well beyond anything resembling irony. Post-positivist ethical theory not only prompts the consideration of how we treat people in these and other governance settings but it prompts us to consider ethical questions in ways that are different than the code based and calculative approaches common to the field.

The size and influence of pubic organizations also remind us that explicit ethical questions often have wider normative connections. The normative is the political in that values and norms very directly shape what we believe the good life—the content of politics—to be, and governance is largely about how we achieve it. Said differently, governance can be thought of as the framing and approach to the pursuit of the good life. Ideology and culture can have distinctions, but they are not isolated. Social, political, and organizational ideologies are inherently linked. What we value, what we privilege has continuity across levels of our thinking, experience, and practice—and probably should. ∎

Reflection Questions

What interconnections, or links, can you identify between these concepts and corresponding practices?

Where do these concepts reinforce or support each other?

What are some benefits that might result from the use of these practices?

What are some new challenges or tensions that result from the adoption of these ideas?

Discussion Questions

1. What other sorts of harms or wrongs might result from the authorities of governance agencies? Think about specific missions of different agencies or organizations.

2. What new tensions emerge from adopting post-positivist thinking about organizations, structures, and practices? For example, what effect will efforts to adopt more precise ethical codes or rules have?

Notes

1. See, for example, the debate between Kenneth Hansen, Hugh Miller, and Orion White. Kenneth N. Hansen, "Identifying Facets of Democratic Administration: Implications for Programs of Public Administration," *Administration and Society* 30 (1998): 443–461; Hugh T. Miller, "Method: The

Tail That Wants to Wag the Dog," *Administration and Society* 30 (1998): 462–470; Orion F. White, "The Ideology of Technocratic Empiricism and the Discourse Movement in Contemporary Public Administration: A Clarification," *Administration and Society* 30 (1998): 471–476.

2. David J. Farmer, *Public Administration in Perspective: Theory and Practice through Multiple Lenses* (Armonk, NY: M.E. Sharpe, 2010).

3. Hubert Dreyfus, *Being in the World* (Cambridge, MA: MIT Press, 1990).

4. Martin Heidegger, *Being and Time,* trans. John Macquarrie and Edward Robinson (New York: Harper & Row, 1962), 347.

5. Susan Gilbertz et al., "Wicked Wisdoms: Illuminations of Conceptual Capacities among Local Leaders of the Yellowstone River," *Studies in the Sociology of Science* 2, no. 2 (2011): 1–10.

6. Hubert Dreyfus, "What Could Be More Intelligible Than Everyday Intelligibility? Reinterpreting Division I of Being and Time in the Light of Division II," *Bulletin of Science Technology Society* 24, no. 3 (2004): 265–274.

7. Ibid., 267.

8. For extensive summaries of the research describing the cognitive processes by which such an awareness can occur, see Timothy D. Wilson, *Strangers to Ourselves: Discovering the Adaptive Unconscious* (Cambridge, MA: Belknap Press, 2002); Gerd Gigerenzer, *Gut Feelings: The Intelligence of the Unconscious* (New York: Viking, 2007).

9. Hubert Dreyfus, *Being in the World: A Commentary on Heidegger's* Being and Time (Cambridge, MA: MIT Press, 1990), 10.

10. Heidegger, *Being and Time.*

11. Margaret Stout and Carrie M. Stanton, "The Ontology of Process Philosophy in Follett's Administrative Theory," *Administrative Theory and Praxis* 33, no. 2 (2011): 268–292.

12. Mary P. Follett, *Creative Experience* (New York: Longman Green and Co., 1924).

13. Michael McGill and Neely D. Gardner, "Od Orienteer," *Public Administration Quarterly* 6, no. 2 (1992): 190.

14. Kurt Lewin, "Conduct, Knowledge and Acceptance of New Values," in *Resolving Social Conflicts,* ed. Gertrud W. Lewin (New York: Harper & Row, 1948), 56–70; Kurt Lewin, "Action Research and Minority Problems," in *Resolving Social Conflicts,* ed. Gertrud W. Lewin (New York: Harper & Row, 1948), 201–216; D. Bargal, "Personal and Intellectual Influences Leading to Lewin's Paradigm of Action Research," *Action Research* 4, no. 4 (2006): 367–388.

15. Norman R. King, "Managing Values at City Hall (With a Lot of Help from Neely)," *Public Administration Quarterly* 16, no. 2 (1992): 235–253; Frank Sherwood, "Institutionalizing Training: Another Gardner Legacy," *Public Administration Quarterly* 16, no. 2 (1992): 164–179.

16. Victor J. Friedman and Tim Rogers. "There Is Nothing so Theoretical as Good Action Research," *Action Research* 7, no. 1 (2009): 31–77.

17. James F. Wolf, "Neely Gardner and Deming's Total Quality Management: Parallels and Connections," *Public Administration Quarterly* 16, no. 2 (1992).

18. Mary Schmidt, "Grout: Alternative Kinds of Knowledge and Why They Are Ignored," *Public Administration Review* 53, no. 6 (1993): 525.

19. Stout and Stanton, "The Ontology of Process Philosophy."

20. Shifting the pronunciation from representation to re-presentation prompts us to more clearly recognize the epistemological character or representation—that is, that something known is re-presented.

21. Ibid., 18.

22. David Schlosberg, "Resurrecting the Pluralist Universe," *Political Research Quarterly* 15, no. 3 (1998): 583–615.

23. Ann Webster-Wright, "Reframing Professional Development Through Understanding Authentic Professional Learning," *Review of Educational Research* 79, no. 2 (June 2009): 726.

24. Webster-Wright refers to research by Nora Hyland and Susan Noffke, "Understanding Diversity Through Social and Community Inquiry: An Action-Research Study," *Journal of Teacher Education* 56, no. 4 (2005): 367–381.

25. Milorad N. Novicevic, Michael Harvey, Ronald Buckley, Daniel Wren, and Leticia Pena, "Communities of Creative Practice: Follett's Seminal Conceptualization," *International Journal of Public Administration* 30, no. 4 (2007): 367–386.

26. Allison Murdach, "Situational Approaches to Direct Practice: Origin, Decline and Re-emergence," *Social Work* 52, no. 3 (2007): 211–218.

27. O. C. McSwite, "Now More Than Ever—Refusal as Redemption," *Administrative Theory and Praxis* 25, no. 2 (2003): 183–204.

28. O. C. McSwite, *Legitimacy in Public Administration: A Discourse Analysis* (Thousand Oaks, CA: Sage, 1997).

29. David Weidner, "Why Jon Corzine Is as Lost as He Seems," *Wall Street Journal,* December 15, 2011, http://online.wsj.com/news/articles/SB10001424052970204844504577098934251914956.

30. Justin Rood, "CEO Salaries Weather Mortgage Crisis," ABC News, July 21, 2008, http://abcnews.go.com/Blotter/story?id=5413172; Nick Timiraos, "Views Conflict on Fannie Meltdown," *Wall Street Journal,* April 14, 2010, http://online.wsj.com/news/articles/SB10001424052702304024604575173623669689564

31. Barry Schwartz, *The Paradox of Choice: Why More Is Less* (New York: Harper Perennial, 2004); Wilson, *Strangers to Ourselves*; Gigerenzer, *Gut Feelings.*

32. David J. Farmer, *To Kill the King: Post-Traditional Governance and Bureaucracy* (Armonk, NY: M.E. Sharpe, 2005).

33. Robert B. Denhardt and Janet V. Denhardt, *The Dance of Leadership: The Art of Leading in Business, Government and Society* (Armonk, NY: M.E. Sharpe, 2006).

34. This is essentially a variation of the legitimacy question in public administration. How are public organizations, which can be quite powerful and influential and that are populated and largely managed by unelected personnel, legitimate in a democracy?

35. Cheryl Simrell King and Camilla Stivers, *Government Is Us: Strategies for an Anti-Government Era* (Thousand Oaks, CA: Sage, 1998); Cheryl Simrell King, Kathryn M. Felty, and Bridget O'Neill Susel, "The Question of Participation: Toward Authentic Public Participation," *Public Administration Review* 58, no. 4 (1998): 317–326; Richard Box, *Citizen Governance: Leading American Communities Into the 21st Century* (Thousand Oaks, CA: Sage, 1998).

36. O. C. McSwite, "Public Administration as the Carrier of the New Social Bond," *Administrative Theory and Praxis* 28, no. 2 (2006): 176–189; Eric K. Austin, "The Possibility of Effective Participatory Governance: The Role of Place and the Social Bond," *Public Administration and Management* 15, no. 1 (2010): 221–258.

37. Fox and Miller use the idea of incommensurable language games in the context of the postmodern condition to describe the robust languages that develop within communities but that become increasingly nonsensical between communities. Examples of such incommensurability could well include breaks between fundamentalist religious groups and wider communities or perhaps even between major political parties—or factions within those parties.

38. Stewart Clegg, *Modern Organizations: Organization Studies in the Postmodern World* (Thousand Oaks, CA: Sage, 1990).

39. These efficiencies have led both to the most superficial creature comforts we enjoy but could live without as well as the quality of nutrition, health care, sanitation, and other aspects of modern society—without which our quality of life would be impossible.

40. Earlier in the book we describe types of theory as including descriptive, predictive, and prescriptive. Each of these types attempts to articulate comprehensive depiction of the world. The notion of *understanding,* by contrast, enables action but does not strive to be or purport to be comprehensive.

41. David J. Farmer, *The Language of Public Administration: Bureaucracy, Modernity and Postmodernity* (Tuscaloosa: University of Alabama Press, 1995).

42. Farmer, *To Kill the King.*

43. O. C. McSwite, "The Psychoanalytic Rationale for Anti-Administration," *Administrative Theory and Praxis* 23, no. 2 (2001): 493–506; Michael W. Spicer, "Value Pluralism and its Implications for American Public Administration," *Administrative Theory and Praxis* 23, no. 2 (2001): 507–528; Richard C. Box, "Private Lives and Anti-Administration," *Administrative Theory and Praxis* 23, no. 2 (2001): 541–558; Janet R. Hutchinson, "Multigendering PA: Anti-Administration, Anti-Blues," *Administrative Theory and Praxis* 23, no. 2 (2001): 589–604; Debra A. Jacobs, "Alterity and the Environment: Making the Case for Anti-Administration," *Administrative Theory and Praxis* 23, no. 2 (2001): 605–620.

44. McSwite, "Public Administration."

45. An interesting parallel can be drawn between Weick's description of the collapse of sensemaking, Lacan's discourse of the hysteric, and Jean Baudrillard's postmodern condition. While Weick is working at a micro level of particular events, an argument can be made that the psychological experience of such collapses and the discourse of the hysteric and life in the postmodern condition are essentially the same.

46. "Confessions: Kim Possible (Episode 507)," narrated by Saul Elbein, *This American Life*, WBEZ, October 11, 2013, http://www.thisamericanlife.org/radio-archives/episode/507/confessions?act=1#play.

47. Pauline Marie Rosenau, *Post-Modernism and the Social Sciences: Insights, Inroads and Intrusions* (Princeton, NJ: Princeton University Press, 1992), xi.

48. Jacques Derrida, "Letter to a Japanese Friend," *Derrida and Difference*, ed. David Wood and Robert Bernasconi (Evanston, IL: Northwestern University Press, 1988), 4.

49. Farmer, *The Language of Public Administration*, 184.

50. Jonathan Culler, *On Deconstruction: Theory and Criticism After Structuralism* (Ithaca, NY: Cornell University Press, 1982), 109.

51. Derrida, "Letter to a Japanese Friend," 86.

52. Lynton K. Caldwell, "Managing the Transition to Post-modern Society," *Public Administration Review* 35, no. 6 (1975): 567.

53. Zygmunt Bauman, *Wasted Lives* (Cambridge, UK: Polity, 2004).

54. James W. Bernauer and Michael Mahon, "Michel Foucault's Ethical Imagination," in *The Cambridge Companion to Foucault*, ed. Gary Gutting (Cambridge, UK: Cambridge University Press, 2003), 149–175.

55. Ibid., 49.

56. Arnold Davidson, "Ethics as Ascetics," in *The Cambridge Companion to Foucault*, ed. Gary Gutting (Cambridge, UK: Cambridge University Press, 2003), 126.

57. Ibid., 133.

58. Ibid., 141.

59. Bernauer and Mahon, "Michel Foucault's Ethical Imagination," 162.

60. McSwite, *Legitimacy in Public Administration*; Michael Harmon and O. C. McSwite, *Wherever Two or More of Us Are Gathered* (Armonk, NY: M.E. Sharpe, 2011).

Chapter 11

Conclusion

This Is the Beginning

Over the past ten chapters, we have introduced a wide range of approaches to both studying and effectively working in governance organizations. In this last chapter, we want to figuratively step back and reflect on that material and consider how this is the beginning of your exploration of organizations, not the end. In order to do that, we start with a top ten list designed to highlight and organize what we view to be some of the key takeaways that emerge through the course of the book. From there, our summary reflections continue with a review of two overlapping themes in the book. One theme has to do with the historical and contextual development of organizational ideas. In part this historical approach is a pedagogical arrangement that we find to be useful as a way of arranging and retaining ideas. Moreover, this historically situated focus should prompt some consideration of whether, and in what ways, the contextualized development of ideas informs our thinking about how those ideas function in some venues and situations and not in others. In other words, if context matters, the logical extension would seem to be that not all ideas function equally well in all settings.

We then turn our attention to the idea of theory competence. Applicability has been an important selection and organizing criterion for us throughout the book, and while applicability is crucial if we want to sustain and enhance the effectiveness of our organizations, we are committed to the importance of theory competence as a critical and reflective means extending practitioners capacity in what we've described as increasingly complex settings. We revisit one model of theory competence and introduce a second as a way of thinking about *praxis*—the intersection of theory and practice. Finally, we return to governance one last time. Beyond the focus on practice and application, we want readers of this book to walk away with a greater lucidity about the importance of how organization theory (OT) and democratic governance are inexorably linked.

Top Ten Things You're Tired of Reading (but Should Remember Anyway)

The various practices and techniques we've discussed through the book are important, but as we ponder conclusions, we want students to think beyond tools. You can fairly easily return to this book or go to other sources to find prescriptive descriptions of tools and how-tos. What's important to us at this point is not any specific set of how-tos but being cognizant of how and why you make choices among techniques and an understanding of the consequences of those choices. As a result, our effort to develop a top ten list is not about which practices or techniques to select and use but instead about how to conceptualize your orientation to the field.

10. *Context matters*—Context shapes both the emergence of ideas (we'll revisit that in the following pages) and also the selection and use of techniques. It's useful to be aware of both the context of the idea's emergence and its current application.

9. *Degrees of constructivism*—Organizations have measurable and observable manifestations but are also socially constructed. Administrators benefit from being attuned to the processes and expressions of construction. Despite being socially constructed, organizations and the structures that comprise them are, for better and worse, robust. They are difficult to destroy and can be correspondingly difficult to change.

8. *Empiricism and knowledge (or wisdom) development*—Constructivism doesn't imply a rejection of rigorous empiricism. Philosophical pragmatism reveals the possibilities of utilizing what can be known through empirical study, while acknowledging that what can be known is also broader and more diverse than our first impressions might suggest.

7. *Visible and invisible organization*—One consequence of broadening our sense of what can be known about our organizations is that we must give attention to both visible and invisible elements of the organization—the formal and informal, explicit and implicit, as well as concrete and symbolic.

6. *Paradox*—One consequence of broadening our view of organizations, as well as what comprises and can be known of them, is that paradox and circumstances that are logically incommensurable but nevertheless simultaneously present become common in our experience.

5. *Frameworks for analysis and action*—There are useful models and taxonomies, such as the frameworks of differing levels of analysis or realms of activity. While necessarily incomplete and imperfect, these frameworks can be productively used to make sense of organizations and then strategies of action can be crafted in them.

4. *Ontological and epistemological implications*—Understanding that there are potentially many forms of knowledge should also drive attentiveness to the assumptions embedded in those forms and the corresponding approaches. Those assumptions determine, for example, what we pay attention to and ignore, what is considered to be possible or not.

3. *New wine in old bottles*—The adoption of new theoretical understandings doesn't necessarily imply the need to develop entirely new practices. It is possible to repurpose practices to new ends so as to create new or different understanding. From the outside,

the bottles look the same as they always have, but from the inside, the substance—and consequently, the experience—is different.

2. *Theory competence*—The ability to "think outside the box" can be understood as the ability to exercise agility in reflexively adapting and adopting different theoretical perspectives.

1. *Normative commitments and democratic governance*—Notions of constructivism, equifinality, antifoundationalism, and epistemic pluralism aside, the praxis of OT in governance settings embraces multiple values within a democratic culture and corresponding institutions. Democratic values are, and will remain, the central, orientating feature of twenty-first-century governance.

Historical and Conceptual Review

One of the central challenges in education is figuring out how to maximize knowledge gain. Given the breadth of material we've covered and the diversity of settings in which it was both developed and can be applied, this is an acute challenge for OT. As such, the summaries presented here are designed to reinforce some of the concepts and applications covered previously, but the summaries are also presented and structured in ways that hopefully provide one or more frameworks simple enough to retain and to repopulate as necessary in real-world settings.

We've developed a twofold approach for our review and summation of the ideas we've covered. The first element of our review is a roughly historical summary based on and extending Frederick Mosher's work. This review is very intentionally informed by a set of contextual factors that give some chronological and contextual structure to what now amounts to more than a century of work. The second element of our historical review is more narrowly organizational and is focused on the emergent and recurrent organizational questions, concerns, and analytical orientations.

In Chapter 1, we briefly described six distinct eras of government described by Mosher, with the addition of a seventh, based on changing conditions beyond the end of Mosher's timeline. We're reexamining those eras here in order to extend our original synopsis with an overview of the theories we described in Part I and the operational concerns covered in Part II. The purpose of this synopsis, however, is not simply to recap the ideas but to emphasize that ideas don't develop or exist in isolation. They are deeply connected to the larger social context. Kevin Kelly describes the advent of new technologies as following a particular logic.[1] Kelly suggests that conditions don't just establish the climate or conditions in which particular ideas emerge and others don't. The evolutionary logic Kelly describes suggests that certain ideas naturally or even necessarily emerge at particular moments. Kelly points to cases in which nearly identical technologies emerge almost simultaneously but in total isolation of each other. This dynamic helps explain the emergence, for example, of classical management theory in Germany with Max Weber, France with Henri Fayol, and the United States with Frederick Taylor so close together. This dynamic also explains how similar ideas emerge nearly simultaneously and isolated from each other across fields. For example, Taylor's notions of scientific management in industrial and production organizations and Gifford Pinchot's description of forest management practices operate from nearly identical principles, with no indication of formal connections between the two men.

More importantly for our purposes at this point, for those of us who make sense of and retain ideas within an historical and contextual timeline, the arc captured by this narrative is one way of organizing the breadth of ideas we've covered. In our reexamination of these time periods, we present a brief sketch of some of the major societal dynamics that both shaped and were shaped by governance and governance organizations at the time.

Government by the Good: 1883–1906

This era marks the movement out of reconstruction and into industrialization at the beginning of the twentieth century. We suggest that the "good" can be understood as being both about the morally upright and the operationally effective. For example, the moral side of the good can be seen in the rise of the temperance movement at the community level and later in government policy. The operational side of the good is exemplified in personnel system reforms like the Pendleton Act and Woodrow Wilson's essay, championing the idea of competent and nonpartisan public administration, and Frank Goodnow's notion of bureaucratic neutrality and expertise.[2, 3] These ideas both reflect and shape the spirit of the era across several areas.

- *Economic*—Industrialization marks a shift from the dominance of agriculture to industrial production as drivers of capital distribution and economic growth. Industrialization sees both a change in sectors of economic activity but also the nature of the activity in that even in agricultural production, industrialization leads to the increasing reliance on machines rather human workers.
- *Sociocultural*—Industrialization coincides with urbanization as agricultural workers move from rural areas to urban areas in search of economic opportunity. When these migrations combine with immigration to the United States, this results in new forms and scales of urban poverty and social and political efforts to mitigate the effects of urbanization. Other aspects of urbanization include new and more expansive forms of gentrification and a wealth gap that peaks just before the Great Depression; heightened moralism in, for example, the temperance movement; and diversification through immigration.
- *Political*—The political response to these trends includes forms of populism and progressivism that ultimately resulted in reform and regulation. The passage of the Pendleton Act, the creation of the Interstate Commerce Commission, and the popularity of—and resistance to—Teddy Roosevelt's antitrust efforts are also examples of these political trends.
- *Science and technology*—Innovations in science and technology such as improvements in metallurgy and subsequently the mass production of high-quality steel are critical for industrialization but also contribute to the ethos of progress in this area. Discoveries in basic science and applied science lead to improvements in medicine (X-rays, germ theory, and aspirin), transportation (the development and improvement of gas and diesel engines and carburetors), communications (wireless radio), and other areas, all of which lead to a sense of promise and possibility.

Implications for Organizations—Concepts and Practices

The implication, directly and indirectly for organizations, is the emergence of what we now describe as classical theories of management and organization. Key among these theories is Weber's depiction of rational-legal forms of authority and outline of bureaucracy that both advances the systemization and rationalization of the structures and practices of organizations and reflects the wider spirit of the era. This also includes Taylor, Fayol, and others' efforts to articulate organizational and management practices including time and motion studies, span of control, and unity of command to operationalize the ideas into effective practices. These efforts operate across all three areas of concern we utilized in Chapter 10—namely information and knowledge activities, people activities, and structural activities. More specifically, the ideas that emerge during this time—roughly corresponding to the being of the classical or orthodox era—are both developing and applying new forms and bodies of knowledge, be that conceptual in Weber's work on authority and structure or Taylor's time and motion studies. Moreover, this knowledge is very much oriented to the concerns of managing people and establishing optimal structural arrangements.

Although we are keenly aware of the limits of these theories with respect to flexibility, responsiveness, and the tendency to dehumanize organizations, these theories represent a huge leap forward in both the conceptualization of organizational settings and practices that improve organization performance. Moreover, when compared to the potential for arbitrary and capricious behavior of traditional or charismatic forms of authority in organizations, classical organization forms and practices signify a dramatic move to more humane methods than existed to that point in time.

This era also sees a critical change in the appearance and role of governance organizations. The Interstate Commerce Commission is created to oversee rail transportation and becomes the first federal agency in what would eventually become a large and sophisticated regulatory system. At the local level, the New York Bureau of Municipal Research is created to conduct organizational and policy analysis. These and other emerging public organizations mark an important departure in the role and scope of government activities from the prior century.

Government by the Efficient: 1906–1937

As we move further into the early twentieth century, the civil service reform and neutral competence emphasized by Wilson, Goodnow, and others corresponds well with what was happening in the private sector trends, with the acceleration of the Industrial Revolution. The emergence of new structures of organization, which separated ownership and management and introduced scientific management procedures, emphasizes efficiency, and production continues and further expands. Luther Gulick, Lyndall Urwick, and others take up these ideas and advance the idea that government should become more businesslike and rational through the use of planning, specialization, and standardization. Here again, political, economic, social, and technological changes both mirror and reinforce the thinking about organizations at this time.

- *Economic*—Through this era, we see both growth and expansion of the economic trends of the prior era but also experience a boom and bust cycle both immediately after the First World War and then more severely with the Great Depression. Late in this era we see the emergence of Keynesian economic concepts in the form of New Deal programs.
- *Sociocultural*—Just as there is both an economic growth as well as new and more expansive economic boom and bust cycles socially, there are moments of both widespread

optimism and dismay during this era. These are exemplified by the emergence of Dadaism following World War I, followed by the exuberance of the Roaring Twenties.

- *Political*—While reform efforts continue and extend, the general trend continues to be one of small government and isolationism. Although the United States does eventually become involved in World War I, President Wilson is unsuccessful getting the Senate to ratify the Treaty of Versailles and with it the League of Nations that would have expanded US involvement in international affairs. President Hoover's response to the 1929 economic crash is characterized by faith that markets can self-correct, and it is not until nearly four years into the Great Depression that limited government involvement finally gives way to large-scale government involvement and the use of Keynesian economic principles under President Roosevelt.

- *Science and technology*—While not having a direct impact on economic, social, or political dynamics, this era sees an explosion of basic science, particularly in physics with Einstein's publication of his general theory of relativity (actually in 1905), as well as the work Niels Bohr, Werner Heisenberg, and Erwin Schrödinger did on quantum mechanics. In applied science and technology we find the development of technologies that shift communications and culture. The radio receiver is invented on the cusp of this era in 1901, but widespread production occurs during this era following the development of a functional tuner in 1916, as well as Edison's development of practical motion pictures in 1910. The cathode ray tube and superheterodyne radio circuit are invented during this era, making television—and later, computer monitors—possible. The first use of magnetic recording tapes occurs in 1934, setting the stage for the storage and distribution of audio, video, and in the late twentieth century, computer information. The Model T goes into production in 1908, changing the possibilities of cheap, long-range personal transportation.

Implications for Organizations—Concepts and Practices

Largely this era sees an extension of the movement to theorize and implement classical concepts including the notion of "one best way." There are, however, new and distinctive ideas as well. Chester Barnard's introduction of new structural and leadership (people) oriented ideas in the addition of cooperation and leadership to the thinking about organizations introduces one bridge to what would eventually become the human relations movement in OT. The surprising findings of the Hawthorne experiments, particularly those revealing the presence of unintended and informal social structures that affected performance, are another link to new possibilities. There are also important contributions specific to public or governance organizations. Gulick and Urwick's work, including the Brownlow report, attempting to establish unified political control of public organizations, reveals one such contribution. The Friedrich-Finer debate (which begins in 1937 and continues into the 1940s), which set the parameters for the legitimacy question in terms of discretion and accountability, also inform the thinking about the nature and function of governance organizations.

Government by the Administrators: 1937–1955

During this era, the demands of the New Deal, the Second World War, and subsequent recovery efforts such as the Marshall Plan move public bureaucrats from being mere technicians to administrators charged with coordinating large, complex, logistical reconstruction and social programs. While there is a growing momentum seeing public administration as being a central player contributing to the quality of life in a developed democracy, there is also a movement to establish presidential or executive control of bureaucracy. Although institutionally the federal bureaucracy retained two masters—the president *and* Congress—Presidents Roosevelt and Eisenhower each convene ad hoc commissions to review the organization of the federal government and to help the president gain greater control of the bureaucracy.

- *Economic*—While the fights between President Roosevelt and Congress over New Deal programs are impassioned, the early portion of this era is characterized by a continuation of Keynesian economic recovery efforts. Changes to monetary policy begin at the end of the previous period, with many nations abandoning the gold standard. The United States acts to temporarily suspend the gold standard in 1935, but the Bretton Woods Agreement negotiates at the end of World War II to ensure global economic and financial security effectively make the change permanent. Following the war, the United States sees a sustained period of economic expansion in part as a result of efforts to support reconstruction in Europe and Japan but also because the United States is the only industrialized power whose productive capacity is not decimated by the war.

- *Sociocultural*—The late 1930s continues to see some degree of mass internal migrations because of continuing economic conditions and the Dust Bowl. Other social problems such as crime, suicide, and abandonments increase as well. These dynamics change as the United States enters World War II and are replaced by social unity and patriotism in the 1940s, as exemplified by bond drives, scrap drives, and victory gardens. Widespread optimism follows the end of the war, but with threads of worry and discontent orbiting around revelations of Holocaust, continuing racism and other forms of discrimination in the United States and the beginnings of the Cold War.

- *Political*—During this period, President Roosevelt was elected to an unprecedented third and fourth terms. Following his death, the Twenty-second Amendment to the Constitution is proposed in 1947 and ratified in 1951, which limits the number of terms a president can serve to two. Although concern about Communism predates this period, the actions of the Soviet Union following the war lead quickly to the beginning of the Cold War, and specifically to US and UN involvement in Korea and the creation of the North Atlantic Treaty Alliance in Europe.

- *Science and technology*—A key technological breakthrough of this era is the ability to harness the atom for weapons and for energy production. The war also leads to advances in cryptography and other information management technologies and contribute to the development of mechanical and later analog computing capacity. In the social and behavioral sciences, behaviorist psychology of B. F. Skinner and Jean Piaget influences the postwar work of Kurt Lewin, Rensis Likert, Douglas McGregor, and others. Although Abraham Maslow ultimately champions the emergence of humanism in psychology, the behaviorist theory that emerged in the 1930s continues to be influential.

Implications for Organizations—Concepts and Practices

For organizations and management, this era is characterized by the continuation of the ideas and practices of the previous era, focused on the practical needs of building the institutions and programs first, of the New Deal, and followed by the conduct of a global war, and finally, reconstruction after the war. The administrative and logistical requirements of these three massive efforts lead many scholars to contribute their expertise to these efforts in various administrative positions. The experience gained would later contribute to organizational attention to, for example, operations research and operations analysis that later led W. Edwards Deming and Joseph Juran to develop the methods of systems, or technological structures focused quality control and total quality management (TQM), or attention to the social-structural dynamics that Norton Long would explore in *Power and Administration*. Following the war, influenced by the findings of Hawthorne, the continuing weight of behaviorism, human relations theory (HRT) becomes a central influence on organization studies and practices. One of the responses can be seen in Simon's efforts to structure organizations, including their knowledge acquisition and analysis processes, in order to maximize organizational rationality. The work at the Tavistock Institute and elsewhere represents an alternative approach to people and structures that improves productivity around structures of relationships rather than rationalizing information analysis.

Government by the Professionals: 1955–1968

During this era, public administration becomes further professionalized and academically institutionalized. In higher education, a growing number of dedicated schools of public administration were established in order to train expert or specialized administrators, and public organizations continued to grow and expanded rapidly. Moreover, there was continued optimism about the direction and future of the nation, a vision that clearly included an active, vibrant public sector. This optimism was tempered and constrained, however, in that the United States was also in the midst of the Cold War. Threats of Soviet military and political incursion into Asia, Africa, and Latin America, as well as technical events like Sputnick's launch in 1957, prompted the United States to believe it was technologically and educationally behind. This, in turn, sparked new public efforts in education, science, and technology that required the need for professionals, the experts, and the white-collar workers with specialized knowledge such as training in medicine, engineering, law, and psychology. While these movements were understandable within the sociopolitical climate of the time, they also exacerbated or perhaps even drove emerging tension between public values and administrative values. This tension can be found, for example, in the disconnect between Robert McNamara's efforts to use management techniques designed to maximize efficiency in the Ford Motor Company, in the conduct of the Vietnam War, and the growing resistance to the war among the wider public.

- *Economic*—The period from the mid-1950s through the late 1960s was largely a period of economic growth. While there were several short recessions in the 1950s and 1960s, Presidents Eisenhower, Kennedy, and Johnson used varying forms of economic policy to stimulate and support stable growth and often had significant budget surpluses to utilize on federal programs.
- *Political*—This period saw a continuation of the Cold War and dramatic increase in US involvement in Southeast Asia. To some degree, the Kennedy administration, but especially the Johnson administration, dramatically expanded social engineering and safety net programs such as Medicare and through the War on Poverty.

- *Sociocultural*—Socially and culturally, this is a period of both optimism and frustration. To a great degree, this is also a period of social and cultural conformity and a sense of great potential. At the same time, there are undercurrents of skepticism and criticism that ultimately manifest in the civil rights, women's liberation, and antiwar movements and the beat movement.
- *Science and technology*—Outside of the behavioral and social sciences, other important events in science and technology reflect economic, political, and cultural trends. For example, the launch of Sputnik drives investment in science and engineering education and research and development (R&D). Other inventions have a profound social effect, such as the invention and approval of the birth control pill in the late 1950s.

Implications for Organizations—Concepts and Practices

At least three trends are notable in OT and practice, all of which reflect the dynamics just described in varying combinations: emphases on effectiveness, scale, and values—especially those of liberal democracies. In part this is seen in theory, which explains and enables practices that support and extend the possibility of large-scale, effective social programming as a way of resolving issues of poverty, peace, and prosperity. Behaviorist and humanist theory supports improvement in the management of organizations purportedly to make them both more humane and more effective. The focus of organizational researchers including Lewin, Likert, and McGregor extended efforts to organize practices focused on interpersonal, structural, and change activities. This research was further augmented with thinking about the inclusion of broader social values in administrative agencies and their work. This inclusion of these values is discernible most clearly during and after the 1968 Minnowbrook Conference and the emergence of the New Public Administration (NPA) movement.

Government of the Hysteric: 1968–Present

This era extends beyond the model that Mosher originally developed. When we introduced it in Chapter 1, we described a set of conditions that emerged out of the social and political turbulence of the 1960s. We also acknowledged this as a comparatively long era relative to those Mosher describes earlier in the twentieth century. Admittedly, we could adopt an interpretation of sociopolitical history and government that would allow us to create reasonable subdivisions within this forty-plus-year period of time. However, we believe that there are important overarching experiential and conceptual themes that hold this time period together as a coherent era rather than it being several shorter eras. As we indicated in Chapter 4, these overarching themes during this period have to do with growing social, economic, technological, and other forms of diversity and complexity, as well as intellectual heterodoxy that range from, in Gibson Burrell and Gareth Morgan's terminology, profound functionalism to extreme interpretivism.[4]

Now that we've described the Lacanian *discourse of the hysteric* in Chapter 9, we have a term that captures the increasingly complex, diverse, heterodox, and even paradoxical character of the era and its experiential conditions—both socially and administratively. Although there are other theoretical narratives that suggest greater or lesser degrees of coherence and stability through this most recent era, we believe that the conditions we just noted lead to and result from and cause and are caused by the ambiguity, uncertainty, ambivalence, incommensurability, and undecidability across these areas.

- *Economic*—Economic conditions and trends both domestically and internationally become increasingly complicated. This era sees the rise of new economic powers internationally and pressure on US markets and industries. This includes the emergence of Japan as an economic power, followed by Asia and other economies including the Persian Gulf states in oil production and Brazil in South America. This is also the era of corporate globalization, where by the beginning of the twenty-first century, 51 of 100 of the largest economic entities were corporations rather than nations. The fall of the Soviet Union and economic changes in Communist China lead to a growing assumption of roughly market dynamics in the global economy. Financial innovation, globalization, and consolidation under a transaction-cost rationale lead to unprecedented corporate profits and massive growth in the value of securities markets, as well as interconnectivity that leads to the "too big to fail" phenomenon early in the twenty-first century.
- *Political*—Domestically, this era begins with the Watergate scandal as well as Ronald Reagan's election as the governor of California. These two political events portend a growing skepticism about federal programs and national politics and move back from the massive, progressive policies of the prior era. Internationally, the Cold War ends, opening a space for regional conflicts in the Balkans and between former Soviet republics as well as a rise of fundamentalism in various parts of the world.
- *Sociocultural*—The sense of conformity that existed in the 1950s and early 1960s gives way to fragmentation. This can be seen in many areas of American culture, whether in popular culture of music and the media or the push and pull of urban-rural or urban-suburban tensions or the emergence of the religious right as a social and moral, as well as political force. This era marks the expansion of political and civil opportunity linked to awareness of race, gender, and emerging awareness of exclusion of those with physical or mental disabilities as well as what would become LGBT (lesbian, gay, bisexual, and transgender) politics starting at the end of the 1990s.
- *Science and technology*—While the scientific and technical breakthroughs of the early and mid-twentieth century resulted in massive, visible changes in society, it may be that the changes of the late twentieth century may be even more profound, though less visible in many ways. The emergence of digital technology and the explosion of its availability and interconnectivity accelerate massively during this time. Our capacity to communicate and coordinate on unprecedented scales, as well as the ability to access, track, and analyze information, that make possible uses of "big data" result in both new forms of political analysis and the National Security Agency (NSA) digital surveillance scandal. Advances in transportation technology, the emergence of biotechnology driven by recombinant DNA technology, the development of nanotechnology, and advances in quantum and cognitive sciences all create new regulatory questions but also shape our approaches to managing organizations. This era sees new knowledge of and consideration of human-caused ecological impacts first with the environmental movement and more recently climate change, with technology both at the heart of the causes and the solutions. For example, the ebb and flow of debates about greenhouse gases and energy production have resulted in an ebb and flow of arguments about fossil fuels (clean coal,

carbon sequestration) and a renewed interest in nuclear power as a non-greenhouse gas source of energy in the early twenty-first century (but before the tsunami crippled the Fukushima nuclear plant).

Implications for Organizations—Concepts and Practices

The implications of these conditions relate to OT and practice in two ways. First, these trends affect the breadth and diversity of OT. The range and variety of theories we include in Chapter 4 give some sense of the conceptual work being done over the last forty-plus years. The wide range of economic, political, social, and scientific trends has resulted in the extension of existing as well as new perspectives from which OT has been developed (e.g., chaos and complexity theories, constructivist theories, and ecological theories). Because of the increasing degree of theoretical variation, our approach has been to suggest that practitioners can make sense of that theory using any of several frameworks. We've used Scott's model that focuses on different levels of analysis and the organizational concerns that correspond to those levels of analysis.[5] We've also suggested the possibility of framing through classification schemes based on broad and overlapping (knowledge, people, and structure) or more narrow and discrete (individual, group, change, and environments) categories. The selection of practices, whether traditional or inchoate, can then be reflexive and intentional rather than either arbitrary or dogmatic.

The second way the conditions we just described relates to cotemporary OT and practice has to do with a growing awareness of the climate and setting. Clearly organizations have always existed in a larger political, social, and economic environment that has subtly or explicitly shaped organization behavior, even if the extant theory assumed that organizations were closed systems. Our attentiveness to the climate and setting has partly to do with a greater awareness and responsiveness on the part of practitioners. Moreover, because that climate and setting is more complex than in the past, developing the theoretical competence to reflexively consider and wisely respond to that complexity is more important than ever.

Organizations and Theory Competence

> Administrative thought must establish a working relationship with every major province in the realm of human learning.
>
> —Dwight Waldo[6]

We began the book by introducing David Farmer's idea of epistemic pluralism—or multiple knowledge frameworks—as a way of leading into our discussion about how students and practitioners might make sense of and navigate the diversity of OTs, as well as settings of practice. The ability to organize the breadth of theories is especially important given that, at the least, they work at distinctly different levels of analysis and consider significantly different concerns. Beyond those differences, we've argued that many of the assumptions underlying these theories are incommensurable, meaning that traversing between and among them requires an awareness of how those assumption play out against our own ideologies, cultures, policies, and practices.

O. C. McSwite argues that these paradigmatic differences and the result incommensurability makes moving between paradigmatically different theories enormously difficult, if not impossible. Farmer, on the other hand, argues that understanding and using these lensesis not only possible, but can give new life to public administration theory and practice. For Farmer, the orthodox or classical period expressed the belief that it was on the cutting edge of social progress and could make a critical contribution to the vitality of the country and world. Early administrative and OT provided the intellectual basis for widespread confidence in the capacity of public administration to contribute to democratic governance. Theoretical diversity can, according to Farmer, "enrich PA theory and practice with fresh and better ideas—with ideas that are not partial and misleading" and serve as a source of justified and renewed confidence in public administration and democratic governance.[7]

More concretely, Farmer suggests that administrators can use these various perspectives, even those considered to be incorrect, to inspire insights, the sort of engagement he describes as "play of the imagination." In exercising imagination and opening the possibility of discovery, Farmer states that "it is not true that one has to be an X on order to take X seriously or to believe that X is true."[8] Instead, we have the ability to reflexively consider the insights and revelations that different theoretical perspectives offer. Although the admonition to "think outside the box" has become so overused as to become largely meaningless, if the box is understood as the assumptions associated with any one particular theoretical perspective, reflexive theoretical flexibility does offer a way to get outside of the box.

The point of our historical treatment and the conceptual examination of content and application of OT is not about finding the right one but instead about having a range of perspectives available such that they can stimulate reflexivity. McSwite adopts this perspective in their 1997 book *Legitimacy in Public Administration* when they make the unusual admission that their work is wrong.[9] They continue by claiming that not only are they wrong, but that everyone else is as well. Most importantly for our purposes, they go on to argue that despite being wrong, they and everyone else has a contribution to make to our thinking about public administration theory, or in this case OT and practice. Moreover, reflexivity allows the avoidance of paralysis by analysis—or the failure to take action for fear of not having enough or the right information. If we understand that sufficient, let alone perfect, information is an impossibility, then we find ourselves understanding that we cannot delay action, and as we noted in Chapter 10, we—the decision maker or makers—become responsible for the consequences of that decision.

McSwite describes the idea of *theory competence* among practitioners and students of public administration as the capacity to function effectively in complex governance and administrative setting as being something more, or better, different than the simple, turnkey application of concepts mastered in formal or informal classrooms.[10] Instead, theory competence by McSwite's estimation is "a certain kind of mind, a conceptual format, that, couple with a particular set of attitudes, changes an MPA-educated administrator's way of thinking through questions of effective action."[11] In the depiction of the approach to developing such competence, McSwite identifies six attributes.

The first is an *awareness of linkages and interconnectedness*. This is the admonition that we need to recognize that we are increasingly aware of the extent to which elements of our environments are intimately interconnected, but as they also point out, social and administrative environments are extensively linked and interconnected in highly complex and, in some cases, unexpected ways.

The second dimension entails developing a *structuralist attitude,* which necessitates "searching out and understanding the underlying codes" that govern or determine social circumstances.[12] These codes reveal the underlying forces, often symbolic ones, that shape the course of events from below the surface. These can be macro level structures that are expressed in the relations between large institutions, or micro level structures found in, for example, the arrangement of rooms or the mix of participants attending an event. These structures or codes don't dictate the outcomes but do strongly set the parameters and possibilities.

The third, *systems thinking,* is one that we've explored in our discussions of TQM. Theory competence along this dimension entails seeking out general causes resulting from system behavior rather than specific causes enacted by a single person. Working along this dimension involves determination of how the system causes variations in quality of outputs and then improving the system. Systems, like structures, can be multiple and overlapping, so this doesn't mean just the formal and explicit systems but informal and implicit as well.

Attentiveness to the social field, the next dimension, has to do with the human and interpersonal side of systems. That is, those who populate the systems and structures of organizations both affect and are attuned to more than the formal and social-structural elements of organizations. They are oriented to the interpersonal tenor, energy, or feel of the setting as well. McSwite points out that, for example, the expression of anxiety by an organizational leader can manifest related, dysfunctional behaviors among the wider membership of the organization. Theory competence and practice must include an awareness of the social field and the potential consequences of action within that field.

The fifth dimension, *dialectical adeptness,* is a recognition that actions and their effects aren't monolithic or unidimensional. We have discussed the logic of taxonomies from Aristotle to present thinking in earlier sections of the book, which create exhaustive and mutually exclusive categories as the basis of understanding and action. Dialectical adeptness is the awareness that actions entail their opposite. For example, efforts to create procedural clarity and precision result in new forms of ambiguity and initiatives to ensure openness generate new forms of concealment and obfuscation.

Lastly, a *mysterian* dimension involves realizing that some aspects of human experience are simply incomprehensible. It acknowledges that beyond the development of robust causal models and the use of inferential statistics, some aspects of human experience simply exceed comprehension. More concretely, though, this dimension prompts us to come to terms with incommensurablites, allowing the tensions between them to stand unresolved and the anxiety associated with not having the *right* answer to be directly and intentionally engaged.

OT and theory competency is not about the abstract examination of the various ideas that have emerged over time about how organizations and the people who populate them behave. Neither is OT about the mastery of what to do in organizations. The tools, techniques, and practices—the instrumental elements of OT—are not the expression of one best way. Finally, the practices are not radically relativistic such that there are no wrong answers. Rather, OT and theory competency is about praxis. It is oriented first toward building the capacity to think about how to think about organizations and ultimately concerned with reflexive action driven by that thinking.

Governance Redux

Mark Bevir defines *governance* as being a broader notion than government. Governance is inclusive of pluralistic patterns of rule, which focuses to a greater degree on robust forms interaction between and among the institutions of but also members within civil societies.[13] Government, by contrast, is a narrower concept and has to do with the instrumental activities and practices of public organizations. Our contention from the outset has been that although an instrumental attitude and influence of the politics-administration dichotomy is still operative, at least to some degree, in contemporary organizations, the legitimacy question is moot.[14] The central question is no longer whether but *how* organizations might contribute to democracy in a contemporary setting. As a result, we're interested in the intersection between the instrumental questions of effective organization practice and the normative questions of how that practice contributes to the democratic politics of determining and pursuing the *good life*. As such, governance, understood as pluralist, interactive, and inclusive is the starting and ending point for our approach to OT and practice.

McSwite, Bevir, Ralph Hummel, Cheryl Simerell King, and Camilla Stivers and other public administration theorists have, over the past twenty years, made a compelling case that public and increasingly nonprofit organizations are uniquely positioned and have come to occupy a distinctive symbolic and structural position from which to support democratic governance.[15] While public organizations have suffered the same decline in public faith and support as elected institutions have, that decline has not been nearly as precipitous when distances are short and direct experience with them is higher. That is, opinion polls have consistently shown that we have greater trust and higher opinions of those organizations close to us and with which we have more direct familiarity. Moreover, governance organizations are positioned partly because of the network of relations they develop over time and partly because of institutionalized public engagement requirements and practices, to directly support the articulation and implementation of the good life in ways no other entity can. This is not to say that governance organizations always, or even routinely, operate in this way. Rather, our point is that they are positioned and in a growing number of instances are demonstrating the capacity to do so.

The position that we've taken here should not be read as somehow rejecting the importance of historical values held by public organizations, such as neutrality and competence. One of the things that makes public administration in the United States unique and effective by comparison to governments in much of the rest of the world is the extent to which it is characterized by high levels of expertise exercised toward the ends of a common good rather than those of special interests. However, we're following NPA theorists in arguing that competence doesn't require willful blindness to historical or current discourses about the nature of the good life, in the name of neutrality. Add to that attentiveness to democratic norms, a broader and antifoundational understanding of knowledge forms, and sources and approaches, what remains is an attitude toward OT and governance rather than a recipe, or even a menu, of techniques. Instead, this attitude or orientation, along with rigorous adherence to robust processes at all levels of organizational activities, can be a crucial venue in which the good life can be constructed and pursued. ■

Notes

1. Kevin Kelly, *What Technology Wants* (New York: Penguin Group, 2010).
2. Woodrow Wilson, "The Study of Administration," *Political Science Quarterly* 2, no. 2 (1887): 197–222.
3. Frank J. Goodnow, *Politics and Administration: A Study in Government* (New York: Russell and Russell, 1900).
4. Gibson Burrell and Gareth Morgan, *Sociological Paradigms and Organizational Analysis* (Brookfield, VT: Arena, 1994).
5. Scott W. Richard, *Organizations: Rational, Natural and Open Systems,* 5th ed. (Upper Saddle River, NJ: Prentice Hall, 2003).
6. As cited in David J. Farmer, *Public Administration in Perspective: Theory and Practice Through Multiple Lenses* (Armonk, NY: M.E. Sharpe, 2010).
7. Ibid., 7.
8. Ibid., 8.
9. O. C. McSwite, *Legitimacy in Public Administration: A Discourse Analysis* (Thousand Oaks, CA: Sage, 1997).
10. O. C. McSwite, "Theory Competency for MPA-Educated Practitioners," *Public Administration Review* 61, no. 1 (2001): 100–115.
11. Ibid., 112.
12. Ibid., 113.
13. Mark Bevir, *Democratic Governance* (Princeton, NJ: Princeton University Press, 2010).
14. We follow McSwite's argument in McSwite, *Legitimacy in Public Administration.*
15. This discourse has been evolving for more than forty years of the Minnowbrook Conference, and the emergence of the NPA movement is taken as the starting place.

Index

About the Authors

Dr. Sandra Parkes Pershing is the Assistant Vice President of Engagement, and a professor in the Master of Public Administration program at The University of Utah. Her work focuses on organizational behavior, leadership, and change. Prior to her current position, Dr. Pershing served as the Assistant Vice President of Continuing Education and Program Manager for the Master of Public Administration Program at the University of Utah. Dr. Pershing also works as an organizational consultant and trainer to public and non-profit organizations to assist them in maximizing their potential. Dr. Pershing co-edited *Classic Readings in Organizational Behavior* (2008) with J. Steven Ott and Richard Simpson, and *Classics in Public Administration* (2003) with Jay Shafritz and Albert Hyde.

Dr. Eric K. Austin is an Associate Professor of Political Science and Coordinator of the Master of Public Administration program at Montana State University, where he teaches courses including organization theory, public management and administrative ethics. His research focuses on inter and intra organizational processes of decision-making in contentious environments, and his work has appeared in *Public Administration and Management, Administrative Theory and Praxis, The Journal of Public Affairs Education* and elsewhere. Dr. Austin's professional career prior to completing his PhD at Virginia Tech included managing program units in both public and non-profit organizations. Dr. Austin has and continues to work as a trainer and consultant providing technical support and capacity building for organizations ranging from large, federal agencies to small, volunteer based non-profits.

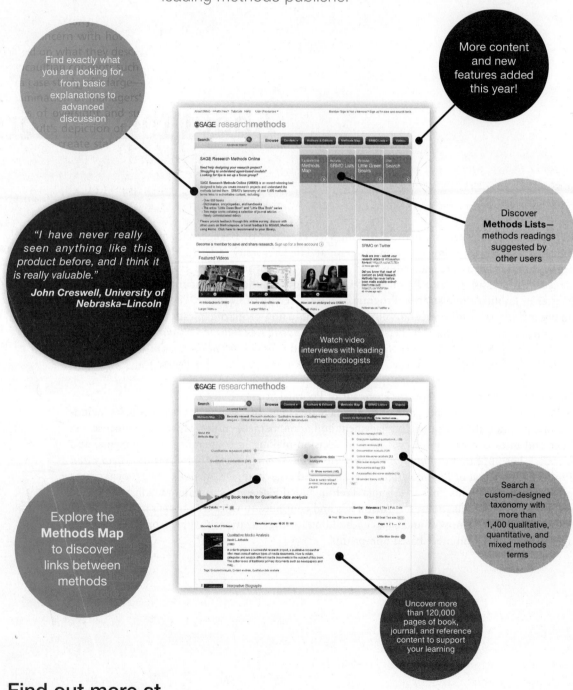